An Introduction to
Music and Art
in the Western World

Seventh Edition
An Introduction to
Music and Art
in the Western World

Milo Wold
Linfield College

Edmund Cykler
University of Oregon, Emeritus

ωcb
Wm. C. Brown Company Publishers
Dubuque, Iowa

Copyright © 1955, 1958, 1967 by Milo Wold and Edmund Cykler

Copyright © 1972, 1976, 1980, 1983 by Wm. C. Brown Company Publishers

Library of Congress Catalog Card Number: 82-72487

ISBN 0—697—03124—1

Printed in the United States of America

2-03124-01

Contents

Figures

Colorplates

Preface

More than twenty-five years have passed since the first edition of this book was published. In these years the technical media of television, tape recording, long-play records, and radio have made music of all periods and types available to everyone everywhere. Rapid communication and reproduction techniques have either brought visual artworks to the public or the public to the artworks and have made all forms of art available to everyone. As a result, we have been inundated with music and art of all kinds as never before. As in the past, the art-consuming public will eventually winnow the wheat from the chaff. The examples of past traditions should help us in this task so that not only the future might benefit from our selection but that we ourselves might recognize and enjoy the best works of our contemporary artists. The perspective of time will prove us right or wrong.

In order to make some sense of this period in which we find ourselves, we have found it necessary in this seventh edition to divide the more than three-quarters of the twentieth century into two chapters. Like the general public, we found ourselves unable to decide between works, styles, and trends. We, too, have often been unable to see the woods for the trees. The newly added last chapter should challenge you to make a selection between lasting and significant art and the plethora of pseudo art with which we are surrounded.

This book is not intended as a history of the fine arts or as a history of music. It is an introduction to the stylistic character and cultural climate of the important art epochs of Western civilization. In addition, it aims to show how the various arts responded to the same sociocultural conditions and how each art is related to the others in the patterns of cultural history.

In order that you may become thoroughly familiar with representative works of music and art, only a few examples have been chosen as illustrations. We suggest that many more examples of both visual art and music be sought out for further study and enjoyment. You are urged to supplement the illustrations of painting, sculpture, and architecture by inexpensive prints available from most bookstores. A list of musical examples in their order of use in the text is included at the end of each chapter. A glossary of both music and art terms as well as a pronunciation guide for proper names has been included in this edition as an aid.

We are deeply indebted to our many colleagues and friends who have so generously given of their time and knowledge to assist in various ways. A special word of appreciation is due to those colleagues in numerous colleges and universities who have used the material in classroom situations and have made constructive criticism and suggestions. Many of the additions and changes in this seventh edition are the result of their kindly interest.

The inclusion of a recording in the seventh edition has made us additionally indebted to our colleague, Prof. James Miller and a number of students of the University of Oregon Music School. The following persons participated in the performance of the examples found on the recording accompanying this edition: Charles Bach, contratenor; Carolyn Carver, violin; Julia Haydon, gamba; James Miller, piano and tenor; Peter Nothnagle, gamba; Ed Kammerer, horn and James Reynolds, tenor. Peter Nothnagle was the recording engineer for the production.

Recordings: Their Source and Use

This Seventh Edition of AN INTRODUCTION OF MUSIC AND ART IN THE WESTERN WORLD has included a recording of some of the examples which are notated in the text. This has been done in keeping with the authors' conviction that every art work which is discussed *MUST* be experienced, if not in reality at least through reproduction.

In respect to painting, sculpture, and architecture this can be accomplished by means of illustrative reproductions and photographs. The situation with music is more complex. Plastic art works are appreciated in space as well as time. Through the original or its reproduction one can study the various elements of form, color, texture, etc., while they are being observed in close detail and in extended time. Music exists only in time, and one cannot observe it "frozen", so to speak, at any one moment. One possibility of studying a piece of music is through notation which, however, is *not* the music, nor even an illustration of it, but merely the contrived and accepted symbols of performance instruction. The real piece of music is the sound which is revealed in time.

This is the reason the authors of this text are so insistent that the students listen attentively to each of the pieces of music which are used for analysis, and to the examples which are notated in the text. Despite the disadvantage that music presents for the discussion and analysis of details, there is the great advantage that today the student *can* listen to the *actual* music, if not in a live performance, at least in recorded version. Moreover the recording, unlike the illustration of art, sculpture, and architecture, *is* the real piece of music; it is not a substitute for the original. Through the example given in the text the authors hope to alert the student to particular details of a composition under discussion. If the student is unfamiliar with musical notation it is hoped that the instructor or fellow student with musical ability will point out the particular detail which the example is presenting in notation, thus enabling the student to *hear* this detail in the music.

Because the compositions discussed in the first seven chapters of the text are very short, they are to be found only in anthologies. The authors have restricted the recordings of these compositions to pieces which are to be found in the three following publications and their recordings.

Masterpieces of Music Before 1750. Designated by MM. Parrish, Carl and Ohl, John. New York: W.W. Norton, 1951. Recorded by the Haydn Society.
Treasury of Early Music. Designated by TEM. Parish, Carl. New York: W.W. Norton, 1958. Recorded by the Haydn Society.
History of Music in Sound. Designated by HMS. 10 volumes. London; Oxford Press, 1953. Recorded by RCA. The anotholgy contains only partial scores but the recordings are complete.

The above texts give the notated scores for the compositions used in the first seven chapters, together with added analyses and descriptions of the works and their composers. These recordings give authentic renditions of the scores.

In the case of the musical works discussed in chapters 8 through 15, the available recorded examples are so numerous that no individual recordings have been listed. The Schwann Record and Tape Guide includes numerous options for each of the works discussed.

The recording included in this Seventh Edition serves only to illustrate some particular point of musical structure which might not be recorded or which might be hidden and difficult to hear in the complete recording in which the example occurs. Where the example is readily observable in the complete recording it has not been included in the accompanying record.

Example 27 is the notation for the first fourteen measures of the first movement of the Mozart *Clarinet Quintet* in which the Mozartian treatment of the melody discussed on page 216 occurs. In this case there was no need to record this example on the accompanying record. Example 31, the theme for Till from *Till Eulenspiegel* will only be heard within the complete composition, along with colorful accompaniment. In this case it was deemed helpful to the student to excerpt the example from the content of the composition and to record it. All recorded Examples are marked by ®.

Suggested audio-visual film strips with sound

Schloat Production, 150 White Plains Road, Tarrytown, New York, 10591

Education Audio Visual Inc., Pleasantville, New York 10570

Guidance Associates, Communications Park, Box 300, White Plains, New York 10607

1

The Humanism of the Arts

Study Objectives

The objectives of this chapter are

1. To learn that the arts are the results of the dominant sociocultural climate of any particular art epoch.
2. To bring about a meaningful aesthetic understanding that can only come about through direct experience with works of art.

Pronunciation Guide

Bach (Bakh)
Beethoven (Bay'-toh-ven)
Boucher (Boo-shay)
Dali (Dah-lee)
Debussy (De-boo-see)
Esterhazy (Es'-ter-hah-zee)
Goya (Goy'-yah)
Handel (Hen'-dul)

Haydn (Hih'-dn)
Mozart (Moh'-tsahrt)
Orozco (Oh-roth'-koh)
Picasso (Pee-kah'-soh)
Vinci, Leonardo da (Veen'-chee,
  Lay-oh-nahr'-doh dah)
Wagner (Vahg'-ner)

This book is intended to correlate music and art with history and to provide you with a useful understanding of the meaning of the arts. Specifically, it has three basic aims: (1) to develop a breadth of understanding and appreciation of the cultural pattern of the Western world; (2) to develop insight into actual works of music and art; (3) to develop a technique of general critical analysis by which you can arrive at your own evaluation and judgment of works of art. It is in no sense a history of music or a history of the fine arts. Its aim is merely to introduce you to the various kinds and periods of art with the hope that you will be encouraged to seek more of the aesthetic experiences which await your participation.

One of the dangers to our democratic society is the lowering of its standards of values by the very means that have made its existence possible, namely, mass production, mass communications, and mass education. At no time in history have the humanities been challenged with a greater opportunity than now presents itself, for it is just this problem of values with which the fields of literature, philosophy, and the arts deal. That this challenge has been accepted is already evidenced in recent trends toward a renaissance of the humanities in the liberal arts which has focused attention on the study of the arts by the general student as a means of broadening his cultural understanding of the heritage of the past and his awareness of the exigencies of the present. This emphasis has also focused attention on the problem of correlating music and art in the pattern of cultural history on a level which takes into consideration the nonprofessional student's limited technical knowledge and experience.

Sociocultural aspects

Art, in any age, is the expression of the characteristic attitudes of the people of that age toward important aspects of life. Since people live and think in social relationships, their music and art is partially determined by social factors. The dominant class usually sets the cultural taste for the masses. This class may or may not be the largest numerical group. More often than not, it is the class that holds the economic, political, or religious balance of power and therefore imposes its likes and dislikes on the rest of society. Consequently, religious and social patterns often determine the function of music and art. For example, in an age when the church is the principal social institution, the problem confronting artists is that of expressing religious sentiments in harmony with the particular doctrine of the dominating religious group. Bach's *Passion According to St. Matthew* was written for the Lutheran Church at Leipzig in the early eighteenth century. This great work is much more than a sincere expression of Bach's own spiritual devotion. It is a musical revelation of a literal acceptance of the doctrines and spiritual beliefs of his age. Another illustration of the social fabric as a determining force in the function of art can be seen in court life. In an age when courtly activity is prevalent, the problem is to create music and art for lovemaking, for dancing, and for the boudoir. Boucher's delicately molded nudes in playful poses represent the lovemaking spirit of the French Rococo court. *Eine kleine Nachtmusik*, a serenade by Mozart, is charming and graceful music for the gay and frivolous parties of Viennese court life.

An example of economic climate affecting the arts can be seen in the post–War II period. There was a tremendous buying power in the hands of the youth, thanks to a growing economy and the advertising success of the mass media. As a result, the so-called pop culture emerged as a vital force in the business of art, especially in the United States. While the popular arts usually have limited lasting qualities, the consequence of the pop culture movement can be seen in its influence on the artistic endeavors of serious artists. One example is the widely acclaimed musical *Mass* by Leonard Bernstein which incorporates a number of elements from the rock music of the fifties and sixties.

In addition to the influence of the dominant group, the arts are affected by their inheritances from the past. Each cultural pattern leaves its mark on the following generation; therefore, the artistic characteristics of any given age are influenced in some degree by the styles, traditions, and forms they inherit. Furthermore, the influence of one art on another is important in determining the artistic trends of a particular art; for example, the influence of Impressionism in painting on Debussy. The aesthetic theories and artistic ideals that control the destiny of one of the arts, such as literature or visual art, often exert the same kind of influence on the other arts.

In order to have an adequate understanding of the sociocultural conditions from which art springs, we must look on history as something more than a chronicle of past events. We must look upon it as a description of the social, political, economic, religious, and artistic environment out of which grew music, painting, sculpture, and architecture. Each of these facets of history leaves its unmistakable imprint upon the role that art plays in an epoch and the very character of art itself.

As the pattern of economic, political, spiritual, and intellectual life changes, so does the art pattern. The art of ancient Greece, for example, is very different from that of the Gothic period. An investigation of the dominant attitudes toward important aspects of life in these two periods reveals differences which are also found in their art. The study of Greek social and intellectual life will give us a preview of the character and quality which will be found in their art.

Conversely, an intimate knowledge of art will provide clues to the intellectual and social life. The music which Bach wrote for his Lutheran congregation during the early eighteenth century is very different from that which Haydn wrote for the court of Prince Esterhazy fifty years later. This is due to the differences in attitudes toward religion and other institutions. Yet both of these men were great creative artists; both were following closely the patterns of their own age and both composed for a patronage which made specific demands upon them. No one will deny that the paintings of Boucher for the court of Louis XV are very different from those of Picasso in the twentieth century, yet each in his own way represents the culture of his time; Boucher portrays charming flirtatious subjects to enhance the art of love, whereas Picasso, putting his artistic finger on the pulse of the machine age, seeks to produce a style commensurate with the scientific spirit.

One often finds that a particular event or crisis will elicit a creative response. Picasso's *Guernica*, a painting that was a reaction to the mass bombing during the Spanish civil war of 1937, and Penderecki's *Threnody for the Victims of Hiroshima*, a musical response to that holocaust, are two such works in the twentieth century. What the long-term meaning of these two works will be may depend on our memories of those two events.

It is not suggested that individual personality does not make for differences within a certain style and period. Every great creative artist leaves the stamp of his own personality and ideals on his art, and yet each has much in common with his contemporaries. Bach and Handel lived at the same time. Their personalities were very different, and their music is different, but fundamentally the same in its basic style. The paintings of Orozco and Dali are certainly not alike, yet the work of each represents an aspect of contemporary life that we can all recognize. Every great artist is to a certain degree the child of his age, and yet every great artist helps to create his age. It is a matter of interaction between cause and effect. Leonardo da Vinci helped to make the Renaissance a great artistic age, and in turn he was made great by the humanism which was set in motion by the Gothic and which eventually flowered into the Renaissance. Richard Wagner, to take another example, epitomized German nationalism through opera, but at the same time he was borne up on a rising tide of nationalism. In the post–World War II era of the twentieth century the music of the Beatles represented a cultural protest against the past, but their music still was derived from traditional harmonic and rhythmic sources. Even the pop visual art represented a type of realism that was prevalent in the late nineteenth century. All artists have something very personal to say, but each conveys his messages through the medium of the style accepted in his age. Even the iconoclast has his roots firmly in the traditions of his own time.

In view of this very close connection between art and life, it is obvious that an understanding of art involves many different facets of experience. It involves all the forces that were brought to bear on any individual artist: religion, economic status, and social status of both the artist and the artist's public. These, and many other forces such as geographic location, mechanical advancement, and political ideas, all play important roles. For instance, after World War II the emergence of developing countries and cultural exchange programs of various kinds brought on a kind of crossfertilization of cultures. Artists and composers whose indigenous culture was non-Western began to create works in the Western idioms and Western artists in return began to incorporate non-Western points of view into their artistic creativity. If you add to these forces the personal history of the artist and cultivate the faculty of actually hearing or seeing the result of these forces on art, you will have arrived at a better understanding of the cultural heritage of Western civilization. One must have a flexible mind and be able to project one's self into the period of art which is being experienced. This flexibility can be cultivated by study and practice.

Function

To gain insight into works of art, one must become familiar with the various functions of the arts. What were they used for and who were the people for whom they were created? Obviously, a church is built for religious purposes, but what kind of religion? A Gothic cathedral serves a different purpose than a Protestant church, and a Buddhist temple is different from a Jewish synagogue.

Architecture is a living art in that during its lifetime it often undergoes considerable change. A building is redecorated or is used for a different purpose and is remodeled to meet the needs of new functions. In some instances a building may be damaged by fire, war, or some disaster and is then restored in a different style according to the cultural pattern of that particular period.

A painting may serve the purpose of religious education; it may satisfy the ego of some wealthy merchant who commissioned it, or it may be propaganda against the horrors of war, as will be observed in the work of both Goya and Picasso. The same thing is true of sculpture; it may commemorate a historic event or symbolize the function of a building. Under certain conditions we find artists who create pure artworks without a practical objective but with a deep and abiding expression of humanity's idealism. In any event, the artist had a certain, well-defined function in mind which was always determined by his age, patronage, and his own personality.

Music is also a functional art. There is music for war, for religion, for dancing, for love, for comedy, and a host of other purposes for which composers created great works of the past and present. In the case of the visual arts, function can usually be determined by subject matter. Instrumental music, being abstract, defines its function in terms of form, melody, harmony, rhythm, expressive quality, and sometimes by means of announced programs or stories. The function of vocal or dramatic music is determined by the meaning of the text itself.

Not all art has a high purpose. There is a great wealth of art, especially music and painting, which aims merely to amuse and to provide a pleasant diversion from life's everyday problems. Popular music, musical comedy, salon music, illustrations, caricatures, and cartoons are by their very nature of a diversionary character and as such have little or no lasting quality. While their purpose is not denied, it must be realized that the very fact of their timeliness militates against their consideration as representative artworks of real consequence. This is especially true of the so-called protest music and art of the 1960s and 1970s. They achieved a popularity in their time, but as the events which triggered the protest were either forgotten by time, or conflicts partially resolved, or new crises arose, the artistic representations in either visual arts or music dimmed in importance.

The term "kitsch" refers to bad art and is sometimes applied to art which caters to the masses. This kind of art is usually aimed at the aesthetically illiterate and is often represented by commercially produced and distorted copies of other works. Kitsch caters to the masses, whose judgment prevails through their tremendous buying power. Those who appeal to the general public through the popular arts in the world of entertainment give the public what they think they want. In general, this kind of art is of little aesthetic value and will not be considered in the present study.

The function of any art is inseparably connected with the social, economic, political, and religious pattern of its age. In the pattern of history there are periods wherein certain artistic functions are most prominent. For example, the Romanesque and Gothic demanded religious art because the Church was the one all-powerful institution. As the Church lost leadership, art for religious purposes diminished both in quantity and quality. Likewise, the Romantic period of the early nineteenth century laid bare such things as social injustice, exploitation of labor, and the struggle for democratic idealism. Consequently, artists provided works of art which highlighted these abuses and served as propaganda for social reforms as well as documents of faith in the democratic ideals. Nationalistic art served the function of uniting minority peoples into social, cultural, and political units. In the periods where these things may have been the prominent reasons for art, we also find music and art which serve other common purposes as well as these specialized functions. As we progress through the pages of history, we will be constantly aware of the function of art as the consequence of cultural patterns.

Art epochs

In this study we will survey the various aspects of art in terms of the great periods or epochs. For the sake of convenience, history will be divided into large and broadly defined periods. In each of these, the dominant trends in religion, economics, and other areas of important activity will be reduced to a general statement or statements. It will then be demonstrated how each of the important arts is affected by these trends. In order to avoid too many complexities, it will be necessary to emphasize only those arts in each period which have been proved to be the most important. Not all the arts are of equal importance in all times. For example, while painting was considered a major art in the time of the Greeks, it is not so considered in our experience of Greek art. From the point of view of the modern concert stage, Greek music almost ceases to exist. Painting was considered a major art in the Renaissance, while in the contemporary scene architecture is perhaps the most influential. There are certain minor arts and crafts which, while no one denies their existence and their beauty, do not represent the most important artistic productivity of the age. Because we are mainly concerned with a broad and generalized picture, some of these by-products can be left for a later and more intensive study.

It is impossible to divide history arbitrarily into periods of time with exact dates as boundaries. It is equally difficult to mark off one period of art from another. History is a process of change that is slowly revealed as time progresses. While one period of art reaches its zenith, another is being born, the result of normal cultural growth and change. It will be noted that while the Gothic ideals were gradually waning, Renaissance humanism was emerging, and during the High Renaissance of the middle and late sixteenth century the seeds of the Baroque were being germinated, and so on down through history. It must be constantly borne in mind that every period has its past, present, and future; furthermore, we must be ever aware that this process moves slowly and that often many characteristics of one artistic period overlap into another.

Terms such as Gothic, Renaissance, Baroque, and Rococo will be used to designate certain artistic styles in periods of time. It will be practical to use dates for this purpose, but the dates used are only to mark off the span of time when each of these stylistic ideals reached a high peak at which we can say, with some degree of certainty, that it represented the dominant cultural pattern of that age. The following periods and dates are those with which we will be concerned:

Greek   (500 B.C.–100 B.C.)
Roman and Early Christian   (100 B.C.–A.D. 500)
Romanesque   (500–1100)
Gothic   (1100–1400)
Renaissance   (1400–1600)
Baroque   (1600–1725)
Rococo-Classic   (1725–1800)
Romantic/Realist and Nationalist/Impressionist   (1800–1900)
Modern to 1945   (1900–1945)
The Arts Today   (1945–   )

A laboratory of experience

The second specific aim of this study is to develop insight into actual works of music and art. This will involve much more than biographical studies of great composers, painters, and sculptors, or the recognition of their works by title, although these are important steps. It will involve much more than a reading of critical reviews. Only when you are on intimate terms with art by actually seeing and hearing does it become a part of your experience. What does the eye see and the ear hear? What constitutes an aesthetic experience in terms of art? These are questions with which we will be concerned, for real insight can come only when you can perceive with your own senses the forms and sounds the artist used to convey his messages. You must become a hearer and a seer (one who sees) as well. You must spend hours in the laboratory of the concert hall and art museum or the equivalent, acquainting yourself with recordings and art reproductions. You must hear a musical work again and again until the details are easily recognized by the ear. The themes and texture of such a work as Beethoven's *Pastoral Symphony*, for example, should be so indelibly impressed upon your memory that you will never forget them. Reproductions of painting and sculpture should not remain in bound volumes but should take their place on the walls of the home, where they become a part of life's everyday experiences. Even better would be a few originals by unknowns, chosen with discrimination and taste. You must become so familiar with the spirit and character of a few well-chosen works that their messages become a part of your life, and only then will you become fully aware of the meaning of such art. In the case of architecture, the various styles and examples in the local community must be sought out and studied. What is observed in this laboratory of experience will, in turn, be made more meaningful in the light of the historical background and personal history of the artist.

Another facet of artistic insight is the ability to analyze the materials of art and to experience the various ways of organization within the context of the cultural pattern. Just as the artist uses the methods of synthesis in creating, so you must learn to synthesize. You must be able to account for what you see and hear in the terms of the larger forces and monuments in Western civilization. You must see and hear with the eyes and ears of the creators. The aesthetic experience reaches full bloom when you can absorb into your own experience all the aspects of an artwork: function, material, form, cultural milieu, and the artist's own personality.

What techniques can you employ in an effort to bring about this synthesis? What practical tools of hearing and seeing can you utilize in your laboratory of experience? These questions bring us to the subject of the following chapter and to the third specific aim of this study: to develop a technique of analysis as a means to general critical judgment.

Suggested readings

Fry, Roger. *Vision and Design.* London: Chatto and Windus, 1928, chapters 1 and 2.

Lang, Paul Henry. *Music in Western Civilization.* New York: W.W. Norton, 1941, introduction.

Leichtentritt, Hugo. *Music, History and Ideas.* Cambridge: Harvard University Press, 1940, chapter 1.

2

The Organization of the Elements of Art and Music

Study Objectives

The objectives of this chapter are

1. To master the principles of design and learn how they are applied to works of art.
2. To develop a technique to analyze the elements of art and music as they appear in specific works.

Pronunciation Guide

Bartok (Bahr'-tok)
Berlioz (Bayr-lee-ohz)
Delacroix (De-lah-krwah)
Duchamp (Doo-chahmp)
Dufay, Guillaume (Dü-fah-ee, Gwee-lohm)
Giorgione (Johr-joh'-ne)
Penderecki (Pen-der-et'-skee)

Praetorius (Prih-tor'-ee-us)
Raphael (Rahf'-ah-el)
Rembrandt (Rem'-brant)
Schubert (Shoo'-bert)
Stockhausen (Shtohck'-how-zen)
Strauss (Shtrows)
Stravinsky (Strah-vin'-skee)
Van Gogh (Van Gokh)

Granting that we have an understanding of the social forces, a knowledge of the artists' lives, and an awareness of the various functions of art, it becomes necessary to examine some of the devices by which we can actually see or hear those forces as they are expressed in artworks. It is also necessary to examine some principles of sensory perception that are involved in an aesthetic experience. This brings us to the third specific aim of this book: to

9

develop a technique of general critical analysis by which you can arrive at your own evaluation. There is no mathematical formula by which this can be done, for art is much too subjective. There are, however, a few fundamental techniques of observation and analysis which can serve as practical tools of understanding. The artist uses raw materials such as stone, paint, or musical tone. These materials are organized into certain basic elements out of which the artist creates a work of art according to principles of design for an expressive end.

Every work of art worthy of the name must have some special characteristic of artistic form and arrangement that distinguishes it from nonartistic forms. For some observers, form can often be an end in itself. There is a pleasure and delight in the sheer magic of technical perfection, or a pleasure in the awareness of the basic elements alone. Rhythmic movement, "voice" movement in music, the interplay of color or movement of dynamic lines can give us a certain amount of aesthetic pleasure. Technical competence, however, is hardly enough for a lasting quality.

Art deals with the whole spectrum of human experience and the artist interprets and expresses these experiences in a distinctive manner. This can range from the kinds of experience that we associate with idealism, to the ordinary experiences of life, even to those that are ugly and revolting. While the various arts vary in their characteristic subject matters because of the differences of media, they are alike in their basic objective. They are all preoccupied with interpreting human experience. The stimuli for such experiences are often varied due to sociocultural influences, but whatever, whenever, and wherever they occur, artists seek to re-create and interpret them for their contemporaries.

To artists, life consists of a variety of sensations which can be reproduced by many different physical means. A shape, a color, a melody, or a chord are only a few of the means by which sensations can be evoked. It is true in music that sound, melody, and chords are not physical means in themselves but become meaningful only upon being heard. The success of a work of art—be it painting, sculpture, or music—can be measured by the extent to which our senses absorb and reveal the experience the artist seeks to portray. In this way our senses become a means to an aesthetic experience. Normal sensations are not artistic in themselves, but by the selection and arrangement of materials artists are able to intensify our sensations, thereby impressing indelibly upon our memories the experience which they seek to bring forth. It follows that creative artists can arouse moods of agitation or calm, of majesty or delicacy with reasonable assurance of our reaction. Psychologically, they can compel us to experience the kind of mood they desire, providing you are not distracted by boredom or fatigue and are willing to approach the work with the proper attitude.

The most widely accepted theory of aesthetic experience is that of the emotive state. While there are those who look upon art merely as a pleasurable sensation, it is recognized that the vast majority of people respond through their emotions. The emotions lend themselves to the arts because they are common to all human experience. While each emotional state is a very personal matter, we also realize that all people can, and usually do, experience the same emotions at one time or another as a result of similar if not identical stimuli. The creative artist arouses in us a specific emotional state, mood, or feeling and it is only when we experience these emotive states that we achieve a real appreciation of the artistic content of a work of art. In music these emotive states can be achieved by tonal and rhythmic patterns. Because of its inherent abstraction, the emotional response to music varies greatly with individuals and, moreover, time and place can vary each individual response. In painting and sculpture, representational forms, as well as pure formal patterns, evoke emotional states. Architecture depends upon the power of architectural form, size, proportion, and social use.

According to Pepper,[1] there are four ways of producing emotions in art: (1) By direct stimulation such as the excitement of a march with its military rhythms and clear-cut phrases or the lilting pattern of a dance tune. In painting, this kind of stimulation can be seen in the use of colors and agitated line. In *Liberty Leading the People* by Delacroix (colorplate 25), the forward diagonal movement from left to right and the atmosphere of somber colors against the smoke-filled background intensify our own feelings about the subject. (2) Types and symbols that through common usage are charged with emotional meaning can also be used to stimulate emotion. For example, the broken sword, the dying horse, and the dead child in Picasso's *Guernica* (fig. 14.3) all suggest a feeling of terror and carnage that was a part of the artist's message. This type of stimulation does not usually apply to music, except that with a verbal text that suggests these symbols. Instrumental music, by its very abstract nature, refuses to be so objectively associated with specific symbols, but even in abstract music, rhythmic or melodic patterns can be symbols of emotional imagery. An obvious example of this is the rhythmic motive at the opening of Beethoven's Fifth Symphony which, by tradition, suggests Fate knocking. (3) Feeling can also be aroused by representation of emotional behavior in a work of art. In Delacroix's *Liberty Leading the People*, the grim determination in the facial expressions and the upraised arm with weapons, together with the shadowy bodies of fallen citizens provide an emotional climax to the painting that has already been suggested by line and color. Berlioz does this musically in the first movement of the *Symphonie fantastique* where the fragmentary and vague harmonies are contrasted with the lyric and intense melody of the "beloved" to call forth a feeling of reverie and passion. He even suggests these states of emotional response by the title "Reveries and Passions." (4) Artists can also evoke an emotional response by evidence of their own feelings. This response can be realized by listening to

Colorplate 25 follows p. 242.

1. Pepper, Stephen C., *Principles of Art Appreciation* (New York: Harcourt, Brace & Co., 1949), p. 128.

Beethoven's Third (*Eroica*) Symphony, where the dynamic power and majesty of the music can be readily associated with the idea of heroism. Van Gogh, for example, is noted for paintings that reveal his own feelings, such as *The Starry Night* (colorplate 27). Bold, swirling strokes and heavy contrasting colors give a kind of elemental strength to this painting that is not unlike van Gogh's own attitude toward life.

There are other and more subtle ways in which aesthetic responses can be awakened, and we must remember that the artist does not rely on any one of these to the exclusion of others. Furthermore, the artist depends upon a gradual awareness of the various facets of an artwork by repeated observations. No work of art can be instinctively meaningful to the observer, for no work of art can communicate with an observer who is not qualified to understand and speak its language. There is nothing inherent in the nature of people that will make Beethoven's *Eroica* meaningful. The listener to whom this work communicates in an aesthetic way has, by one means or another, become acquainted with the musical language. This may come in part unconsciously as a member of the society of the Western world and in part by personal effort. The greater the mastery of the musical language, the more understanding can be brought to the experience of hearing and the greater is the aesthetic response.

Every scrap of relevant information concerning an artwork can be helpful in assisting you, the conscientious and sympathetic observer, to enlarge and heighten your aesthetic response to any artistic experience, to any art object—visual or aural. It is therefore important to understand that the appreciation of art, the realization of an aesthetic experience, and the awareness of the communication of the work of art are phenomena for which you must work, for which an effort must be made. These phenomena do not occur through the efforts of the creative artist alone. The completed communication depends upon the efforts of both creator and observer. It is never passive and can be made real only through active participation. One uses talents of creating communicative objects and the other uses talents of understanding the communication. The artist arranges material in such a manner as to combat boredom and fatigue and at the same time to assist the observer to remember details and to anticipate emotional states. The observation of principles of design and the basic elements of the arts, when fused into the perceptual process, will lead you from the objective to the subjective understanding of art.

Principles of design

Artistic design is the arrangement of materials and elements into a pattern which conveys a function and meaning of art. While there is an endless variety of artistic possibilities in material, subject matter, and function, there are only a few basic principles of design by which every artist is guided. Every work of art must have enough variety to interest the observer and

Colorplate 34 follows p. 306.

enough unity to avoid chaos. Simply stated then, every artist seeks to achieve enough unity and coherence to present a logical case for an objective and, at the same time, seeks to achieve enough variety to combat monotony. There are two basic ways in which this paradox of unity in variety can be solved: (1) by the principle of repetition and contrast; (2) by the principle of theme and variations.

Repetition and contrast is one of the simplest methods of achieving a satisfying design in that the contrast provides variety while the repetition supplies the unity. This principle is very apparent in popular music, where a melody is stated and then repeated after the statement of a melody of contrasting nature. A painting may achieve this contrast and repetition by utilizing only two or three basic colors or by a limited number of contrasting patterns of line.

The theme and variation principle of achieving unity in variety is one of the most technically demanding accomplishments required of the artist, for it consists of a skillful handling of one motive with the ever-present danger of monotony. A painter may use only one basic color with varying values, hues, and intensities, as will be observed in Rembrandt's work. On the other hand, the artist may use only one motif of line in varying patterns, sizes, and positions. The composer may use only one simple theme and build variations on that theme by playing it backwards, upside down, in fragments, or in various rhythmic patterns. The same harmonic formula may be varied by use of different instruments or of a higher or lower register.

The presence of dynamics, or emphasis, is another way in which both unity and variety can be accentuated. The impression of unity can be intensified by drawing attention to the motives by the use of such devices as size, color, or a focal point; in music, by loudness, tone color, or accented rhythms. Dynamics can also contribute to variety by gradations of intensity of such elements as line, color, and tone.

These two principles of design are by no means independent of each other but are mutually dependent one on another. All works of art employ dynamics to some degree and many combine the theme and variations principle with that of repetition and contrast. As the various facts and trends of history are correlated with art, you will see that certain art epochs reveal strong tendencies toward the almost exclusive use of one or the other of these two principles.

Basic elements in visual art

Line

One of the most simple and common elements used by all artists to create form is line. Painters use graphic line to mold various plastic forms. Sculptors create line in defining form with their material. Even the architect's organization of space results in the lines of a building. There are many different aspects of line. Lines may be curved, with a smooth-flowing rhythm, or they may be straight, with sharp, dynamic angles; they may be clearly defined or vague and diffused; they may be simple and direct or they may show a great amount of detail and ornament.

By the use of line artists can create basic shapes such as spheres, triangles, square, etc. Shapes created by line may be representational or non-representational and abstract. They may also be three-dimensional or two-dimensional and, in the case of some twentieth-century art, they may suggest four dimensions, imaginatively adding the illusion of action to three-dimensional forms. The quality of line may be delicate and refined or it may be broad, showing great strength and solidarity. Color, texture and values, or intensity of line also determines quality.

Line also has expressive qualities. Horizontal lines suggest repose and stability (fig. 2.1). A sense of strength is shown by vertical lines (fig. 2.2). Diagonal lines reflect tension and action (fig. 2.3). Long curves express relaxation and a sense of calm, while short, quick curves are often used to express dynamic agitation. Whatever the qualities may be, artists usually identify themselves with a stylistic line in conformity with their personality, philosophy, and epoch.

Space

Space is three-dimensional volume which is real enough to be experienced physically in architecture and sculpture, but an illusion which can be experienced only by suggestion in painting. Sculptural space is suggested by movement of line. The architect deals in the organization of space into areas, as do the landscape gardener and the city planner. For example, space may appear restricted by being enclosed within heavy walls with few windows. In contrast, it may be expanded by letting one room flow into another, eliminating doors and using large amounts of glass, as in much modern architecture. The landscape architect can contract space by restricting portions of the garden with borders and hedges or expand the concept of spatial volume by providing easy access to all areas, both physically and visually. Space in painting may be an illusion of the third dimension, as recession into the distance or as projection forward.

Infinite space gives a sensation of looking through an opening into a landscape without end. This is accomplished by the relationship of size and position, lack of detail in distance, overlapping of shapes, and receding color intensity (colorplate 1). A more controlled three-dimensional spatial character is achieved by means of rules of perspective. *School of Athens* by Raphael (colorplate 2) demonstrates a more controlled three-dimensional spatial character by means of rules of perspective. Groups of figures are organized in such manner that the figures of Plato and Aristotle are framed by the rounded arch in the background. In contrast, space may be denied by a flat plane on which figures and objects are placed in such a manner as to have relationships

Colorplates 1, 2 follows p. 18.

Figure 2.1 *Venus* [1508–10]—Giorgione. (Courtesy of Alinari/Editorial Photocolor Archives)

Figure 2.2 *American Gothic* [1930]—Grant Wood. (Courtesy The Art Institute of Chicago)

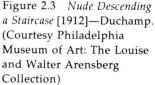

Figure 2.3 *Nude Descending a Staircase* [1912]—Duchamp. (Courtesy Philadelphia Museum of Art: The Louise and Walter Arensberg Collection)

only on a two-dimensional plane. Most visual art suggests either a great or a small amount of space which seems either to expand or to contract. Vertical and horizontal space is contracting if the eye is drawn inward, and expanding if objects or scenes are suggested to exist outside the boundaries of the artwork.

Color

Basically there are two types of color organization: monochromatic and polychromatic. Monochromaticism means that the colors are derived mainly from one primary color, with different values and a unity of hues. Moreover, the hues are usually of low intensity, with small amounts of contrast. Polychromaticism comes from many contrasting colors and high-intensity hues, with generally high values used in various combinations to form a color pattern. In addition to contributing to the reality of form, color has a great number of other functions. It can define form and line; it can create eye rhythm by cleverly shifting the emphasis from one color mass to another; it can add to the sense of motion by expanding or contracting space, using dark colors for contraction and lighter colors for expansion. Color can also contribute to formal organization and unity; for example, polychromaticism usually leads to closed form and separate organization, while monochromaticism leads to open form and fused organization.

Color can also contribute to the emotional or expressive quality of a work. For example, high intensities of bright colors can evoke a sense of excitement, while low intensities and somber colors can suggest serenity, calmness, or even mystery. In traditional art, color is often used to symbolize ideas, such as purple for royalty, blue for faith, white for purity, and a host of other symbolic ideas and objects with color associations.

Medium

The quality of material in a physical sense applies especially to architecture and sculpture. The physical properties of materials such as stone, wood, metal, and plastic determine the manner in which the basic elements will be organized. In painting, the physical properties of such materials as oil and watercolor will determine the technique and provide a discipline for the artist which, in turn, is reflected in the expressive qualities of the artwork.

Recent technological developments have greatly increased the resources of visual media. New materials such as acrylics and plastics have challenged the creativity of the artist. Collage in which materials of different tactile values are used in combination with each other and with painting has led to many interesting kinds of visual expressions. Moreover, multimedia artworks in which visual forms combine with movement and sound have opened even more possibilities.

Formal organization

Form has two meanings in art. The first, formal organization, is the composite of all elements into an expressive whole. This total organization may draw attention toward a focal point, creating closed form, or it may lead the observer out and beyond the immediate scope of the artwork. The latter creates open form. Form may have a geometric balance of mass and void or it may be off-balance and asymmetrical.

Formal organization also concerns itself with the juxtaposition of the various parts into a whole. There may be an organization of separately articulated parts, any one of which can be removed without destroying the reality of the remaining parts. A painting is said to possess separate organization when each figure or object is complete in itself but retains a significant relationship to the whole. In contrast, organization may be fused, the component parts merging one into another.

The second meaning, plastic form, is used to designate the shape or mass of an object. Almost all objects take on certain basic forms such as the sphere, cone, cylinder, rectangle, or square. The sculptor molds plastic form into these shapes. The architect encloses space within the confines of these primary forms. The painter creates the illusion of plastic forms with line and color. The differences between these two definitions must be kept in mind: the use of formal organization for the total picture and plastic form to designate masses.

Not all of the foregoing concepts apply to the visual arts in the same degree. For example, color is less important in sculpture than in painting, and the physical character of material is more important in sculpture and architecture than in painting. It must also be remembered that all the basic elements add to the total character of each individual element.

Expressive content in visual art

To these basic elements we must add the expressive content which is the result of the organization, the function, and the artist's personality. This is an intangible but very real quality of art, for the expressive content is the message which the artist wishes to convey. Whether it is a character study in painting, a heroic group in sculpture, or a private dwelling, the object of the artist is to make the character real, to evoke a sense of heroism, or to give the building the warmth and intimacy of a home. The success of the works of art is in direct proportion to the achieving of these aims. The creative artist possesses the intuitive power to sense relationships and the technique of organizing materials in such a way as to make a work of art communicate some message or experience. In the final analysis, the only really important aspect of art is this expressive content; all other elements and devices are only a means to that end.

The manner in which an artist employs the principles of design and the aspects of the basic elements most commonly used determine his or her style of art. Artists who are subjected to identical cultural forces usually organize the materials and elements in much the same manner, subject, of course, to the function of the artworks as well as to the individual difference and personality of the artist. There are cases in which an artist continues in a style that was prevalent in a bygone era and refuses to conform to the present culture, but such artists are not the accepted great men of art. More often great artists go ahead of their time and provide the connecting link between one artistic age and another. They have the intuition and the courage to recognize that times are changing, that new forces are at work. A da Vinci or a Beethoven then becomes a prophet of a new era. In that case, an analysis of the basic elements will reveal nonconformity to the accepted contemporary style and will show some stylistic characteristics of the subsequent art epoch. Leonardo da Vinci was such a prophet of a new era. His famous *Mona Lisa* does not fulfill all the qualifications of Renaissance painting, but exposes an early view of some qualities later called Baroque. The same is true of Beethoven. He was trained in the classicism of eighteenth-century music, and yet his later works fulfill many of the demands of romanticism. Thus he became the prophet of the new romantic spirit in music. In the case of some

Colorplate 1 *Wheatfields* [1670]—Ruisdael. (Courtesy The Metropolitan Museum of Art, Bequest of Benjamin Altman)

Colorplate 2 *School of Athens* [1510–1511]—Raphael. (Courtesy Scala/Editorial Photocolor Archives)

Colorplate 3   *Sistine Madonna* [1513]—Raphael. (Courtesy Scala/Editorial Photocolor Archives)

twentieth-century artists, such as Picasso and Stravinsky, their works reveal a variety of styles that kept pace with the extreme rapidity of cultural change that characterizes this century.

Enough suggestions have been made here to give some idea of the basic elements and principles of design in the arts. The important thing to remember is that everything cannot be grasped at once and that all elements are not always of equal importance. A general conception of these elements is all that is necessary for the beginner. As you grow in your ability to analyze works of art, you will be able to make a more detailed study of each of the above principles and elements.

An example in painting

Taking the *Sistine Madonna* (colorplate 3) by Raphael as an example, let us make an analysis of the organization, function, and elements, according to what we actually see. The function of this work is apparently religious. The subject is the Madonna and the baby Jesus. Note that the artist, in order that there will be no doubt as to the subject, has surrounded the head of each figure with a halo—all except the two little angels, whose wings identify them as heavenly. There is nothing else to identify the figures as being holy. They are mere humans—real people whom Raphael knew and chose to use as models.

Line

One of the prominent elements of this work is line. Note that the lines are very sharp, clearly defining the outlines of the various forms, separating them from the background. They are also primarily curved, suggesting a smooth-flowing vertical motion. Linear unity is achieved by a rhythm of motives, and variety by a contrast of visual pauses between these motifs.

Space

The space element is not great in this case. The figures are bounded by the drapery and by the painted-in frame at the bottom. The background, made up of a myriad of faces of cherubs, is quite flat and does not suggest any sense of limitless space. The figures, however, are so molded as to seem real in a plastic sense, giving a three-dimensional effect. In addition, they seem to project forward, a projection implied by the gesture and look of the two figures on either side of the Madonna. This spatial quality is also implied by the emergence of the major figure from the sea of cherubic faces.

Color

The color is polychromatic, for the colors do not blend but give a rich color harmony by means of contrast, especially between the red and blue. Note that the principle of repetition and contrast of color provides both unity and variety.

Colorplate 3 follows p. 18.

Medium

In this instance the material is oil on canvas, painted in such a manner that brushstrokes are blended together and are not visible.

Formal organization

The lines of the figures draw the eye inward toward the figure of the Madonna and Child. All motion is centered toward this group, which then provides the dynamic quality. The gaze of the figure on the left, the vertical line of the right figure, the upward look of the cherubs, even the drapery above bring the eye toward the focal point. Obviously, this is closed form. It is also balanced form, for the two figures on the side equalize the vertical axis of the central group. Here again the drapery serves to emphasize the perfect balance of form. The organization of this painting is one of separately articulated parts. No figure is merged with another; each is complete in itself and could be removed without destroying the reality of any other—not, however, without destroying the formal balance of the whole.

Summarizing, what do we have? We have an oil painting of a religious subject that is primarily linear in character. It has closed form, separate organization, little spatial sense, and its colors are polychromatic. It utilizes all of the basic principles of design, with repetition and contrast dominating. The reality of the human form is perhaps the strongest impression one gets. The expression of religious feeling is poetic, beautiful, but not overwhelmingly powerful. Raphael's painting is a good example of Renaissance art, and we shall later see that this particular pattern of art is indigenous to the sociocultural trends of that period. The above analysis can be easily accounted for in the religious, intellectual, social, and economic life of the Renaissance and in the life of Raphael. This synthesis of all elements, both objective and subjective, results in a keener insight to the meaning and a broader understanding of the art. If, for example, a work of the Romantic period had been analyzed, we would have found a very different subject for a different function. This, in turn, could be explained by the spirit of romanticism.

Basic elements in music

Music is the most abstract of all the arts and exists only through the medium of performance. It moves in time, with constant shifting and changing which makes it difficult for a listener to make an objective analysis. The scope of our attention is very limited, making it impossible to grasp all the details at once. Consequently, music requires repeated hearings to enjoy the full impact of its message. Nevertheless, there are materials and musical concepts which can be observed and used objectively in making an expressive and stylistic analysis.

Since few persons can look at a piece of notated music and imagine or actually hear what the notation means auditorily, it becomes necessary for you, the listener, to hear the following examples either through your own performance or that of someone else. Compare the musical examples with the analytical schematas and listen to them with the schematas in mind.

The principles of design that are valid for visual art are also inherent in any musical work worthy of our attention. The problem of achieving unity and variety is the same, and, in general, the composers solve their problems in much the same manner as the painter, sculptor, and architect.

Rhythm

In music rhythm has two common meanings. In the broader sense rhythm is the movement of the formal organization, the ebb and flow of the musical elements in the overall structure of the composition. In a narrower sense, rhythm refers to the patterns within the accented and unaccented metric organization of a work. The simplest metrical schemes are those of either two or three pulses per measure.

Example 2.1: Two Pulses Per Measure®

(Ukranian Folk Song)

In example 2.1 the metric organization is one of two pulses per measure, one accented and one unaccented. In the 2/4 of the metric signature, the 2 indicates the number of pulses and the 4 indicates that these pulses are represented by quarter notes.[2] In the narrow sense there are three different rhythmic patterns within the metric organization, namely:

a) ♩ ♩ b) ♩ ♩ c) ♩ ♩

2. See appendix for note values.

In pattern a) the metric pulses (¼ notes) are divided between two ⅛ notes. In pattern b) one pulse is divided by two ⅛ notes and one is represented by a ¼ note. In c) the pulse and rhythmic pattern are identical. Each consists of two ¼ notes.

Following is a diagrammatic representation of the metric scheme and the rhythmic patterns of example 2.1. The ′ indicates accented and the ˘ indicates unaccented pulses.

The overall rhythm is represented by the brackets underlying the diagram.

Example 2.2: Three Pulses Per Measure®

The Blue Danube, Johann Strauss

Example 2.2 has a metric scheme of three pulses per measure, one accented and two unaccented. There are only two rhythmic patterns in this case and they do not coincide with the metrical divisions. The rhythmic patterns are: a) ♩ | ♩ ♩ ♩ | 𝅝 and b) ♩ | 𝅗𝅥 The complete diagram of meter and rhythm would look as follows:

Meter

Rhythm

Even in such a simple melodic idea as example 2.2 it will be readily heard that the metric and rhythmic schemes are overlapping and not identical. The intriguing charm of the Viennese Waltz is the very defeat of the restrictive and repetitive scheme of accented and unaccented pulses by the broader rhythmic organization, and especially by the freedom of interpretation by the performer. Such contrast between meter and rhythm is recognized by the artistic reader of poetry who is conscious of the underlying metric scheme but never subservient to it. It is the difference between reading the words and reading the meaning.

It is this recognition of the overall sense of rhythm that makes for artistic interpretation and for satisfying listening. This overall rhythm may be symmetrical or asymmetrical.

Example 2.3: Symmetrical®

(Hungarian Folk Song)

Example 2.4: Asymmetrical®

(Rumanian Folk Song)

Some periods of Western music have tended to use symmetrical rhythms, while others have made great use of asymmetrical patterns. Some rhythmic patterns, such as those of a march, are very simple, regular, and strongly marked. Complex rhythms are often so subtly marked off that the patterns are hardly noticeable.

Not only can overall rhythmic organization be asymmetrical, metric organization can also be complex in that the metric schemes of different values can be mixed together in a composition as in example 2.5. Such metric schemes as five and seven are actually composed of two or more simple patterns—five equals two plus three, seven equals three plus two plus two, or two plus two plus three, or two plus three plus two.

Example 2.5: Bartók, *Dance #1* from the *Six Dances in Bulgarian Rhythm*®

The tempo with which the rhythmic patterns recur is an important element of the expressive content of music. Fast tempi or rapidly recurring patterns give a feeling of excitement, while slow tempi tend to suggest repose. It must be remembered that rhythm is the one element without which music cannot exist. It is an indispensable factor in the character of every other element of music.

Pitch

Pitch is traditionally referred to as high or low. In actuality it is the number of vibrations of the sounding body (a string, a membrane, a column of air, or an electronic modulator among many others) that determines the pitch of a tone. Tones generated by a great number of vibrations are said to be higher than those of fewer vibrations. While the human ear can hear a very large range of vibrations, music up to the advent of electronic synthesizers in mid-twentieth century has traditionally used only those tones between approximately twenty to eight thousand vibrations per second. Moreover, only a very limited number of sounds or tones from among the infinite possibility are actually used. The keyboard of the piano with its eighty-eight pitches a half step apart from each other constitute the pitched material that was exclusively used in Western music for over one thousand years.

Melody

Melody is a series of single tones sounded successively and organized rhythmically which expresses a musical idea. It can be either sung or played. It may be simple, without ornamentation, or it may be elaborate, with a great deal of ornamentation. It may be smooth-flowing and lyric in quality, with only small skips or pitch intervals between successive tones or very angular, with many large pitch intervals, or, in extended melodies, a combination of both.

The following example shows a melody that is both simple, without ornamentation, and smooth and lyric:

Example 2.6: *London Bridge*®

Example 2.7 below is a melody with elaborate ornamentation:

Example 2.7: Handel, *Messiah* (Aria, *Every Valley*)®

Example 2.8 is a melody with many large pitch intervals as is often characteristic in instrumental works. While the human voice is generally restricted to a range of about two octaves, instruments are generally capable of a much greater range.

Example 2.8 is a melody with many large pitch intervals:

Example 2.8: Richard Strauss, *Don Juan* (first theme)®

In the history of Western music, melody has been employed in three different textures: (1) monophony, (2) polyphony, and (3) homophony.

A musical work consisting exclusively of a single melody without accompaniment is monophonic in texture:

Example 2.9: Hymnus, *In adventu Domini*®

Polyphony is a musical texture in which two or more melodic lines are sounded simultaneously. The simplest example of such a texture is that of the *round* or *canon* in which the same melody is heard in two or more voice parts simultaneously but at different points in time, and often at different pitch levels. Example 2.10 is a canon in three voices. The second and third voices sing the same melody as the first voice but each enters two measures later than the preceding one. Canons were first written to be sung, but later composers also wrote instrumental canons. Due to their vocal origin the individual melodic lines continued to be called "voices."

In example 2.11 Dufay has taken the melody of example 2.9 and added two different lines of melody to give it a polyphonic texture. He has changed its rhythmic structure and given it a metric organization of three pulses to

Example 2.10: Michael Praetorius, *Viva la musica*®

Vi - va, vi - va la | mu - si - ca, | vi - va, vi - va la | mu - si - ca,

Vi - va, vi - va la | mu - si - ca,

Example 2.10 (Continued)

vi - va   la   mu - si - ca,   vi - va, vi - va la   mu - si - ca,

vi - va, vi - va la   mu - si - ca,   vi - va   la   mu - si - ca,

vi - va, vi - va la   mu - si - ca,   vi - va, vi - va la   mu - si - ca,

vi - va, vi - va la   mu - si - ca,   vi - va   la   mu - si - ca,

vi - va, vi - va la   mu - si - ca,   vi - va, vi - va la   mu - si - ca,

vi - va   la   mu - si - ca,   vi - va, vi - va la   mu - si - ca,

Example 2.11: Guillaume Dufay®

1. Con - di - tor   al - me   si - de - rum,   ae -

1. Con - di - tor   al - me   si - de - rum,   ae -

Example 2.11 (Continued)

ter - na   lux   cre - den - ti - um.   Chri - ste,   Re - demp - tor

ter - na   lux   cre - den- ti -   um.   Chri- ste,___ Re - demp - tor

em - ni - um,   ex - au - di   pre - ces   sup - pli -   cum.

em - ni- um,   ex - au - di   pre - ces   sup - pli - cum.

the measure. At the same time he has altered the melodic line of the original chant to fit the polyphonic texture.

The use of a single melody supported by harmonic accompaniment is called homophony, as in example 2.12.

Example 2.12: Stephen Foster, *Jeanie with the Light Brown Hair*®

1. I   dream   of   Jea - nie with   the   light   brown   hair,

Harmony

While melody is a series of single tones sounded successively, harmony is a series of simultaneously sounded tones (a chord) of two or more pitches. When present, harmony may be the result of the weaving together of melodic lines, or it may be the result of vertical chords, or a combination of both. Various systems of harmonic organization have been used in Western music. These have been commonly referred to as modality, tonality, and atonality. Modality is a type of harmony based on the use of the eight church modes (see ex. 5.1) which were scales in common usage during the medieval periods of the Romanesque and Gothic. Each mode gave rise to a slightly different harmonic organization, since each modal scale was different in structure.

While modal harmony predominated in the vocal writing of the polyphonic masters of the fifteenth and sixteenth centuries, tonal harmony (tonality) increasingly displaced it in the seventeenth century and became the controlling practice of the eighteenth and nineteenth centuries. Tonality is a harmonic-melodic system in which the vertical structure of chords and the melodic movement of tones are organized around a central tone to which both the harmony and the melody gravitate. This tone or tonic is derived exclusively from the major-minor scales. Tonality is a unified system for all major-minor scales, since all major-minor scale patterns are the same in structure.

Listen to example 2.13 and experience the urge in measures three, four and seven to return to the central tone G which is the basis for the harmonic chordal structure of measures one, two, five, six, and most importantly eight, as well as the central tone to which the melody relentlessly moves.

Example 2.13: *Here we go 'round the mulberry bush*®

Consonance and dissonance are used in both modality and tonality. Consonance gives a feeling of repose, while dissonance gives a feeling of tension. Atonality is a system of combining tones harmonically without the use of the traditional tonal centers of either modality or tonality. Judged on the basis of either modality or tonality, atonal music strikes the listener as completely dissonant. Atonal music, however, uses combinations of pitches as ends in themselves, rather than as means to an end within the modal or tonal systems of harmony. Twelve-tone, or dodecaphonic music is often referred to as atonal. Other harmonic practices less structured than twelve-tone music achieve atonality through the use of experimental devices such as cluster tones, chance or aleatory combinations, and electronically produced sounds. Atonal and twelve-tone music belongs exclusively to the musical development of the twentieth century.

Dynamics

Dynamics in music is synonymous with gradations in sound volume. Dynamics became an increasingly important factor in music as the desire for intensity of expression grew in the eighteenth and particularly in the nineteenth and twentieth centuries. Composers found dynamic variation a vital tool for intensifying emotional expression and gave explicit directions about its use in their compositions. While there can be no specific indication of dynamic level, directions for loud and soft performance as indicated by the traditional marks of *p* (the initial of the Italian word "piano" meaning soft) and *f* (initial of the Italian word "forte" meaning loud) and their multiple use inform the performer of the general intent of the composer in the degree of loudness or softness.

Tone color

Tone color is the quality of sound produced by various instruments, voices and all other devices to generate sounds in musical performance. Physically tone color is determined by many factors which result in the presence or absence, as well as the intensification, of certain overtones in the sound as heard by the human ear. The specific tone color of an instrument is dependent upon the method of producing the sound and by the material and construction of the instrument. Three main divisions have been traditionally recognized based on the method of sound production: (1) strings, (2) winds, (3) percussion.[3] The sounds may blend together into a single sonority, or they may retain their individual qualities even when played or sung together. The tonal quality of the human voice is determined in part by the range of the voice—whether soprano, alto, tenor, or bass, as well as by human individuality.

3. See appendix for a list of instruments and their characteristic tone color.

Within the twentieth century, a whole new range of tone color has been introduced into music through the employment of electronic devices. True electronic music is that which is generated by the electronic medium itself. The production of sound on the Moog synthesizer is of this nature, as in the *Brandenburg Concerto* no. 3 by J. S. Bach recorded under the title *Switched-on Bach.*

Electronic media are also used for the manipulation of pre-created sounds. This can be illustrated by the use of tape recorder, amplification, electronic resonating devices, and filters. An example of this is *Gesang der Jünglinge* by Stockhausen (see p. 369).

Traditional instruments have been used to produce new tonal effects. Performing techniques such as glissandos on both woodwind and brass instruments, bowing on the untuned portion of the strings behind the bridge of stringed instruments, or the plucking of the strings of the piano with fingers or plectrums are only a few of the new techniques in use today. New tonal effects are also obtained by adding devices normally foreign to traditional instruments.

Beyond this, composers have called for a great number of sounds generated by what would have traditionally been considered nonmusical instruments or devices, among which are typewriters, wind machines, automobile horns, and shattering of glass. In their search for new tonal colors and combinations of sounds, composers have often joined together any and all of these devices. They are also combining these new sounds with those of traditional instruments.

Formal organization

Musical form is the manner in which materials of melody, harmony, rhythm, and tone color are organized. While there are many variants, there are only two elementary treatments of formal organization—which would indicate a simplicity of all artistic forms. One type of formal organization is variation; the other is repetition and contrast. Obviously, both of these devices can be employed with very brief musical ideas or motives. Moreover these two means of organization can be quite independently pursued or combined. Both variation and repetition and contrast can be achieved in melody, harmony, rhythm, or tone color or any combination of these.

Extended formal design leads to such individual and traditional forms as dance, rondo, song form, theme and variation, sonata form, etc. In large compositions such as the symphony, opera, or mass, to mention but a few, a number of separate movements, sometimes of different formal design, are joined together for a unified common purpose or expression.

Expressive content in music

The expressive quality or musical message is contained in our response to the foregoing materials and their organization. A musical scholar, or one who has an adequate technical knowledge of music, may enjoy music from an intellectual point of view, but most people respond to music through the emotions and receive their aesthetic experience in terms of subjective feelings, for music possesses tremendous powers of sensuous appeal through rhythm, melody, harmony, and sheer sonority of sound. It often happens that these feelings become visual by association. A certain rhythmic pattern, for example, may remind you of a galloping horse, and you may experience a visual impression from the music. An example of this is found in the piano accompaniment to Schubert's *Erlkönig*. In *Threnody for the Victims of Hiroshima* by Penderecki, the varying intensities of bands of sound result in a tonal coloring that intensifies the feeling of lament for the victims. For some listeners it may even trigger the imagination to the degree that they may experience the sounds and sights of that holocaust. In Beethoven's own words, the Sixth or *Pastoral* Symphony is based on his "feelings when in the country." The average listener associates a visual impression of these feelings with a personal experience in nature. If you have not seen the countryside near Vienna where Beethoven walked, you might associate the music with nature of your own environment. Even in such abstract emotional feelings as love, tragedy, and joy, you might associate particular scenes and events from your own experience.

Composers organize their materials in such a way as to evoke the emotion or visual image which best conveys their message. They do this in much the same manner as visual artists use materials to convey messages. Messages are the expressive content of the music, and composers bring all of their technique, intuition, ideals, and personality into the creative process in achieving this end.

Examples in music

A simple example of a purely abstract design in musical composition is the first movement of Mozart's *Eine kleine Nachtmusik*, which literally means *A Little Night Music* (a simple nocturne). The entire work, which is in four movements, is written for a string quartet of string orchestra and constitutes what is known as a classical sonata. (See pages 208–210.) Without going into a detailed analysis of the first movement let us observe its features from the standpoint of the basic elements in music just discussed.

Rhythm

The music moves in a very lively four pulse meter throughout, and is absolutely constant and regular. Mozart employed a great number of rhythmic patterns in the narrow sense. While the overall rhythmic organization gives a distinct feeling of balance, constant variations of the larger patterns are achieved by repetitions of the smaller rhythmic elements, so that a short rhythmic phrase is often balanced by a larger one or vice versa. This constant actual asymmetry versus the feeling of complete balance lends rhythmic vitality to the movement.

Melody

The principal melodic material is heard almost exclusively in the upper or first violin part. It is characteristically instrumental throughout, with patterns and ranges that preclude any vocal derivation or association. There are many instances of ornamentation—trills and very rapidly repeated notes and scale patterns. While the movement is basically homophonic in texture, Mozart's skill in writing for those instruments which are not engaged in playing the melody is such that one is rarely conscious of a subordinate accompaniment. His homophonic texture is realized through what is almost pure counterpoint in which each instrument participates in the accompanying structure through a part that is essentially melodic.

Harmony

The harmony is purely tonal. The first part of the movement which is repeated presents two groups of thematic materials. The first is in the basic key of G major, and the second in the closely related key of D major. A short passage which ends the G major section, bridges the transition to the key of D major. Such a bridge, leading to the establishment of the new key of D major is known as a modulation. The two keys so established arouse a feeling of contrast and unrest. This feeling is intensified in the short section that follows the repeated first part and is resolved in the final section where all the thematic material is heard in the tonic key of G major. The general harmonic feeling is one of respose rather than restlessness.

Dynamics

Mozart made considerable use of dynamic contrasts, but the overall effect is one of conscious reserve rather than dynamic exaggeration. The contrasts tend to arouse a coquettish expression rather than one of deep emotional feeling.

Tone color

There is no attempt to develop any tonal color beyond that of the normal string quality. Mozart exploited a responsive and expressive string quality by employing the most comfortable and typical range for each of the string instruments.

Formal organization

The movement is that of a very simple sonata-allegro form. (See pages 208–210.) The basic treatment is that of statement-repetition and contrast. This is accomplished through rhythmic, melodic, harmonic, dynamic, and even coloristic statements of very short sections which constitute the structure known as sonata-allegro form. Subtle variations within the repetitions of materials lends interest to the work which, however, is decidedly straight-forward and simple in presentation.

An example of Impressionism in music is *Nuages* (*Clouds*) by Debussy, which presents a much more complex use of the basic elements of music. This work can serve as a laboratory experiment in the observation of the various musical elements and the manner in which Debussy handles them. Remember that you may not be strongly conscious of all these elements on the first hearing. Repeated hearings are a basic necessity to complete comprehension. The function of Debussy's *Nuages* is to give you a musical impression of the feeling caused by the movement of white fleecy clouds on a summer day— clouds that shift and change without effort. Debussy probably expected that a serene, languid feeling would result from hearing the music.

Melody

There are several melodies present, but usually only one at a time. Melody is not constant, but appears very clearly for brief moments and then becomes lost in the welter of sound. The contour, or lines, of the melodies encompasses a wide range, giving them a distinct instrumental quality.

Harmony (consonance and dissonance)

The harmonies of *Nuages* are very luxurious, full of rich mellow sounds built upon chords with large numbers of tones. The sense of consonance and dissonance is very interesting here. Note that there is a slight feeling of tension most of the time, giving a sense of harmonic motion. The periods of repose, or consonance, are few and usually very soft. All this lessens the finality of phrasing and adds to the impression of vagueness and constant movement.

Rhythm

In this instance, rhythm is very complex, even though the music moves rather slowly. This is not dance music. It is difficult to keep time to because there are few regular strong accents.

Tone color

Debussy utilized every resource of the modern orchestra, using all instrumental colors available. Note the clear-cut tone in the melodic lines, usually from the woodwinds. The strings are often used in a sweeping manner, suggesting the feeling of celestial motion.

Formal organization

Debussy used a modified repetition and contrast principle of design on which to base his musical form. The form is not clear-cut; rather, it is vague and suggestive, like the subject itself. Note that when a climax is expected or a melodic phrase is expected to be completed, the music suddenly changes, taking up a new melody and harmonic background. This near formlessness also adds to the original idea of the subject matter. Here we have an example of fused organization applied to music.

The total effect of the way in which Debussy used these musical materials is the expressive content. He succeeded in the functional task before him. He created a bit of music that suggests the vague wandering motion of clouds—a motion which is experienced visually. Owing to the fact that the harmonic tension is never very strong, you get no strong emotional response. Because the melodies are vague and because the form is indistinct, you get the suggestion of atmosphere. The tone color supplies the impressions of the colors of the beautiful azure sky and billowing white clouds.

A suggested analogy

Because of the difference in technical terminology and the lack of a traditional correlation between the arts, it is extremely difficult, and often dangerous, to attempt an analogy between the basic elements of music and the basic elements of the visual arts. There is agreement as to the sociocultural force which affects both types of art, but there has been little attempt to draw analogies between the materials and elements of each in a manner that is useful to the student. It is not necessary that an exact comparison be made, but you will become more aware of the affinity between the arts if some analogy is suggested.

Visual line has its counterpart in the melody and rhythm of music. The spatial element is suggested in music by the tension of dissonant harmony, which seems to bring things forward in a plastic sense, and by gradation of tone color. The same is true of painting. Visual form is closely allied to aural form, for the same principles of design are utilized in both. Unity of organization has no direct counterpart in music, but the sense of either fused unity or separate unity is suggested by the clarity of melody and harmonic texture, by the consistence of rhythm, and by the contrast of one musical element with another. Visual color has its direct analogy in timbre, or tone color, of instruments both separately and in combination. The materials of visual art are also analogous to the kinds of musical tones which are produced by mechanical devices, such as drawing a bow over a string or setting a column of air into vibration by a reed, lips, vocal chords, or by a percussive action on a string or other vibrating material.

It is not suggested that a comparative analysis of a symphony and a work of sculpture both from the year 1800 will reveal conformity in every basic element. There are too many objective and subjective factors for this to be true. If, however, the two works grew out of much the same social condition, they will show a surprising amount of conformity in the matter of design and general organization of their component parts. Our study will show clearly the relationship between the Gregorian chant and the Romanesque cathedral. A Bach fugue and a Rembrandt painting both arise out of the spirit of the Baroque, and both conform to the pattern of organization typical of the period. It will be noted that both op art and electronic music of the twentieth century are closely related to physics. One produces optical effects of illusion through color and line manipulation through a variety of technological devices, and the other evokes aural sensations by electronic manipulation of sounds. If you can both see and hear the objective elements in these works, if you can relate them to the cultural scene, the resultant aesthetic experience will be unforgettably real.

Bear in mind that the three examples which were analyzed, the *Sistine Madonna, Eine kleine Nachtmusik,* and the *Nuages,* parallel most other works of their same periods in history. The other historical periods have their own patterns which we will try to differentiate, recognize, and understand as we journey through history. As you become more and more aware of the organizational patterns of the elements of art and learn to account for these patterns within the social milieu, you will come to a breadth of understanding of our cultural heritage.

Recorded musical examples

Switched-on Bach, Brandenburg Concerto no. 3

Stockhausen, *Gesang der Junglinge (Song of Youth)*

Debussy, *Nuages*

Mozart, *Eine kleine Nachtmusik*

Suggested readings

Boyden, David. *Introduction to Music,* 2nd ed. New York: Knopf, 1970, pp. 9–107.

Broekema, Andrew J. *The Music Listener.* Dubuque, Ia.: Wm. C. Brown Company Publishers, 1978, pp. 27–140.

Langer, Susanne K. *Philosophy in a New Key.* Cambridge: Harvard University Press, 1960, pp. 204–45.

Myers, Leonard B. *Emotion and Meaning in Music.* Chicago: University of Chicago Press, 1956, pp. 1–82.

Pepper, Stephen C. *Principles of Art Appreciation.* New York: Harcourt, Brace and Co., 1949, pp. 49–57, 147–96.

Wölfflin, Heinrich. *Principles of Art History.* New York: Dover Publications, n.d.

Suggested examples for further analysis

Painting: Rembrandt, *The Noble Slav;* Duchamp, *Nude Descending a Staircase*

Architecture: Bernini, Plaza of St. Peter's in Rome; Frank Lloyd Wright, Kaufmann House, Bear Run, Pa.

Sculpture: Michelangelo, *Bound Slave;* Mestrovic, *The Maiden of Kossovo*

Music: Beethoven, Symphony no. 6 (*Pastoral*); Britten, *Young Person's Guide to the Orchestra;* Penderecki, *Threnody for the Victims of Hiroshima;* Schubert, *Erlkönig*

3

The Greeks
(500–100 B.C.)

Chronology of the Greeks

B.C.

582	Pythagoras (c.582–c.500)	470	Socrates (470–390)
	Greek modal scales	427	Plato (427–347)
525	Aeschylus (525–456)	404	Athens at war with Sparta
496	Sophocles (496–406)	390	Praxiteles (390–330)
490	Persian Wars	384	Aristotle (384–322)
	Phidias (490–432)	360	Lysippus (c.360–c.316)

Study Objectives

The objectives of this chapter are

1. To define humanism and its realization in Greek art.
2. To understand the intellectual concept as revealed in Greek life and art.

Pronunciation Guide

Aphrodite (Ahf-roh-dih′-tee)
Apollo (Ah-pol′-loh)
Aristotle (Ah′-ris-tot-tul)
Athena (Ah-thee′-nah)
Dionysus (Dih-oh-nih′-sus)
Hermes (Hur′-meez)

Lysippus (Li-sip′-pus)
Mercury (Mur′-ku-ree)
Nike Of Samothrace (Nih′-kee of
  Sah′-moh-thrays)
Parthenon (Pahr′-the-non)
Pergamum (Pur′-gah-mum)

Pericles (Pay'-rik-lees)
Phidias (Fi'-dee-us)
Plato (Play'-toh)
Praxiteles (Prax-i'-tay-lees)

Prometheus (Proh-may'-thee-us)
Pythagoras (Pi-thag'-oh-rus)
Venus de Medici (Vay'-nus day
    May'-dee-chee)

Because the Western world has always looked upon Hellenic culture as the cradle of our own cultural development, our study of art epochs will start with the art of Greece.

The Archaic Age of Greek art, extending from about 1000 to 800 B.C., is the age in which an indigenous Grecian art was slowly developing. The second period, often called the Lyric Age and extending from 800 to the sixth century B.C., is noted for its expressiveness and realism. This was the great age of lyric poetry from which the period takes its name. However, neither of these two early cultures reached a pinnacle of quality and perfection that makes them an indispensable prelude to our own culture. The Golden Age, or the Age of Pericles, which flourished in the fifth century and extended over into the fourth century, is the age which we will consider as the high point of Greek culture. During this era there occurred such a development in drama, architecture, sculpture, and music that it is still looked upon as the cultural spring from which our own culture has emerged. The Hellenistic period of Greek culture can be dated from about 325 B.C. to 100 B.C. and is generally considered to be a period of decadent Greek art.

The end of the Persian wars in 480 B.C. precipitated a flood of artistic energy that was to be called the Golden Age of Greek art. The spoils of war provided the necessary wealth for artistic patronage. Then, too, a feeling of peace settled on the Greeks which gave them confidence and incentive for artistic production. After all, the gods must have approved of their actions to have given them victory over the Persians. It was a fitting memorial that a great program of public building should be undertaken and dedicated to the gods in appreciation for their protection and guidance. When Pericles came to power about 460 B.C., he embarked on a program which was designed to make Athens the cultural and artistic center of Greece. The core of the program was the construction of a group of buildings on the Acropolis, of which the *Parthenon* was the largest and most nearly perfect. With such a fertile ground for artistic activity, it is not surprising that the finest scholars and artists were attracted from the entire known world. This was the age of Plato, Aristotle, Pythagoras, and Praxiteles, to mention but a few. With the finest minds in the world centered in one city of about 100,000 inhabitants, it is not surprising that Athens held the position of the cultural capital of the world.

If we recognize that art is a reflection of the attitudes of a people toward important aspects of life, we must focus our attention for a moment on the religious, philosophic, social, and economic status of Athenian society. By

Athenian society we do not mean all of the people living in Athens. Slavery was a recognized institution, and the peasants were but little better off. Foreigners could live there and transact business but could not hold office or take part in public affairs. It was the freeborn citizens who constituted the Athenian society as patrons of the arts. The dominant attitude of this group can be summed up by saying it was one of "this-worldliness." The Greeks were concerned mainly with problems of human life, of life in this world with all that this implies. To live beautifully and happily was the aim of Athenians, and their motto was man is the measure of all things. The Greek temperament sought to master the world by knowing it and reducing it to a simple mathematical formula.

The Greeks did not harbor the fear and awe of the supernatural that is found in early cultures. Life after death held little interest for them, for the Greek religion did not confront, as did the Christian religion, the mystery of death and suffering. The Greek gods and goddesses dwelt in eternal bloom. A Greek tombstone makes no allusions to the darkness of the grave and offers no hope of a glorious resurrection. It shows the commemorated person in some delightful image of the life once lived—a lady selecting a pearl from a basket, a young man stripped for a foot race with his favorite dog beside him. The Greeks did not look upon death with faith in the future, but neither did they dwell upon it with morbid regret. Sorrow for the departed was dignified by the restrained and simple grace with which their memory was portrayed in reliefs of marble.

Their gods were merely human beings endowed with a greater physical beauty and a little more wisdom than ordinary mortals. When the Greeks strove toward the heights of the gods, they sought to rival them for their greater power, not for their moral perfection. The gods themselves were anthropomorphic; that is, they were represented as humans—ideal humans, for the Greeks saw in their gods the ideal likeness of themselves. A different god was created for every aspect of nature and human activity. Zeus was the king of the gods who ruled from Mount Olympus over such gods as Apollo, the sun god; Mercury, the patron god of commerce and trade; Aphrodite, goddess of love and beauty; Athena, patron goddess of Athens. Besides these, there was a host of lesser gods and goddesses. Greek citizens did not rely on any one god for all of their spiritual needs, for the gods themselves were not always infallible and could not always be trusted. They could even be outwitted on occasion, as they were by Prometheus when he stole fire from them. Yet the Greeks were a very religious people, building temples and celebrating festivals in honor of the gods. A daily visit to the temple was a part of each day's routine.

Greek thinkers refused to accept the blind will of their gods as an explanation of the universe. They pursued knowledge, finding order and recurrent patterns in all spheres of intellectual activity. It was this basic structure which they were seeking, and to them geometry and mathematics described it. They brought reason to the fore, using numbers as symbols of the cosmic force which they believed was operating throughout the universe. This mathematical reasoning dominated their whole life, including their art. The Greeks pushed earlier superstitions and magic aside in favor of logic and reason.

It is not difficult to find the results of this basic philosophy in Greek art. It was life that fascinated the Greek artist, and this life was seen in physical perfection. A perfect body was the incarnation of the perfect mind. What was perfect was both beautiful and good. Their art demonstrates again and again this ideal of youthful physical perfection through which the Greeks expressed eternal love, eternal youth, and eternal play. Being interested primarily in the human being they naturally thought that they should study and theorize upon the effects of art, especially music, on people. This led to the basic concepts of aesthetics as advanced by such philosophers as Plato and Aristotle. The deep-rooted instinct that the gods were ideal humans was responsible for the emphasis on human form in sculpture—an emphasis that gave rise to the concept of the ideal body in art.

Because Greek philosophy was concerned with the mind, it is natural that their art should reflect proportion and mathematical precision. All art, architecture, sculpture, as well as music, is permeated with this element of mathematical exactness. On the other hand, the idea of space was difficult for Greeks to experience in their limited world as is shown in their architecture and vase-painting. It was intangible and did not have convincing reality; therefore, this element of art was often lacking, especially in architecture.

Architecture

The Parthenon (fig. 3.1), dedicated to Athena, the patron goddess of Athens, was the most beautiful and most perfect of all the temples on the Acropolis. Because the highest function of a Greek god or goddess was the protection of the city or state, it can be said that the temples were actually office buildings which they occupied for that purpose. The famous maxim about the Greek citizens, "They kept their bodies in hovels but their souls on the Acropolis," is only another way of saying that religion, exemplified in great public and civic works, was more important in their lives than the desire for personal gain or glory. The idea of a city living under divine sanction and of public service as a virtue implies that artists were also servants of the state. The highest talents of the artist and craftsman were necessary to fulfill the highest duties toward the gods.

We are likely to think of religious buildings as designed to hold congregations. We usually think of decorations and furnishings of a sanctuary as being closely associated with the particular religious emotion and faith which brings people within its door and possesses their minds during the service. To understand the connection of art with religion in a Greek temple, we must forget this modern version of religious architecture. The Greek temple was definitely the home of the god or goddess who was there, whatever the feeling of the people. Everything in the design and decoration of the temple was determined by this fact.

The Parthenon was built on a hill to lift it above human dwellings. In dimensions, it is about 220 by 90 feet and is a rectangular chamber surrounded by a free-standing colonnade. A considerable portion was walled off and used as a public treasury. The small amount of space left makes it clear that nothing in the way of large congregations was intended or expected. Processions and the ritual of popular worship took place outside, with the temple as the center. It was designed to be viewed from outside rather than from within. Consequently, the shed roof and columns were fittingly used, giving it a quiet serenity, rather than the arch, which shows vigor and strength, especially from within.

All Greek architecture employs a type of construction called the post and lintel in which two or more vertical columns support a horizontal beam. Because of its availability and quantity, stone was the usual building material, but because of its brittle quality it had limitations. The distance between vertical members was determined by the tensile strength of the horizontal beam. In the case of stone, which is very heavy, the distance could not be great because the weight of the stone itself would cause it to break. Consequently, if a building of any size were to be constructed, it was necessary to have a great many columns with comparatively little distance between them.

Figure 3.1   Parthenon [c.440B.C.]—Restored model. (Courtesy Metropolitan Museum of Art, purchase 1890, Levi Hale Willard Bequest)

Figure 3.2   The Greek orders. (Courtesy University Prints)

Also, it was not practical to have a building of any great height because of the weight which would be placed upon the columns. Note that the limitations of the material fit into the basic attitudes of the time. There is little sense of space in the Parthenon, and it stands close to the earth; both of these ideas are reflected in the Greek concept of this-worldliness. It was only when a different philosophy prevailed, when different methods and materials were used, that religious architecture began to point toward the heavens.

Special attention was centered on the columns and their entablatures. This led to the creation of three distinct styles, or orders, each having a specific type of decoration which identified it as Doric, Ionic, or Corinthian (fig. 3.2).

Each order represented the culture of the group which used it most extensively. The Doric order, used in Athens, was sturdy and strong and was thus characterized as masculine. It was the most simple of all. The fluted columns rested without a base on the stylobate.[1] The capital of the column was a curved echinus[2] with a square abacus[3] on top. The Ionic order was very slender and graceful, giving it a feminine character. The Corinthian order, used widely in the luxury-loving city of Corinth, had a very ornate design,

1. Stylobate: The platform or step upon which the classic column is placed.
2. Echinus: The upper portion of the capital that supports the abacus.
3. Abacus: A thin slab of stone that rests on top of the capital of a classic column.

with an elaborate column resting on a decorated base with a richly carved capital.

The most remarkable feature of the Parthenon, which utilized the Doric order, is its apparent perfection of proportion. The relation between the height of the columns, their thickness, the height of the pediments,[4] and the dimensions of the temple was determined with such unerring judgment that the whole is neither too light nor too heavy. The lines harmonize in such a manner as to give the impression at once of strength and grace. The technical perfection of the temple is no less amazing. The blocks of marble and the drums of the column are joined and adjusted without cement as exactly as the most delicate of jeweler's art. This feature is even more amazing when we remember that the post and lintel type of construction called for the use of heavy stone slabs balanced on marble columns.

Even here the architects were concerned with the reality of our experience. A succession of vertical columns creates an illusion of tilting. In order to avoid this effect, the columns were not placed exactly the same distance from each other. They were also tilted back slightly to give a sense of perfect balance which one does not get from a row of perfectly balanced vertical columns. A slight bulge in each column gives realness to the pressure caused by the weight of the stone pediment on the columns. Edwin Teague in his book, *Design This Day*, devotes a whole chapter to the mathematical proportions of the Parthenon. The perfection of building is again a demonstration of the Greek attitude of concern for things of this world, since the human mind is the measure of all things. For the mind, to the Greeks, could produce perfection—and they very nearly did just this.

The Parthenon stands as a symbol of a civilization unique in all history in that it embodied three facets of life which have never existed simultaneously in any other place in the world. It united the religious life with intellectual aims; it reconciled the physical body with spiritual life; and it saturated a whole society with the substance of art as a part of their everyday existence.

The same style, the same general proportions, and the same intellectual and mathematical approach were used in almost all the rest of Greek architecture of this period—never with the same perfection, but with basically the same aim. The philosophy of the Greeks, coupled with their limited knowledge of materials, stabilized their architecture into a pattern that fits almost every example.

Sculpture

Though Greek sculpture was mainly religious in character, monumental sculpture in honor of national achievements and favorite personalities—important citizens, scholars, athletes, and other people of distinction—was popular. The deep-rooted instinct that the gods could be best approached

4. Pediment: A triangular space formed by the gable of a two-pitched roof in classical architecture.

through an image in stone brought forth the highest talents of artists of this medium.

Of all the visual arts, sculpture was one of the best suited to the embodiment of Greek thought. The most significant sculpture appears to be that which is parallel to the anthropocentric philosophy of the Greek that man is the measure of all things. To the Greek, then, that which was significant in experience was that which could be grasped by the senses, the degrees of its reality depending on the directness of its impact upon the human mind. To be convincingly real, an object therefore must have convincing form; sculpture had this quality.

Sculpture existed not only as an art by and of itself, but it was also incorporated into the architectural design of the temple. This was done by means of sculptural friezes placed in panels on the exterior as well as on the interior walls of the temple. Because their temples were dedicated to the gods, the Greeks adorned every available space in the pediment and metope[5] with figures representing the gods and their activities. In addition, plastic representations of the gods and goddesses were placed in prominent sections, or rooms, of the building.

There is one notable example where sculpture became a part of the structural plan of a temple, as well as a decorative addition—the Erechtheum (fig. 3.3), with its famous Porch of Maidens. The carved figures carry the weight of the entablature on their heads with such ease that we are completely unaware of the downward thrust. Notice also the graceful stance of the figures, each delicately balanced with one foot behind the other. Each of the bodies carries its burden with the same grace and vitality found in the Parthenon columns.

Sculpture formed an integral part of the Parthenon design. The frieze around the wall contained many forms. In addition, each metope was intricately carved with scenes from the life of the gods and incidents pertaining to their origin. There were ninety-two in all, in addition to groups of figures in both the east and west pediments. The artist responsible for the planning and execution of the sculpture of the Parthenon was Phidias, one of the greatest of all Greek artists. While he planned and directed most of the work, it is very probable that he was not the sole executor of his own plans. Nevertheless, he left the mark of his genius in the frieze and other decoration of the temple. This was a body of sculpture in amount and quality superior to that of any other temple in the Grecian world. Color was used as an accessory to carvings in all parts of the building, as some remaining patches indicate. The effect must have been very different from the monotonous whiteness that is a part of the current notions of Greek art.

The concern for this life is shown in these sculptures by the use of the human body and by the lifelike quality achieved. Since the gods were like

5. Metope: An area between two roof joists, usually square and often decorated with sculpture in Greek architecture.

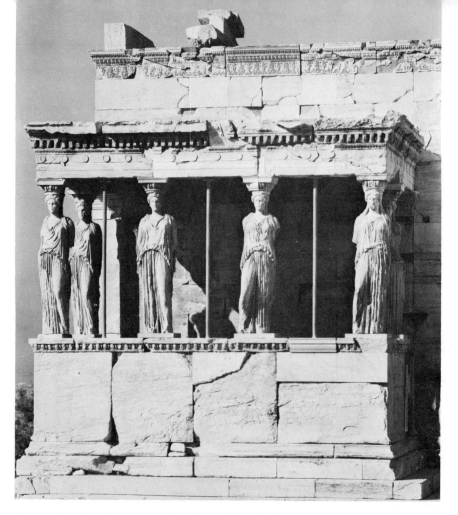

Figure 3.3 The Porch of the Maidens [421 B.C.]—The Erechtheum. (Courtesy Marburg-Art Reference Bureau)

man, their statues must be reasonably realistic. The forms are molded and are in perfect accord with the proportions of the human body. Even though they are conceived in stone, one has the feeling that there is flesh and blood beneath the surface. *The Three Fates* (fig. 3.4), which adorns the east pediment and which represents the goddesses present at every birth, is an excellent example of realism. The bodies seem warm and lifelike beneath the flowing robes, themselves very realistic. The whole group is majestic, serene, and very much alive, a natural way for Greek artists to portray their goddesses.

Praxiteles was one of the greatest artists of the Golden Age. His statue of *Hermes* (fig. 3.5) is the only existent statue known to be from the hand of this great master. It is of marble and represents the god Hermes carrying the infant Dionysus on his left arm. The child is reaching for some object, probably a bunch of grapes which Hermes may have held in his missing right

Figure 3.4 *The Three Fates* [c.440 B.C.]—Parthenon. (Courtesy Metropolitan Museum of Art)

Figure 3.5 *Hermes* [c. 340 B.C.]—Praxiteles (Courtesy Editorial Photocolor Archives)

hand. Using some of our basic concepts, let us look at this work of art. Line, always clearly defined in this kind of art, is very delicately molded, as if the skin were stretched over the inner body. The form is human, but what we call closed. There is nothing outside of the work itself; all action and direction is centered toward the middle of the statue: the reaching of the child, the direction of the look—even the object, missing as it is, was without doubt in the very center of the work. As everything is centered in the plastic form, there is no space-awareness. The parts fuse. One plane melts into another, for the artist was concerned with the total visual effect of the completed perfect body—mind and all—and not with the sum total of separate parts.

The Greeks did not model their human bodies after real people. They created an ideal human form from their own imagination—an ideal which could only be associated with the gods. It is for this reason that their sculpture seems to lack personality and individuality of character. These are qualities reserved for humans, because they are mortal and possess faults and imperfections of both body and character. The statues of the gods, like the figure of *Hermes*, represent the highest ideal of both mind and body; consequently, no mere mortal could serve as a model.

Figure 3.6 *Aphrodite* (*Venus de Medici*) [c. 200 B.C.] (Courtesy Editorial Photocolor Archives)

Figure 3.7 Two figures of *Hermes Fastening his Sandal* [c. 300 B.C.]. (Courtesy Editorial Photocolor Archives)

Another great sculptor of the fourth century was Lysippus. The *Aphrodite* (*Venus de Medici*) (fig. 3.6) and the two figures of *Hermes Fastening his Sandal* (fig. 3.7) are two works that are probably copies of, or in the style of, this master. Both of these works show the same general characteristics that are in the other examples we have seen. The *Aphrodite* is quite typical of Greek classicism. The emphasis is on the human form, on a posed figure that is static, with no movement. It shows classical proportions of the body, with perfect balance in a mathematical sense. Its form is closed; there is no interest or suggestion of anything outside of the figure—it is complete in itself. Again referring to the balance, notice how the weight of the body is placed on the left foot, with the right foot slightly behind it, in opposition for the sake of balance. There is no emotion expressed; the figure is serene, refined, and very real, but hardly alive.

The two figures of *Hermes* are of the same type, although on first glance we see more reason for action, because the subject is one of action—that of tying a sandal. We are strongly aware that there is flesh and blood beneath the stone, yet there is no feeling of being alive, because the figures do not imply movement. Hermes is posed in the act of tying the sandal; this is not a candid camera shot of a person doing the deed, unconscious of the fact that he is a subject. A little later, we shall find figures such as these in the act of motion, arrested in stone. We shall find facial and bodily expressions that give us a sense of a living person experiencing emotion. The Greek figures are not yet humanized to that extent, in spite of the dominant attitude of concern for things of this life. The spirit was there, but the method was mathematical. Reason held the answer to all things, and through it everything could be achieved. The spiritual element in the modern sense was lacking, for the gods of the Greeks were too human. The Greeks did not look with awe, or fear, or reverence upon them. They were merely mortals with more intelligence and understanding than humans. The human form was worshipped for itself and not for the soul that dwelt within it.

The Athenians were defeated by the Spartans in 404 B.C., an event that triggered the dissolution of Athenian democracy. This event, together with the later conquests of Alexander the Great, caused Greek culture to be spread over all of Asia Minor. The Hellenic world became a world of international merchants, industrialists, and warriors. Individualism and personal wealth supplanted civic duty and religious devotion. The calm reason and idealism of the Golden Age fades, and in its place there arose a taste for garish emotionalism, for the exotic, for the vulgar, and for the dramatic.

The temple at Pergamum in Asia Minor shows how the Greek style had changed from the days of the Parthenon. *The Altar of Zeus* from Pergamum about 170 B.C. (fig. 3.8) has been reconstructed from archeological records. It was free standing, not attached to the temple proper. It stood on a high platform approached by an impressive flight of steps. The sculptured figures, which dominate the altar, represent the struggle between gods and humans; deeply carved figures with wild movement enhance the feeling of violence and agony of the battle. Gone is the restraint of the earlier Greeks. Space, movement, and emotion replace the reasoned balance of the Parthenon.

Perhaps the finest example of Hellenistic sculpture is *Nike of Samothrace* (fig. 3.9) often called the *Winged Victory*. The figure of Victory is shown as if at the moment of alighting on the prow of a ship. The spreading wings and the forward movement of the body that causes the drapery to move against the wind give the work a feeling of vibrant life, motion, and space. Contrast this with the calm restraint of *Hermes* (fig. 3.5). Greek art had undergone a great change from the Golden Age and was to be further integrated with

Figure 3.8 *The Altar of Zeus* at Pergamum. (Courtesy Bruchman Art Reference Bureau)

non-Grecian cultural ideals under the influence of the Romans in the first century B.C.

Music

The very word *music* is of Greek origin, but we have no way of knowing just exactly what Greek music sounded like. All the information we have about Greek music comes through the writings of philosophers and scholars, together with a few fragments of stone that contain their version of notation. Two of these fragments, *A Hymn to the Sun* and *Skolion of Seikilos,* have been reconstructed according to the best musical research and made available in recordings, but even this reconstruction seems to be merely conjecture.

The word *music* was applied to a combination of poetry, music, and dancing, of which poetry was considered the ruler, music the accompaniment, and dancing the rhythmical expression of the vocal incantation. As in architecture and sculpture, music was closely connected with religion. It was used as a sort of charm between the Greeks and their gods. Greek festivals were religious and almost always in honor of some god or goddess such as Dionysus, Apollo, Athena, or Aphrodite. Everyone took part in those festivals as religious and social affairs, giving music a religious and a social function.

Greek music sounded very different from what we are accustomed to hearing, for it was based on very different organization of the basic materials. (1) This music was always monophonic (one melody) and vocal. Most music was accompanied with poetry. (2) Rhythm was determined by the poetic

Figure 3.9   *Nike of Samothrace (Winged Victory)* [c.200–190 B.C.]. (Courtesy of Alinar/ Editorial Photocolor Archives)

meter of the text. (3) The melodic line was determined by the inflection of speech. (4) Since the music was monophonic, there was no harmony in our modern sense. The idea of consonance and dissonance played no part in musical experience. (5) Notation, based on the letters of the alphabet, was very limited and vague. Some instruments, like the lyre and the aulos (an instrument somewhat like our oboe), were used, but not in any harmonic sense. They were merely weak doublings of what the voice sang. In dramas the music was very important and was probably sung by a number of voices in unison.

In spite of this music being unlike our own, we owe a great deal to it. Their concern for proportion and mathematical exactness led the Greeks to develop the diatonic scale, which is the basis of our modern scale system. Pythagoras, a Greek mathematician, is credited with formulating the mathematical ratios of the fundamental intervals of the scale. The intervals of the octave, fourth, and fifth were considered as consonances, or perfect, and all others were dissonances or imperfect. The interval of the octave, with its ratio of two to one, has been universally accepted as the limit of any scale. Within the octave, all scales, Western and non-Western, are constructed. Pythagoras's conclusions were based on observations of the length of strings and number of oscillations for each note. Our modern science of acoustics is founded on these scientific inquiries into the nature of sound.

Another very important musical concept which came from the Greeks is their *doctrine of ethos*. The Greeks held the notion that certain modes, or scales, possessed moral and ethical values in terms of the emotional response of the listeners. Music had a very definite influence on character, and according to their writers the will could be influenced by music in at least three ways. Music could spur to action; it could lead to the strengthening of the whole being, just as it could undermine mental and spiritual balance; it could suspend completely the normal willpower, so as to render people unconscious of their acts. This doctrine explains the important role music played in the Greeks' system of education and government. Plato, in the *Republic* and the *Laws*, assigns a vital role to the type of music that could be used in education. We still hold to these basic theories, although we do not give this power to scales but to certain combinations of melody, rhythm, harmony, and tone color. Modern science is demonstrating that the values given to music by the Greeks do exist in some measure. Physicians are turning to music as a therapeutic agent in relief of pain, lessening of fatigue, and preservation of mental health. Our modern industrialist is recognizing the value of music in industry as a means of combating fatigue and, consequently, as a means to greater production.

Summary

The Greeks developed a set of intellectual and emotional concepts which, in their freedom from superstition and intolerance, have never been surpassed. They produced an expressive and lasting art because of a high degree of realism, of imagination, and of humanism. Greek citizens exemplified such real devotion to the principles of truth and beauty and such freedom of intellectual processes that they have become a desirable prototype for all time.

The education of Greek citizens was such as to make them aware that what we call culture was an essential part of living and not something that was to be extraneously sought after, once the material demands of life had been satisfied. It has been said that the every free citizen in Athens could play the aulos and take part in the chorus at the drama. The visual beauties of the Parthenon and other temples were matters of ordinary experience to those people. No wonder that creative art flourished as it did and reached the heights of excellence that have seldom been surpassed.

In review of the basic elements of the arts, we find that in general Greek architecture and sculpture showed little sense of space and an almost perfect mathematical balance. Art was, for the most part, calm and ordered with clarity of line and restrained movement. Even music was subjected to mathematics and avoided the appeal to emotion. Only in the Hellenistic era do we experience violent motion, emotion, and the suggestions of expanding space.

Because the economic and material foundation of Greek life was inadequate, their society collapsed. The artistic glory that lived with Plato and Aristotle faded into an era of sensuousness and sentimentality. The Greeks themselves fell victim to their Roman conquerors, but the art of the Golden Age remains as a symbol of a culture which has hardly been equaled for its devotion to truth and beauty.

Suggested readings

Barnes, H.E. *An Intellectual and Cultural History of the Western World,* rev. ed. New York: Reynal & Hitchcock, 1941, pp. 160–94.

Breasted, J.H. *Conquest of Civilization,* rev. ed. New York: Harper & Bros., 1938, pp. 339–63.

Grout, D.J. *A History of Western Music,* 3rd. ed. New York: W.W. Norton, 1980, pp. 1–34.

Janson, H.W. *History of Art.* Englewood Cliffs: Prentice-Hall, Inc., 1962, pp. 67–122.

Lang, Paul Henry. *Music in Western Civilization.* New York: W.W. Norton, 1941, pp. 1–21.

Upjohn, Wingert and Mahler. *History of World Art*. New York: Oxford University Press, 1940, pp. 67–76.

Wold and Cykler. *An Outline History of Music*, 5th ed. Dubuque, Ia.: Wm. C. Brown Company Publishers, 1982, pp. 1–10.

Suggested examples for further analysis

Architecture: *Temple of Zeus*, Olympia

Sculpture: *Aphrodite of Melos*

Examples of Greek music can be found in Volume I of *The History of Music in Sound* (R.C.A.), and in *2000 Years of Music* (Folkway Records)

Film strip with sound

Ancient Greece: The Age and its Art. Schloat Productions.

4

Roman and Early Christian
(100 B.C.–A.D. 500)

Chronology of Romans and Early Christians

B.C.

146	Carthage destroyed	76	Publius Hadrian (76–138)
106	Marcus Tullius Cicero (106–43)	120	Pantheon built
100	Julius Caesar (100–44)	274	Constantine I—The Great (c. 274–337)
70	Publius Virgil (70–19)	313	Edict of Milan
c. 4	Birth of Christ	330	Constantinople established as capital of the Roman Empire
A.D.			
c. 29	Crucifixion of Christ		
74	Colosseum built (74–80)	325	First Council of Nicaea

Study Objectives

The objectives of this chapter are

1. To learn about the Roman genius for political and economic techniques as represented in their artistic activities.
2. To learn about the contributions and limitations of the early Christians in art and music.

Pronunciation Guide

Ara Pacis (Ah'-rah Pah'-chis)
Colosseum (Ko-lahs-say'-um)
Constantine (Kahn'-stan-teen)

Etruscan (Et-rus'-kan)
Jupiter (Joo'-pi-ter)
Mars (Mahrz)

Pantheon (Pan'-thay-ohn)   San Vitale (Sahn Vee-tah'-lay)
Pont du Gard (Pont dü Gard)   Sophia (Soh-fee'-ah)

The rise and fall of Roman civilization, as well as the rise of the Christian church and its spread throughout Europe, are of primary importance to the understanding of the cultural development of the long and mystical period we call the Middle Ages. Because there were few significant artistic innovations resulting from Roman domination and because the early Church had little organized art, these movements can be dismissed with a minimum of detail. This does not mean, however, that their contributions were not considerable. A serious investigation of visual art or music reveals tendencies that, while they were not fully developed, eventually played a major role in the later epochs. The arts made few aesthetic advances during the days of the Roman Empire, but the manner in which art was utilized was indigenous to the spirit and temperament of its people.

Rome first rose to a position of importance about 400 B.C. A small nation of landowners and farmers, the Romans became aware of their strength by suppressing the Etruscans. They gradually came to think of themselves as a people with a destiny to fulfill—a mission to bring law and order to the world. They set out to conquer and rule the whole then-known world. One of their first aims was to gain economic power by destroying their economic rivals. Carthage, Rome's great commercial competitor, was finally destroyed in 146 B.C. By means of their armies, the Romans further spread their political and economic control. One by one the Grecian city states, which were already losing their will to remain free, fell under the Roman yoke.

The influence of Greek culture was spread throughout the Western world by their conquerors. The Romans recognized the superiority of Hellenic culture, and they sought to acquire the glories of Greek art by possessing its creators as well as the works themselves. When Greek cities were captured, it was the practice to strip the temples and public buildings of their statues. There are records of Roman generals returning with enormous quantities of art objects, which then found their way into Roman homes. When this supply was exhausted, the Romans began importing artists to make copies of captured art and to create works in the Grecian style. Scholars, artists, and artisans were brought to Rome as slaves and set to the task of supplying the increased demand for Hellenic art. The Imperial City was also immeasurably enriched by the public works engineered by Roman masters and executed by Greek slaves. Some slaves, who gained their freedom through the generosity of their masters, became teachers of the Roman youth, thus enriching the cultural and intellectual life of the Italian city.

The Romans were concerned mainly with increasing their power and controlling large areas of space, politically and economically. They were a practical, proud, and mercenary people with a love for sensual pleasures, lavish living, gladiatorial games, and triumphal parades. They were supreme egoists, spending both time and money in furthering their own ends.

Their religion was akin to that of the Greeks, but they placed more faith in the strength of their armies than in their gods. Like the Greeks, they also were "this-worldly." They had only a vague notion about life after death and put little credence in any idea of immortality. Religion was centered around the home, with special household gods for each family activity. Consequently, worship was carried on in the home even more than in the temple. Not content to borrow only art from the Greeks, they borrowed gods as well. Some Greek gods, like Apollo, were Romanized, and they also took over many other minor gods. They added some of their own to serve their own special interests. The most important of these were Mars, god of war, and Jupiter, god of nature, who could protect them from unseen dangers and the mysteries of nature.

The Romans were also systematizers, excelling in the know-how of engineering and law. They left us monuments of engineering which have become the marvel of the ages. They crisscrossed Europe with a system of military roads, many of which are still extant. They built aqueducts for bringing water into cities from long distances, and they engineered drainage systems that reclaimed thousands of acres of otherwise useless swamplands. Note that these activities were all closely allied with their self-styled destiny as empire builders.

Roman law has been the basis of all subsequent legal systems of Western civilization. The Romans could never have subjected the peoples they did had they not perfected a practical system of law and justice. Their law was based on the assumption that standards of justice were determined by the common citizen with good sense and not by divine revelation. As their laws were put into practice and legal procedures were standardized, the law was codified and systematized by what we might call "legal engineering." This codification also reveals their fundamental character as a nation of coldly practical people.

How did these facets of Roman life influence the arts? We shall see that the manner in which the Romans treated their borrowed Greek art demonstrates these basic attitudes and characters. Furthermore, their own contributions to architecture and sculpture reflect functions that were purely Roman.

Roman architecture

The architectural demands of the Romans were very different from those of the Greeks. Temples were not so much in demand as were public baths, arenas, and private dwellings. They wanted public buildings where thousands could be accommodated as spectators at public games and entertainments.

The Roman arch grew from the needs of a people who excelled in large-scale planning and engineering, both materially and politically. The Greek type of post and lintel construction was incapable, as we have seen, of spanning large areas of space. The Romans solved this problem by using the arch vault of their Etruscan ancestors (fig 4.1). By crossing two such arches, they produced the groined vault, which is capable of spanning large volumes of space, horizontally and vertically. This technique gave rise to the dome, since recognized as a symbol of authority because of its wide use by the Romans in their public buildings.

The Pantheon (fig. 4.2) is an excellent example of the adaptation of the Greek design to their own use. The portico is of Greek design, with Corinthian columns supporting a pediment which lacks the proportion and unity of the Parthenon. The main part of the edifice is a huge oval-shaped structure capped by a dome. Because columns were not necessary to support the roof in this type of building, there was a great open hall, capable of accommodating huge crowds. The temple, unlike the Greek temple, was to be viewed from within, for the interior is much more impressive than the exterior. It is as high as it is wide, giving a sense of expanding space which is even more enhanced by the light which streams in through a circular opening in the dome. The plane of the interior wall is broken by semicircular niches which contained the statues of the Roman gods. It is plain that the *Pantheon* was rather a temple to hold a congregation, more in the manner of our day, than an office for a Greek god. While the *Pantheon* is one of the best-known examples of Roman

Figure 4.1   Roman arch—Sandgren

Figure 4.2   Pantheon [A.D. 120]—Rome. (Courtesy of Alinari/Editorial Photocolor Archives)

religious building, most others lacked the balance and poise of those built by the Greeks. In spite of the fact that they used the Greek orders on their columns, the ornaments were crude in comparison and were not perfectly integrated into the architectural plan. It becomes obvious that the Romans were not natural artists but buyers and borrowers whose copies were always less expressive than the original.

Another monument to the Roman urge for space and pleasure is the Colosseum (fig. 4.3), the great open-air arena used for games, gladiatorial combats, and finally for the persecution of the Christians. It is one of the most remarkable structures of its age because of its size and utility. It was constructed on the principle of the round or barreled arch. Such arches were placed side by side on columns. By making tiers of arches, it was possible to construct a building four stories high. It is a vast oval structure about 600 feet long with a seating capacity of about 70,000. Underneath the bleachers there were countless rooms for attendants, cages for wild animals, and even small shops. It was also built in such a manner that the floor of the arena could be flooded. On these occasions the people could enjoy the sight of naval battles being fought before their very eyes. There was little decoration on the Colosseum, for the plain rhythmic flow of columns and arches was sufficient eye appeal. The whole edifice is a reflection of the Roman efficiency of engineering in solving their spatial and structural problems.

An even more practical use of the Roman arch can be seen in Pont du Gard at Nimes (fig. 4.4). This was essentially a utilitarian use of the arch in an engineering sense. It was built in the first century A.D. and was part of a system to bring water to Nimes. The portion that crosses the river Gard is about 900 feet long and 180 feet high, certainly a tribute to the Roman engineering skill and sense of order that has an inherent beauty of its own.

The Roman house (fig. 4.5) was also more luxurious and spacious than the Greek house. In this respect it is an evidence of concern for personal magnificence as well as spatial control. Because much of the owner's personal

Figure 4.3   Colosseum [A.D. 75–82]—Rome. (Courtesy University Prints)

Figure 4.4   Pont du Gard (Courtesy Marburg-Art Reference)

business as well as worship was carried on in the home, it was natural to spend large sums of money on domestic housing. The lavishly built houses contained many of the conveniences which we think of as modern, such as central heating, running water, and sanitation. The basic plan was usually that of a central court surrounded by a columned structure in the Grecian fashion. In keeping with their love for luxury, there were elaborate rooms for dining and entertaining. Large parcels of land were reserved for gardens, walks, and pools. The size and extent of the villa were usually in direct proportion to the wealth and political power of its owner. This fact has been well established by the excavation of the lava-covered city of Pompeii, as well as through contemporary writings. A sincere appreciation of the finer values of life did not always seem to exist along with wealth and power, for it is evident that many Roman villas were sadly lacking in artistic values.

Roman sculpture

Because art in Rome was not confined to the temples but was in great demand for private use, it was expedient to have copies made of Greek statues and objects of art brought to Rome as war booty. This was done in part by the enslaved artists, but, to expedite the copying process, the Romans devised a method of casting in which a mold was made from the original and then a plaster copy of the original. This innovation made it possible to have copies as they wished. Generally speaking, Roman taste leaned toward the lesser Greek art. It has been pointed out, for example, that it was not the sculpture from the Parthenon that was copied. More often it was art from the first century B.C. when Greece had already lost much of her will to remain free. It was a decadent Greek art that the Romans copied; the more lavish and sensual, the more demand there was for it.

Not all Roman art was imitative. The Romans excelled in portrait sculpture (fig. 4.6), and for a very good reason. In order that they might honor their soldiers, prominent citizens, and merchants, they created sculptural likenesses of them for prominent places in public buildings as well as homes. Morever, it was not unusual for wealthy people to commission a number of statues while still living so that a realistic likeness would be available after death. Some even went so far as to have their own tombs constructed and

Figure 4.5   House of the Vettii [A.D. 65]—Pompeii. (Courtesy University Prints)

Figure 4.6 *Augustus* of Primaporta (Courtesy of Alinari/Editorial Photocolor Archives)

decorated with reliefs showing their heroic deeds. This kind of sculpture was very realistic in its feeling for every minute line, blemish, or physical oddity. The ideal form did not interest them in the slightest, but rather the heroes were to be portrayed as they actually lived and walked among the people. In order to meet the demands for this kind of sculpture, artists often created a number of torsos of various kinds, such as soldiers, and other important citizens. When a certain kind of statue was called for, it was necessary only to model the face. It was then placed on a torso that fit the subject, and the job was finished.

Another lasting innovation was the effect of space created in relief sculptural groups. By making distant figures smaller and placing them behind foreground figures, the illusion of space became quite real. A famous example of this is seen in the *Ara Pacis Frieze* (fig. 4.7). There is a sense of recession. The foreground figures are placed in high relief which gives them the appearance of coming forward in a plastic sense. The effect is heightened by the artist turning the feet of these figures outward and beyond the flat surface of the marble slab. Furthermore, the background figures are shown in profile, while the others have their faces turned toward the observer. This adds to the concept of space.

We have briefly discussed some of the Roman artistic activities. The development of the arch and dome was more of an engineering feat than an artistic development. The Romans added their concept of space to sculpture but, in the total picture of Western art, they added amazingly little for a nation that was one of the greatest of all time. This was perhaps due to the fact that they used Greek models. A truly great artistic development can come only from the hearts and character of a people. The Romans were borrowers, and while they placed the stamp of their own temperament and philosophy on the borrowed ideals, the original always remains more beautiful and glorious than the imitation.

Roman music

Roman music, like the visual arts, was borrowed mainly from the Greeks, and, as with the visual arts, the decadent Greek music appealed more than any other. Roman taste tended toward the spectacular rather than the restrained and balanced lyricism of the Greeks. As might be expected, the function of music was to provide music for war and pleasure. The trumpet and drum were more useful than the lyre. The Greek tragedies deteriorated into dance pantomimes which became more popular with the Romans as they became more obscene and sensual. It was this source from which most of Rome's musical life took its nourishment.

Even if it was of rather dubious quality, music was cultivated by the Romans as a mark of education. Witness the character of Nero who thought

Figure 4.7 *Ara Pacis Frieze, Procession* [c. 10 B.C.]. (Courtesy Editorial Photocolor Archives)

Colorplate 4 San Vitale [c. 547]—Ravenna. (Courtesy Scala/Editorial Photocolor Archives)

Colorplate 5 *Empress Theodora and Retinue* [c. 547]—San Vitale, Ravenna. (Courtesy Scala/Editorial Photocolor Archives)

of himself as a great artist above all else. It is one of the ironies of musical art that the early Christians died in flames and at the fangs of wild animals to the accompaniment of music—an art which was to owe its greatest development to the Christian Church.

Early Christian art

The rise of Christian art is another story. We have a combination of Greek idealism with that of Christianity, which had a distinct Oriental flavor and was tinged with Judaism. The early rise of Christianity was phenomenal. From a small group of disillusioned disciples who were left after the crucifixion of Christ, it mushroomed in less than 300 years to a well-organized religion of universal appeal. The Romans must have felt that the death of Paul, the burning of Jerusalem, and the agonizing death of hundreds of the cult's followers would be sufficient to discourage it. But they were very wrong, and many eventually became converted to the movement.

During its early days, the Church had little place for art of any kind. It had no architecture except the catacombs of Rome, which originally were burial places. It had no wealth, for its early converts were from the lower and middle classes, and art cannot thrive without wealth. Artistic expression had been the prerogative and luxury of the Roman citizen; consequently the middle class had little or no artistic experience. Another and more fundamental reason for the lack of art was its association with everything pagan and corrupt. Because Christianity was in direct opposition to the existing religious and social structure, anything which formed an integral part of that structure was damned, together with Roman society itself. It was only after the upper-class Roman became converted and after the authorities ceased to persecute the Christians that art began to flourish at all.

Christian art revolves around the ritual and teaching of its various doctrines. Ritual, theology, and symbolism were borrowed freely from the Jews and the Greeks. The part which was played by Judaism is well known. Needless to say, the Old Testament is Hebraic, and certain portions of our present-day ritual evolve from the Jewish synagogue. The influence of the Hebrew culture came mainly through its literature, especially the Old Testament. Because Jews abided by the Mosaic Law that forbade images, there was hardly any representational art. Since the first Christians were Jews they brought a good deal of what they had been accustomed to in the Jewish service to the Christian service. The elaborate chanting of the Psalms was among these contributions.

The religious practices of the Greeks, notably the rites of Baptism and the Eucharist, also contributed to the Christian ritual. The cross itself became, symbolically, the floor plan for the Christian church, or Basilica, as it was called. Here we see the Roman as well as the Greek influence. Most churches in Italy used the Roman cross in which the upright is longer than the crossarm. Those in the East and in Greece used the Greek cross in which the arm is equal in length to the upright (fig. 4.8).

In 313 A.D., the Roman Emperor Constantine signed the now-famous Edict of Milan, an act which legalized Christianity throughout the Roman Empire. Because the center of Roman power was shifting toward the East, Constantine moved his capital to Byzantium, which was later called Constantinople and is now called Istanbul. It was amid these surroundings and under these circumstances that the art of the Orient came to play an important role in

Figure 4.8   Greek and Latin crosses—Sandgren

FIG. 21   Greek and Latin Crosses
—Sandgren

Christian art, especially the visual arts of architecture and painting. Later we shall see that the Jew made a substantial contribution in music, for the Asiatic system was completely foreign to Western ears.

The style of art and architecture which we call Byzantine was the result of this influence of Oriental artistic convention on the demands and ideals of the new religion. After the Church became well organized and included more wealthy converts, there was the desire to build churches in a more elaborate fashion. The Asiatic love of brilliant colors, rigid patterns, and sensuous feeling for expression aroused the spirit of mystic exaltation and emotion which was inherent in a religion that held out the promise of immortality beyond the grave. Santa Sophia (fig. 4.9), located in Istanbul, is the prototype of the influence of this Eastern temperament on Christian art. The floor plan was in the form of the Greek cross, with a huge dome centered over the entire square formed by the cross. Like the Roman Pantheon, Santa Sophia was most impressive from the interior. The marble walls were richly decorated with paintings of multicolored mosaics of tile against a background of gold leaf. Light, which was let in by a row of windows set in the base of the dome, played on the jewellike colors of the interior like the rays of sun on a brilliant diamond. In addition, the sacred relics, altars, crosses, and statues were ornamented with precious stones set in backgrounds of richly carved gold and silver.

All of these treasures disappeared during the centuries of Turkish and Arabic rule. Most of the mosaic decoration was covered by decoration symbolic of Mohammedanism. The present-day spires and minarets were added by the Arabs and Moors and have no Christian significance. In recent years the Turkish government has allowed the layers of later decoration to be removed, showing portions of the original Byzantine art.

Another superb example of the Byzantine style is San Vitale in Ravenna, Italy (colorplate 4). It was modeled after Santa Sophia and was richly decorated with colorful mosaics. A sense of great height is made more real by rows of windows at every level which flood the interior with light. The effect on the multicolored mosaics is that of jewels in the sunlight.

Byzantine painting was primarily in the form of mosaic, which is painting by means of small colored bits of tile and glass in the manner of later stained-glass windows. *Empress Theodora and Her Retinue* (colorplate 5) is a typical example of this kind of art. There is no lifelike quality, no depth, no movement. It has very sharp lines and is multicolored. The unity is slight, but what there is, is separate; each individual is alone. There is an unreal quality about this art that is very different from the Roman and Greek emphasis on human form. It therefore found favor in the early Church, for the Christian looked upon human life merely as a transition to the glories of heaven. We will find this unreal quality in most Christian art until the late Gothic and Renaissance.

Colorplates 4, 5 follows p. 66.

Figure 4.9 Santa Sophia [c. 535]—Istanbul. (Courtesy University Prints)

Early Christian music

The early Christians, as we have seen, had little opportunity to develop art. This applied to music also. Early Christian history gives us only an extremely vague notion of the use of music, partly because of the inadequate system of notation which made preservation almost impossible. It is known that some of the Jewish chants were used as settings of the Psalms. In fact, these chants probably served as their greatest source of musical material. It is also known that the Byzantine church had some influence on early Church music; just how much is hard to say because of the lack of source material. However, the florid ornaments of the chants are certainly analogous to the brilliant colors and design of Byzantine architecture.

The melodic line of this early music must have been almost nil, using a very narrow range with emphasis on the words at the expense of the music. It was monodic and therefore had no harmony. It was also vocal, for instruments were associated with pagan rites. In Rome, the early Christians were a clandestine group, meeting secretly in the catacombs and always in fear of detection by the Romans. That they had any music is a wonder, but its power was evident even in the earliest days. Like the Greeks, they saw in music a tremendous force for shaping one's moral life and a means of coming into a mystical contact with God.

The main problem of this music was to keep it simple and not to let it become too emotional. As Christianity grew, there were many who came into the Church with a background of the popular songs of the day. Recognizing these songs as evil influences, the Church made every effort to purge this pagan music from the service. Music existed for one purpose only, and that was to serve God. It could not exist for its own sake as an expressive art form. It is not surprising, then, to find little advance in the scope of music during these early times. As an expressive art, music received no encouragement. On the contrary, music for pleasure was a sin, to be dealt with by the Church authorities. It was only after Christianity became the Roman state religion that music, as well as other arts, became an integral part of the ritual and a moving force in the development and spread of Christianity.

Summary

The Romans came to be the empire builders of western Europe from about 100 B.C. to 300 A.D. They were mainly concerned with increasing their power and controlling large areas of space, politically and economically. As a result they became master politicians, lawmakers, and engineers. They were a proud and practical people with ambition for personal wealth and power. Their artistic activity revealed this philosophy of power, wealth, and pleasure. One of their greatest achievements was in the area of architecture and engineering. With the invention of the arch and vault they constructed impressive arenas, baths, and public buildings, and they spanned great areas of space with aqueducts, bridges, and roads.

The Romans admired and copied the Grecian style of sculpture and decoration, especially from the Hellenistic period. However, they did make notable contributions of their own in portrait sculpture of their important citizens, generals, and heroes. They also created monumental friezes that depicted the triumphs of their rulers and armies as they expanded their power over Western Europe. There was very little artistic activity that did not serve a functional and practical purpose for the pleasure and glory of the Empire. Space in their art was as real as their ambition to rule the then-known world.

The earliest Christian art was not a style in itself, but utilized some of the symbolism of the pagan world. In reality there was very little artistic activity until Constantine moved the capital of Christianity to Byzantium. The Byzantine architecture shows the Roman-Greek and Oriental influence. The multicolored mosaic decorations show the Oriental love of stylistic patterns of brightly contrasted color. While the churches showed great domed space, there was no three-dimensional quality about the mosaic decoration. Music in the early Christian Church was confined to vocal chants which were most likely borrowed from the Jewish liturgy. The details of the music itself are not known, due to the complete lack of notation and historical records.

Suggested readings

Barnes, H. E. *An Intellectual and Cultural History of the Western World*, rev. ed. New York: Reynal and Hitchcock, 1941, pp. 203–6, 248–54, 315–19.

Grout, D.J. *A History of Western Music*, 3rd ed. New York: W.W. Norton, 1980, pp. 1–34

Janson, H.W. *History of Art*. Englewood Cliffs, N.J.: Prentice-Hall, Inc., 1962, pp. 157–85.

Lang, Paul Henry. *Music in Western Civilization*. New York: W.W. Norton, 1941, pp. 81–110

Upjohn, Wingert and Mahler. *History of World Art*. New York: Oxford University Press, 1949, pp. 81–110.

Wold and Cykler. *An Outline History of Music*, 5th ed. Dubuque, Ia.: Wm. C. Brown Company Publishers, 1982, pp. 1–10.

Suggested examples for further analysis

Roman

Architecture: Baths of Caracalla, Rome; Arch of Constantine, Rome
Sculpture: *Dying Gaul*, Pergamum; *Emperor's Triumph*, Arch of Titus

Early Christian

Architecture: Sant' Apollinare in Classe, Ravenna; Cathedral of Torcello
Mosaic: Apse Mosaic, San Vitale, Ravenna; Apse Mosaic, Cathedral of Torcello
Music: Examples of Byzantine chant can be found in vol. 2 of the *History of Music in Sound (R.C.A.)*

Film strip with sound

Ancient Rome: The Age and its Art. Schloat Productions

5
Romanesque
(500–1100)

Chronology of the Romanesque

354	St. Augustine (354–430)	742	Charlemagne (742–814)
410	Fall of Rome	787	Second Council of
480	Boethius (c. 480–524)		Nicaea
540	Pope Gregory (c.	900	Feudalism established
	540–604)	912	Otto the Great
	Gregorian Chant		(912–1073)
650	Rise of the Monasteries	955	Guido of Arezzo
			(955–1050)

Study Objectives

The objectives of this chapter are

1. To study Romanesque art as the mirror of the religious beliefs and practices of the Church, which was the sole medieval artistic patron.
2. To study the symbolism in Church architecture.

Pronunciation Guide

Ambrogio (Ahm-broh'-zhee-oh)
Aquinas (Ah-kwih'-nahs)
Charlemagne (Shar-lah-mayn)
La Madeleine (Lah Mah-de-layn)

The Mass
    Kyrie eleison (Ki'-ree-ay e-lay'-ee-zon)
    Gloria in excelsis (Gloh'-ree-ah in eks-chel'-sis)

73

Credo (Kray'-doh)
Sanctus (Sahnk'-toos)
Agnus Dei (Ahn'-yoos Day'-
ee)
Ite, Missa est (Ee'-te, Mee'-sah
est)

Nicaea (Nih-see'-ah)
Notre Dame la Grande (Noh-trah
Dahm lah Grahnd)
Pisa (Pee'-zah)
Poitiers (Pwah-tyerz)
San Trophime (Sahn Troh-feem)
Vezelay (Ve-ze-lah-ee)

The Church and medieval art

The span of history which we call the medieval period extends from about 500 to 1400. This rather long and mystic period is divided into two important subperiods, the Romanesque (500–1100) and the Gothic (1100–1400). The Middle Ages still fascinates us, not only because of its civilization, but because we are still bound with invisible ties to the institutions and people of that age. Any historical study will surely include such medieval personalities as St. Augustine, St. Thomas Aquinas, St. Francis, and Dante. Feudalism has lived until our own day. Our bourgeoisie emerged from the ranks of the medieval city burghers: even the condition of the proletariat, which is not merely a by-product of our modern industrialism, manifested its burning problems during these times. Furthermore, many of our social, religious, and economic institutions date back to medieval days. Our labor unions have their origin in the guild systems of the thirteenth century, and it was also during these times that the Christian Church became an organized institution. The universities of today owe many of their traditions to their medieval counterpart; in fact, not a few European universities have had a continuous existence, since the medieval period.

In contrast to previous art epochs, we will discover a great change in the conditions on which music and the visual arts depended for their prosperous existence and growth. It is these basic conditions of social, religious, economic, and political life that we must survey in order to have a real understanding of the artistic aims and practices of this fascinating age.

Any study of the trends of artistic development of the medieval age must necessarily include an examination of the basic attitudes of the Church, for the Church was almost the sole patron of the arts and was to remain so until the eighteenth century. All activities of life were inseparably connected with the one supreme and new ecclesiastical power which in a thousand years was to give an entirely new aspect to all of Europe. The Church was not merely a religious idea. Soon after the larger masses of people were moved by the Christian concept, it became an institution for the preservation and propagation of the Christian religion. There then emerged an organization which had the authority to teach, order, and spread its doctrines over the whole then-known world.

The Church became the ruler not only over spiritual life but also over economic, political, and social life as well as the artistic life. A philosophy of otherworldliness in contrast to the worldly attitude of the Greeks and Romans was to be the guiding principle. The doctrine of salvation formed the very core of Christianity, and around this doctrine the early rituals and institutions were built. Medieval Christianity did not offer a promise of material well-being. On the contrary, it taught that this life was a dirty, sordid mess—to be endured, not enjoyed, until the final day. Human suffering would have the tendency to help the Christian concentrate on religion and on the hope of salvation.

Poverty was a virtue because it was less likely that people would be tempted toward evil living if they had little of this world's goods. The idea that a rich person has as much chance of going to heaven as a camel had of going through a needle's eye was more than an epigram. If admonition was not enough, there was always the prospect of hell to consider. The medieval Church emphasized the idea of the Devil, who was always on hand to waylay the faithful. He was especially active whenever there were pleasurable pursuits at hand. All avenues of pleasure were therefore closely guarded, and many faithful became hermits in the wilderness to avoid the Devil's persuasive manner.

The result of this doctrine was the rise of the monastic movement. Groups of devout worshippers banded together in communal enterprises where they lived, worked, and worshipped jointly. The monks, as they were called, took vows of poverty, obedience, industry, and chastity. In this environment one could contemplate God and bring his soul into harmony with the spirit of the Church. One did not labor because labor was a healthy and happy occupation, nor because it would help others. The virtue of labor was that it reduced the fires of passion within one's own soul. The monasteries provided a safe refuge for those who felt the need for spiritual protection.

While the monks spent most of their time in prayer and manual labor, they also found time to pursue intellectual activities. In fact, the learning of the medieval age was centered largely in the monasteries. It was in such an environment that men like St. Augustine and St. Benedict wrote the treatises which were to give them recognition as Church fathers.

Because it was pagan in nature, Greek culture was generally condemned. The works of Plato and Aristotle were banned until the time of St. Thomas Aquinas, in the thirteenth century, and then they were approved only through the interpretation of Aquinas. Doctrines that differed in any way from those laid down by the Church were labeled as heresies. The punishment for such beliefs often was burning at the stake or, at best, some form of torture that would drive out the evil spirits. If the guilty were spared, it was because of repentance and some form of penitence. The Church had an elaborate organization to safeguard the faithful from evil. As Barnes puts it: "It was the great stronghold that guaranteed to the pious the protection against earthly evils and definite assurance of eternal salvation. The Church was like a well-lighted house, looming in the darkness to a man wandering, terror-stricken, in a dark and stormy night."[1]

Another medieval institution which left its imprint on art was feudalism, which reached its zenith about the twelfth century. This system provided a certain amount of protection and economic stability for the lower classes of society. It also enabled the nobility to exploit the helpless for economic and military purposes. Secular wealth was concentrated in the hands of the feudal lords, who enjoyed complete sovereignty in their own domain. Among the artistic monuments left by feudalism are the massive castles that graced the mountain slopes of medieval Europe. They served much the same purpose as the monasteries in that they provided safety from the hostile forces of neighboring nobles as well as wandering bands of highwaymen.

Because feudal lords held power by the grace of the Church, it is not surprising to find the Church closely allied to the feudal system. Many of the more powerful lords were also bishops and archbishops. We see here a double concentration of wealth and power. The Church and civil authority were, for all practical purposes, one and the same. The nobles often supplied the wealth, while the monks planned and directed the construction and decoration of the churches. More important was the merging of the Church with feudalism into a fortress of economic and political power which was based on agrarian control. The Church emerged as the guardian of the land as well as the custodian of salvation. To protect its power, it even suggested that people should be content with the station of life into which they were born. As the Church expanded its ecclesiastical, civil, and economic authority, it became the supreme power of medieval Europe.

Because the church was the one supreme power, it follows that creative art must have had a religious function. This was true in almost every aspect of medieval art and music. Religious architecture was the only type of building that really mattered. Where people lived was of little consequence, for the comforts of life were of evil import. Illiteracy was almost universal, except among the monks, and thus the biblical stories could best be taught through visual art. Painting and sculpture therefore served as documents of religious education.

Since the Church was the sole patron of the arts, it could well control the style of painting and sculpture. In 787, the Second Council of Nicaea laid down a set of rules for artistic representation of religious subjects that was to be binding upon artists for almost 500 years should be:

The substance of religious scenes is not left to the initiative of the artists; it derives from the principles laid down by the Catholic Church and religious tradition. . . . His [sic] art alone belongs to the painter, its organization and arrangement belong to the clergy.

1. Barnes, H. E., *An Intellectual and Cultural History of the Western World*, rev. ed. (New York: Reynal and Hitchcock, 1941), p. 295.

This was a very logical rule, since the Church and not the individual was looked upon as the guardian of the sacred truth upon which the safety of society and the salvation of the soul depended. Nobody thought of artists as being divinely inspired and knowing more than the Church fathers. It was logical, therefore, that artists were given exact specifications as to what they could represent.

But this was not all; having been given subject matter and theme, the artist was bound further by strict conventions as to how sacred subjects were to be depicted. Jesus on the Cross had to be shown with his Mother on the right and St. John on the left. The soldier pierced His left side. His halo contained a cross as the mark of divinity, whereas the saints had a halo without a cross. Only God, Jesus, the angels, and the apostles could be shown with bare feet. It was sheer heresy, therefore, to depict the Virgin or the saints without coverings on their feet. It was the purpose of these conventions to help the observer identify the figure. Thus, St. Peter was given a short beard. St. Paul was always bald, with a long beard. There were numerous other conventions which denied artists any great liberty or imagination in their work.

The cathedral itself was also subject to conventions of style and decoration determined not by artistic taste but by theology. The usual floor plan was that of a Latin cross, itself a symbol of salvation in the Church. Christian liturgy determined many of the stylistic practices of the builders. The ritualistic practice of separating those participating in the service from those of the congregation made necessary the portion called the chancel. This served as a place for the altar where the service was held as well as the place where the choir was seated.

Because it was the tradition that the priests and the congregation should face the east, churches were usually oriented with the altar in the east and the main portal to the west. The symbolism of the Holy Trinity was used at every convenient opportunity. Wherever possible the number three was in evidence—in triple arches, triple portals, and many other details.

Reverence for holy relics, such as a portion of a holy man's body, was also responsible for architectural detail. Relics had the supposed power of performing miracles for those who paid homage to them, and great crowds of pilgrims would often be attracted to a church because of some special holy relic housed within its walls. To accommodate the crowd, it was necessary to provide smaller chapels which pilgrims could enter without disturbing the main service. To accomplish this purpose, small chapels were constructed along the ambulatory, which is the passageway around the apse[2] of the church (fig. 5.1). There are other evidences of design arising from religious doctrine, but needless to say all details of design were completely functional. They served to impress upon the faithful an unquestioning faith in salvation by the cross.

2. Apse: A semicircular portion of the church, usually at the end of the rear axis of the plan.

Figure 5.1. Plans of Romanesque churches. (Courtesy University Prints)

Music also served a religious function during the medieval period. It was a sort of personal communication with God. As with painting and architecture, the Church exercised rigid control over the types and character of music, keeping it simple, unpretentious, and vocal. The liturgical service determined the formal structure as well as the subject matter and the very text itself.

Large-scale planning often resulted in a complex of structures around the church. This was especially true in the Italian Romanesque, and a fine example is at Pisa (fig. 5.2). The Cathedral is flanked on one side by the Baptistry and on the other side by the famous Leaning Tower.

Romanesque Period

For the purpose of this study, the Romanesque period can be said to span from about 500 to 1100. The Byzantine style of the early Church remained through the formative years, but it was modified by Roman practices and ideas. As events of history moved toward the year 1000, there were other artistic styles that are sometimes recognized by the art historian, which are here being included in the concept of the Romanesque. These styles include the Carolingian during the reign of Charlemagne and the Ottoman, which received its name from the Ottoman Empire. The term Romanesque refers to the artistic style influenced by the Romans, a style marked by its stark simplicity. Because the Roman Empire left its imprint on all of Europe during the medieval age, it is not out of order to use the term for this whole period.

Although the Romanesque style dominated from about 500 to 1100, it was not until about the tenth century that there appeared a well-developed body of creative art in the Western church. History has shown again and again that artistic activity is possible only in a well-organized and fairly wealthy society. This society began to appear about 1000 in the monastic institutions. Through the gradual reestablishment of law and order in a Europe that had seen so much of the art and civilization of the Greek and Roman world disappear in the barbaric invasions, a foundation for a new and vital civilization was made. This foundation was brought about by a number of events and achievements. The turning back of the barbarians made possible the building of roads in northern Europe and fostered a gradual growth of trade and commerce. The monastic movement and feudalism combined to reclaim the land and to establish a fairly stable agrarian society. Both of these

Figure 5.2. Baptistry, Cathedral, and Tower at Pisa. (1053–1272) (Courtesy of Alinari/Editorial Photocolor Archives)

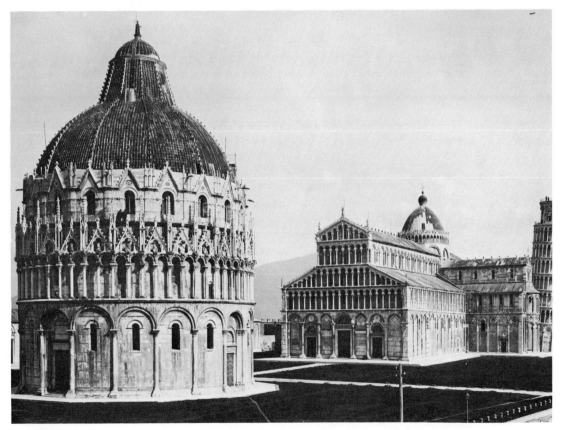

movements helped to provide the economic stabilization for a new cultural effort.

The Church, now well organized, reeducated its people in the realm of mind, manners, and morals. This reeducation provided a moral and spiritual motivation for a new civilization that was again to give opportunity for the development of creative art forms. Because wealth and social organization were centered largely in the monastic establishments of the Church, it was natural, then, that the architecture, sculpture, painting, literature, and music of the Romanesque should reflect the culture of the cloister.

Romanesque Architecture

Romanesque architects and builders, most of them monks or friars, adapted the stone arch of the Romans in much the same manner as the earlier Byzantine builders. This was an arch of great solidarity and strength, capable of bearing tremendous weight (fig. 5.3). The necessity for fireproof buildings resulted in the use of heavy stone roofs. In order to support the great weight, exceedingly thick walls without windows were used. The heavily vaulted ceiling and massive walls indicated the severe asceticism of the monastic builders. The impressive distances and gloomy spaces suggested a spirit of quiet renunciation of the world. It was a place devoted to the worship of God. There is none of the cheerful brightness of the later Gothic or Renaissance churches. In the dim twilight of the Romanesque aisles, one could feel the very presence of the Most High and the shadow of the Almighty.

The exterior of Notre Dame la Grande at Poitiers (fig. 5.4), built in the eleventh century, is a fine example of this Romanesque spirit in architecture. The triple arches of the facade suggest the symbolism of the Trinity. Close examination reveals that the two outer arches are not the same height. This is often the case with the Romanesque arches, for the churches were not always planned as an organic unit of perfect symmetry and balance. The upward thrust of the towers does not seem to give the structure a feeling of height, for the towers are too low for the rest of the building. The total height is about the same as the width. The lines do not seem to flow smoothly from one part to another. On the contrary, there is an abruptness of line which detracts from eye appeal. There is balance between arches and towers, but its effect is minimized by a lack of precision. The church was obviously not planned as a thing of sensuous beauty for the eye, but as a cubicle in which people could come into the presence of God.

The interior of San Ambrogio (fig. 5.5) at Milan again shows the treatment of the round arch. The nave is a series of bays, or areas between the heavy piers. A system of round arches forms the vault for each bay so that the appearance is one of great hollow areas with a massive ceiling. There is little light from windows, and there are innumerable dark recesses where there is no illumination except that furnished by burning tapers. Altogether this is a forbidding atmosphere. A cloisterlike feeling pervades the total space enclosed.

Figure 5.3.   Cross section of Romanesque church—Beplat.

Compare these two buildings or any other Romanesque churches with an example from the Greek civilization, such as the Parthenon. Great differences are at once apparent. The Greek is open, resting gracefully on the earth, giving a sense of peace and repose. Here was a temple that served the needs of the Greeks as they came to worship and then went their way without fear of the wrath of the gods. It was functional in that it housed the gods, but it also gave great delight to the aesthetic sense of the Greek citizen. The Romanesque, on the other hand, is heavy and dark. It shuts out the light of the world around, physically and symbolically. It was a place where medieval men and women could come to contemplate God and find a haven from the realities of life. This was a functional building also, but for a far different purpose than the Greek temple. Each in its way reflects the philosophy and belief of those who worshiped.

Figure 5.4. Notre Dame la Grande [11th century]—Poitiers. (Courtesy Marburg-Art Reference Bureau)

Romanesque Sculpture

Because sculpture and painting are arts of representation, we might expect both to deal with the same general subjects in the Romanesque. They were both purely functional in that they served an educational purpose. According to Pope Gregory, who lived about 600, painting and sculpture were to take the role of a teacher: "What those who can read learn by means of writing, that do the uneducated learn by looking at pictures."

Sculpture was functional in another manner also. All Romanesque sculpture was subordinated to architecture and was almost always conceived as a portion of the architectural decoration as well as an educational device.

Just as the Romanesque churches themselves were architecturally simple and crude, so the sculpture seems archaic in comparison to the rounded forms of a later date. The monks decorated the facades of their churches with sculptural representations of biblical scenes in simple and unsophisticated terms. It served to remind all who entered the portals that salvation lay within. The figures portrayed on the facades and columns of the cathedrals were emaciated, elongated, and seemingly more like a skeleton of bone covered with fabric than a living form.

This distortion of human form was caused by two important considerations. First, because medieval people denied this life, we would expect any

Colorplate 6 *Crucifixion* [c. 800]—Anon—Santa Maria Antiqua, Rome. (Courtesy Scala/Editorial Photocolor Archives)

human representation to be unlike life itself. This is exactly the case. Unlike Greek sculpture, with its delicately molded forms, this sculpture used symbols as an abstract expression of feeling.

The second reason for sculptural distortion is the affinity between sculptor and architect. It will be noted in most examples that the figures themselves form a part of the scheme of design and often help to support the thrust of arches and columns. Because it was general practice to carve columns after they had been placed into position, it can be readily understood that the form was often dictated by the structural design. However, there seems to have been little conflict, for the limitations of design served only to emphasize the basic forms for which Romanesque faith called.

Figure 5.5.   Interior of San Ambrogio [11th—12th century]—Milan. (Courtesy Marburg-Art Reference Bureau)

Figure 5.6. Portal of St. Trophime [c. 1105]—Arles. (Courtesy Metropolitan Museum of Art)

The portal of St. Trophime at Arles (fig. 5.6) shows how sculptured figures were brought into the total design as an integral part of the building. Note the stylized rows of elongated figures stretching across the top of the columns. The figures of the apostles are not humanistic. The bodies are flat, with the various members radically out of proportion with each other. One is hardly aware of plastic form. The heads of the figures are greatly enlarged, but they do seem to blend into the massiveness of the total structure.

The tympanum[3] of La Madeleine at Vézelay (fig. 5.7) is one of the most famous examples of Romanesque architectural sculpture. The subject, the Pentecostal scene, shows Christ bestowing his spirit upon the apostles by means of rays coming from his fingertips. The body of Christ is exceedingly unrealistic. It appears in a very awkward position and gives the impression of a fabric-covered frame of bones. Close examination of the other figures reveals

3. Tympanum: The area enclosed by an arch over the lintel of a doorway.

the same lack of humanism. The sculptured figures of the tympanum were symbols of faith. They were the emotional symbols of the reality of a faith which denied earthly pleasures but which promised eternal salvation to all who entered within.

Painting became more and more important in the scheme of Christian art. It was purely functional in that it served the same educational purpose as sculpture. There are very few original Romanesque paintings extant today, because they were usually painted on wood. Either fire or normal decay destroyed most of them.

The *Crucifixion* from Santa Maria Antiqua (colorplate 6) is one fairly good example that has come down to us. Naturally, the crucifixion was a popular

Colorplate 6 follows p. 82.

Figure 5.7. Tympanum of La Madeleine, *Christ Sending Forth the Apostles* [c. 1130]— Vézelay. (Courtesy Metropolitan Museum of Art)

subject due to the concept of salvation as the focal point of the Church's doctrine. Here, as in sculpture, we find a denial of the flesh in art. These figures are not at all real. As in the earlier mosaics, there is no sense of space. The painting has a vague feeling of closed form and a slight impression of unity. There is classical balance with the figure of Christ on the cross as the focal point of interest. Notice how the human form has been distorted and elongated in an effort to deny the reality of the flesh and to give a realistic picture of the agony and suffering of that occasion. This was a painting less likely to please the aesthetic sense than to impress upon the beholders the moving significance of the cross in their own doctrine of salvation.

Both painting and sculpture were hardly independent arts in the Romanesque. They were an integral part of architecture in order to increase the spiritual value of the church itself.

Medieval music

As the medieval Church exerted its influence, the conditions for the development of music changed as they did for the visual arts.

Under the patronage of a fairly well-organized Church, music was ordered according to specifications of the service and in keeping with a simple, ascetic faith. The medieval denial of physical matter is again apparent in the lack of instrumental music. Because instruments had a bodily shape, they were banned in order that worship might not be distracted by a concern with bodily matters. In addition, the use of instruments by the pagan Greeks and Romans militated against their use as a religious medium of musical expressiveness. Vocal music was the only kind permitted in the religious service. It had to be simple and unpretentious in its expression of religious sentiment.

In general, it may be said that Christian music took its forms and liturgical order from the Byzantine church and the Jewish temple. The Byzantines contributed the use of the hymn tune, but more important, many of the melodies stemmed directly from the Jewish-Oriental chants which were highly ornamental (melismatic). The theoretical basis and musical system were acquired from the Greeks. In fact the names of the modes were taken from the Greeks, but did not indicate the same tonal relationships as used in medieval music. The basis of tonal relationships of Western music was the result of the acoustical mathematics of Pythagoras.

It took a long time for music to reach a degree of importance comparable to architecture and sculpture. Several styles of chant were developed in the Western Church in keeping with the variety of liturgical practices and language usages. In Spain, for example, the chant was known as Mozarabic, in northern Europe as Gallican. The chant used in Rome came to be called Gregorian chant because it was due to the encouragement and leadership of Pope Gregory (540–604) that these chants were gathered together and codified. While the Gregorian chants, which eventually became the exclusive song of the Western Church, flourished most richly in the period from the fifth to the eighth century, their composition continued until the twelfth century. No composers, however, are attached to these melodies, for like folk songs they have an anonymity which tends to give them a traditional and timeless character.

The Gregorian chants were based on a series of scale patterns known as the church or ecclesiastical modes. Each of these modal scales represented a different scheme of arrangement of the seven tones of the octave system. Each mode is a different octave of the diatonic scale (i.e., the notes represented by the white keys of the piano keyboard). The octaves D-d, E-e, F-f, G-g became the basis of the eight church modes. Each chant has its own final by which the mode of the chant is determined.

Example 5.1: Charts of modes

For the medieval Church, these modal scales had a certain emotional significance. Consequently, melodies or chants constructed on these modal scales assumed these attributed characteristics.

The function of the Gregorian chant was to express a simple faith in God in keeping with the otherworldly spirit of the age. The musical forms consisted of settings of the various parts of the service. As the Church grew into an organized body of well-regulated religious practices, one of the important developments was that of a liturgy, or order of service, called the Mass. Eleven pieces of music were normally needed for the celebration of solemn Mass. These were divided into two sections. The *Ordinary*, consisting of the Kyrie, Gloria in Excelsis, Credo,[4] Sanctus, and Agnus Dei, was constant, using the same texts for every service. The second section, the *Proper*, changed texts from service to service according to the Church calendar. It consisted of the Introit, Gradual, Alleluia, Offertory, and Communion.

Sung		Recited	
Proper	*Ordinary*	*Proper*	*Ordinary*
1. Introit			
	2. Kyrie		
	3. Gloria		
		4. Collects, Prayers, etc.	
		5. Epistle	
6. Gradual			
7. Alleluia or Tract (in Lent) with Sequence.			
		8. Gospel	
	9. Credo		
10. Offertory			
			11. Prayers
		12. Secret	
		13. Preface	
	14. Sanctus and Benedictus		
			15. Canon
			16. Pater Noster
	17. Agnus Dei		
18. Communion			
		19. Post Communion	
	20. Ite, Missa est or Benediction		

Figure 5.8.   Sung and recited parts in the normal presentation of the Mass.

4. The Credo was added to the Mass after the adoption of the Nicene Creed in A.D. 325.

Example 5.2 is a Kyrie from the Ordinary of the Mass and comes from the tenth century. It is in the neumatic notation on a four-line staff as commonly used in the tenth century and as finally adopted by the Roman Catholic Church. Example 5.3 is the same chant on the five-line staff which gradually became the standard for Western notation. This Kyrie is an example of a highly melismatic type. The long florid melodic passages which are sung to the final vowel *e* of the words Kyrie and Christe are typical of such chants. It is to these passages that words were often added in medieval times, and the first words often gave the name to the chant. In the case of example 5.2 it became known as the *Kyrie fons bonitatis* (Kyrie of the fountain of goodness) since these words began the text which was placed under the notes of the long decorative melisma. Later church edicts forbade the use of verbal additions, but the chants often retain the name even though the text has disappeared from use. Note that the chant is in three parts as it was finally traditionalized in the service of the Mass. The text is from Greek and represents one of the oldest parts of the Mass. Kyrie eleison (God have mercy) is repeated three times, followed by Christe eleison (Christ have mercy) also repeated three times. The opening Kyrie is then repeated three times, twice to an altered version of the opening setting and finally to another slightly altered version. However, both of these employ the final half of the opening Kyrie melody. The chant is strictly in the Phrygian modes (see ex. 5.1). The final tone is on the note *e* not only at the final cadence but at the end of each of the three sections. The note *c* constitutes the dominant tone of the mode about which the climaxes of the chant center. The range of the chant is predominantly upward from the final tone *e* which is characteristic of Mode

Example 5.2: Neumatic notation®

Kyrie fons bonitatis   X. S.

III. The use of three repetitions for each of the textual phrases shows the symbolism of the number three in the art of the Church. The musical structure of A (first Kyrie) B (Christe) and A (final Kyrie) is another example of the symbolic use of the number three. At the same time this three part formal structure has a very satisfying aesthetic justification of statement, degression, and restatement; statement, tension, and repose, a device which will be found in architecture, sculpture, and painting of the Romanesque as well as in the following centuries of Western civilization.

Example 5.3: Modern notation®

Kyrie fons bonitatis

The Gregorian chant was used for the setting of the *Proper* and *Ordinary* sung parts of the Mass, and in addition there were many chant settings of hymns, liturgical parts of Office Hours of the Church, and chant settings for other special occasions. The chants varied in style from intonations, in which the same tone was used to set long prose passages, such as the psalms, to simple settings in which a single tone accompanied each syllable of the text, to very elaborate chants in which single syllables were often prolonged by florid vocalizations called *melismas*.

This music, like Romanesque architecture, is simple, straightforward, and nonsensuous. In listening to it, we find ourselves far removed from the secular surroundings and the hectic world we know. This music is a fitting commentary on the stark beauty of the architecture and sculpture—the three arts combine to lift the devout into a spiritual exultation that is completely detached from everyday existence.

Summary

During the medieval period which includes both the Romanesque and Gothic, the Church was the primary patron of all the arts. Moreover, because the Church held the political, economic, social, as well as the spiritual power, it was able to dictate the function, the subjects, and the style of most art and music. A philosophy of otherworldliness dominated and permeated both religion and the arts. Almost all the clergy were members of monastic orders which functioned as havens from worldly temptation. It is to the monastic orders that we owe a debt for the preservation of classic learning and letters. They were the principal architects of the nonsecular buildings as well as the secular. All art and education were under the influence and guidance of the clergy; consequently religious doctrine dictated the rules by which religious personages and subjects were to be represented. The same is true for music. The growth and development of music composition and performance of sacred music was within the province of the monastic clergy.

Feudalism was another institution that left its mark on medieval civilization. Its function was to give some stability and economic protection to the lower classes as well as to consolidate the wealth and strength of the nobility. However there was usually a close relationship between the feudal lords and the Church, for they ruled their domain with the blessing of the Church.

Romanesque builders used the Roman arch and vault as the principal method of construction which resulted in massive walls and dark interiors. There was little sense of classic balance and symmetry of design. Churches were not planned for their beauty, but as havens for the faithful.

The main function of sculpture and painting was that of religious education. Figures were usually distorted, without physical reality, almost to the point of denying the reality of the flesh which was in keeping with the philosophy of otherworldliness. Religious symbolism played a great part in all the arts, in the architectural plans, in the details of sculptural and painted figures, and even in the music.

Music was ordered according to the specifications of the liturgy and in keeping with a simple and ascetic faith. The Gregorian chant emerged as the most widely used in the Western Church and was based on ecclesiastical modes or scales. The liturgical texts dictated the choice of modes, formal organization, and style. The chants varied from a simple syllabic to highly ornamental with many notes to a single syllable. The music of the chants was monophonic and is a fitting parallel to the simplicity of the Romanesque architecture, sculpture, and painting.

Both the visual arts and music of the Romanesque are faithful expressions of this early medieval spirit. The monastic simplicity of life finds its counterpart in unsophisticated facades, in ascetic-looking sculpture, and in monodic melodies of the Gregorian chant. As the Christian Church fastened its hold on every facet of spiritual life, it also controlled the artistic expression of that faith. As time progressed, the feeling of otherworldliness became less powerful. New cultural and intellectual ideas spread over Europe on the heels of the Crusades. New economic forces were to cast a different light on the social, political, and religious pattern of life. The result was the age of the Gothic—still a medieval spirit, but tempered with an intellectualism and humanism that was to reach its full fruition only in the Renaissance.

Musical examples

Examples of Gregorian chant can be found in *Masterpieces of Music Before 1750* (Haydn Society), and vol. 1 of *History of Music in Sound* (R.C.A.).

Examples of Gallican and Mozarabic chants can be found in *Treasury of Early Music* (Haydn Society).

Suggested readings

Grout, D. J. *A History of Western Music*, 3rd ed. New York: W. W. Norton, 1980, pp. 34–64.

Janson, H. W. *History of Art.* Englewood Cliffs, N.J.: Prentice-Hall, Inc., 1962, pp. 195–228.

Lang, Paul Henry. *Music in Western Civilization.* New York: W. W. Norton, 1941, chap. 5, pp. 62–68, "Gregorian Chant."

Upjohn, Wingert and Mahler. *History of World Art.* New York: Oxford University Press, 1949, chap. 8, pp. 111–29, "Romanesque Art."

Wold and Cykler, *An Outline History of Music.* 5th ed. Dubuque, Ia.: Wm. C. Brown Company Publishers, 1982, pp. 13–26.

Suggested examples for further analysis

Architecture: Cathedral of Pisa; St. Mark's Cathedral of Venice.

Sculpture: Tympanum of St. Pierre at Moissac; *The Sin of Adam and Eve*, facade, Modena Cathedral.

Film strip with sound

The Middle Ages: The Age and its Art. Schloat Productions
Medieval Art and Music. Educational Audio Visual, Inc.

6
Gothic
(1100–1400)

Chronology of the Gothic

1100	Crusades (1100–1300)	1265	Dante Alighieri (1265–1321)
1170	Perotin (c. 1170)		
1182	Organum	1266	Giotto (1266–1337)
1200	Trouveres, troubadors, and minnesingers (c. 1200)	1300	Guillaume Machaut (1300–1377)
		1304	Francesco Petrarch (1304–1374)
1205	Nicolo Pisano (1205–1278)		
1214	Roger Bacon (1214–1294)	1305	Papacy in Avignon
1215	Magna Carta	1313	Giovanni Boccaccio (1313–1375)
1220	Salisbury built		
1225	St. Thomas Aquinas (1225–1274)	1340	Geoffrey Chaucer (1340–1400)
1240	Chartres rebuilt	1348	Black Death

Study Objectives

The objectives of this chapter are

1. To learn about the Gothic arch, which provided the skeletal frame that made great height and enormous window space possible in architecture.
2. To understand how music becomes an artistic form in which interwoven melodies and rhythmic elements are organized.
3. To study how humanism and secularism find their way into the arts.

Pronunciation Guide

Amiens (Ah-myăh)

Chartres (Shahr-tr)

Cimabue (Chee'-mah-boo-ay)

Giotto (Joht'-toh)

Machaut (Mah-Shoh)

Michelangelo
    (Mih-kel-ahn'-jel-oh)

Or la truix (Ohr lah troo-ee)

Perotin (Pe'-roh-teen)

Pisano (Pee-sah'-noh)

Rheims (Răms)

Rouen (Roo-ăh)

Siena (See-en'-ah)

It has already been mentioned that the dominant attitude of otherworldliness was not as strong and sure during the Gothic. The Romanesque concept of the world was that of a God-inspired mystery that could be expressed in terms of simple and direct art. The Renaissance concept that followed the Gothic was, like the Greek, a concept of rationalism and humanism worthy of being cultivated for its own sake. In between these two came the Gothic, in which there was a gradual swing toward humanism. In place of a blind faith in life hereafter, there arose an intellectuality and a religious skepticism that eventually caused the separation of Church and State. The artistic consequence was a body of creative art that was both intellectually ordered and full of secular influences, but was still fundamentally an art which expressed the religious fervor of the age.

This change in degree of otherworldliness did not come about as a catastrophic change but through the subtle influence of a variety of trends and events. When the year 1000 dawned and passed into history without the predicted end of the world, people began to think in terms of a more pleasurable life. While salvation through the remission of sins was still paramount in their thinking, they reduced the process to a formula. They organized theological doctrines into a scientific system of philosophy called *scholasticism*. It argued that while religious dogma was unquestionable and infallible, it could be explained and clarified by means of logic and reason. Spiritual life and salvation were thus reduced to a state of academic prescription.

Scholasticism was the product of the medieval university that had evolved from the earlier monastic schools. The medieval curriculum was divided into the so-called quadrivium and trivium. The quadrivium included arithmetic, geometry, astronomy, and music—all under the heading of mathematics. The trivium included rhetoric, grammar, and logic. Note that all of these subjects were looked upon as systematic studies, all influenced by the idea of order. Not only religion, but architecture, painting, sculpture, and music were reduced to a set of strict rules and formulas. The same protocol that bound the Romanesque painter applied to the Gothic. In addition, architecture was subjected to an elaborate plan of religious symbolism, and even music was ordered according to strict canons of procedure. The very fact that the subject of music was listed under the heading of mathematics is evidence of the influence of scholasticism.

This philosophy gave rise to innumerable minutiae in all areas of artistic effort. In addition, these minutiae lent weight and proof to the logic of the religious doctrine. Consequently, there was less individual creative imagination in the arts than we normally attribute to such endeavor. It is not until the Renaissance that artworks begin to reveal the individuality of their creators and express the warmth of human emotion. The Gothic was still subject to the collective creative effort of the people, directed and inspired by the Church.

While scholastic philosophy systematized salvation, it did not bring forth the deep and abiding faith that many believed it would. Worship tended toward an empty formalism. The letter of the doctrine superseded the spirit of Christianity. Men like Dante were conscious of the paradox that existed between the Christian ideal and the Christian practice. The clergy themselves were often corrupt beyond belief, some of them actually engaged in practicing piracy when not engaged in reading their services. High positions in the Papal State were openly obtained by a process of barter and trade. The Church was losing its moral and political power, as well as its spiritual significance. At one time, three different popes were engaged in the shocking spectacle of trying to excommunicate each other. Even in the face of such conduct, scholasticism gave tacit approval by holding that the scaraments were still valid even if the clergy administering them were immoral.

This decline of spiritual values gave rise to a skepticism of spiritual authority and law. It cannot be said that the Church lost its hold, but certainly the faithful were less concerned with the self-denial of the earlier ages and more interested in their own happiness and well-being. The arts, in turn, responded with a more humanistic expression.

Another factor which helped to soften the spirit of otherworldliness was the movement of the Crusades. These pilgrimages to wrest the Holy Land from infidel Turks were unsuccessful in their main objective, but they did open up new vistas in social and cultural thought. Material wealth through trade, a love of a full life, and high adventure were but a few of the results. The Crusaders came into contact with Oriental civilization. They tasted luxury and experienced a culture and social code that contrasted sharply with the uncouth customs of their own land and with the spiritual concepts in which they had been trained. The Crusaders copied social customs and forms of entertainment which they had come to know in the East.

Those returning from these pilgrimages showed signs of becoming intellectually and economically more independent. Their new experiences, as well as scholasticism, made them skeptical of the religious doctrine that threatened the punishment of hell for every impulse conducive to a life of pleasure.

The cult of the Virgin Mary was, at least in part, a consequence of the Crusades. The idea of courtly love was an Oriental concept, which made its way westward. People had been fearful of the Church. The spiritual and temporal power of the Church, its authority to save or damn, its teaching of hell, its doctrine of an avenging God—all this awed and frightened medieval people. They feared God, but did not love him. Under the influence of the courtly love idea they could, and did, make Mary the object of their affection. Mary, Mother of God, was a humanizing influence by her sympathy and loveliness. No burden was too great to bring to her in prayer. They loved Mary, admired Jesus, and feared God.

Closely allied with the Crusades was the development of towns and the building of a more adequate system of roads, especially in northern Europe. Romanesque art, as we have seen, was mainly monastic, but the Gothic cathedral of the twelfth to fourteenth centuries was the creation of the towns and bishops. With the growth of commerce and industry and a corresponding growth of towns, especially in northern Europe, the bishops, bourgeoisie, and guilds grew steadily more wealthy. All classes were united in an ardent religious faith and in an equally ardent feeling of local pride. The towns enthusiastically built more churches than we would imagine they needed, partly to express the fervor of their faith and partly to surpass rival towns in magnificence. A spiritual fervor lasted in spite of a growing secularization and criticism of the clergy. Being the product of communal effort, the Gothic cathedral was placed on the public square, surrounded by the homes of its builders, and paid for by public subscription. It became the religious, civic, and social center of a community life. It functioned as church, picture gallery, concert hall, theater, library, and school—truly a multipurpose artwork.

The sum total of the influence of the aforesaid aspects of Gothic culture on art is vividly emblazoned on its subjects, forms, and expressions. The Gothic artist found beauty in the human spirit, not in the physical body. The emotional tone became one of warmth and mystic longing. Gothic artists recreated the adventure and excitement of their age by towering spires, dynamic decoration, and complicated sinews of masonry. Gothic artists sought to integrate religious emotion with the reality of life by putting side by side the noble and ignoble, the real and the mystic. In the spirit of their age, Gothic artists strove to rise above the coarseness of this life and project the observer into the beauties of heaven.

Architecture

The Gothic cathedral is a physical testimonial to the urge for rising above the earthly, with its towering spires rising majestically over the towns of northern Europe. It was in France that the Gothic style came into being. Ecclesiastic architecture in Italy was dominated too much by the Byzantine-Romanesque to be a leader in the new movement. In fact, the term *Gothic* was used by the Italians of the Renaissance and later classicists as a description for a style which they thought to be vulgar, barbaric, and lacking in refined taste. It was only after the Gothic was well established in France, Germany, and England that southern Europe responded at all, and then only mildly.

The round arch of the Romanesque was quite inelastic because the height of the arch could not be more than half of its width. This limitation hampered the Gothic builders who sought to reach great heights. Ingenuity and experiments brought about the pointed arch (fig. 6.1), which made possible the vaulting of any space at almost any height. One of the main problems was how to withstand the lateral thrust of the arch. The heavy walls served this purpose in the Romanesque. Using the pointed arch made the problem even more acute, for the higher the structure, the more lateral thrust to be neutralized. Gothic builders solved this by a series of supporting arches and

Figure 6.1 Cross section of a Gothic church—Beplat

buttresses which exerted a counterthrust. The building was so delicately balanced by this system of bracing that theoretically it would collapse if any one of the supporting arches were removed.

This knowledge of thrusts and counterthrusts suggested a skeleton frame of masonry piers, ribs, and buttresses that would stand alone and tower toward the heavens. In place of the massive columns and thick walls of the Romanesque, the Gothic technique resulted in slim, slender piers that suggested a web of ribs that held windows, letting light add to the already expanding sense of spaciousness. The amount of space, both vertical and horizontal, was determined only by the wealth and ingenuity of the builders. The Gothic was so closely allied with the technique of achieving these effects of lightness that it can be called a system rather than a style.

One of the most famous Gothic cathedrals is Amiens (fig. 6.2), built in Picardy between 1220 and 1269. Much of the ornamental design of the exterior was added about a century later. Note the open spaces—the amount of window space and the height of the edifice in comparison to the Romanesque Notre Dame la Grande. The basic plan is the same for both, but Amiens reaches upward toward the heavens, while Notre Dame la Grande sits heavily on its massive foundations. Amiens appears to grow out of the earth, held up by a vast web of piers, ribs, and buttresses. The turrets, pinnacles, and decorative ornamentation combine with the structural details to give a filigree, or lacework, effect of clear-cut lines. There is an impression of energy forcing its way upward. Starting at the base, with its trinity of vaulted arches as entrances, this upward movement is assisted by rows of arches alternating with rows of sculptured figures. Above it all stands the intricate rose window, flanked on either side by lofty arches and stately spires. Note that vertical lines dominate the facade. Horizontal lines are permitted to exert their influence, but are broken by the upward thrust. The feeling of weight is defeated at every turn. Unity is that of separate parts, but they are fused into one gigantic panorama by the energy of the upward movement.

The interior of Amiens (fig. 6.3) intensifies and repeats the same energy. The sense of vertical space is even more impressive here than it appears to be from the exterior. The eye of the observer is drawn upward by the massive piers, which become more slender and lighter as they progress higher and higher. Their outline eventually becomes diffused by distance and ornamentation. The sweep of pointed arches leads the eye and the spirit of the observer even higher, until they are fused with the heavens. Ribs of masonry frame the multicolored stained-glass windows that capture the sunlight, diffusing its rays into all colors of the spectrum.

The cathedral at Salisbury, England (fig. 6.4), is one of the few Gothic structures with a completed set of spires. Set in the center of a spacious park, its unusually tall steeple over the main transport gives an upward thrust to the whole. All lines lead the eye up until they converge at the tip. Even here the momentum is sufficient to carry the eye up into the heavens.

Figure 6.2   Cathedral at Amiens [c. 1225]. (Courtesy Metropolitan Museum of Art)

Figure 6.3   Interior of Amiens [c. 1225]. (Art Reference Bureau)

Each Gothic cathedral had its own personality. Each strove to express the communal faith of its builders. The cathedrals often vied one with another to surpass in beauty and magnificence. Yet each followed the same basic plan and technique of construction. The cathedrals of Chartres, Rouen, Rheims, and Notre Dame of Paris are among the most glorious examples of that type of ecclesiastical architecture—a type that has become synonomous with church architecture throughout the whole Christian world. There are many imitations built in later time, but none as sincerely wrought as those of the Gothic age.

Stained glass

The most remarkable artistic effort in visual representation is seen in the stained-glass windows of the Gothic. These windows served many purposes. They admitted the much-needed light that was almost absent in the Romanesque. They were not only magnificent decorations which gave the interior a warm, humanistic atmosphere, but they were also a means of instruction as illuminated paintings for religious education. In addition, the windows more and more took the place of walls; they occupied all the free space between the piers supporting the arches.

Stained glass was a craft which developed from the stylized mosaics of the Byzantine and Romanesque. The glass painter assembled bits of colored translucent glass into a window panel in such a way as to define a subject with the sharp lines of contrasting glass. The lines of the figures were always strongly marked, and the draperies clearly indicated. Because line and color had to be so sharply divided, it was very difficult to achieve any amount of

Figure 6.4   Salisbury Cathedral [from 1220]. (Courtesy Marburg-Art Reference Bureau)

expressive detail. The element of space was nonexistent because of the lack of perspective.

As in the Romanesque concept of human form, the figures remained out of proportion and distorted. There is no movement suggested. In every case, there is an archaic juxtaposition of forms with little relationship between figures. This leads to separate organization.

An interesting device which shows the communal effort of the Gothic is the trademark of the donor. Many windows, or sets of windows, were the gift of a local guild or a wealthy patron. The egoism of wanting a gift to be a memorial to one's memory is shown by the trademark or crest of the donor. This was usually placed in a prominent position in each window, often just below the central figure of the panel.

A window from Chartres depicting the *Death of the Virgin* (colorplate 7) shows the technique of this remarkable craft. With all its brilliant polychromatic coloring, the representation is stiff and unreal. The figures are stylized without expression and show the absence of perspective in the manner in which they are grouped around the deathbed. In spite of these artistic defects from our point of view, this was a meaningful message for the faithful. The donor, in this instance the shoemakers' guild, is memorialized by the figure of a cobbler at his bench.

The rose window of the south transept of Chartres (colorplate 8) shows how the windows were a part of the architectural plan, fitting as they do into the open spaces of the arches. All windows were symbolic of the Scriptures, for they not only stood as barriers from the elements of the world, but they taught the true way of salvation. The rose window was the special symbol of the glories of heaven. As the faithful were bathed in the radiance of its rays, they were reminded, no doubt, of the description in Revelation: "And the twelve gates were twelve pearls; each one of the several gates was of one pearl; and the street of the city was pure gold, as it were transparent glass."[1]

The architecture and stained glass of the Gothic was a complete expression of their faith. The spirit of scholasticism is deeply ingrained in the logic of their building technique—a technique that caused the thrust and counterthrust to be so calculated that the whole edifice stood as a pattern of sinews and ribs, each supporting the other. This system, combined with the rich coloring of the stained glass and the physical reaching for the heavens, attests to the harmonious appeal of the Gothic—an appeal to the mind, eye, and spirit.

Sculpture

The basic elements of sculpture were treated essentially the same in the Gothic as they had been during the Romanesque. There was an added predilection for expressive feeling and naturalism that was lacking in the mon-

Colorplates 7, 8
follows p. 114.

1. Revelation 22:21.

astic art. Figures were no longer merely symbols. They were people of character who served as reminders of moral truth. The saints came to have idyllic countenances and personalities that suggested their own spiritual character. All personages were presented with a naturalism that made them alive and real. In keeping with the "otherworldly" philosophy, however, the soul was still in conflict with the body; therefore, a moral character was conveyed by expression, not by bodily form or pure symbolism. Gothic interest was still in the message of faith and in the solace of salvation.

Naturalism was not confined to human personality but was also present in the decorative details that were carved on the moldings and capitals of the pillars. Realistic vines and flowers were often used to break up the smooth surface and give energy to an otherwise static bit of stone. Nature in perspective was still unknown, but Gothic artists were aware that they were living in an organic world which was in constant flux.

As it was during the Romanesque, sculpture was an integral part of architecture. Every portal, every niche, every space not taken by stained glass carried a message in stone. The influence of scholasticism made Gothic artists conscious of minutiae, both artistic and theological. Every movement, every detail was made a symbol of faith that conformed to the doctrine. Stories from the Old and New Testament and scenes from the lives of the saints were depicted as sermons in stone. In addition, the influence of the cult of the Virgin Mary is apparent everywhere. Almost every cathedral had a special Virgin prominently displayed. In fact, the Virgin became so popular that the artistic portrayal of Jesus was largely replaced by that of His Virgin Mother. Unlike the Romanesque, Gothic sculptors created their figures independently of the columns, placing them upon pillars or in niches that were an integral part of the structure. This innovation made it possible to achieve effects of movement and space that were unknown earlier. Movement and plasticity were also enhanced by the Gothic treatment of drapery. Instead of large ornamental scrolls which seemed to symbolize only form, Gothic drapery was deeply carved, permitting light and shade to suggest space and movement.

The elongation of the body, which has the tendency to endow it with lightness and immateriality, was still used with striking success. Gothic sculptural figures seemed to grow from their bases, as the cathedral itself did from the earth. Bodily elongation also had the tendency to conventionalize bodily form. While there was often real personality revealed in facial features and in the position of the body, no real individuality could be achieved through the form itself. In keeping with the Catholic faith, the Gothic sculptor gave little attention to sex characteristics. The Madonnas and female saints show only very slight physical indications of sex. Breasts are usually very small and are often set too high on the chest. They were only symbols of sex, not physical characteristics.

The sculpture of Amiens fits well into the structural pattern of the cathedral and also reveals the Gothic spirit as it is manifest in stone. Figure 6.5

Figure 6.5 *Apostles, Portal of LeBeau Dieu* [1225]—Cathedral, Amiens. (Courtesy University Prints)

shows the Apostles from the central portal of Amiens. The individual figures are set apart from the wall and are covered with a Gothic-type canopy to integrate them with the architecture. Note that while the bodies are completely impersonal, the position of the hands and turning of the heads make them seem alive and real. The full folds of drapery, which fall gracefully about the forms, give a feeling of plasticity and refinement.

The central portal is taken over by *The Last Judgment.* The space immediately over the door is divided, according to scholastic theology, into three separate panels. The lower one depicts the judgment of souls; the second, the separation of the saved from the damned. Christ, the Judge, looks down upon the scene from the topmost panel. Flanking the portal are figures of saints and martyrs, each identified by some symbol of a particular martyrdom or saintly acts.

On the central part which divides the doors is the justly famous *Amiens Christ* (fig. 6.6). This is different from earlier portrayals of the Saviour, for it pictures him as a kindly ruler who judges according to the Book of Laws, which is held in his left hand. He is standing upon the heads of a serpent and a snake, symbols of the evil which He vanquished. The figure is modeled in broad, simple forms. The head is a bit too large for the body but commands attention by its deeply carved features and by its size. The folds of drapery, which are drawn about the waist, catch and absorb light and shade to suggest space and movement. The body itself, however, remains obscure. The kindly face, the upraised hand in a gesture of promise, and the book combine to make a focal area. There is no feeling of asceticism. Here is the promise of security and joy for a good life. Here is Gothic humanism in contrast to the Romanesque "fleshless hand."

The Italian sculptors of the Gothic period did not respond to the severe style of the northern Europeans any more than the architects. However, the wave of humanism did make its appearance in the thirteenth century. The *Annunciation, Nativity, and Shepherds* from the pulpit at Siena (fig. 6.7) is Italian medieval sculpture with the humanistic influence. The artist Nicola Pisano (1205–78) made his figures dignified and serene, suggesting the forms of the body beneath the draperies, in the style of the Greeks. In true Gothic style, Pisano shows no spatial perspective, for he crowds the three stories into one scene. Like the figures of Amiens, however, there is freedom of movement in the deeply carved folds and the flow of line from one form to another—a movement which actually brings the three scenes together into a time concept which does not fit the subjects.

Painting

The art of painting, except for the illumination of manuscripts, was a minor art in the Gothic north. It remained for the Italians of the thirteenth and fourteenth centuries to raise painting to an equal footing with sculpture. Perhaps it was the lack of great amounts of stained glass in Italy that gave artists the impetus to decorate the walls of churches with Biblical scenes as an educational device. In any event, the famous wall painting at Padua served the same religious purposes as the stained glass of Amiens.

Like architecture and sculpture, Gothic painting adhered to the canons of medieval theology. Symbols of sacred stories were arranged according to the traditional manner of biblical storytelling, and the protagonists were presented according to theological specifications. The difference between the painting of Italy and northern Europe was in the naturalism and the feeling for human emotion. The Italians learned the lesson of expression from the northern sculptors and then applied it to painting.

Figure 6.6 *Amiens Christ* [c. 1225]—Cathedral, Amiens. (Courtesy Metropolitan Museum of Art)

The Annunciation of the Siena cathedral altar (colorplate 9) is a case in point. All the medieval symbolism is present. The Archangel Gabriel holds the olive branch as a symbol of peace; the vase of lilies, symbols of virginity, stands between the two figures. Over the central scene stands the trinity of Gothic arches with a dove, the symbol of the Holy Ghost, at the point of the central arch. It is the natural arrangement and the feeling for emotion that bring this painting beyond the realm of mediocrity. The Virgin shrinks back with a look of awe as the angel raises his hand in preparation for speaking. Expression is real, even if the forms themselves are not plastic in a physical sense. The denial of the flesh is still apparent. Note that the vase and the lilies are more convincingly real than the human forms. Symbolism is also apparent in the separate unity of the painting. Each figure, each item, is separate and complete in itself, adding to the spiritual implications of the story. Line is clearly defined, defeating any suggestion of motion and space.

The most famous painter of the Gothic is the Italian, Giotto (c. 1266–1337). Art historians usually look upon this famous master's work as the beginning

Colorplate 9 follows p. 114.

Figure 6.7 *Annunciation, Nativity, and Shepherds* [1260]—from pulpit at Siena-Pisano. (Alinari/Editorial Photocolor Archives)

of a new era in painting. This is true; like many great masters, Giotto was a prophet of a new age. He lived during a time when the Gothic spirit was at its peak, but he was so humanistic, so individual, that he can rightfully be called the link between the Gothic and the Renaissance.

Giotto's most famous work is the monumental fresco of the *Life of Christ* on the walls of the church at Padua. Fresco is a name for painting that is put on wet or fresh plaster. This technique is exceedingly difficult, for an error means that new plaster must be applied and then painted over. Another distinct disadvantage to fresco painting is that plaster has the tendency to crack and absorb moisture. We will see in a later chapter how the works of Leonardo da Vinci and Michelangelo have been damaged in this way.

One of the remarkable scenes from Giotto's *Life of Christ* is the *Disposition*, or the laying away, of Christ's body in the tomb (colorplate 10). Giotto has presented this theme in such a natural manner that we feel witnesses to a real drama. He created a three-dimensional group that moves in space. Closed form centers attention on the body of Christ. Every movement, every gaze is focused upon him. Even the angels are drawn toward him. There are expressions of grief on each face. In true Gothic tradition, facial expressions of grief are alike in each—lips parted slightly, eyes narrowed and drawn back. Giotto did not yet recognize the real individuality of grief. Organization of separate parts with each individual being apart from the others, was at least true of the heads. Lines are clear-cut and sharply define the polychromatic coloring. The painting is still Gothic in its essential features of symbolism. The halos and angels attest to this. The stylized humans are still unreal in comparison with the Greeks' portrayal of physical reality. There is more humanism than was found in Romanesque sculpture, or even the Gothic sculpture of Amiens. Giotto was on the threshold of the Renaissance. He organized the basic elements of painting in much the same manner as later artists. However, in adherence to traditional scenes and symbolisms, he is tied with invisible bonds to the spirit of the northern Gothic.

Music

As the Gothic concept of art broke with the past in its inclination toward humanism and yet held to the scholastic attitude of the Middle Ages, so did the Gothic music exhibit these same tendencies. In this period are found the first expressions in artistic form of one of the basic elements of western European music—the simultaneous sounding together of tones of different pitch, a phenomenon which we call *harmony*. While it is possible that this device had been used previously in some form, it is probably the most characteristic element whereby European music can be differentiated from all other musical systems.

Colorplate 10
follows p. 114.

There are two schemes whereby harmony is achieved in the history of Western music. One, which is called polyphony or counterpoint, implies the use of two or more simultaneously sounded melodic lines, a scheme which deals with the musical materials in a linear fashion. The other, which we will call homophony, deals with the musical materials in a chordal-harmonic or vertical-block fashion. Both achieve the result of having tones of different pitch sounded simultaneously, a phenomenon which was described in chapter 2 as harmony, under the basic elements of music.

Both of these schemes demand a certain definiteness of notation in order that composers may communicate their ideas to the musical performers. As long as music was made up exclusively of single melodic lines, no necessity was felt for a system of symbols which did more than remind performers of the traditional melodies. With the advent of musician-composers, who thought of themselves as individual artists concerned with the organization of musical sounds in complex tonal patterns, notation became a necessity. The countless anonymous composers of the chants of the Middle Ages are an embodiment of a "God-inspired" mysterious creative power disassociated from the human being. On the contrary, Gothic composers were individuals struggling with an artistic problem, and they needed to communicate their solution to other people. Notation made possible the preservation of works and names of specific Gothic composers. A further example of the concern with things of this world was the emphasis on artistic treatment of secular music, both by recognized composers and the great body of poet-musicians, the minstrel singers of the twelfth and thirteenth centuries.

In contrast to these humanizing tendencies, the rigid subscription to rules and devices of composition can be likened to the acceptance of the stylized symbols of Gothic painting. The organization of the musical materials by composers of the Gothic era was accomplished by strict adherence to arbitrary rules and practice, many of which had symbolic meanings. For example, Church music always used triple meter for its rhythmic structure, symbolizing the Trinity. Of the two schemes of achieving the element of harmony, the Gothic composers chose that of polyphony. This polyphony was greatly influenced by the traditional music of the medieval Church, the Gregorian chant. The weaving together of lines of melody, one of which is a traditional chant of the Church, is characteristic of the works of the composers of this period. The addition to the original chant which was called the cantus firmus (basic chant), of one, two, or even three lines of melody, all of which return at cadence points to the perfect intervals of the unison, fifth, or octave, is, in a sense, the musical parallel of the subdivisions of the Gothic arch that is so characteristic of architecture at this time (ex. 6.1). This early style of polyphonic music was known as organum and was the basic style from the twelfth through the fourteenth centuries.

Example 6.1: Organum, Sequence, *Rex Caeli, Domine*®

Original chant

Added voice.

1. Rex cae - li Do - mi - ne ma - ris un - di - so - ni,
2. Ti - ta - nis ni - ti - di squa - li - di - que so - li.

3. Te hu - mi - les fa - mu - li mo - du - lis ve - ne - ran - do pi - is.
4. Se ju - be - as fla - gi - tant va - ri - is li - be - ra - re ma - lis. (etc.)

* = cadence point.

An example of polyphonic music is the *Alleluia* of Pérotin (c. 1170). This early work is one in which the original modal chant, the cantus firmus, is sung as a very slow-moving voice, while the added parts move in a decorative manner in faster note values, always returning at the cadences to the inevitable perfect intervals of unison, fifth, or octave. While the mode of this chant was determined by its final tone, there was no scheme of chordal structure or accompaniment. This music, unlike the greater portion of Western music with which we are familiar, is not organized on the basis of a feeling for tonality or key in which harmonic structure determines the central or tonic tone. There are no vertical chordal considerations which determine the harmony. The organization is one of pure linear style. The harmony, which is a result of the combining of the upper melodic line with the traditional chant, is merely coincidental, a by-product, as it were, of a system of organization which is concerned only with the intervallic relation between the original chant and its added decorative melodies. Moreover, these relationships are of concern only at the beginning and the end of each phrase. The intervals of the unison, fourth, fifth, and eighth, being considered consonant, determine the relationships at these points which are further defined by dynamic interpretation. To ears accustomed to tonal organization, this music may sound empty and crude at first. Listen for the accented cadences with their archaic consonances, and soon the intervening melodic passages with their dissonant transient harmonies will reveal themselves.

In the matter of rhythmical organization, this *Alleluia* is a fine example of the rigid scholastic application in the upper two voices of an arbitrary poetic rhythmic pattern, the dactyl. The lower voice in the greater portion of this work is unmeasured.

The form of the *Alleluia* is exceedingly free, consisting of slightly varied repetitions of a rhythmic pattern so short and so limited in its pitch range that only the skill of performance can counterbalance the tendency toward monotony.

While there are no given instructions for the performance of this early polyphonic music, it is obvious from sculpture and paintings of the period that instruments were used in its performance. This could have been accomplished either by doubling the voice parts or substituting instruments for voices in one or more parts. Certainly the slow-moving note values of a cantus firmus would be well adapted to rendition by such instruments as the viols, sackbuts, or other wind instruments.

Another example of a setting of a liturgical text is the *Agnus Dei* by Machaut (c. 1300–c. 77), the greatest composer of the Gothic period. This work is from the first composed polyphonic setting of the entire ordinary of the Mass. It represents a much less repetitious and monotonous organization of the musical materials than that of Pérotin, even though the basic scheme is the same—that of polyphonic linear structure. The composer has substituted a much freer and larger rhythmic pattern for the short poetic foot of the dactyl. Since the harmonic organization is still intervallic, there is as yet no feeling for tonality in our present-day meaning, and the cadences are marked by the perfect intervals, particularly the fifth and octave. There is, however, some concern about the transient harmonies engendered by the flow of the four voices, and the interval of the third, which is so pleasing to the more modern ear, is to be heard occasionally. A rhythmic melodic figure of four smaller note values acts as an element of form by its frequent varied repetitions.

In contrast to these works of Pérotin and Machaut is the great wealth of secular songs of the Gothic period. Minstrel singers who were variously known as troubadours, trouvères, and minnesingers set poems of secular themes to melodies which they themselves composed or to tunes which were well-known common property. While all medieval secular songs were not the product of these aristocratic and courtly singers, it is from them that the greatest number of settings have come down to us. The troubadours originated in southern France, and their influence spread all over Europe. In northern France the comparable singers were known as trouvères and in Germany as minnesingers. These minstrels were often more concerned with poetic expression than with the musical settings. From the troubadours and trouvères alone a treasury of more than 1,500 melodies and 7,500 poems are known today. The subjects of these lyrics vary from political satire to love, the latter a favorite theme. Many songs are concerned with religious subject matter. This is especially true of the laudas of Italy. Since they are nonliturgical, however, they are included under the term "secular."

A common characteristic of all these songs, whether from France, Italy, Germany, or Spain, is their monodic or single melodic line structure. The trouvère song "*Or la truix*" is representative of this type of musical expression. It is music of the court and typical of many of the minstrel singers' compositions. It consists of a single line of melody, the form of which is dictated by the poetic construction of the verse. The form of this song is definitely that of repetition and contrast. The opening phrase contrasts with the second and is followed by two repetitions of the first phrase. Various patterns of such repetition and contrast are to be found in all these secular songs, depending on the structure of the lyric. While there is no chordal notation given, the melody may well have been sung to some form of simple accompaniment of harp or lute, since numerous pictures show singers and other performers with such instruments capable of producing chordal harmony. The melodies, while predominantly modal, often tend to fall into our present-day concept of minor and even major tonality.

Summary

The Church, during the Gothic, retained its position as the principal patron of the arts. It was still the most powerful political, economic, educational, artistic, and religious institution. While the canons and symbolisms by which religious doctrines were realized artistically remained basically the same as in the Romanesque, there was more emphasis on magnificence and beauty. The trend was toward more humanism. The rise of towns and the Crusades were developments that saw more secular ideas and foreign cultural practices integrated into the sociocultural scene of the West. Gothic churches were more the result of the communal effort of the towns than the product of the monasteries. The Gothic church served as the educational and social, as well as the religious center of the community. Its splendor was a testimony to the wealth and power of the Church itself.

The development of the Gothic arch resulted in a skeletal frame that made it possible to reach great heights with the upward thrust of high ceilings and tall spires. It also made it possible to have whole walls of magnificent stained-glass windows, usually with memorials to the donors, such as trade guilds or noble families, placed in a prominent position below each scene.

Gothic sculpture was usually freestanding with movement of free-flowing drapery and some evidence of bodily movement. Sculpture was still somewhat distorted as to physical reality, but to a lesser extent than in the Romanesque. Real beauty was still of the spirit and not of the flesh. The subject matter of both sculpture and painting was enhanced by the devotion to the Virgin Mary as an object of courtly love. Painting also showed more three-dimensional character with humanistic tendencies. The spatial concept, however, was still very slight. Clearly defined lines and contrasting colors gave the effect of a controlled space with little sense of movement. The expressive feeling in painting, sculpture, and stained glass was brought about more by symbolism than the realism of emotional reaction.

The development of polyphony, rhythmic organization, as well as form, was an achievement of Gothic music. These innovations were made possible through the invention of a system of notation. Still, music was more of a science than an art. Rigid rules controlled the intervallic relationships, rhythm and formal organization in polyphonic sacred music which was organized around liturgical texts. There was also a great wealth of secular song set to the poems of troubadours, trouvéres, and minnesingers. These songs were usually of a courtly nature, but many were related to religious subjects, especially to the love of the Virgin Mary.

We have seen how the architecture, sculpture, painting, and music of the Gothic have been the expression of the religion, mysticism, and scholasticism that permeated the age. All art was a veritable encyclopedia of religious beliefs. Humanism was beginning to blossom, but it remained for the Renaissance artist to capture and express this new spirit in its entirety.

Musical examples

Pérotin, *Alleluia.* M.M. 22–26

Trouvère song, *Or la truix.* M.M. 11–12

Machaut, *Agnus Dei.* M.M. 36–39

Suggested readings

Grout, D. J. *A History of Western Music,* 3rd ed. New York: W. W. Norton, 1980, pp. 64–144.

Janson, H. W. *History of Art.* Englewood Cliffs, N.J.: Prentice-Hall, Inc., 1962, pp. 229–304.

Lang, Paul Henry. *Music in Western Civilization.* New York: W. W. Norton, 1941, chapter 7, pp. 122–44.

Leichtentritt, Hugo. *Music, History and Ideas.* Cambridge: Harvard University Press, 1940, chapter 3, pp. 51–73.

Upjohn, Wingert and Mahler. *History of World Art.* New York: Oxford University Press, 1949, chapter 9, pp. 130–47.

Wold and Cykler. *An Outline History of Music,* 5th ed. Dubuque, Ia.: Wm. C. Brown Company Publishers, 1982, pp. 29–51.

Suggested examples for further analysis

Architecture: Chartres Cathedral; Rouen Cathedral

Sculpture: *Coronation of the Virgin*, Notre Dame, Paris; *Kings and Queens*, west portal of Chartres Cathedral; *Vièrge Dorée*, Amiens Cathedral

Painting: Cimabue, Giovanni, *Madonna Enthroned*; Giotto, *The Death of St. Francis*

Stained Glass: Stained-glass windows of Amiens; stained-glass windows of Chartres

Music: School of Notre Dame, Motet, *En non Diu! Quant voi; Eius in Oriente*; Bernart de Ventadorn, Troubadour Canso, *Be m'an perdut*

These examples can be found in *Masterpieces of Music Before 1750* and *Treasury of Early Music* (Haydn Society). Other examples of Gothic music can be found in *History of Music in Sound* (R.C.A.)

Additional sources for visual illustrations

Cole, Bruce. *Giotto and Florentine Painting.* New York: Harper and Row, 1976

Film strips with sound

Middle Ages: The Age and its Art. Schloat Productions

Medieval Art and Music. Educational Audio Visual Inc.

The Age of Dante and Giotto. Guidance Associates

Colorplate 7 *Death of the Virgin* [c. 1200]—Chartres Cathedral. (Courtesy Scala/ Editorial Photocolor Archives)

Colorplate 8   South Rose Window and Lancets [c. 1220]—Chartres Cathedral.
(Courtesy Scala/Editorial Photocolor Archives)

Colorplate 9   *The Annunciation* [1333]—Simone Martini e Lippo Memmi. (Courtesy Scala/Editorial Photocolor Archives)

Colorplate 10 *Disposition* [1303–1306]—Giotto. (Courtesy Scala/Editorial Photocolor Archives)

7
Renaissance
(1400–1600)

Chronology of the Renaissance

1378	Lorenzo Ghiberti (1378–1455)	1471	Albrecht Dürer (1471–1528)
1386	Donato di Nicolo Donatello (1386–1466)	1473	Nicolaus Copernicus (1473–1543)
1400	Guillaume Dufay (c.1400–1474)	1475	Michelangelo Buonarroti (1475–1564)
1430	Rule of the Medici family (1430–1495)	1477	Tiziano Vecelli (Titian) (1477–1576)
1435	Andrea del Verrochio (1435–1488)	1478	Giorgo Giorgione (1478–1511)
1440	Sandro Botticelli (1440–1510)	1480	Mathis Grünewald (1480–1528)
1444	Donato Bramante (1444–1514)	1483	Raphael Sanzio (1483–1520)
1449	Lorenzo de' Medici (1449–1492)		Martin Luther (1483–1546)
1450	Josquin des Prés (1450–1521)	1492	First voyage of Columbus
	Heinrich Isaac (1450–1517)	1496	Johann Walter (1496–1570)
1452	Leonardo da Vinci (1452–1519)	1497	Da Gama voyage to India
		1498	Execution of Savonarola
1469	Niccolo Machiavelli (1469–1527)	1503	Julius II as Pope
		1513	*The Prince* by Machiavelli

1517	Luther posts his *Ninety-Five Theses*	1540	Founding of the Jesuit Society
1520	Brueghel, Pieter (c. 1524–1569)	1545	Council of Trent
1520	Andrea Gabrieli (1520–1586)	1548	El Greco (1548–1614)
1525	Giovanni Perluigi Palestrina (1525–1594)	1553	Luca Marenzio (1553–1599)
1532	Orlando di Lasso (1532–1590)	1560	Don Carlo Gesualdo (1560–1613)
1534	Church of England separates from the Papacy	1564	William Shakespeare (1564–1616)
		1577	Drake starts world voyage

Study Objectives

The objectives of this chapter are

1. To understand that this period marks the return to the ideals of Greek humanism and individualism and that the search for personal identity dominated the arts during this period.
2. To study how scientific research influences art through perspective and anatomy and music in harmonic structure.
3. To understand that the patronage of artists and musicians was divided between the Church and the aristocracy, but their objectives were similarly humanistic.

Pronunciation Guide

Botticelli (Bot-tee-chel'-lee)
Crequillon (Krek-kee-ŏ)
Dürer (Dü'-rer)
El Greco (El Gre'-koh)
Erasmus (E-ras'-moos)
Farnese (Fahr-nay'-ze)
Gabrieli, Giovanni (Gah-bree-ay'-lee, Joh-vah-nee)
Gesualdo (Jez-wahl'-doh)
Ghirlandaio (Geer-lahn-dah'-ee-oh)
Gott Schöpfer, Heiliger Geist (Got Shöp'-fer, Hih'-li-ger Gihst)
Gozzoli (Got-zoh'-lee)
Grünewald (Grü'-ne-vald)

Isaac (Ee-zahk')
Josquin des Prés (Jos-ka day Pray)
Machiavelli (Mah'-kee-ah-vel'-lee)
Magi (Mah'-jee)
Medici, Lorenzo (May'-dee-chee, Loh-ren'-zoh)
Palestrina (Pahl-es-tree'-nah)
Palladio (Pahl-lah'-dee-oh)
Perugino (Pay-roo-jee'-noh)
Prinzen Tanz, Proportz (Print'-zen Tahnz, Proh'-portz)
Santa Maria delle Grazia (Sahn'-tah Mah-ree'-ah del-le Graht'-zee-ah)

Savanarola (Sah'-vahn-ah-roh'-lah)
Sforza, Ludovico (Sfor'-zah, Loo-
    doh-vee'-koh)
Simonetta (See-moh-net'-tah)
Tintoretto (Teen-toh-ret'-toh)

Veni Sponsa Christi (Vay'-nee
    Spon'-sah Krees'-tee)
Verrochio (Ver-roh'-kee-oh)
Vicenza (Vee-chen'-zah)
Walter (Vahl' -ter)

The flowering of humanism, which had its faint beginnings in the Gothic, reached full bloom in the succeeding epoch, which we call the Italian Renaissance (1400–1600). Like the spirit of Greek culture, the Renaissance spirit was one of this-worldliness, but it was quite different in that individuality and the worth of human personality were its motivating forces. You will remember the Greeks were interested in the various facets of the ideal human, but the Renaissance attitude was one of concern for the real human. Interest was shown in the individual's personality, mind, body, social relationships, personal religion, economic condition, and place in the political scheme of things. The term *Renaissance* is used to designate a period of time, but remember that it was a humanistic spirit, even more real than that of the medieval. It was an idea, a philosophy, a way of life that changed and molded the individual's whole outlook and attitude toward himself, his community, and his God.

Because of the complexity of the Renaissance, there have been numerous interpretations of its cultural fabric. The most popular has been that it was the period in history dedicated to the rebirth of classical learning. In fact, the term itself has this connotation. This interpretation is quite true. The scholars of the Renaissance did rediscover the classical learning of the Greeks, but probably only because they were interested in the things of this world, as were the Greeks. Therefore, the Renaissance interest was not merely one of veneration for antiques, but one of a kindred spirit. The Parthenon, with its sculpture, stood in Athens all through the Middle Ages, but medieval man denied its beauty and value because it was not ascetic enough. It was too much concerned with worldly affairs and not sufficiently concerned with salvation. No, the Renaissance did not suddenly discover Greek culture as if it had been long lost in some stuffy attic. It was cultivated because they found themselves in sympathy with the same general attitude toward life as that of the Greeks.

To some writers and scholars, the Renaissance is the period of a resurgence of interest in man and the world in which he lived. This concern enabled man to look on life as a period of joyous existence and not merely as a painful preparation for a life to come. This is a philosophic attitude and is perfectly true but not quite sufficient to explain the humanistic development. The Renaissance concern for this life must have arisen from some fundamental cause, from outward happenings that forced the change from the medieval philosophy. It has already been noted how this humanistic change had come gradually through the spread of Eastern culture and the development of towns.

Another explanation is that it was a period when men began again to show interest in the knowledge of natural phenomena and in the techniques of civilization. The Renaissance spirit brought forth the heliocentric theory of the universe and established beyond a shadow of doubt that the world was round. The voyages of Columbus and da Gama into unknown seas were outward, physical manifestations of the Renaissance spirit. The introduction into western Europe of gunpowder, the invention of the printing press, and the systematic progress of physical science were also proof that the Renaissance man was concentrating upon his own mind and earthly problems. Political science was not neglected either. Machiavelli's *The Prince* was a book of advice for the ambitious ruler.

Others see the Renaissance as a crucible of religious, economic, and social conflict. Surely the Protestant Reformation was a manifestation of the humanistic spirit in northern Europe and was clearly associated with trends in the economic, social, and political scene. The powerful ruling families of the Italian city-states were in a continuing struggle with each other for political and economic supremacy—a struggle that often had the control of the Vatican itself as the ultimate prize.

In reality, the Renaissance was all of the above mentioned and more. It was a process of change and integration. It was a time for new discoveries and inventions that had a profound effect on every phase of human experience. All of these ideas and events were both cause and effect. There was an interaction among them. Each was partially responsible for the Renaissance spirit of humanism and, at the same time, its result.

The net result of these varied activities caused something to happen to Renaissance man. He became a materialist and an individualist. The gradual spread of humanistic thought and the advances made in astronomy and other sciences removed some of the wonder and mystery from his understanding of the universe. This, coupled with a weakening of loyalty to spiritual authority due to the constant struggle between the Church and State for supremacy, made him a materialist. The development of trade and commerce, with the resultant increase in his standard of living, also strengthened his materialistic philosophy. Man became an individualist for many of the same reasons. Set free from the authority of the Church, he began to question all authority. If he could no longer look to either the Church or the State for leadership, he felt free to have confidence in his own rationalizations as valid authority. Consequently he became an individualist.

Materialism and individualism brought new incentives for living. The acquiring of personal wealth became a goal for which all strived. Worldly wisdom and temporal power were cultivated for the personal satisfaction they could bring. New dreamers rose, but their world was one of business and politics rather than religion.

Italy, through its fortunate position along the trade route from the East, was the center from which this tremendous activity spread and, naturally, the home of the financiers who made it possible. The movement was not confined to Italy alone. Northern Europe responded to the same forces in much the same way with its particular stamp of cultural personality. All through Europe it was a period of great vitality, forcefulness, unsentimental business, and often extreme cruelty. There arose paradoxes that almost defy explanation. Beauty, whether pagan or Christian, was cultivated for its own sake and not for the sake of what it could teach. The arts were enthusiastically cultivated by the rich patrons of the time—patrons who were often paganized princes and popes who, even when they were religious, were hardly Christian in spirit. As in the Middle Ages, the Church remained as the greatest single patron of all the arts, not in any sense of spiritual values, but as the most powerfully rich patron available.

How, then, do the varied facets of Renaissance humanism reflect themselves in the creative efforts of its artists? How do they reveal themselves in the function, subject matter, and expressive content of those works of art that we recognize as being among the greatest of all time?

One of the most obvious results of the Renaissance spirit is seen in the influence of wealthy patronage upon the function and subject matter of art. The portrait, which had not been in favor since early Roman times, again assumed a prominent place as an art subject. No doubt it was due, in part, to the egotistic desire of the wealthy to leave likenesses of themselves as reminders of their worldly successes. Patrons were anxious to have the artist present them in the most favorable light, as devout Christians or as benefactors of mankind, often without any real basis in fact except their own egos. It was looked upon as a signal honor to be represented as a personage from pagan mythology or as a figure from a Biblical scene. Botticelli put the whole Medici family into his *Adoration of the Magi* (fig. 7.1) and included himself as well.

Artists were retained to furnish designs for elaborate costumes and even to plan parades and festivals in such a way as to enhance the glory and prestige of the patron. They were called upon to make pictorial records of ordinary events as well as events that were a part of the social activity of the upper classes. Consequently, much of this art was popular, descriptive, and sometimes superficial. The *Journey of the Magi* (fig. 7.2) by Gozzoli is one of this type. Its theme is an elaborate parade in honor of Lorenzo the Magnificent of Florence and his honored guests. The title is religious, for it symbolizes the journey of the wise men to Jerusalem. Obviously, the title was only a pretext for celebrating the wealth and power of the ruling Medici family, the artist's benefactors. The most brilliantly colored and largest figure in the group is Lorenzo himself, with the lesser personages painted in a splendor proportionate to their importance. Individual faces are shown very realistically, but the landscape portion is quite primitive from our point of view.

Figure 7.1 *Adoration of the Magi* [1478]—Botticelli. (Courtesy Alinari/Editorial Photocolor Archives)

This mood of worldly culture had little in common with the soul-searching mysticism of the earlier Gothic artists. This art was illustrative, decorative, popular, and served as a memorial to the wealth and splendor of its patron.

Religious painting ceased to be the main concern of artists. If there seems to be a great number of artworks with religious titles, it is only because the Church was still the richest institution to patronize art, not because of any profound sense of spiritual awareness. Pope Julius II (1503–1513) caused a new St. Peter's to be planned in Rome. It was to be a magnificent structure, not to the glory of God, but to the glory of Julius. Ironically, Julius died before his plans could be executed. Even the *Last Supper* (fig. 7.4) of Leonardo da Vinci has little to do with the spiritual significance of that event but was a psychological study of the reaction of the disciples to the statement, "One of you shall betray me."

Music was not neglected either, and its function was also strongly influenced by secular patronage. Music moved out of the Church into the home as a necessary adjunct to social life. Great social importance was attached to making music after meals. Dance music gained popularity both in the home and at festivals and pageants. There was an increase in the number of composers who were attached to wealthy households to provide music for entertainment and to teach the youth. Even municipalities retained bands of musicians to announce honored guests and to perform for special celebrations.

Art also reflected the humanistic spirit by the personalities of its creators. The Renaissance has often been referred to as an age of geniuses. This is due to the individualism fostered by humanism. For the first time in centuries of art, we come upon creative personalities who capture the imagination, not only of their contemporaries but our own as well. Leonardo da Vinci, Michel-

Figure 7.2 *Journey of the Magi* [1469]—Gozzoli. (Courtesy Alinari/Editorial Photocolor Archives)

angelo, Raphael, Botticelli—to mention a few—were artists of such personalized character that they have colored the whole of subsequent art history. The awakening of the individual artist's personality and his own awareness of personal creative powers and imagination is one of the important qualities of the Renaissance artist. It is for this reason that we must pay detailed attention to specific artists. From this time on, art was no longer the collective effort of many people but was the personal creative effort of individuals. Differences between specific works are seen in the differences between personalities, but all were subjected to much the same basic cultural pattern of the period.

Renaissance artists also caught the spirit of scientific research and exploration. Realism in art was the direct result. Rules of perspective and foreshortening were formulated with mathematical exactness. This enabled artists to be more realistic in the illusion of space. They also made extensive studies and measurements of classical architecture and sculpture to arrive at workable rules of proportion and balance. Unity and form were reduced to certain basic laws of art.

Studies in anatomy were of fundamental importance to art. Medieval prejudice and Church opposition were overridden in the thirst for knowledge. Artists believed that realism of the human form could not be fully attained without a sound knowledge of intimate physical details. This of necessity demanded laboratory dissection. Laborious drawings of muscles, tissue, and bony structure were among the required studies of every artist. The studies in anatomy made by Leonardo da Vinci were so meticulously drawn that they have been used in medical textbooks until fairly recent times. Because the Renaissance was interested in the real human form, the nude regained its place in art and lost its medieval connotation of shame. The essence of humanism—the entire human being with perfect proportion of the various members of the body—could be completely represented only in the nude. Renaissance nudity, like the Greek, was unashamed nakedness. It was the complete human.

The entire Renaissance culture was so intimately mirrored in the works of its artists that its history can be clearly told in terms of their creative efforts. The slow but infallible processes of time have proven that of all Renaissance activity, its artists have left us the most valuable legacy and the finest interpretation of their age. There were more first-rate artists during this epoch than during any preceding period. However, our study of specific artists will be confined to a few uncontested great men and their works. This selection is for the purpose of basing our concepts of Renaissance art on a relatively few representative examples and in no way does it question the importance or the quality of others. The painters whose works will be analyzed are Botticelli (1440–1510), Leonardo da Vinci (1452–1519), Mathis Grünewald (1460–1528), Albrecht Dürer (1471–1528), Michelangelo (1475–1564), Titian (1477–1576), Raphael (1483–1520), Pieter Brueghel (c. 1524–1569).

Painting

Renaissance artists used the same basic elements of line, space, color, and formal organization that were used by Gothic artists and those in the ancient world. Humanism, however, brought a new, fresh approach to the organization of these elements. In order to emphasize form, the element of line was usually clearly defined and curvilinear, giving an effect of smooth-flowing motion. Space was organized on a plane, with little sense of recession into the distance. When the subject itself presupposed a spatial quality, as in Gozzoli's *Journey of the Magi,* it was often unconvincing. Form was generally closed, with attention focused on a central figure or point of interest, thus creating a balanced or symmetrical plan of organization. The idea of formal organization is one of juxtaposition of the individual parts into a whole. Brilliant polychromatic coloring is also a general characteristic of Renaissance painting. More often than not, painters used color as a line to separate figures one from another. This led to a rich palette of contrasting colors that also served to detach principal forms from their backgrounds.

There is another group of concepts which became an integral part of painting in the Renaissance and remained until late in the nineteenth century. The first of these is the idea that all painting must be based on plastic representation. Subjects must be presented in a manner that is true to nature. This idea again reinforces the humanism of the period. Another concept followed by painters was the use of fragments as symbols of something not actually present in the scene but necessary to complete understanding. For example, the headgear in the *Sistine Madonna* (colorplate 3) is that of the Eastern church and symbolizes its unity with the Western church. The last of these general concepts is that form, or the total organization of an artwork, must express its function. This is illustrated by Gozzoli's work, which expresses its function as a social painting.

The principle of organization or design most commonly found in Renaissance painting is that of repetition and contrast. Polychromatic colors, separate unity, sharply defined lines, closed forms, and minimum spatial awareness lend themselves to this method of design. We can use the term "classic" to define the stylistic character of such art, for it strives for the complete unity of separate parts in harmony with the whole. As we will observe in later analyses, Renaissance artists were occupied with the problem of how to portray a subject more than what to portray. Now then, let us analyze some Renaissance paintings according to the above basic elements and principles. The differences between them and the art of earlier periods will be the basic differences between the cultures of each epoch.

In chapter 2 we studied the *Sistine Madonna* by Raphael as a typical example of Renaissance style. It is primarily linear in character, with closed form, multiple organization, and little spatial sense. Its colors are essentially polychromatic. The principle of design, or organization, is that of contrast and repetition. While the subject is religious, the viewer is impressed more by the beauty of forms and color than by its religious meaning. The impression is one of humanism, of the poetic beauty of human form, of beauty for and by itself.

Botticelli

Another fine example of these same elements is found in *The Birth of Venus* by Botticelli (colorplate 11), painted earlier than the *Sistine Madonna*. Botticelli was a lyric painter with a sensitive feeling for poetic beauty. He was also enamored with the idealized beauty of pagan mythology and used it as a vehicle to express his own love of the beauty inherent in the human form. Botticelli came under the spell of the reformer, Savonarola, in Florence and turned to religious painting. On the whole, his mythological works are the best examples of his style. *The Birth of Venus* depicts the Greek myth which told of Venus born from the foam of the sea and gently carried to shore on a sea shell with the Winds rippling the waves and mythical Hours waiting to cover her with a star-studded garment.

Pictorial representation is the dominant force in this painting. Fragments such as the sea shell and the figures representing the Winds and Hours are used symbolically. The function was to put the Greek myth on canvas and to reveal the beauty of Venus. It is probable that the model of Venus was Simonetta, a great Florentine beauty of the artist's acquaintance. Turning to the organization of the elements, we find that the lines are sharply drawn. They are curvilinear and sparkle with life and movement. Even the figures representing the Winds, which are almost as one, not blended, but each is defined by structural line and color. There is great detail in this work, and each is made important by clear flowing lines. While the space element is present, according to our experience it is not convincingly real. The shoreline in the background is more artificial than nature's creation. In contrast to the unreal landscape, notice the realness of the human form, even to the color of the flesh. The form is closed, for there is nothing to take your eye outside the picture itself. While one could destroy the balance by removing any one of the objects, such removal would not destroy the plasticity of the remaining objects. The color is polychromatic. It is a painting of contrasting colors rather than a blend of different values of the same basic color.

The Birth of Venus also used the principle of contrast and repetition. The vertically curved lines of Venus contrast sharply with the horizontal line of the horizon. The contrast is repeated in the diagonal lines of the figures. The straight lines of the trees repeat and also oppose the curved and vertical lines of Venus. Botticelli has presented his story in a graphic manner, with all the essential symbols of the myth present. The viewer, however, is more

Colorplate 11 follows p. 130.

enchanted by the physical forms than by the story. True to the Renaissance spirit, the artist has reflected the Greek influence in his subject and humanism in his treatment of it. The human body becomes the real subject. The painting is classic in style of its arrangement of individual forms into harmonious unity. It is a painting devoted to the ideal of beauty for its own sake.

Albrecht Dürer

Renaissance painters of northern Europe did not respond to the revival of the Greek ideals as quickly as those in Italy. While the trend toward humanism and realism were undoubtedly the result of Italian influence, the expressiveness was still Gothic. Religious subjects with an almost morbid concern for suffering and death were common. We must remember that the Reformation was an influence in northern Europe, and the problems of sin, suffering, and salvation were still very real, especially in north Germany, where Luther's teaching precipitated strong religious feelings.

Albrecht Dürer was a German Renaissance artist, a friend of Luther and Erasmus, who embraced the Protestant religion. His early studies in Italy brought him into contact with the humanism of Italian art and, moreover, introduced him to the disciplined objectivity of line and perspective of the Italian Renaissance. Among the media he used, in addition to painting, were the intaglio arts of engraving, etching, and woodcutting. His engraving *Knight, Death and the Devil* (fig. 7.3) shows his careful molding of physical forms, the controlled spatial effect, and the clear character of line. The subject is representative of the concern for the eternal struggle between good and evil. The Christian knight is undaunted in his journey toward salvation by the specter of the horseman of Death and the temptation of the grotesque Devil behind him. Even his faithful dog seems unafraid and confident in faith.

Mathis Grünewald

The *Crucifixion* by Mathis Grünewald (colorplate 12) gives us an excellent example of the style of northern Renaissance painting. While Dürer represented the Protestant element, Grünewald associated himself with Catholic patronage in Germany. The artist's portrayal of the agony on the cross is medieval, but the emotional response of the onlookers seems more humanistic. The figure of Christ is oversize to emphasize its importance and is shockingly real as a festering corpse. On the other hand, the surrounding figures are soft, alive, and grieving as humans. Notice the sweeping curves and the use of polychromatic coloring to highlight line. There is also a sense of perspective and three-dimensional form that was usually lacking in medieval painting. Unity of separate parts with the figures on either side act as a balance to the central figure of the dead Christ.

Colorplate 12 follows p. 130.

Figure 7.3 *Knight, Death and the Devil* [1513]—Dürer. (Courtesy Museum of Fine Arts, Boston, Bequest of Horatio G. Curtis)

Pieter Brueghel

Pieter Brueghel the Elder represents a significant facet of the Protestant North in Renaissance art during the sixteenth century. Many of his works are related to the struggle between the Catholics and Protestants in the Low Countries. These paintings were sometimes filled with symbolic figures which were related to the conflicts that arose during the Spanish Inquisition.

However, Brueghel was also a master of landscapes, and some of his best recorded the scenery of the Low Countries. He was close to the folk customs and the lives of humble people. *Winter* (The Return of the Hunters) (colorplate 13) shows us a landscape with ordinary peasants and their simple, everyday life in a setting of the cold and damp of winter. However, the basic Renaissance idea of space controlled by the repetition of similar shapes and recession into the distance, is very apparent.

Leonardo da Vinci

If one man could be singled out as the quintessence of the Renaissance spirit, that man would be Leonardo da Vinci. He was a painter, sculptor, scientist, engineer, and poet, to mention only a few of the fields of human endeavor that claimed his attention. Leonardo received his early training in the studio of Verrocchio, the most celebrated teacher of art in Florence. The studio which Verrocchio conducted was a meeting place for the great intellectuals and artists of that time. Thus Leonardo was able to make contact with the finest minds of the age—minds from which he acquired the habits of scientific investigation as well as the finest training in the canons of painting and sculpture.

After leaving Verrocchio's studio, Leonardo worked as an independent artist in Florence. After painting his first masterpiece *Adoration of the King,* he went to Milan under the patronage of the Duke of Milan, Lodovico Sforza. He remained there for seventeen years, and during this time he performed many duties, some artistic and some military. His later years were divided between Milan and Florence, and he maintained studios in both cities. Ironically, Leonardo did not live out his life in Italy. Disappointed by his relations with his patrons and willing to serve anyone who loved beauty, he accompanied Francis I to France, where he ended a long and useful career in 1519.

A recital of Leonardo's activities and accomplishments would fill many pages. He executed designs for public buildings; he built dams and constructed a canal; he rebuilt the fortifications of Milan and devised new instruments of war; he invented an aircraft and a submarine; he wrote treatises on anatomy, optics, geology, physics, and painting. His notebooks, which have been preserved for us, are an encyclopedia of Renaissance thought and culture. Leonardo even found time to create some of the greatest art masterpieces of all time, including the portrait of *Mona Lisa* and one of his greatest works *The Last Supper.*

Colorplate 13 follows p. 130.

In the same vein as the *Mona Lisa* is Leonardo's *Ginevra de' Benci* (colorplate 14). He succeeded in capturing her mysterious beauty by subtle gradation of light and dark, together with filigree lines which bring out the character of the subject. He has painted more than a portrait—his is a psychological study of the character of his subject.

Leonardo da Vinci believed that all art should have its roots in scientific study of nature, human nature included. However, he had no intention of confining himself to the surface qualities. His studies convinced him that nature's secrets were well hidden and could be revealed only by painstaking investigation. He spent weeks and often months over some minor detail at which lesser men would have guessed. In the process, he added a vast amount of knowledge to the art of painting and to the storehouse of man's intellectual achievements.

Of the few completed works to come from the hand of Leonardo da Vinci, *The Last Supper* (fig. 7.4) is his greatest and one of the most monumental artworks of all time. It is a large work painted on a wall in the refectory of Santa Maria delle Grazie in Milan. Because Leonardo used an experimental method in painting on fresh plaster, the painting has not withstood the ravages of time very well, but we can still get some of the drama of the scene from what is left. *The Last Supper* is Leonardo's contribution to the science and art of painting. It is not a photographic study of those twelve disciples and Jesus, but a psychological study of the effect of Christ's words: "One of you shall betray me." The sudden shock of those words and the varied response of each disciple, reacting according to his own nature, is the subject of the painting. The disciples are not merely ordinary men used as models; they are individuals. Leonardo studied each and every personality involved in the scene. He spent long hours probing their personalities according to the Biblical record. The whole work took years to complete because there were certain men, especially Judas, whose character Leonardo had difficulty in grasping from a psychological point of view. Strictly speaking, this is not fundamentally a religious picture. It is the scientific observation of one of the most profound scientists of his century. It is a pictorial study of emotional response to a shocking statement. It is a revelation of each man's physical and emotional reaction under the impact of this accusation.

From a formal point of view, the painting is classical in design. The figure of Christ is in the center, his head silhouetted against the sky through the open window. Notice that he is isolated physically as well as psychologically. By itself, the room is a masterpiece of perspective. The lines of the walls and table converge to a point behind the head of Christ. This is not infinite space, but a carefully controlled chamber of space created by clearly defined lines. The form is closed, with all attention centered on the figure of Christ. Formal organization is multiple, but not to the same degree as other examples we have seen. The bodies of the men seem to merge together, but

Colorplate 14 follows p. 130.

Figure 7.4 *The Last Supper* [1495–1498]—Leonardo da Vinci. (Courtesy Alinari/ Editorial Photocolor Archives)

note that their heads are separate and individual. Leonardo's problem was to present an individual portrait of each and yet mold the separate units into a whole. This he has done by means of the table and the narrow room, which force the lines of perspective toward the center. The work is a monument not only to Leonardo's skill as a painter and his painstaking research as a scientist but also to his profound understanding of human nature.

Michelangelo

One of the last of the great sixteenth-century painters was Michelangelo, who stands with Leonardo da Vinci at the pinnacle of the Renaissance ideal. Born in 1475, near Florence, Michelangelo entered the studio of Ghirlandaio at the age of thirteen. He later became a favorite of Lorenzo the Magnificent, who had in his private gallery a large collection of Greek sculpture. Michelangelo's preference for sculpture probably dates from this experience. He also studied the usual canons of art and was given an opportunity to study anatomy firsthand. It was due to the kindness of a friendly monk that he was permitted to perform dissections of human bodies in an effort to discover for himself the mysteries of the human form.

Michelangelo, like Leonardo, had a variety of talents. He was a painter, architect, and sculptor, but considered himself a sculptor. He saw the human form through the eyes of one who worked with marble and a chisel. His omission of nature as a background, his manner of painting the nude in a strong three-dimensional form, and his preoccupation with the human form has led to his painting being called "painted sculpture." He is said to have stated on more than one occasion, "The only fit subject for an artist is man." He could hardly have made a remark more in keeping with the Renaissance spirit, for the statement is humanism at its most eloquent.

Michelangelo's personal life was filled with hardship. Poverty was his faithful companion, made even more menacing by selfish relatives and friends. There were also conflicts of personalities within himself, conflicts with which he grappled almost constantly during his eighty-nine years of life. Many of his works reflect these conflicting forces within his own consciousness. Some pieces are extremely morbid, while others have a tone of strength and solidarity. As an artist, he was generally above personal problems, for he was a universalist in his outlook. His art transcends the superficial, and he embodies in his painting and sculpture an awareness of the forces of the universal tragedy. This is perhaps best expressed in the *Last Judgment* painted on the east wall of the Sistine Chapel. Here human form becomes almost a musical motive as Michelangelo sees mankind's mighty movement on the day of judgment. There is wave after wave of rhythmic movement as the blessed are separated from the damned.

His greatest work is his fresco in the Sistine Chapel, with scenes depicting the epic of mankind from the creation to the day of judgment. As a sculptor, he protested bitterly when Pope Julius II ordered him to this task, for he claimed he was not a painter. The completed work is testimony enough that he was a great painter as well.

The *Creation* (colorplate 15) is one of the panels on the ceiling of the Sistine Chapel. This is an interesting composition because it clearly shows the artist's qualities in painting, and it also displays his complete concern for the humanism of man. Adam rests upon the earth, symbolic of man, while his outstretched hand receives the life-giving touch from Jehovah. The group of figures, including Jehovah, has a quality of buoyancy about it that suggests the infinity of God's world. The face of Adam does not show the joy of life but is, rather, a little pensive in recognition and anticipation of the trials and sorrows of the earthly life he is gaining. The artist has made the physical figures of Adam and Jehovah the focal points in the panel. The bodies are exceedingly plastic in the sense of three-dimensional space. One even feels their weight. The anatomy is superb—perfect in every detail, down to the rippling of the flexed muscles. In general, the lines are sharply defined. Color is polychromatic, even though its years on plaster have caused it to fade.

Colorplate 15 follows p. 130.

Colorplate 11 *Birth of Venus* [1485]—Botticelli. (Courtesy Scala/Editorial Photocolor Archives)

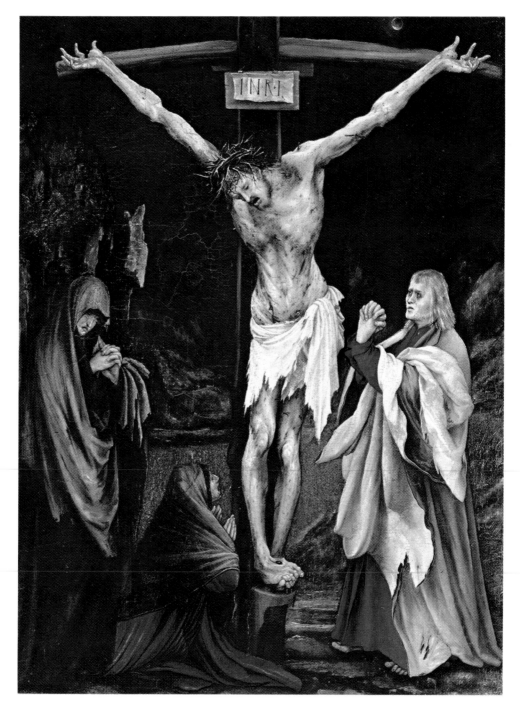

Colorplate 12 *The Crucifixion* [1507]—Grünewald. (Courtesy National Gallery of Art, Washington, D.C., Samuel H. Kress Collection)

Colorplate 13 Winter (Return of the Hunters) [1565]—Pieter Brueghel the Elder.
(Courtesy Scala/Editorial Photocolor Archives)

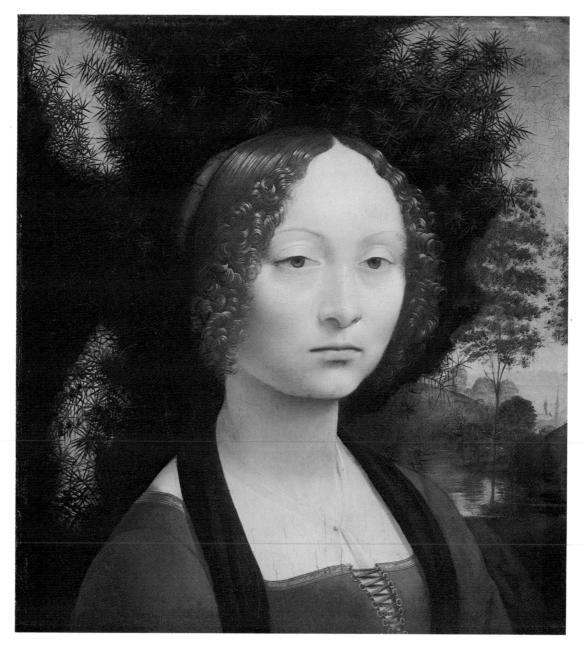

Colorplate 14 *Ginevra de'Benci* [c. 1480]—Leonardo da Vinci. (Courtesy National Gallery of Art, Washington/Ailsa Mellon Bruce Fund)

Colorplate 15 *Creation* [1508–1512]—Michelangelo. (Courtesy Scala/Editorial Photocolor Archives)

Colorplate 16 *Venus and Adonis* [c. 1560]—Titian. (Courtesy National Gallery of Art, Washington/Widener Collection)

Organization is multiple, and the form is closed. The effect of distance is canceled by the predominance of the two molded forms. With all its symbolism, this is not a great religious painting in the sense that it might portray the act of life-giving. It is one of the most perfect representations of the human form, but one feels that the subject is the form, not the act of creation as the title suggests. True to the Renaissance ideal, Michelangelo has created a great work of art with a religious subject but in a secular spirit.

Titian

Titian (1477–1576) seems to represent a departure from the sharply defined line and static quality of the middle Renaissance. There is more movement, more energy than was found in Botticelli and Michelangelo. During his life of ninety-nine years he created thousands of paintings, including portraits, as well as religious and mythological subjects. His *Venus and Adonis* (plate 16) treats figures of mythology as human beings of flesh and blood, with a quality of sensuality that was usually lacking in earlier Renaissance painting. While the principle of design is still that of closed form with a pyramidal format, lines are less sharply defined and blend into a shadowy background. He was a colorist, and his forms, instead of being linear in character, seem to be created as color. Titian's art signaled the end of the high Renaissance and served as a transition to the Baroque of Tintoretto and El Greco. He even anticipated the coloring and sensuousness of Rubens and Delacroix.

Sculpture

Renaissance sculpture discloses the same concern for humanism that was found in its painting. Because of the predilection for the molded form in all Renaissance art, it was not uncommon that an artist be equally facile with a chisel and a brush. Both Leonardo da Vinci and Michelangelo were artists of this caliber. While the medium of sculpture is quite different from that of painting, Renaissance sculpture confirms the character of basic elements that were observed in painting.

Leonardo's teacher, Verrocchio (1435–1488), has provided us with a fine example of the Renaissance spirit as exemplified in sculpture by his *David* (fig. 7.5). Verrocchio uses bronze to depict the youthfulness of David. He shows him as a lithe, immature lad, but possessed with great courage and determination. The head of Goliath lies at his feet as a symbol of the encounter and victory over great odds. Somehow we are compelled to believe that this David could not have accomplished such a deed with his adolescent body alone; he must have had divine help in achieving victory. Notice how the

Colorplate 16 follows p. 130.

Figure 7.5 *David* [1465]—Verrocchio.
(Courtesy Editorial Photocolor Archives)

Figure 7.6 *David* [1501–1503]—
Michelangelo. (Courtesy Metropolitan
Museum of Art)

artist has emphasized the immature qualities of David's body and the boyish candor of his facial expression. Realism of form is shown by the bony structure of the body. Every skeletal portion that would normally appear is present. The collarbone, the elbow, the knuckles, even the ribs are clearly molded beneath the garment. Muscular structure is also very prominent. Note how the veins of the arm stand out and how the muscles of the neck give the effect of tension.

Verrocchio was able to portray the human form with life and expression. This is not an ideal David, but a real person who has participated in an exciting event. Like the other artists of his epoch, he has expressed through sculpture the essence of humanism.

Michelangelo's *David* (fig. 7.6) is, on the other hand, a different sort of a person. He saw David as a mature man with great physical strength. This fact is emphasized by the monumental size of the statue. It is made from a huge block of marble and stands eighteen feet high. He also depicts his subject before the action takes place. David stands with a stone in his left hand looking out over the scene, in contemplation of the coming action. The highly developed bodily features show a greater degree of physical maturity. David also has real personality; he has a look of determination to achieve his goal. In a way Michelangelo's figure is even more in the Renaissance spirit, for it is an expression of individualism. David shows confidence in his own physical prowess.

Both of these examples, Verrocchio's adolescent *David* and Michelangelo's adult *David*, are of the same spirit. Yet each represents the individual differences between their creators. Both works have closed form and classic balance. Lines are clear and detailed, and there is a tranquility present in both—perhaps more in Michelangelo's. It will be noted in the next chapter, on Baroque art, how a later artist treats the same subject from the point of view of a different cultural pattern.

Architecture

While buildings for religious purposes still held the major attention of architecture, there was another field to which architects devoted themselves, namely palaces and villas for elaborate and comfortable living. This function of architecture is, in itself, a part of the sixteenth-century scene. Along with individualism and the desire for worldly possessions, there came a natural trend among the wealthy toward providing elaborate domestic housing.

One of the architects to devote his talents to this type of building was Andrea Palladio (1518–1580). It is most fitting that Palladio be studied in connection with Renaissance architecture, because he has had the greatest influence on later generations. In both England and America, the "classic style" can be traced directly to his work. A number of the great estates in seventeenth century England became the setting for some of the finest examples of the Palladian style of architecture. *Monticello,* Thomas Jefferson's home, is in this style, and he even suggested a Palladian-type building for the White House. Like many other artists of his time, Palladio wrote treatises about his art. In his *Four Books on Architecture* he laid down the classic canons of the builder's art in much the same fashion as Leonardo did for painting in his treatise on that art.

The *Villa Rotonda* (fig. 7.7) in Vicenza is the best known of his works and is a fine example of his own theories of architecture. One of the most striking aspects of the *Villa Rotonda* is its debt to antiquity. Its dome is modeled after the Pantheon in Rome (fig. 4.2). The Greek influence is apparent in the use of freestanding columns supporting the pediment of the porticos. The building is classic in proportion, for its various rooms are laid out in a symmetrical

Figure 7.7 *Villa Rotonda* in Vicenza [1552]—Palladio. (Courtesy Metropolitan Museum of Art)

manner around the central rotunda. Palladio used the cube and cylinder as his basic forms. It is a square plan with four identical porticos placed on the two axes of the rotunda. He did not obscure the simplicity of the plan with elaborate decoration but used ornament sparingly. Notice how the structure sits lightly upon the earth, with none of the towering spires of the Gothic. This is a functional, but a spacious and formal, building. It is Renaissance in its classic proportion and dignity and in absence of mystic symbolism.

Another example of classic proportion in architecture is found in the Farnese Palace in Rome (fig. 7.8). Michelangelo was responsible for a portion of this building; he designed the third story. Note the symmetry of the facade. Each story is clearly separated from the others by a broad band. The window

Figure 7.8 *Farnese Palace* in Rome. [c. 1520] (Courtesy Metropolitan Museum of Art)

treatment of the first floor is one of exact repetition of the lintel idea. The third floor uses the Grecian pediment design. The second floor, however, alternates the pediment with an arch-type motif. Repetition and contrast is the apparent principle of design for the facade. The eye is relieved as it moves from the top by the contrast of the second floor. This creates variety, through slight change, and unity at the same time. In its eye appeal, as well as in its function and arrangement, the Farnese Palace mirrors the classic idealism of its age.

Music

As suggested earlier in this chapter, music moves out of the church into the households of the aristocracy and the upper classes. This does not mean that music ceases to be important in the Church, but it does mean that music as an art is no longer under the exclusive patronage of the Church. As a consequence, a large musical literature, both instrumental and vocal, devoted to secular purposes arises alongside the continued output of Church works.

The music of the Catholic church continued to serve much the same purpose as in previous periods. Composers continued to set, in motets and Masses, those parts of the liturgy which had been permitted them. In the one Protestant sect where music was not regarded as either popish or satanical, namely the Lutheran church, music of a folklike simplicity was given back to the congregation as its rightful heritage. Here in the Lutheran church of the sixteenth century, music was accumulated to act as a great fountainhead for the Baroque art of Bach and his contemporaries. The great emphasis toward secularization in the Renaissance was also carried over into the religious works of the time. While the technique of contrapuntal treatment in the early Renaissance still has something of the academic scholasticism of the Gothic period, there is evidence in the sixteenth century of a complete mastery of technical devices which makes possible a truly expressive handling of the musical materials where this is desired.

The religious music speaks not only of the serenity of God, but of human serenity: not only of the mysterious detachment of a supreme being, but of the anguish, aspirations, and hopes of the human soul. On the other hand, the secular music treats of the human joys and sorrows of this earthly existence in song and dance.

Despite the emphasis upon humanism, which in the other arts has tended to make us very conscious of the great wealth of production in painting, sculpture, and architecture, the religious music of the Renaissance was rarely heard outside the Roman Catholic church until recent times. This was undoubtedly due to the disparity between the style of the music of the fifteenth and sixteenth centuries and that of the eighteenth and nineteenth, which constituted the great bulk of musical fare. This disparity is evidenced primarily in the modal polyphony of the Renaissance as against the tonal polyphony and homophony of the post-Renaissance.

Since the seventeenth century, Western composers have organized their musical materials on the basis of a tonal center. Renaissance composers dealt exclusively with polyphonic treatment of musical ideas. They organized their melodic materials not on the basis of an underlying or gravitational harmonic concept but on the basis of certain intervallic relations between voices. Certain intervals, the unison, fourth, fifth, and octave, were considered to be of consonant nature, and specifically named the "perfect" intervals. All others were of varying degrees of dissonance. A great body of practical rules and regulations determined the manner in which the dissonant intervals were used and called for their careful introduction and inevitable resolution into the perfect consonances. It might be said that as space was organized on a single plane in painting, so was tonal material organized in a purely melodic way in music. The lack of recession or depth in Renaissance painting is paralleled in music by a lack of tonal harmonic organization. Toward the end of the Renaissance, certain practices already indicate the tendency toward a distinct feeling for tonality, a phenomenon which determined the creative thinking of composers from that time to the beginning of the twentieth century and has controlled the listening attitude of the public to the present.

The most generally used principle of organization in Renaissance music is that of repetition and contrast. This is perhaps best illustrated in the motet *Ave Maria* by Josquin des Prés (c.1450–1521) which is made up of a number of contrasting sections, each of which is knit together by rather strict imitation between the several voices. These sections overlap one another so as to cover up the seams of the work. Actually, the entire work, both music and words, is derived directly from the Gregorian chant setting of the Ave Maria. Note how the section which uses only the words and corresponding melody "Ave Maria gratia plena" is first treated in rather close imitation between all voices and takes up the first few measures of the work. Following this section, the second line of the verse, "Dominus tecum, benedicta tu," and its original melody are introduced, overlapping the conclusion of the first section and constructed out of wholly new and contrasting material which is treated, however, in the same imitative fashion as the first section. The composer thus exhaustively treats the chant, line by line, until its conclusion. While it would seem that several methods of organization are present in this work, actually the principle of repetition within each of the sections and that of contrast between the sections themselves constitute the basic devices used. These are devices peculiar to polyphony which were developed to their ultimate during the Renaissance. It will be noticed that this manner of joining together rather unrelated and contrasting sections, which in themselves are closely knit together by imitation, is characteristic of all the vocal forms, whether secular or sacred, and is well suited to musical works which accompany a literary text. There seemed no need for an overall principle of theme and variation or of repetition after contrast. When instrumental music severs the connection between text and music, a larger overall design will become necessary.

An example of sacred music from the Mass is Palestrina's (c. 1525–1594) setting of the Agnus Dei from the Mass *Veni sponsa Christi*. This is a work of the high Renaissance in music. Palestrina, who with the exception of a few books of madrigals, devoted himself exclusively to sacred music, is regarded by the Catholic church as the ideal composer of liturgical composition. His music has a certain detached and calm sublimity which makes it the sacred music par excellence. The lines of melody are smooth-flowing, quite limited in range, and characteristically lacking in wide steps. The voice parts rarely cross each other, which tends to give a transparency to the texture of the whole work, and dissonance is handled in such a fashion as to make it very unobtrusive. The organization, however, is very like that of the previous two works, particularly the motet. Actually this entire Mass, of which the Agnus Dei is the final section, is based upon a motet of Palestrina's which he in turn based on a Gregorian chant. There are three sections in the Agnus Dei, each developed in an imitative style. The first part is set to the words Agnus Dei ("Lamb of God"); the second to the words "qui tollis peccata mundi" ("who taketh away the sins of the world"); the third to "miserere nobis" ("have mercy on us"). There is considerable repetition of text to enable the composer to spin out his musical idea. The three sections are in general contrast to one another, but careful listening will be rewarded by the discovery that there is a rhythmic-melodic pattern of four notes which is found in each of the three sections. Its appearance is varied by occurring both as an ascending and descending scale passage, by the varied note values in which it occurs, and by its presence in each of the four voice parts at different pitch levels and on accented rhythmic points.

Of the several Protestant groups arising from the Reformation, the Lutheran church influenced the musical development of western Europe most. During the period of the Renaissance, this influence consisted almost exclusively of settings of hymn texts in what became known as the German Protestant or Lutheran Chorales. Luther was particularly instrumental in building up a large collection of these chorales through his intense interest in music generally as a vehicle for religious expression and his immediate interest in the writing of chorale texts. The tunes for the chorales came from several sources. One was the Gregorian hymn tunes of the Catholic church, another the melodies of secular and folk songs, and a final source the tunes composed by Protestant musicians. While the tunes with their vernacular texts served as unison hymns for the congregation, they also served the composers as bases for motet-like settings. An example of this kind of setting is the chorale *Komm, Gott Schöpfer, heiliger Geist—Come, O Creator Spirit*, composed by Johann Walter (1496–1570) to the old Latin hymn text, *Veni Creator Spiritus*, translated into German by Martin Luther. To this text, Walter adapted the original chant tune as a cantus firmus in a polyphonic motet. Every note of the original tune is used as a cantus firmus in the tenor voice. While this is an elaborate use of the simple hymn tune, it was not long before regular four-part settings with the melody in the soprano became the conventional congregational hymn. We shall witness the importance of such settings made by Bach in the Baroque period.

Secular folk songs were often adapted by composers as a basis, or cantus firmus, for polyphonic settings both secular and religious. A folk song which, in the course of centuries, has been used in this fashion innumerable times is the song *Innsbruck, I Must Leave Thee* In its original form it was a love folk song. Its first notated setting was made as a polyphonic lied by Henrich Isaac to words by the Emperor Maximilian. It is in this form that it has come to be known by the title of the *Innsbruck Lied.* Isaac himself employed it in a polyphonic setting in the Kyrie of the *Missa Carminum,* a polyphonic Mass which employed a number of secular songs. Subsequently the *Innsbruck Lied* was adapted to other words and choral settings. Most noteworthy are those by J. S. Bach in *The Passion According to St. Matthew.*

In the secular field, music served a society which actively engaged in its production. Secular music was not a mere pastime or entertainment for a passive patron. Instrumental and vocal secular music in the form of chanson, madrigal, canzona, ricercare, and countless dances was played and sung by every well-educated and refined gentleman and lady whose education included some skill in music making. While there were occasions in which only professional singers or players would perform, there was, during the Renaissance, no organized social event comparable to the public concert or opera of today. The truly Renaissance secular music was an intimate music meant for a small, interested, and, for the most part, participating group.

The texts of the chansons and madrigals likewise reflected this intimacy, speaking as they generally do of unrequited love and melancholy. Even when they are of a more jolly nature, they are inclined to be of a wistful humor, and words, such as "sighing," "alas," "sorrow," "cruel," "slay," "pain," etc., tend to be stressed by one means or another. All of this indicates the general tendency to inject into these secular works a certain degree of human expression.

There were no large forms comparable to the Mass in the area of secular composition. The madrigal, chanson, and polyphonic lied, however, were secular counterparts to the motet, which was religious. The devices of polyphonic composition in these secular works were the same as those used in the sacred motets. The differences between the secular and the sacred works lie in the vernacular texts which often dealt with themes of love (usually unrequited love), in the rhythmic freedoms employed, and in the many attempts to write music which reflected the spirit of the text if not the specific meaning of a word or phrase.

The madrigal, *Thyrsis, Sleepest Thou?,* by John Bennet (c. 1575–c. 1625) is representative of the great flowering of English composition in the late six-

sixteenth century. The madrigal, like the chanson, was social music of a secular nature meant to be sung and played by the upper and middle classes of society. A great wealth of madrigals was published in Italy where the form originated and later in England where it became popular. In this work, the unity of style with the motet and chanson will be easily recognized. The same imitative devices unify the contrasting section of the textual setting. The intrusion of passages which are in true chordal style foreshadows the Baroque era with its chordal harmonic technique. Realistic musical writing in conformity with the words are indications of the dissolution of the Renaissance style in favor of the more expressive and dramatic manner of the coming Baroque era. Such devices in the madrigal are well illustrated by examples 7.1, 7.2, and 7.3, from *Thyrsis Sleepest Thou.*

Example 7.1 introduces a pattern of rhythmic lilt to fit the words "hola, hola." In example 7.2 the words "hold up thy head man," are given a melodic fragment which ascends by a wide skip upwards musically and is imitated in each voice. Example 7.3 is another naive attempt at word imitation or association in the setting of the text, "hark how the cuckoo singeth cuckoo," where the last "cuckoo" is actually sung to the musical imitation of the cuckoo's call in the soprano and alto voice, even to the extent of keeping the call, a falling minor third, always at the same pitch as though it were an actual bird.

In the chanson by Crequillon (d. c. 1557), *Pour ung plaisir* (For a delight) the imitative treatment within sections will be noted. In this work, a secular one and much more lightly treated than the motet of des Prés, one recognizes a somewhat larger element of repetition and contrast than in the motet. The music for the first two lines of the poem is repeated literally for the second pair of lines; there follows a constrasting section, and the whole is concluded with a third contrasting section which repeats both words and music. It is interesting to note that the entire work is used with some changes, mainly in the addition of some faster rhythmic patterns, as an instrumental form known as a *canzona francese*, showing that the unity of style in the Renaissance extended to all forms, both vocal and instrumental.

Example 7.1

Example 7.2

Example 7.3

While the madrigal, chanson, and polyphonic lied were all meant to be sung, and therefore had no instrumental parts written, it was common practice to double the voice parts or even to substitute for them on instruments. Among the favorite instruments used for this purpose were the large families of viols and recorders, the lute, and the harpsichord. The size and construction was in no way standardized, and individual instruments varied greatly from one to another.

These instruments, along with others such as the shawms, crumhorns, cornets, and sackbutts which were more often played by professional performers, were also used for an ever-growing supply of purely instrumental works. These instrumental forms were largely based on dances and performed on various solo instruments and by small ensembles. The dance named *Der Prinzen-Tanz; Proportz* (c. 1550) is by an anonymous composer and notated in this instance for the lute, the favorite and typical instrument of the Renaissance. (The lute held a position of importance in the fifteenth and sixteenth centuries which the piano held in the nineteenth.) This short but typical dance, one of thousands of such works that were extremely popular during the sixteenth century, is constructed in a true repetition and contrast design.

(fol. 142ᵇ) Die geschicklheit in der musiken und was in seinen ingenien und durch
in erfunden und gepessert worden ist.
(Cod. 3033.)

Figure 7.9   Illustration—Hans Burgkmair from *Der Weisskunig*.
Woodcut. (The Metropolitan Museum of Art; Dick Fund.)

The first phrase of four measures is repeated, and the second phrase of nine measures is also repeated. While one complements the other, there are readily recognizable elements that are common to both parts. At the conclusion of the second phrase, the whole dance is repeated but in a different metric pattern. While it was originally in a measure of four, it is now in a measure of three. Imitation between what are still essentially four-voice parts, even though played on a single instrument, is common throughout the work.

Like the madrigals, the dances were inclined to reflect the tendency toward a feeling of tonality. Unlike the more truly polyphonic vocal works, the dance forms, by means of this stronger feeling for tonality, organized the melodic material in well-defined phrases which tended to balance one another in symmetrical fashion. This was, after all, a part of the encroaching Baroque style, which was to sweep away the dependence on modality and substitute an organization of musical materials on the basis of tonality.

Figure 7.10   Lute; probably made about 1596. Ivory, wood; length 2'5", width 12". (The Metropolitan Museum of Art; Gift of Mrs. Lucy Drexel, 1889)

Figure 7.11   Double spinet or virginal made by Ludovicus Grovvelus (Lodewijck Grauwels). (The Metropolitan Museum of Art; The Crosby Brown Collection of Musical Instruments, 1889)

Mannerism — a transition

It must be remembered that one art epoch is not usually clearly delineated from the epoch that follows. As the Renaissance ran its course, there were artists who began to imitate the accepted great masters of the time. There were also those who sought to escape from the domination of such masters as Raphael, Michelangelo, and da Vinci. There was a searching for freedom from the rational objectivity of the Renaissance, a moving toward more subjectivity and mysticism, and the establishment of personal stylistic idiosyncrasies. Many art historians call this transitional period *Mannerism*. The term actually has two meanings. First, it is applied to those who academically imitated the masters of the High Renaissance. Second, it is applied to those who were moving away from the past and were responding to the new movements in religion, politics, economics, and science. Mannerism, consequently, can be interpreted both as the end of the Renaissance and the beginning of the Baroque. Both Tintoretto and El Greco are sometimes called mannerists because they demonstrated the stylistic changes that were to come to fruition in the Baroque. In music, composers such as the madrigalist Gesualdo, with his chromatic harmonies, seem to precede the expressiveness of the composers of the Baroque. While Giovanni Gabrieli is thought of as a Baroque composer, he lived the greater portion of his life in the late sixteenth century, and his music suggests the sonorities of tonal coloring analogous to the major and minor tonalities of the Baroque.

Summary

The Renaissance was an age of humanism and individualism with a search for personal identity and a desire for wealth and power. It was also a period in which there was an insatiable search for knowledge in the areas of science, natural phenomena, and human behavior. Because their basic philosophy was this-worldly, there was a rebirth of the ideals of the Greeks, especially in philosophy, literature, and art.

Artistic patronage came from the many wealthy Renaissance families who ruled the various city-states, such as the Medici. However, the Church was still the most powerful patron of the arts, but a Church that was often more concerned with this-worldly humanism, rather than with salvation as in the Romanesque and Gothic. Secular and mythological subjects in art were often intertwined with religious scenes. Moreover, portrait painting was popular, even to the point of including prominent people in religious and mythological scenes.

There was almost a "cult of personalities" in the Renaissance. Artists such as Michelangelo and Leonardo da Vinci became prototypes of the "Renaissance man" even in their own time. Their wide range of artistic activities and their intense quest for knowledge about science, nature, and man made them almost legendary and they have remained so to this day.

There was an emphasis on representationalism in both painting and sculpture. In painting line was clearly defined, smooth-flowing, and curvilinear. Space was organized on a plane and the development of perspective gave the illusion of an orderly and controlled volume of space. Brilliant polychromatic coloring of highlighted figures often served as line to separate figures from each other and their background. Form was usually closed with a unity of separately articulated parts balanced against each other.

Renaissance sculpture showed the same humanism as painting, in fact some of the finest sculptors were also painters. Sculpture was closely related to Grecian models with the finely molded forms showing all the physical details of the human figure. Some were so delicately wrought that you can almost sense the living body beneath the stone and metal. It must be noted, however, that in both painting and sculpture there was an absence of strong emotion expressed. There was feeling, but it was usually well controlled and mild.

Churches still held the major attention of Renaissance architects, but in keeping with the new materialism, there were a great many palaces and villas built for comfortable living and pleasurable pursuits. The influence of the classic Greek style is very strong with Grecian porticos, symmetry and classic simplicity with balance of design. Religious architecture was sometime a combination of this classic style with the Romanesque dome and vault.

Sacred music still retained its importance, but music moved into the households of the aristocracy and the upper classes. As in the other arts, the Church was no longer the sole patron. As a consequence a large body of secular music literature, both vocal and instrumental arose along with Church music. Composers of sacred music continued to set in polyphonic style those portions of the liturgy that had become standard. The older polyphonic style was still used, but with more freedom and individualism in the treatment of intervallic relationships. The sometimes barren and harsh intervals of the Gothic were softened to please the ear. The principle of organization most often used was that of repetition and contrast, repetition of melodic lines by various voices with a contrast of melodies within the various sections of the text. Expression was often achieved by word-painting, such as a melodic turn, or a harmonic tension to suggest the meaning of individual words. This was especially true in the madrigal and chanson. The dominant musical medium was vocal, but instrumental music was abundant and was usually a transcription of vocal polyphony for instruments, such as the harpsichord or consort of viols.

Musical examples

Josquin des Prés, *Ave Maria* M.M. pp. 58–63

Palestrina, *Agnus Dei* from *Veni sponsa Christi* M.M. pp. 86–90

Walter, *Komm, Gott Schöpfer, heiliger Geist* T.A.M. pp. 120–125

Bennet, "Thyrsis, Sleepest Thou?" M.M. pp. 109–114

Crequillon, "Pour ung plaisir" M.M. pp. 64–73

Canzona francese based upon "Pour ung plaisir" M.M. pp. 64–73

"Der Prinzen-Tanz; Proportz" M.M. pp. 74–77

Isaac "Innsbruck I Must Leave Thee" H.M.S. Vol 3. p. 75

Suggested readings

Grout, D. J. *A History of Western Music,* 3rd ed. New York: W. W. Norton, 1980, pp. 145–292.

Janson, H. W. *History of Art.* Englewood Cliffs, N. J.: Prentice-Hall, Inc., 1962, pp. 305–73.

Lang, Paul Henry. *Music in Western Civilization.* New York: W. W. Norton, 1941, chapter 9, pp. 168–77; 226–50.

Leichtentritt, Hugo. *Music, History and Ideas.* Cambridge, Mass.: Harvard University Press, 1940, chapter 4, pp. 74–93.

Upjohn, Wingert and Mahler. *History of World Art.* New York: Oxford University Press, 1949, chapter 12, pp. 195–229.

Wold and Cykler. *An Outline History of Music,* 5th ed. Dubuque, Ia.: Wm. C. Brown Company Publishers, 1982, pp. 53–92.

Suggested examples for further analysis

Painting: Giorgione, *Sleeping Venus;* Perugino, *Crucifixion;* Fra Angelico, *Annunciation;* Titian, *Bacchanal;* Pieter Bruegel the Elder, *Peasant Wedding*

Sculpture: Donatello, *David;* Michelangelo, *Bound Slave;* Ghiberti, *Gates of Paradise;* Baptistry, Florence

Architecture; St. Peter's, Rome Valmarana Palace, Rome

Music: Marenzio, *S'io parto, i' moro;* Orlandus Lassus, Motet: *Tristis est anima mea;* Palestrina, *Missa Papae Marcelli;* Gesualdo, *Moro Lasso*

These examples can be found in *Masterpieces of Music Before 1750* and in *A Treasury of Early Music* (Haydn Society)

Film strips with sound

Age of Leonardo and Michelangelo. Guidance Associates

Renaissance Art and Music. Educational Audio Visual Inc.

Additional sources for visual illustrations

Akgan, G. C. *Botticelli, Biographical and Critical Study.* Geneva: Skira 1957

Beck, James H. *Raphael.* New York: Abrams, 1976

Hartt, Frederick. *Michelangelo.* New York: Abrams, 1970

Rosand, David. *Titian.* New York: Abrams, 1978

Stechow, Walter. *Breugel the Elder.* New York: Abrams, 1970

Wasserman, Jack. *Leonardo da Vinci.* New York: Abrams, 1975

Wind, E. *Giorgione's Tempesta.* Oxford: Clarendon Press, 1969

8

The Baroque
(1600-1725)

Chronology of the Baroque

1557	Giovanni Gabrieli (c1557–1612)	1602	Galilei discovers law of falling bodies
1561	Francis Bacon (1561–1626)	1606	Rembrandt van Rijn (1606–1669)
1564	Galileo Galilei (1564–1642) William Shakespeare (1564–1616)		Macbeth written by Shakespeare
1567	Claudio Monteverdi (1567–1643)	1608	John Milton (1608–1674)
		1609	Henrik Hudson explores the Hudson River
1571	Johann Kepler (1571–1630)	1618	Beginning of the Thirty Years' War
1577	Peter Paul Rubens (1577–1640)	1620	Pilgrims landed at Plymouth
1578	William Harvey (1578–1654)	1622	Jean Baptiste Molière (1622–1673)
1585	Heinrich Schütz (1585–1673)	1626	Peter Minuit buys Manhattan Island
1596	René Descartes (1596–1650)	1628	William Harvey discovers circulation of the blood
1598	Giovanni Lorenzo Bernini (1598–1690)	1630	Boston founded
1599	Francesco Borromini (1599–1667) Diego Velasquez (1599–1660)	1632	Jean Baptiste Lully (1632–1687) Baruch Spinoza (1632–1677)
		1634	Taj Mahal begun

1636	Harvard University founded	1685	Johann Sebastian Bach (1685–1750)
1637	Dietrich Buxtehude (1637–1707)		George Friederich Handel (1685–1759)
	First public opera house opened in Venice		Domenico Scarlatti (1685–1759)
1638	Louis XIV (1638–1715)	1689	Peter I (The Great) Tsar of Russia
1642	Isaac Newton (1642–1727)		
1648	End of the Thirty Years' War	1700	Sauveur measures musical vibrations
1653	Arcangelo Corelli (1653–1713)	1701	Yale University founded
1659	Henry Purcell (1659–1695)	1708	First German theater opens in Vienna
1661	Reign of Louis XIV (1661–1715)	1709	Christofori builds the first pianoforte
1667	Milton writes *Paradise Lost*	1715	Louis XV reigns until 1774
1668	François Couperin (1668–1733)	1719	Pompeii rediscovered
1672	Newton propounds law of gravitation	1730	Guarnerius family makes violins in Cremona
1675	Sir Christopher Wren begins St. Paul's Cathedral	1738	First spinning machine patented
1676	Antonio Vivaldi (1676–1741)		Methodist Church founded by John Wesley
1678	First German opera house opens in Hamburg.	1740	University of Pennsylvania founded
1682	Philadelphia founded		Frederick the Great rules to 1786
1683	Jean Philippe Rameau (1683–1741)	1745	Princeton University founded

Study Objectives

The objectives of this chapter are

1. To study the systematic development of forms and methods of creativity as revealed in specific works of art and music.
2. To learn that perspective in art and tonality in music were fully achieved during this period.
3. To learn that drama and motion permeate all of the arts during this period.

Pronunciation Guide

Anhalt-Cöthen (Ahn'-hahlt-Koe'-ten)
Bernini (Bayr-nee'-nee)
Borromini, Francesco (Boh-roh-mee'-nee, Fran-ches'-koh)
Calvin (Kal-vin)
Colbert (Kohl-bayr)
Corelli, Arcangelo (Koh-rel'-lee, Ahr-kahn'-jel-loh)
Courante (Koo-rahnt)
Descartes (Day-kahrt)
Frescobaldi (Fres-koh-bahl'-dee)
Froberger (Froh'-ber-ger)
Giacoma della Porta (Jah-koh'-mah del-lah Por'-tah)
Gigue (Zheeg)
Giorgio Maggiore (Jor'-joh Mah-joh'-ray)
Giorgione (Jor-joh'-nay)
Gluck (Glook)
Ignazio (Eeg-naht'-zee-oh)
Il Gesu (Eel Jay'-zoo)

Leipzig (Lihp'-tzeeg)
Leucippus (Loo-tsip'-pus)
Loyola, Ignatius (Loy-oh'-lah, Eeg-nah'-tsee-us)
Monteverdi (Mon-te-ver'-dee)
Orfeo (Or-fay'-oh)
Pascal (Pahs-kahl)
Passacaglia (Pah-sah-kah'-lee-yah)
Peri (Pay'-ree)
Pozzo, Andrea (Poht'-zoh, Ahn-dray'-ah)
Ritornello (Ri-tohr-nel'-loh)
Rubens (Roo'-benz)
Scarlatti, Domenico (Skahr-laht'-tee, Doh-may'-nee-koh)
Schütz, Heinrich (Shütz, Hihn'-rikh)
Spinoza (Spi-noh'-zah)
Velasquez (Vay-las'-keth)
Vignola (Vee-nyoh'-lah)
Vivaldi (Vee-vahl'-dee)
Wölfflin (Voel'-flin)

The term *Baroque* (from the Portuguese *barroco,* a pearl of irregular form) was first used to describe a style of art overladen with ornament. It was applied especially to the seventeenth-century style of architecture and meant to denote vulgar or debased Renaissance style. In the last sixty years, art historians, notably Wölfflin,[1] have rescued the term from denotations of inferiority. It is now used to designate simply an art epoch, along with such terms as *Gothic* and *Renaissance.*

The last decades of the sixteenth century were filled with doubt and contradictions and contained the ingredients out of which arose the Baroque. The State and the Catholic church were facing almost certain separation; not only that—their very existence as authoritarian institutions was in jeopardy. New prophets in religion, politics, economics, science, arts, and letters were staging a revolution against the established authority of the Renaissance. The Protestant Reformation, the rise of the capitalistic system, the establishment of absolutism in government, and advances in science were all movements out of which a new spirit was to emerge in the seventeenth century.

1. Wölfflin, Heinrich, *Principles of Art History,* New York: Dover Publications.

What were the causes of this change? The Renaissance had failed; it had failed to fulfill the hopes, dreams, and ideals of its founders. Remember that the Renaissance had not produced a great spiritual generation. Never had there been a greater partronage of arts and letters by the Church, as well as by wealthy princes. It is ironical that these patrons, many of whom had won the right to the cardinal's hat and the pope's chair, were often the age's greatest scoundrels and most corrupt politicians. The Renaissance had been an age of the cult of beauty in opposition to medieval asceticism. Egocentricity supplanted humility; Renaissance humanism had taken the place of medieval scholasticism without making men prophets of a better age. The coming changes in social history were the natural development of Renaissance trends. Progress in science had been mainly theoretical; developments in art and letters had been intellectual. Even the economic and political schemes had been more theoretical than real. For example, Machiavelli's *The Prince* was a theory rather than a practical experiment. The struggle between the Church and the State had as yet been mainly a battle of words. The next step was to cultivate action—action in every sphere of human activity.

The seventeenth century was ushered in on a wave of tremendous intellectual, spiritual, and physical activity. In this age we will find those activities which seem to be the practical basis of our systematic civilization. The result in art was a style full of vigor, full of strong emotions, full of symbolism and subtleties we call Baroque.

Some of those who made real and practical contributions to this flood tide of activity were scientists. Bacon's scientific method of inquiry, that of experimentation, laid the foundation for our modern scientific age. Descartes and Pascal made notable advances in mathematics, as did Kepler in astronomy. Harvey heralded a new era in biology, and Newton founded the modern science of physics. Colbert established the mercantile system upon which the world empires of the seventeenth and eighteenth centuries were built. Spinoza systematized modern philosophy. In short, all intellectual activity was concerned with order and the techniques of achieving that order. This was truly a prelude to the twentieth century.

There was also a great religious activity which marks the seventeenth century as one of the most spiritually minded ages of all history. The Thirty Years' War (1618-1648) resulted in the establishment of Protestantism in northern Europe. Calvinism had risen in Geneva. It spread to England, Holland, and, eventually, to America. All of Protestantism was engaged in a vast program of evangelism and expansion. The Catholic Counter-Reformation was the answer to Protestant criticism and expansion. Out of this movement there rose the powerfully militant order of the Jesuits, which systematically reached into every country of the world, civilized or pagan. Each of these great spiritual revivals was based on the same principle—that of a systematic marshaling of religious forces toward a more profound and personal religious experience.

The program of English and Dutch colonization of the Americas and the East Indies is another evidence of the great physical and material activity of the seventeenth century. The application of mercantilism to empire building results in a shift of wealth from southern European countries to the Low Countries and to England. Men of adventure rose in all parts of Europe and extended their influences to every corner of the globe. Not the least of the effects of this activity was the establishment of absolutism in government. No longer was this a theory: it became a reality on the rising tide of economic and physical expansion. This whole concept of physical, economic, and political expansion was also based on a systematic program of action which held great promise of personal rewards in fame and fortune. If one realizes the significance of such events in economics, politics, science, and religion, it will not be difficult to find the echoes of such events in the music and art of the seventeenth and early eighteenth centuries.

Let us continue to demonstrate our thesis that the arts are an expression of the dominating cultural events and attitudes by observing the strong influence of the above activities on the arts. Some of the more tangible results are to be found in the impact of religion on music and art. As has already been stated, the patrons of the Baroque were somewhat different from those of the Renaissance. Religion still provided an outlet for the greatest works of art, but it was not the Church as an institution but the Church as a personal religious experience which provided the impetus. The superficiality of Renaissance religious art gave way to the sincerity of the Baroque. Rembrandt, for example, makes his paintings of religious subjects personal and meaningful experiences to the beholder, not merely symbolic and beautiful scenes. His *Supper at Emmaus* (fig. 8.2) breathes the very spirit of personal faith and humility. The Protestant Reformation had placed an emphasis on the individuality of religious expression. To fulfill life's mission, one must first conquer himself. Suffering was part of life, and there was an ecstasy and joy in pain. The artistic consequence of this Lutheran attitude was an intense personalized expression of religious subjects in all the arts—an expression that was filled with the pathos and joy of man's struggle and victory over his inner self.

The Jesuit Counter-Reformation, with its spiritual exercises, closely identified artistic expression with personal religious experiences. The effect of the Jesuit spiritual exercises, especially in Catholic countries, was profound. These exercises were a series of mental states which the devout would assume as a part of daily religious experience. There were rules of conduct for every phase of life which were designed to intensify concentration on spiritual matters. There were records kept of sins, and there was an examination of conscience according to a schedule which showed weak points and progress made. Those who consciously practiced these exercises experienced heaven and hell with all the senses. St. Ignatius Loyola, founder of the movement, said, "As the body can be exercised by going, walking, running, so by exercises the will may be disposed to find the divine will." The Jesuit lived in a state of intense concentration of mind and believed that visual and emotional revelation were possible for all pious people.

The artistic result of the Jesuit movement was a personal expression of all human experiences. Jesuits used any and all techniques at their disposal to impress upon the observer the intensity of emotional expression. El Greco (1541–1614), who lived most of his creative life in Spain, where the Jesuits gained their strength, became the ideal artistic voice of the movement. He intensified the mystic asceticism in all of his paintings, whether subject was religious or not. His *Laocoön* (plate 17) expresses the struggle of the high priest of Troy with his sons by the elongation of the human form, by diagonal movement of line, and by the upward movement of light with the view of Toledo in the background. The brownish grey of the body color adds to the feeling of mysticism and asceticism. Art became a living thing by taking on a new vitality. Art was luxurious in form, color, melody, and harmony so that people might have a vicarious experience and a satisfaction of desires.

The Calvinist movement, however, provided a different attitude—one which affected the arts in a negative manner. Calvin preached the doctrine of predestination and freedom of conscience. He set a high value on the individual soul which had been the object of God's choice as the recipient of salvation. Education in spiritual and civil affairs was the Calvinistic technique of bringing God's will into reality on earth. This doctrine brought forth a group which was religious, narrow in personal conduct, successful in business and government. Goodness came to be a matter of following certain rules of conduct, and all avenues of sense perception were carefully guarded and often completely closed. The beauty that Catholicism had utilized as a religious force was looked on as a product of the devil. Images and figures disappeared from the church and the home; they were looked upon as idols, too easily worshiped for their own sake. Music, because it made its appeal directly to the emotions, was looked upon with great suspicion. Except for psalm singing, "in one voice and with plain tune," music was banished from the church. Organs were either destroyed or removed from places of worship. This religious doctrine serves to explain the lack of Church patronage of music and art in those countries, such as England and the Low Countries, in which Calvinism had a strong hold. It remained for the Lutheran and Catholic churches to provide the impetus for artists to embody their religious ideals in art.

The center of wealth had shifted from Italy to the north, consequently the center of art shifted from Italy to Germany and to the Netherlands, where Rembrandt and Rubens represented the Dutch and Flemish, respectively. The arts in these centers reached far greater heights of achievement than any of the Italian arts of the age. During the great religious struggles of the late sixteenth century, the Low Countries were broken up into two sections according to religious leanings. The Dutch were Protestant, while the Flemish

Colorplate 17 follows p. 162.

remained Catholic. Consequently, in Holland we find a distinctly antiroyalist, anti-Catholic, middle-class society dominated by the prosperity of the Dutch colonial empire and the middle-class merchant. The art of Holland and North Germany represents this middle-class Protestant point of view. It is natural, also, that Flanders, south Germany, and Austria would be Catholic and aristocratic. The Flemish artists, such as Rubens, painted their Biblical and holy pictures with models taken from the aristocratic circle rather than the poor or middle-class people used by the Dutch painters.

In comparison with Renaissance painters, all Baroque painters turned more and more toward the common man for patronage because of the concentration of wealth in middle-class hands—whether Protestant or Catholic. This interest in the middle class was also due to the fact that the average person was taking a more important place in the destiny of civilization. This middle-class art appreciation brought new patrons as well as new subject matters. Common everyday scenes, events, and experiences, such as a picnic or a drunken beggar, were sufficient reason for creative effort. As artists became more and more sensitive to the real and basic experiences, their art became more sensitive in its expressions. As the horizon of experience became wider, attention was turned from individuals to include their surroundings. Landscapes became a prominent part of painting. Even portraits were often made with the subject standing by a tree or on a riverbank, with the rolling expanse of an estate in the distance. This was especially true in the north where a considerable portion of the wealth was concentrated in the land.

Music as well as the visual arts appealed to the uncultivated emotions of the common person. For the same reasons that painting appealed to the middle-class merchant and the aristocrat, music reached out for this kind of an audience. In the north, especially in Germany, music provided the devout Protestant with a personal religious experience through a tonal art. Melodies were broad and singable, harmonies were rich and full of pathos. Bach and Handel, both representatives of Protestant Germany, have given us some of the world's most meaningful sacred music because of this appeal to the emotions. The *Messiah* and the *Mass in b Minor* stand as symbols of the spiritual expressiveness of music. In the southern countries, music was still more concerned with spectacle and dancing, reflecting the more aristocratic society for which it was written.

The Baroque urge toward a systematizing of every aspect of human experience also had its effect on the arts. We have seen that science, philosophy, economics, government, and even religion showed a strong urge to methodize. The arts, likewise, used a multiplicity of means and techniques. The theme and variations principle of design became an artistic creed, whether in painting, sculpture, architecture, or music. The ingenious handling of basically simple materials resulted in a homogeneity of all elements, in a singleness of purpose. The purpose was a personal expression, not only for the creator but for the observer. The artist invites the observer to enter into the action and partake of the aesthetic experience, just as the Jesuit was invited to enter into a religious experience and the Lutheran to partake of the inner struggle. The Baroque was not a cult of beauty but an art of simple realism. The realism of all aspects of Baroque life, from business to religion, is expressed in its art.

A desire for magnificence, which was brought about by the rise of a wealthy middle class, was also a characteristic of the Baroque. This led to ornamentation often carried to a point of vulgarity and was responsible for the lack of recognition of the basic values in Baroque art until recent times. Architecture was often loaded with ornamental gingerbread; melodic lines in music were ornamented with trills, turns, and other devices. Such ornamentation is perhaps the weakest part of Baroque art, but beneath these ornamental effects are melodies and visual lines that are truly expressive and beautiful.

Because of the many-sided contradictions of the Baroque, it is difficult to single out one artist, or even one art, as the quintessence of the seventeenth-century spirit. There are, however, a few artists whose works not only reveal the spiritual content of the age, but span the breadth of all the contrasts and contradictions. Tintoretto (1518-1594), Rembrandt (1606-1669), Rubens (1577- 1640), and Velasquez (1599-1660) in painting; Bernini (1595-1680) in sculpture; Monteverdi (1567-1643), Froberger (1616-1667), Corelli (1653-1713), Giovanni Gabrieli (1557-1612), Henrich Schütz (1585-1672), Vivaldi (1676-1741), Bach (1685-1750), Handel (1685-1759), and Domenico Scarlatti (1685-1757) in music—all have won places in the small number of truly great artists of all ages.

Painting

Baroque painters used the same basic elements of line, color, form, organization, and space that had been used before. Because of different influences on their life and art, however, they used them in a different manner. In Baroque painting, line is generally diffused, one form melting into another without clear lines of demarcation. Color is usually monochromatic, the result of variation in hue and value of one basic color. The tremendous vitality of Baroque painting is shown in open form, with action extending beyond the visible limits of the canvas. Organization is multiple, with the forms merging one into another. The results of open form, multiple organization, and diffused line can be seen in a strong sense of space which is often extended both into the distance and also forward in a plastic sense.

Tintoretto

An example of the early Baroque style, in contrast to the Renaissance, can be seen in Tintoretto's *Last Supper* (colorplate 18) at the Church of San Giorgio Maggiore in Venice. Tintoretto was a Venetian and, as such, was deeply indebted to the spectacular and colorful style that characterized all Venetian

Colorplate 18
follows p. 162.

art. He was also one of the last of the great Italian painters, for artistic activity was, as we have seen, gradually moving toward the northern countries.

Note the difference in concept between Tintoretto's *Last Supper* and the one by Leonardo da Vinci. Tintoretto impresses us with the dramatic vitality of the moment. The spiritual impact is here as well as the human reaction of the disciples. The figures stand out in sudden lights, like fireworks, and the whole scene presents a spiritual and emotional interpretation that is quite opposite to the calm and serene expression of Leonardo. Tintoretto has moved away from the classic balance of earlier painters and makes his figures move about the canvas, vibrant and alive. Space recedes diagonally into the distance, drawing the viewer into the action. Symbolically, this space is even more extended by the physical presence of angels in motion over the scene as the figures melt, one into another, without any great degree of demarcation. This effect calls for diffused lines and multiple organization. Color is still quite polychromatic, but without the sharp contrast that is usually present in Renaissance art.

One might even suggest an analogy between this painting and Baroque music, where sheer sonority of sound arouses and intensifies emotion. Thus Tintoretto with his force of color, light, space, and dramatic action leads the spectator into the scene as an actual participant in this deeply moving drama.

Rembrandt

From an early age, Rembrandt showed a sensitivity to beauty and truth. One of the most important early influences on his life was the memory of his mother reading to him from her Bible. The biblical stories left vivid impressions that were later to bear great artistic fruit. Rembrandt's parents had hopes that he would become a lawyer or doctor, or perhaps a preacher. They were disappointed when he showed little interest in anything except art. He was finally apprenticed to a painter, and later was sent to Amsterdam to study with the great celebrity Lastman. After six months Rembrandt left, disgusted with his teacher's methods and artistic ideals. In 1632, he returned to Amsterdam where he was definitely launched on a career of art.

He received many commissions from wealthy families for portraits and scenes representing the business and professional life of Amsterdam. His most famous work of this period is the *Anatomy Lesson* in which he portrayed a well-known doctor demonstrating the technique of surgery. Rembrandt, at this stage of his development, painted in a clear-cut masterly manner, but without the later expressiveness. He was popular and successful, buying a large home in the Jewish section of the city and marrying into a very wealthy family. Business was good—too good to last. Rembrandt, always a student of people, began to be influenced by the people around him. His style changed from the pretty manner to one of character study. The *Night Watch* was one of the results of this change in style, and as a result he lost favor with his wealthy clients.

Consider *Night Watch* (colorplate 19) by Rembrandt as an example of the northern Baroque style. The subject is a group of merchants who have banded together in order to patrol the streets of Amsterdam for the purpose of keeping law and order. Rembrandt was commissioned to paint a canvas of the group as a memorial to their patriotic spirit. It was to be hung in the city hall, and he was to have been paid a hundred florins by each member. Rembrandt painted them as they were—a patrol emerging from the shadows of dark streets into a light, but this was not as they wanted to be portrayed. They were prominent men and wished to be painted in a clear light, with much flattery. Rembrandt was a realist and could only paint what he really saw. The *Night Watch* is based on the keynote of reality—not superficiality.

The lines are very diffused, with one body melting into another to a point where it is impossible to distinguish the dividing line. Sharp edges are lost in the atmosphere of shadow and merging color. This is what the eye sees, not what the mind's eye knows. Because of the diffused lines, the organization is fused. Here is a total organization of forms and symbols into a unit. It gives a sense of infinite space, of recession into the distance. By the skillful use of light and shade, Rembrandt has given a sense of depth that was unknown in earlier art. Space extending horizontally is demonstrated by representing only a part of the action in the picture. The figures on both right and left are only partially seen and are cut off by the frame. Because of infinite space, the form is open. True, the center is a highlight and is shown with greater detail and larger figures, but observation reveals that there is attention to events outside the space enclosed by the picture. There is life and action, both physical and expressive, in every figure represented. The color is quite monochromatic. Rembrandt has used one basic color to fuse the figures together. Color adds to the sense of fused unity and diffused line and is also a reminder of the theme and variations technique of the Baroque—variations of shading on one basic color.

With a sense of direction that was born of the analytical and scientific spirit of the Baroque, Rembrandt strove systematically to make himself a master of reality in every aspect. He sketched and painted hundreds of works in an effort to perfect a technique that would bring reality, action, and vigor to his art. With the aid of mirrors, he made innumerable sketches of himself in order to reduce the texture of flesh and hair to a systematic arrangement under various light conditions. He was one of the first artists to realize the function of light and shade as a medium of extending space, both in recession

Colorplate 19 follows p. 162.

and projection. He was also one of the first artists to recognize light and shade as a unifying agent in painting, and he achieved a fused unity through this technique.

The works of his later period show the results of these intense studies. They are deep and need extended contemplation for a full realization of their meaning. From a purely human point of view, from the standpoint of human sympathy and understanding, nothing can approach the quiet, compassionate beauty of his religious art.

The *Descent from the Cross* (plate 20) is a fine example of Rembrandt's use of light and shade, not only as a unifying agent, but as a means of intensifying the powerful emotional content of the painting. The figure of Christ is highlighted, but still with lost edges and diffused lines. With different degrees of intensity of monochromatic coloring, Rembrandt succeeds in making the faces of each participant in the action reveal their own personal grief over the tragedy. This is truly one of Rembrandt's great religious paintings. Another excellent example is the *Supper at Emmaus* (fig. 8.1). The story of the disciples' meal at Emmaus is one of the tenderest in the New Testament. The two disciples have come together, speaking of the Master who is no longer dwelling among them. Thinking of his words, "Where two or three are gathered together in my name, there am I in the midst of them," the disciples sit at the table with the apparition of the Lord, who has made himself known to them. Rembrandt retains the quiet, tranquil mood of the story. The architecture has solemnity, with the huge arch outlining the figure of the Master. There is no action except a soft movement of light which comes from the radiation of the halo. The disciples are quiet and deeply touched. Christ is presented in the simplest view, full-faced and in the highest light. Space has been dematerialized in this work. Rembrandt has caught not only the spirit of the story but also the atmosphere of the setting. It is a real spiritual experience not only for the disciples but also for the countless thousands who have seen, and have been moved by, this great work.

This painting is only one of the more than 300 works that bear testimony to Rembrandt's greatness. Worldly success did not last. In the end, he had only a few faithful friends—just a few who believed in him. But Rembrandt had a great faith in his mission; he believed that his art was his destiny, and he was faithful to that ideal. Finally, in 1669, he painted his last picture, a self-portrait showing an old, broken, wrinkled man—smiling. Society forced him into a pauper's grave, but his faith has brought him into the ranks of the few great of all time. Like most prophets, he caught the real spirit of his own age and left lasting memorials of it.

Rubens

Colorplate 20 follows p. 162.

We have seen Rembrandt as the product of Dutch Protestantism. Peter Paul Rubens, on the other hand, is one of the greatest painters to come from the Flemish Counter-Reformation. Combining the best elements of the Italian

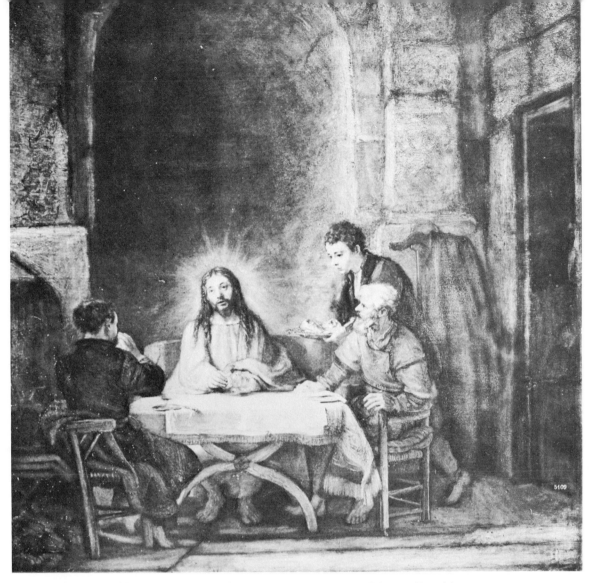

Figure 8.1 *Supper at Emmaus* [1661]—Rembrandt. (Courtesy Metropolitan Museum of Art)

schools of art, he brought forth some of the most stimulating and significant art of any period. From the point of view of sheer animal vigor, there is no painter as exciting as Rubens, while as an interpreter of the violently anti-Protestant movement of Spanish Flanders he has left one of the most moving religious arts of that period.

At the age of twenty-three Rubens, already a master painter, went to Italy. He was engaged by the Duke of Mantua in Venice, who gave him every opportunity to travel and study the work of Italian masters. On one occasion, he made a trip to Spain on a diplomatic mission for the Duke. The success of this trip brought great favor from both the Duke and the Spanish court—a favor that was to prove profitable artistically. While in Spain, he did a number of portraits and palace decorations. From there, he traveled to England in the service of the Spanish king and incidentally assumed the job of decorating the ceiling of the banquet hall in Whitehall Palace. He later settled in Antwerp, where artists and students came to him from all over Europe.

Because of his enormous popularity as a painter, Rubens had many more orders than he could fill by his own creative efforts. He organized a commercial art studio operated on the assembly-line method. This studio, which accepted all commissions and orders, is a demonstration of the Baroque spirit of systematization. The general structure or plan for a work was done by Rubens. He would make preliminary sketches and cartoons, but the canvas was made ready by assistants who would then execute the underpainting, including the background and figures. There were usually twelve such assistants employed, each with a special capacity for doing certain types of painting. When all was finished, Rubens would put the work together by his own hand, putting on the finishing touches. Needless to say, Rubens continued his own creative work in a personal way, but the studio supplied a vast number of excellent pictures. The patron's ability to pay often determined the extent of Ruben's personal interest and therefore often determined the degree of excellence.

Rubens was not a Jesuit, but he was in great sympathy with the Jesuit movement. Consequently, he was commissioned to do a number of paintings for their church in Antwerp. He was a thoroughly Baroque artist. His works abound in colors that blend together in a monochromatic manner. They are filled with action and movement which approach animal vigor. The forms are fused together with subtle light and shading as well as with the "lost edge" technique. He identifies himself with the subject in the Jesuit manner. His effects are so intensely real that the observer is drawn into the feeling and action of the picture.

The *Rape of the Daughters of Leucippus* (colorplate 21) shows the robust animalism of the Baroque spirit. Here is nothing more than physical exuberance, the sensuousness of flesh against flesh. Note the complete absence of static line. Everything moves with a sheer delight in motion. Here, also, the variation technique is employed. Every movement is carried on by short, curved lines of arms, legs, and torsos. This technique is applied even to the contour of the ground and the clouds in the sky. The larger movement speeds diagonally across the canvas through the twisted and unnatural positions of the nudes. The physical reality of form is highlighted by the flashing torsos contrasted against the swarthy mass of men and animals. Form melts into form by diffused line and sheer energy. The observer is drawn into the action by its sensuous appeal to the eyes, not the mind.

Colorplate 21 follows p. 162.

Note the theme and variation technique of the *Assumption of the Virgin* (colorplate 22). The human figure is used almost as a musical motif, each person blending one into another either by motion or by light and shade. Each figure seems to have its own identity, and yet the whole canvas is a fusion of figures into one gigantic movement. The human motif creates open form by moving rhythmically in an upward and clockwise motion. The movement expresses vividly the ecstasy of the Virgin's ascent into heaven, accompanied by the cascade of angelic cherubs. Rubens ingeniously uses all the artistic elements at his command—monochromatic color, diffused line, fused organization, and open form—to create a canvas of exciting action, both physically and spiritually.

This most typical Baroque painter died in 1640. It is recorded that the Jesuits of Antwerp said 700 Masses for the repose of his soul. Like Rembrandt, his greatest works were those created in the service of the Church, but created out of the sincere conviction of his own spiritual experiences.

Velasquez

Another important painter in the Baroque was Diego Velasquez who lived and worked in Spain. He was not a mystic, nor a Jesuit, nor did he express the bold ornamentation and action of the Baroque. Like Rembrandt he was a master of light and shade with a feel for space and realism. He painted what he saw, not what he imagined. *Maids of Honor* (fig. 8.2) is a portrait of the Infanta Margarita and her attendants. The soft pastel dress of the Infanta contrasts with the darker colors of the attendants. However, there are soft edges that blend one figure into another. The faces of the King and Queen, who are observing, are reflected in the mirror. Velasquez manages a fine illusion of reality by his treatment of space and his arrangement of the figures.

Among the most spectacular examples of Baroque soaring energy and religious ecstacy can be found in the ceiling paintings of many Baroque churches, especially those of the Jesuit Order. These ceilings were often created by relatively unknown artists, or even groups of artists. A fine example of this is the Church of San Ignazio in Rome by Andrea Pozzo (colorplate 23). The scene represents the ascension of Ignatius Loyola into heaven. The upward motion of saints, angels, and cherubs give the impression that the dome has been opened to the heavens and all its glory. Here again the human figure is used as a motif in a gigantic panorama of religious mysticism.

Sculpture

There is action, expressiveness, and individuality in all Baroque sculpture as well as painting. The most famous sculptor in this age is Bernini. Bernini was a Jesuit, and his works are impregnated with a devout and intense personal religious expressiveness, enhanced by the spiritual exercises. Compare the

Colorplates 22, 23 follows p. 162.

Figure 8.2 *Maids of Honor* [1656]—Velasquez. (Courtesy Alinari/Editorial Photocolor Archives)

Colorplate 17 *Laocoön* [c. 1610]—El Greco. (Courtesy National Gallery of Art, Washington/Samuel H. Kress Collection)

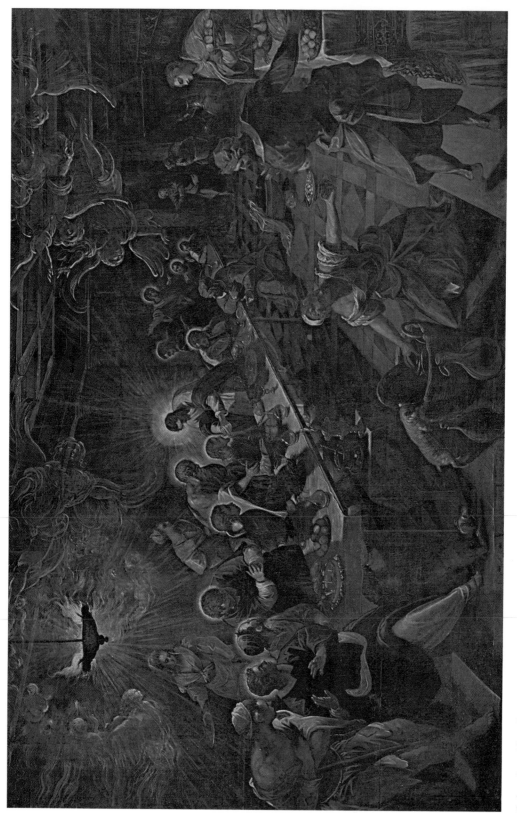

Colorplate 18 *Last Supper* [1594]—Tintoretto. (Courtesy Scala/Editorial Photocolor Archives)

Colorplate 19 *Night Watch* [1642]—Rembrandt. (Courtesy Rijksmuseum, Amsterdam)

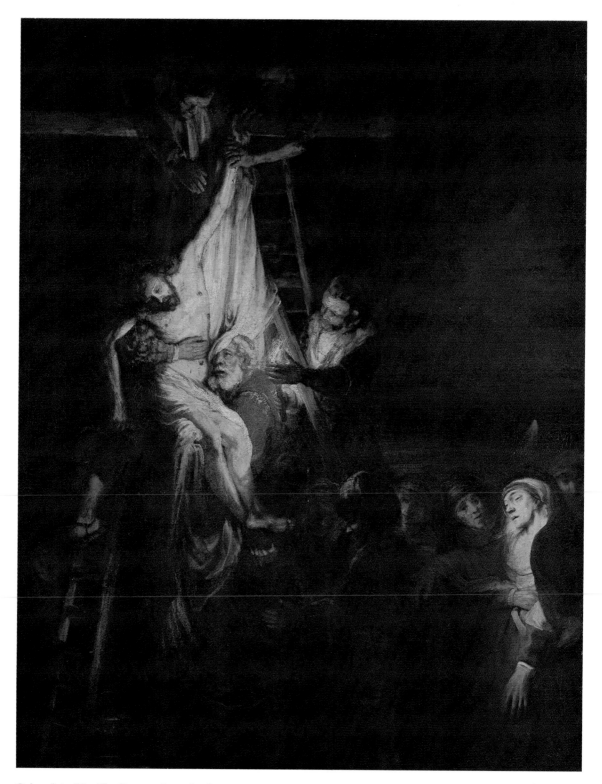

Colorplate 20 *The Descent from the Cross* [1650–1660]—Rembrandt van Rijn.
(Courtesy National Gallery of Art, Washington/Widener Collection)

Colorplate 21 *Rape of the Daughters of Leucippus* [1618]—Rubens. (Courtesy Scala/ Editorial Photocolor Archives)

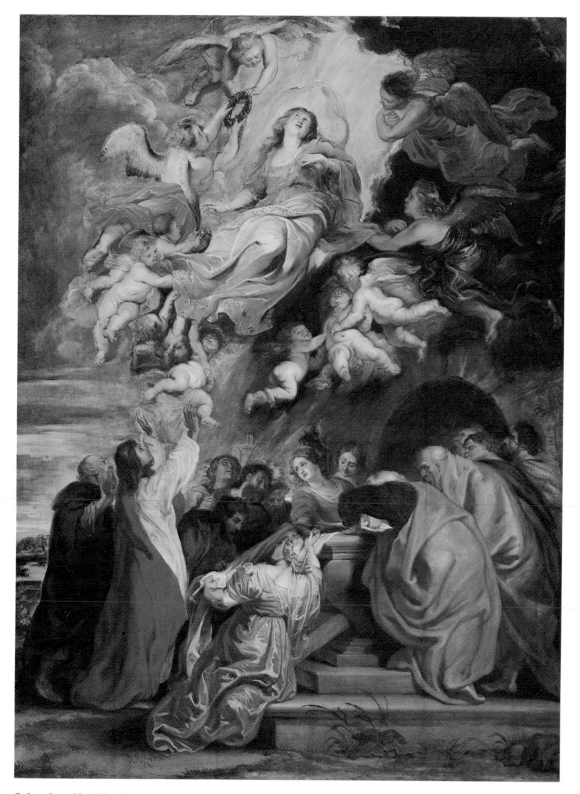

Colorplate 22 *The Assumption of the Virgin* [c. 1606]—Rubens. (Courtesy National
Gallery of Art, Washington/Samuel H. Kress Collection)

Colorplate 23   *Apotheosis of Saint Ignatius*, Saint Ignatius, Rome [1691]—Pozzo.
(Courtesy of Scala/Editorial Photocolor Archives)

David (fig. 7.6) of Michelangelo with Bernini's *David* (fig. 8.3) for the contrast between Renaissance and Baroque. Michelangelo's work is monumental but static, while Bernini's shows great physical and nervous reality. In Bernini there is action—David is tense with pent-up energy about to be released. His eyes are focused on the object of the action, the figure of Goliath, which remains out and beyond the artwork itself.

One of the most famous works by Bernini is the *Ecstasy of St. Theresa* (fig. 8.4). The Baroque spirit of intense emotional ecstasy and imagination is exemplified by this work. The subject is St. Theresa's dream in which an angel appeared before her holding a dart, symbolic of divine life, with which he pierced her heart. The saint is in an ecstasy of pain; the pathetic expression on her face, the upraised shoulder in anticipation of the next thrust are testimony to the emotional sensitivity of Bernini's art. The artist has used every device at his disposal in an effort to intensify this expression. The impression of infinite space is shown by the heavenly cloud on which the action takes place. Space is made even more real by the hanging draperies and the suspended feet of the saint. The poised dart, the angelic face, the flowing drapery—all are combined to make this a work of dynamic motion, not physical, but spiritual. The passion of the moment almost forces the eye to the distance out between the sculptured figures into the limitless space beyond.

Architecture

While architectural design was to remain classic in its basic forms well into the twentieth century, the Baroque spirit added a vigor and motion to architecture that deserves mention. The same predilection for movement, light and shade, and plasticity of form that characterizes Baroque painting and sculpture is present in its buildings. Architectural function was not only to enclose space but also to present a dramatic spectacle to the eye. This was particularly true of the churches. Spiritual salvation lay within the doors, but, added to that, the glory and magnificence of heaven was to be suggested to the eye by the facade.

The Greek temple, along with the Roman dome, was almost always utilized as the basic structure of Baroque builders. It was the manner in which they arranged and decorated these basically simple forms that suggests the Baroque variation technique. An example of early Italian Baroque that was based on classic principles but was energized by the Baroque spirit is the Church of Il Gesù in Rome (fig. 8.5). A Jesuit church, it was designed by da Vignola, but the facade was redesigned by Giacoma della Porta. Notice the mixing of the Renaissance and the Baroque by the triangular design over a low-arched pediment. The curved scrolls on either side act as buttresses and also draw the eye from the wide base of the nave to a screen that hides the

Figure 8.3 *David* [1624]—Bernini. (Courtesy Alinari/Editorial Photocolor Archives)

Figure 8.4 *Ecstasy of St. Theresa* [1646]—Bernini. (Courtesy Alinari/Editorial Photocolor Archives)

Figure 8.5 Il Gesù in Rome [c. 1575–1584]. (Courtesy Marburg-Art Reference Bureau)

vault over the nave. While Il Gesù is not overly ornate, it did become a model from which many other Baroque churches were designed.

Sant' Agnese (fig. 8.6) in Rome is a typical example of the middle Baroque period. It was designed by Francesco Borromini and completed in 1657. One is immediately conscious of the classic columns and the huge dome. Look carefully, however, for purely decorative design. The columns have been doubled to make a richer appearance. The towers on either side of the dome are set ahead and the facade is curved to connect with the central section. In a sense, this is comparable to the painter's use of light and shade for depth. Note also that while the bottom portion of each tower is square, the top is rounded, suggesting a twisting movement. The whole breadth of the facade is covered with repeated ornamental carvings to mold the component parts together and to give a sense of undulating motion to the eye.

Figure 8.6   Sant' Agnese in Rome [1653]. (Courtesy Keystone View Company)

The Monastery Church of Melk in Austria (fig. 8.7) gives us an excellent example of the northern Baroque that followed the basic plan of Il Gesù. The richly decorative and ornamental interior is a highly complex series of variations on the curve of the round arch. The effect is one of dynamic motion from the floor of the wide nave to the well-illuminated and elaborately decorated vaulting above, perhaps suggesting the splendors of heaven itself.

Bernini's Plaza of St. Peter's (fig. 8.8), situated in front of St. Peter's in Rome, is another example of Baroque architecture. Here Bernini shows the Baroque tendency to strive for monumental forms. It is an attempt to dominate great spaces, akin to the Jesuit idea of dominating the world. The facade of St. Peter's and the double rows of colonnades, extending outward like great pincers, are all conceived as one gigantic work of art. The colonnades, topped by rows of figures of the saints, sweep up toward St. Peter's with a curvilinear motion that swiftly draws the observer into the confines of its portals.

Figure 8.7   Monastery Church of Melk [1702–c. 1738]. (Courtesy Marburg-Art Reference Bureau)

Figure 8.8   Plaza of St. Peter's in Rome [1656–63]. (Courtesy University Prints)

Baroque music

There were two main lines of musical development during the Baroque. One was the development of dramatic vocal music, both secular and religious, such as the opera, oratorio, and cantata. The other was the emancipation of instrumental music from its nearly exclusive use of vocal forms, leading it to a position of dominance by the end of the period.

For the first time in musical history, two styles were purposely used side by side, the antique style of the Renaissance and the modern style of the Baroque. For the first time also, composers became conscious of musical conventions. However, certain characteristics of style were developed in this period of a century and a quarter that tied together such seemingly disparate composers as Peri, Monteverdi, and Frescobaldi of the early seventeenth century with Bach, Handel, and Domenico Scarlatti of the first half of the eighteenth century.

The more obvious of these unifying elements can be listed in general terms as follows: the establishment of *tonality* as the basic concept of musical organization, the use of the *basso continuo*, the development of *recitative*, and the development of true vocal and instrumental idioms.

The establishment of tonality as the basis for musical organization sets Baroque music off in complete contrast to that of the Renaissance in which the intervallic harmony was dictated by the use of modes. The idea of harmonic depth is as clearly developed in music as plastic perspective in painting. Contrast the perspective of *The Assumption of the Virgin* (colorplate 22) with that of the *Journey of the Magi* (fig. 7.2). Note the plasticity of the figures, the feeling of depth, and the sense of planes of distance in the former, the lack of true plasticity and depth in the latter. Similarly, contrast the opening chorus, verse 1, of the cantata *Christ Lay in the Bonds of Death* with the *Agnus Dei* from the Palestrina Mass *Veni sponsa Christi*. The overwhelming feeling for key center in the cantata—in this case, E minor—is evidence of the importance of tonality to the Baroque style of Bach, while the Palestrina work with its modal harmony, evidences a completely different concept of tonal organization.

The establishment of tonality as a basic concept in Baroque music gave rise to a number of new methods of handling the tonal material. Homophony became equal in importance to polyphony. In the opera and in instrumental music such as the dance suite and those forms based on the idea of *basso continuo*, homophony reigned supreme. The system of chordal relationships around a well-defined tonal center emphasized the growing importance of chordal harmony and the dissonant treatment of chords. Tonality was applied to harmony by constructing a series of chords under the melodic line. The series was so designed as to create a sense of tension and release, of motion and repose, through the use of chordal dissonance and consonance. The tonal center, or tonic chord, acted as a point of gravitation for the harmony, whose function it was to define this focal point. This concern with tonality not only determined the organization of homophonic composition but determined the treatment of counterpoint as well. The counterpoint of Bach and Handel was tonal rather than modal. The combinations of lines of melody in a Bach fugal passage such as the "Hallelujah" at the end of the first chorus in the cantata *Christ Lay in the Bonds of Death* were determined by chordal and tonal considerations. In contrast, the counterpoint of Palestrina's *Agnus Dei* was determined by the modal polyphony of the Renaissance.

To systematize tonality further, there arose a contrapuntal relationship between the bass line and the melody. A system of musical shorthand called *basso continuo*, or figured bass, was invented, by which the performer could determine the chordal structure of the music. The figured bass was "realized" by the keyboard instrumentalist who played the harmonies indicated by figures under the bass line in support of the melody. The *basso continuo* part was continuous because its function was to supply the harmony with both its basic written tones and chordal formulae. This bass line was reinforced by instruments such as the cello, bassoon, or string bass to supply tonal coloring and volume. The solid character of the bass in the homophonic Baroque style is due to this emphasis placed upon it. Actually, there arose a sort of polarity between the bass and the melody, with the inner parts assuming minor importance. This characteristic becomes a striking and readily recognizable feature of Baroque homophonic music, whether vocal or instrumental, whether from the early seventeenth or the early eighteenth century. The system of figured bass became so much a part of this new harmonic concept that it was, in one variant or another, the basis of the teaching of harmony for the next 200 years.

One of the most striking and effective devices originating in the early Baroque was that of the *recitative*. The recitative was an attempt to give musical setting to texts of dramatic significance so that the words would be clearly intelligible and yet have the assistance of musical texture. This was accomplished by setting the texts to a declamatory type of vocal solo in which the natural inflections were emphasized, but balance and contour of melodic line were avoided. Recitatives were accompanied by either simple figured bass realized on a keyboard instrument or by an orchestral texture. The development of the recitative was the direct result of the efforts of a literary and artistic group in Florence, known as the Camerata, who wanted to give effective representation to the words of their new dramatic venture, *dramma per musica*, which was to be known as opera.

This new form, opera, was a fusion of drama and music through the use of recitatives which carried the narrative text of the drama, arias and solo ensembles which were the expression of highly emotional situations, and choral ensembles which provided massed effects. The desire to fuse text and music into an indissoluble whole in the early music drama was the counterpart of the same tendency to fuse elements of architecture, sculpture, and painting together in the Baroque visual arts. For dramatic purposes, it is clear that a single vocal line serves to convey the meaning of words far better than a contrapuntal texture. At first this led to the highly inflected declamation represented by the recitative. Gradually, more lyric and florid sections developed in contrast to the narrative character of the pure recitative until, by the middle of the seventeenth century, two distinct types of dramatic vocal settings were already evident—the pure recitative and the aria.

The development of two distinct idioms, one vocal and one instrumental, is still another purely Baroque characteristic. Previously, instrumental or vocal music could be played or sung interchangeably. While in the Baroque the vocal style might be applied to instrumental works and vice versa, instrumental and vocal music was written specifically for each medium and could no longer be played, or sung, interchangeably. A *concerto grosso* or a *sonata* for violin and cembalo could not be conceived as vocal. The Passacaglia and Fugue in C Minor by Bach can be performed only as an instrumental work, though some of the idioms used are vocal in origin. For example, the last section of this work is a fugue in which separate lines of melody are used as "voices." On the other hand, such excerpts from Handel's *Messiah* as the recitative *Comfort Ye My People* and the following aria, *Every Valley,* can be suitable only for a vocal performance.

Within these general stylistic characteristics that are common to the whole Baroque era, composers with their technical mastery of chromatic harmonies and musically dramatic situations tried to lead the listeners out of and beyond themselves, to make them forget the limits of ordinary existence, and to open new aesthetic experiences through the emotions. The cultural and ultrarefined art of the elite was no longer satisfying. Together with the rise of the middle class came a desire among artists to identify themselves with their new world of the spirit and intensified experience. What the result was can be seen in the music of the seventeenth-century Baroque, an art of ecstasy and exuberance, of dynamic tension and monumental forms, an art of longing and self-denial in contrast to the assuredness and self-reliance of the Renaissance. Quite naturally, therefore, Baroque music became enriched by expressive melody, pathetic recitative, frequent chromaticisms, and capricious rhythms.

The growing humanism of the Renaissance had resulted in a greater interest in entertainment that would appeal to all classes of people, whether cultured or uncultured. The complexities of the polyphonic style did not appeal to the common people who were more interested in dance forms and popular songs than in madrigals and Masses. Moreover, the Reformation had weakened the authority of the Roman church. Since ecclesiastical domination over the world of art was no longer possible, the work of the artist became increasingly secularized. Finally, the Renaissance veneration for classical antiquity, especially for Greek drama, set the stage for the invention of opera. Music was on its way to becoming an expression of human experience, an art of romantic idealism, a language of emotions. The beginning of the seventeenth century thus saw the fading of one epoch of music and the laying of the foundation for a musical revolution from which there eventually arose the whole edifice of modern music.

Within the two main lines of musical development during the Baroque, the rise of the secular dramatic form of the opera was of earliest importance. In fact, it was the rapid increase of interest in this form that did much to spur on the interest in instruments themselves and, finally, in the great wave of independent instrumental composition that was to dominate the latter part of the Baroque period.

Monteverdi

The greatest of the early operatic composers was Claudio Monteverdi (1567–1643), who laid down the basic principles for combining the most important innovations of the Baroque. Monteverdi's great masterpiece *Orfeo* will probably be of little more than antiquarian interest to the twentieth-century listener. This may be due to the stilted formality of the drama as well as the obvious stress on a series of short independent forms in the music which gives a "posed" character to the opera. As in the Renaissance, this music is broken up into many short pieces, such as dances, madrigallike choruses, recitatives, and instrumental interludes called *ritornelli*, each of which can be removed without damaging the unity of form. The fact that Monteverdi was able to make these formal miniatures serve a truly dramatic purpose attests to his own genius and to the power of the Baroque spirit.

Monteverdi used recitative as the vehicle for carrying the most intensely dramatic and emotional scenes of the drama. This is unlike the later development when the aria, the more lyric form of vocal style, became the idiom for intensified emotional expression and the recitative was used only to carry the narrative. His use of this new recitative style was the realization of the desire to unify music, word, and action into one form. Opera was not yet a composition designed for entertainment. No need was felt to please the ear with pleasant song or spectacular vocal display. However, this new musical dramatic form was so successful that by the end of the Baroque it had become the most popular form of musical entertainment. By this time, the sound principles of Monteverdi had been laid aside to give vocal and visual thrills for a great popular audience. It was not until Gluck restated the principles of Monteverdi in the middle of the eighteenth century that opera gained a new vitality. Despite its great popularity, or perhaps just because of it, the operas of the Baroque, with a few rare exceptions, are completely forgotten items of performance today and have seldom been performed since the middle of the eighteenth century.

One must listen to Monteverdi's *Orfeo* within the framework of the early seventeenth century. Contrasted to the serenity and restraint of the Renaissance choral music, religious or secular *Ave Maria* by Des Pres or *Pour ung plaisir* by Crequillon), *Orfeo* presents a dramatic power that is as dynamic as that of Tintoretto's *Last Supper* (colorplate 14) in contrast to Leonardo da Vinci's work on the same subject (fig. 7.4). The unity of the entire opera depends upon several factors. Most important is the purposeful attempt to make the music, text, and dramatic action combine into a completed expression. In much the same manner, Tintoretto repeats lines and masses of color to link his figures in the dynamic emotions of the *Last Supper*.

Opera's dramatic appeal then was in the vigorous, spectacular, and romantic dramas presented. The plots, gleaned from Greek mythology and historic events, presented a variety of actions and emotions which could be intensified by music and staging. Everything about Baroque opera was impressive and dazzling. Unique stage machinery produced weird effects of supernaturalism and realism. Stage settings taxed the Baroque artists to produce canvases that would reveal the excitement and pathos of the dramas. Music, staging, and the text—in short, everything—marshaled all their forces in a tremendous onslaught on the ear, eye, and mind.

Gabrieli

While Monteverdi succeeds in arousing and intensifying emotion through the combination of words and music, another early Baroque composer illustrates the same success by other means. Giovanni Gabrieli (1557–1612), a Venetian like Tintoretto, overwhelms the listener with sheer masses of sound, both vocal and instrumental. The effect of rich and colorful sonority which he achieves in his *Symphoniae sacrae (Sacred Symphonies)* is that of highly intensified dramatic emotion. Rich and dissonant harmony, rhythmic irregularity, melodic motives, and rhythmic patterns all combine in a dramatic force that is different from that of Monteverdi but just as effective. The Baroque spirit of both masters is clearly apparent in their great power to move the emotions of their listeners.

The *Symphoniae sacrae* were published in two parts. Part one contains forty-five vocal and sixteen instrumental compositions, while part two contains twenty-one purely instrumental compositions. The fact that some are instrumental and others vocal does not alter Gabrieli's preoccupation with tonal masses. The music is polyphonic; some of the sections have as many as sixteen independent voice parts. However, the obvious emphasis is upon a harmonic texture which can result only from a purposeful and planned harmonic and tonal concept. This concept of tonal mass is truly Baroque. In these early Baroque instrumental works by Gabrieli, one already senses the exploitation of sonority and mass of tonal color as a quality that finds even greater expression in the instrumental *concerti grossi* of the later Baroque of Corelli, Vivaldi, Bach, and Handel.

Schütz

The Baroque dramatic element was further revealed in other religious music, especially in the oratorio, passion music, and cantata. The oratorio and passion music were, in effect, opera without staging and action. An early master of these forms for the Lutheran Church was Heinrich Schütz (1585–1672), whose use of polyphonic choruses and the homophonic recitative and aria presaged the enormous output of Lutheran church music which came to full bloom with Bach. The cantata became particularly identified with the church in Germany. In a sense it was a miniature liturgical oratorio, often based on a short hymn text. The massive strength of the Barque church cantata is often due to the use of Lutheran choral tunes as thematic material.

The Baroque musical activity most important to our musical heritage is the development of instrumental music, both solo and orchestral. The forms were derived from the vocal styles of earlier times, both homophonic and polyphonic. Because of the technical demands made by the Baroque spirit, many of our common instruments reached a degree of mechanical perfection which has never been surpassed. This is particularly true of the stringed instruments such as the violin, viola, and cello. Because of the musical demands of the Church, the organ also reached a high state of perfection.

Baroque instrumental music falls into two general styles of textures, both equally popular in use. The first is the homophonic texture with an extended and predominant melodic line. The second is the polyphonic texture, which develops a short thematic motive in various voices.

In the homophonic forms the polarity of the outer parts, the melody and the bass, suggests a contrapuntal relationship between them. In fact the techniques of contrapuntal treatment are often found mixed in the texture of homophonic forms and vice versa. In this type of musical texture the treatment of melodic line is generally of such a nature that a simple statement of thematic material at contrasting dynamic levels and in a few closely related keys is sufficient for an achievement of unity and variety in the composition. This tends to keep the homophonic compositions, or movements, comparatively short and concise. As yet no extended development of themes and motives for the purpose of supplying length will be found, as is common in the eighteenth-century classic sonata.

The homophonic texture of Baroque instrumental music is best exemplified in the forms of the solo sonata, the suite, and the concerto. The sonata derived its name from the Italian word *sonare*, to sound, and was applied to instrumental music in contrast to vocal music. No specific form was implied in using the term, and compositions called sonatas varied from single movement works, for a solo instrument, to works for small ensembles in several movements. Keyboard sonatas which were played upon the clavichord or harpsichord were among the most popular, and the hundreds of harpsichord sonatas composed by Domenico Scarlatti (1685–1757) are among the finest examples of this genre. The Sonata in C minor is typical of the binary or two-part form of these works. Both A and B parts are repeated. The harmonic contrast of the dominant key of G major, with which the A or first half of the sonata ends, the tonic key of C minor, with which the B or second half concludes, is striking evidence of the importance of tonality in Baroque music.

The work is also characterized by the use of specific technical devices which are peculiar to the keyboard instrument, such as crossing of hands and the use of rapid scale and full chordal passages.

The suite, which was essentially a composition made up of a number of short dances, is found in its purest form in the many keyboard suites written for the harpsichord during the Baroque. In its final form in the late Baroque it was based on four specific dances appearing in the following order; Allemande, Courante, Sarabande, and Gigue (Jig). The dance movements were often preceded by a Prelude and sometimes additional dances were interspersed. This was usually the case when the suite was written for an instrumental ensemble or orchestra. Ensemble suites were often called by such names as Sonata da Camera, Sinfonia, and Overture. The four basic dances were representative of four different nationalities: German, French, Spanish, and Irish-English.

A typical suite for the keyboard is the Suite in E minor by J. J. Froberger (1616–1667). This short work makes exclusive use of the four basic dances each in two parts which are invariably repeated. Their unanimity of key serves as the only element of unity in the complete work. Tempo, meter, and thematic material differ entirely from one dance to the other. While each dance is essentially homophonic in texture there are short imitative figures which appear frequently and give the feeling of a texture of several voices. This is especially true in the slower allemande and sarabande. Ornamentation is frequent, often notated, and at other times merely suggested. Such ornamentation was an integral part of the Baroque performance technique and was one of the mannerisms affected by the virtuoso performers of the Baroque of whom Froberger was an early example. Later suites, such as those by J. S. Bach, retained the fundamental characteristics of Froberger, but the dance movements were greatly extended and almost without exception other dances were interpolated.

The concertato style of the early Baroque in which competing or contrasting groups of instruments and voices were played off, one against the other, developed gradually into the purely instrumental concerto idea in which a single instrument or a group of solo instruments were contrasted with a large accompanying body or orchestra. The use of a single solo instrument with orchestra was called a solo concerto. When several solo instruments were used the work was called a concerto grosso. The principle of style and form in each case was similar. The solo, or soloists, were contrasted with the orchestral body in dynamic and thematic material. Passages in which all the instruments, both orchestral and solo, were used were known as the tutti (entire) passages, and passages in which the solo or soloists dominated were called the solo or concertino passages. Such selections alternated in the course of each movement. Concertos were usually in three movements of fast, slow, and fast tempos. Beside the contrast of dynamic and thematic material there was also contrast of tonal color between the solo and the orchestra. Sometimes this was achieved by different use of the solo and orchestral bodies and sometimes by the use of totally different instruments in the solo parts. The latter was especially true in the concerto grosso, where several solo instruments were used, and gave the composer an additional opportunity for tonal contrast.

One of the earliest composers of the concerto grosso was Arcangello Corelli (1653–1713). His twelve Concerti Grossi are written for a solo concertino group of violins and cello with an accompanying group of first and second violins, violas, and a figured bass part which is played by cellos, string bass, and harpsichord. The Concerto VIII is one of Corelli's most popular works. It is titled *Composed for Christmas Eve*. While it has more than the usual three movements, these fall into the three general sections of fast, slow, and fast with an additional movement labeled Pastorale ad libitum—Pastoral to be played if desired. Actually it is this additional movement that gives the work the character of a Christmas concerto since the pastoral movement was commonly associated with works written for the Christmas season. Note the pastoral symphony in Handel's *Messiah* and the similar movement in Bach's *Christmas Oratorio*.

While Corelli used the usual three alternating tempos of fast, slow, and fast, he deviated from the pattern of only one tempo to each movement. The first fast tempo section is introduced by two short passages, vivace and grave, played in unison by the concertino and concerto grosso. Then follows the typical first movement in allegro with its alternation of soloists and accompanying orchestra. The slow movement, marked adagio, has a brief, fast passage in which the soloists and orchestra are again joined in unison. This separates the two presentations of the slow movement proper in which the solo instruments are played off against the accompaniment. The final fast section of the work is actually two short movements in very quick tempos. They are again typical of the concerto grosso style in juxtaposing the soloists and orchestra. The second fast movement likewise is characteristic of the driving rhythm that is usually associated with the final movement of the concerto grosso.

Concluding the work is the pastoral movement in the regular lullaby rhythmic pattern of such movements, in which the soloists are given even more conspicuous passages than in the main body of the work. The contrast of tonal color and dynamic levels between soloists and orchestra, the rhythmic drive of the fast movement in contrast to the expressive character of the slow movement, and the allusion to scene painting in the final movement, all make this work a fitting musical counterpart of the highly ornamental and expressive Baroque murals of the seventeenth- and eighteenth-century churches. Corelli was in the employ of a cardinal of the Church and in this position found a great demand for these compositions for church and festive occasions.

The concertos of Antonio Vivaldi (1676–1741) are perhaps the most varied and colorful of those composed in the last fifty years of the Baroque. In the Venetian tradition of a predilection for tonal color, Vivaldi employs an exhaustive variety of solo and concertino instruments, as well as varied orchestral groups for the concerto grosso. Brass, woodwinds common during his time—flute, piccolo, oboe, and bassoon—as well as such little-used stringed instruments as the mandolin are used with equal success. In all of these concertos, which usually have three movements, the distinguishing feature of the form is the contrast between the solo, or soloists, and the main orchestral body, or tutti. The contrast is due not only to the difference in tonal color and tonal mass but also to the difference in treatment of the melodic material. While Vivaldi wrote over 450 concertos, the great preponderance of the works are for solo instruments. Even in those works which are properly called concerti grossi the solo instruments are given much that is in a virtuoso style and foreshadows the solo treatment in the classical concertos of later times.

Among the concertos that Vivaldi wrote are a number which are grouped under specific titles that indicate the composer's acknowledgment of the Baroque tendency to combine the arts. This desire, which is expressed in the dramatic combination of word and music in vocal works for the stage and the Church, finds a naive counterpart in some of the purely instrumental music of the period. Vivaldi wrote a series of twelve concertos, each for a solo violin, with the exception of one for oboe, under the title of *Il Cimento dell' Armonica a dell' Invenzione* (The *Contest between Harmony and Invention*) and grouped these works further into sets of four. The first is entitled *The Four Seasons* in which each season is represented by a single concerto. Apart from the evident desire to have the music portray the general events as well as specific details of the respective seasons, these are all cast in the traditional fast-slow-fast sequence of the concerto form.

Vivaldi wrote poems, or had them written, for each movement of these four concertos. In the first concerto called *Spring* the poems set the general tone of the movement and furnish the detail for musical expression or, what is even more probable, relate in words what Vivaldi had already accomplished in music.

Quotations from the poems are printed in accordance with Vivaldi's instructions at the beginning and in the course of each movement where appropriate. Translated, the poem for the first movement reads as follows: "Spring has returned and the birds joyously salute him with their gay songs. The streams set free by the breath of spring flow again with their sweet murmur. Thunder and lightning cover the sky with veils of darkness and proclaim him king. Their fury is soon spent and the birds once more sing sweetly." Vivaldi had this poem printed line for line at the appropriate sections of the first movement for the instruction of the performers. In addition, specific program details are noted such as the passage in example 8.1 which designates the "Song of the Birds." Other such details as the "Flowing of the Stream" and "The Thunderstorm" are also printed in the score.

It will be noted that the first movement contains as much material for the orchestra as for the solo instrument. Most of the solo passages are virtuoso sections that elaborate upon the musical material of the movement in a very

Example 8.1 *Canto Dè Gl'uccelli (Song of the Birds)*

CANTO DÈ GL'UCCELLI (Song of The Birds)

decorative fashion, accentuating the program at hand. The slow second movement is in the form of a two-part arioso that is played by the solo violin to an accompaniment of violins and violas. The solo part represents the sleeping goatherd while the two violin parts are labeled "the murmuring of the forest trees" and the viola part "the barking of the goatherd's dog." The final allegro is a shepherds' dance in a gay jig tempo and rhythm in which the solo violin is exploited and contrasted in virtuoso passages with the string orchestra.

Quite apart from the naive program and the pictorial musical passages, Vivaldi has, with his usual mastery, written a work which is musically and aesthetically satisfying in its handling of form, brilliant tonal color, and expressive quality. He is certainly one of the great representatives of the Baroque love of dramatic tension and elaborate ornamentation. This is an example of the use of Renaissance word painting in the madrigal now used in a purely instrumental manner.

The second style of Baroque instrumental texture, the polyphonic, which develops motives and thematic subjects in various voices, is completely contrapuntal in nature. In fact, the fugue, which is one of the best known of these forms, can be regarded as more of a device of contrapuntal writing than as an actual form. In addition, the fugue is not exclusively an instrumental form since it is found in Baroque vocal music as well.

The devices of fugal writing were derived from earlier polyphonic writing and the fugue itself is described as written in two or more *voices*, even though designed exclusively for instrumental performance. The fugue is essentially a contrapuntal work built on a single theme, which is called the subject. The compositional devices employed in a contrapuntal texture are very important in achieving unity and variety in the presentation of the single theme. The fundamental unifying device is that of imitation of the theme or subject between voices. The subject is characteristically a melodic idea which is stated in the tonic key and ends in the dominant. Its answer is an imitation of itself which begins in the dominant key and ends in the tonic. While such contrast already provides a measure of variety, the single theme or subject is consistently treated in more varied fashion. The subject or parts of it may appear in different keys after different intervals of time. It may be played twice as slowly as the original statement (augmentation) or twice as fast (diminution). The subject may be used upside down (inversion), or it may be used in its reverse order (retrogression). The subject and answer may appear quite separately in succession, or the answer may begin before the subject is completed (stretto).

Fugue Number 8 (ex. 8.2) from the first book of "The Well-Tempered Clavier" shows some of these devices that Bach used. The notes marked "x" are those of the subject and answer in various key relationships. Notes marked "o" represent the subject in inverted form. In this case, the ascending intervals of the original subject now descend and vice versa. The notes marked "⊗" are those of the original subject in augmented form. Their note values are twice that of the original subject. In addition to these devices, Bach overlaps his subject and answer in a number of places forming strettos. The Italian name indicates "hurry." Bach achieves tension when he hurriedly introduces the answer before the subject is concluded. Strettos are found in measures 20–22, 27–30, 44–46, 52–54, 61–64, 67–72, and 77–83.

Example 8.2 Fugue No. 8 in d# Minor

Example 8.2 (Continued)

Example 8.2 (Continued)

Example 8.2 (Continued)

In addition to the fugue, the canon, chaconne, and passacaglia are also representative counterpuntal forms. An example of this style is Bach's *Passacaglia and Fugue in c Minor* (ex. 8.3), which provides an excellent study in the theme and variation method of Baroque composing with a polyphonic texture. The composition was originally written for organ, but it has been transcribed for orchestra and is often performed as an orchestral work. A passacaglia is a dance form in which the melody appears in the bass and is constantly repeated in voices or parts. The first announcement of the theme comes in the bass with no accompaniment.

Example 8.3

Note the quality of the melody with its rather large skips, both upward and downward. In spite of these skips, it has a sustained quality and a good deal of pathetic expressiveness. Bach is not trying to tell a story; he is merely creating a melody and then using all his skill to develop that melody and still retain musical interest. Listen carefully as the music progresses and you will hear constant repetition, usually in the bass but, on occasion, in other voices. After a climax of a robust announcement of the theme, along with massive chords, Bach launches into a double fugue. For his subject he takes the first half of the main melody and combines it with a newly created theme. He then proceeds to develop these two ideas simultaneously. The music is not monotonous because he has created a contrasting interest with vigorous variations by differences in loudness, texture, and speed. This is merely one example of the technical way in which Baroque music is put together. Its expressive qualities come from the sincerity of expression put into the basic themes themselves and the rich, full, harmonic substance.

The harmonic structure of Baroque music also needs a little explanation. Just as melodies need contrast of one kind or another, so the harmony must have contrast. This contrast is achieved by dissonance and consonance in proper relation to each other. Dissonance sets up tension, while consonance affords release or repose. In the Passacaglia, Bach has just the right amount of both. Even the melody itself suggests some dissonance in the large skips. As Bach develops the melody in the polyphonic style, he also varies the harmonic structure and, consequently, the relation between consonance and dissonance.

This music creates a chamber of sound by the very massiveness of the tonal fabric. An infinite sense of space (musically) is created by this mass of sound as it rises and falls in degrees, only to reach a powerful climax. The listener is led on by the flowing lines of melody and the lines of the combination of sounds.

Bach

It would be difficult to propose a spot more fitting for the birthplace of Bach (1685–1750) than Eisenach. Romance, religion, and music had all put their special stamp upon this town in the heart of Germany. Just outside of the town was the stately Wartburg Castle. Here lived the saintly Elizabeth of the Tannhauser legend, here the famous tourney of song was held, and here the German minstrels and meistersingers sang their many songs. It was in this castle that Luther came to hide from the wrath of the pope and made the first translation of the Bible into German. Here, also, Luther composed many of the old hymn tunes that were to shake the world's religious life as well as provide material for the works of Bach. The most important influence on Bach was the work of Martin Luther, for without the foundations laid down by the Lutheran church it is hardly possible that Bach would have done what he did. He was full of the newness of Protestantism on the one hand, and yet steeped in the tradition of Catholicism on the other—truly a combination that had the possibilities of producing inspired works.

Bach gave his life to composing music for the Church. Most of his great music was written from necessity. Being an organist, he had to supply music for the Sunday services, and in order to have music he had to compose his own. Most of it remained unpublished until long after his death. He had little intercourse with other musicians of his time, being unable to travel and mingle in places where they were to be found. He never realized his own greatness, and it never entered his mind that his music had qualities that were to place it among the most inspired of the world.

Bach's pen was prolific. His music includes cantatas for every Sunday and Church festival of the year, three Passions (music for Holy Week), including the magnificent *Passion According to St. Matthew*, the great *Mass in b Minor*, and many lesser choral works. Among the instrumental works we find "The Well-Tempered Clavier," violin sonatas, choral preludes, orchestral suites, and numerous pieces for piano and organ.

At a very early age, Bach dedicated himself to the task of creating "a regulated Church music in the honor of God." By "regulated" he meant systematized music form and expression. In the spirit of the Baroque, Bach achieved a technical mastery of all available devices and forms of his time and molded them into an expression of a great religious faith. He invented nothing new but organized and codified the art of music in such a way that to this day he is looked upon as the final authority in the craft of musical composition. The subjective relation between music and text makes his technical mastery more of a means to an end than an end in itself. His craftsmanship was always subjected to the meaning of the text, or subject. This is more apparent in the sacred music, where the spiritual meaning was the objective. He utilized every device in melody, harmony, rhythm, and form to achieve this meaning.

An excellent example of Bach's spiritual pathos and dramatic power is found in the Easter cantata *Christ lag in Todesbanden, Christ Lay in the Bonds of Death.* While the structure of this cantata is unique among the more than 200 extant cantatas that Bach wrote, it brilliantly illustrates his most consistent compositional device by which he linked the cantata both to the scripture lesson of the particular Sunday's service and to the musical tradition of the Lutheran congregation. In most cantatas Bach was content to paraphrase a choral tune—whose text was a commentary on the scriptural lesson of the day—in the large-scale opening chorus. In this cantata, *Christ Lay in the Bonds of Death,* for chorus and small orchestra, however, each of the first six choral movements is a paraphrase or variation on the chorale melody, and beyond that each of these movements employs one of the first six verses of the original hymn text. The theme of these variations is found in the setting of the seventh and final verse, where it appears in the simple four-part setting of the chorale or hymn (ex. 8.4).

An orchestral prelude that is also a paraphrase of the chorale tune presents the whole emotional tone in a chromatically drooping figure. The chromatic movement of this idea creates a tension which is itself suggestive of death. In the opening verse there is a decorative but sturdy statement of the chorale tune in the soprano part which is in contrast to the highly complex counterpoint of the other three voices. The succeeding five verses in their variations on the chorale tune vividly describe the texts of the hymn.

Example 8.4 Versus VII

The second verse weaves the melody over a mystic sort of death-stalking *basso ostinato* figure. In the third verse it is the driving and jubilantly decorative line of the unison violins which goes far beyond the words set to the original tune in announcing Christ as the heroic conqueror of Death. A short halt in the driving rhythm at the word "Tod" (death) in the German text only tends to accentuate the complete destruction of death and give contrast to the subsequent jubilation of the final line and the "hallelujah." Verse four depicts the struggle between life and death in which the soprano, tenor, and bass voices in a powerful fugal writing use many of the devices of counterpoint to accompany the alto's presentation of the simple chorale tune. Canon and stretto tend to intensify the struggle and wrestling between the opponents. This is especially true in the setting of the last line of the text: "The one death consumed the other," where the canonic stretto disintegrates to nothing, just as death was consumed and was destroyed. Note also the use of the major chord at the final cadence of this verse. The elimination of death by the power of Christ calls for a "Hallelujah" on a cheerful major chord after the consistent minor tonality.

In verse five the opening death-haunted figure is again heard as the music expresses Christ on the cross in atonement for our sins. The chromatic elements of melody and bass create a sense of harmonic tension which emphasizes the pathetic character of sin and death. Movement suggested by the impelling bass figure along with the melody, creates a special chamber of sound into which the listener enters. The total effect suggests an emotional tone or state that can be translated in terms of the text. Compare this with the emotional state of Bernini's *St. Theresa*. The harmonic chamber of sound becomes comparable to the supernatural atmosphere which Bernini achieved by light and shade. The implied motion of the angel and St. Theresa establishes the same tension as the chromatic motion of melodic line and rhythm.

The completed work presents a moving expression of the sense of sin, atonement, and the joyous hope of salvation by the cross. This was music that not only expressed Bach's own religious faith, but the very essence of Protestantism. This kind of music is the peak of the Baroque spirit in religious music, for it faithfully interprets the true meaning of that spirit in music.

Typical of many of the cantatas of Bach is the work *Sleepers Awake*. While *Christ Lay in the Bonds of Death* was among the earliest of Bach's cantatas and bears the number 4, *Sleepers Awake*, which is numbered 140, was written during his more mature years. It, too, incorporates a chorale tune and text. In this case the text is appropriate to the gospel for the twenty-seventh Sunday after Trinity, which deals with the comparison of the ten virgins (Matthew 25, 1-13). In this setting, however, Bach uses the tune and text of the old chorale in only the first, fourth, and final movements of the cantata. The second and fifth movements are recitatives and the third and sixth are duets in the form of arias in which the musical themes and texts are in no way derived from the chorale. In each instance the recitatives act as introductions to the duets whose solo voices portray the characters of the Church (soprano) and Christ (bass). Both duets are accompanied by solo instruments in a very elaborate style. The first movement is a setting of the first verse of the chorale as a chorale fantasy. The soprano voices sing the chorale in very slow note values. The three other voices and the entire orchestral body accompany this presentation in a very decorative manner. As was usual in the Bach cantatas this opening chorus was the longest and the most imposing part of the cantata. The second chorale verse, movement four of the cantata, consisted of a simple singing of the tune and its text by the tenor voices accompanied by the violins and violas in a melodic idea quite independent of the chorale tune but in beautiful harmony with it. The final verse of the chorale, as was customary in the Bach cantatas, was a hymnlike setting for voices and instruments in which the congregation could participate.

The inclusion of recitatives and the aria-duets with their sensuous mood of love indicate the close connection of church and secular dramatic music of the Baroque period.

In spite of his avowed goal of music for the glory of God, Bach did accept a number of positions where church music was minimized. The influence of his employers is plainly imprinted on his creative works, wherever he worked. When he was organist at Arnstadt most of his music was written for the organ. When he moved to the Court of Weimar as organist and violinist, he conformed to the needs of the duke. It was a Lutheran court which had a strong religious tone; he naturally wrote some church music especially for organ and some short works for voices. It was, however, a court position and there was a demand for entertainment music—music with a virtuoso display and music for dancing. His violin sonatas, chamber orchestra concertos, and clavichord (early piano) music filled these needs.

The fugue is perhaps the most intellectual and most technical form in all music. In keeping with the Baroque mood of systematizing, this form reached its perfection in the hands of Bach. Bach's greatness lay in the fact that he could be subjected to a strict discipline of writing and still achieve lasting musical effects. His fugues gain intensity as they move along and reach a high point of cumulative power at the end.

When Bach went to the court at Anhalt-Cöthen, he found a Calvinist establishment that did not have a chapel or an organ. Because the Calvinists permitted very little music in their churches, there was no opportunity for sacred music. Bach then turned his attention to the clavichord, orchestra, and secular music for voices. Because part of his duties were pedagogic in nature, he wrote a number of pieces for teaching purposes, notably the *Inventions* and *Clavier Exercises.* When he finally was granted the position at the Church of St. Thomas in Leipzig, his whole output was sacred music because that was all that was demanded of him. This is, without doubt, his greatest creative period, because he was a mature composer by this time and because he was finally doing the kind of work to which he had dedicated his life many years before.

The remarkable thing about his music is that even in secular works, there is a sense of spiritual strength and joy. His own piety permeates everything he did. He gathered together, as it were, the varying and conflicting threads—Protestant, Catholic, and secular—and wove them into a complete musical expression full of the pathos and joy in the spiritual life.

Handel

George Frederick Handel was a contemporary of Bach, having been born in the same year, 1685, in Halle, Saxony. Handel had to overcome the opposition of his parents to a musical career. He learned to play the violin, piano, and organ at an early age and studied law to satisfy his father's wishes. He studied music and law at the same time, but after the death of his father he gave up law and went to Italy to study music. Here he learned to write opera in the Italian style and, after three years, went to England, where financial success beckoned to him because of the popularity of Italian opera. He became an English subject and lived in England until his death in 1759.

While we know Handel as a composer of choral music, he wrote operas until he was fifty. He had made a large fortune, and had decided to become an opera director. It was his failure at this time that caused him to turn to writing oratorios. He admitted he had always wanted to write in this form but financial gain had kept him composing opera. In the dozen years before his death, he composed about nineteen oratorios, the *Messiah* being the greatest of all. The *Messiah* is one of the most popular of all oratorios. It was written in 1741 in the space of twenty-four days. Its appeal to both singer and audience has made it the favorite with choral organizations, and it has probably been sung more often than any other choral work.

The style of music in the *Messiah* is a combination of German polyphony and the Italian opera tradition. The choruses are usually in the polyphonic style. It is in the recitatives and arias that the full forces of the Italian opera show their influence. While Handel's melodies certainly are singable, they have a strong tendency toward being instrumental in character. His harmonic structure is blocklike and simple, giving a feeling of great majesty but without the intense pathos of Bach.

The recitative *Comfort Ye My People* and the following air *Every Valley* are fine examples of the Baroque dramatic element as it was applied to the oratorio. The recitative is accompanied by a series of chords, giving the singer freedom for declamation in a personal manner. The air *Every Valley* is built upon a short lilting melody that is repeated and extended by a variety of quick-running passages and ornamentations. It is in the form of the operatic aria, with a contrasting middle section and repetition of the first melody. Handel does not repeat exactly but makes a few changes for interest and textual demands. The total effect is of great musical lyricism but combined with vivid realism of the text. The bass aria *Why Do the Nations* has been often quoted as a typical example of the florid, agitated "rage" aria of Baroque opera. Handel often achieves an objective realism by suggesting the verbalism of the text in the music. *The People Who Walked in Darkness* shows this realism. A bass voice with the lower strings on a wandering chromatic figure which imitates the visual impression of mystery and darkness serves to make this aria undeniably realistic.

His knowledge of voices enabled him to place the various vocal parts for the maximum effect at all times. The polyphonic chorus *For unto Us a Son Is Born* with its climactic sonority on the words, *Wonderful, Counselor, the mighty God, the Prince of Peace*, can certainly be classed with those few great choruses of all time. In the *Hallelujah Chorus,* one of the most exuberant choruses in all music, Handel has caught the simple majesty of the text by clear-cut melodic motives stated in vigorous rhythmic patterns. In his development of this material he never loses sight of this majesty. No wonder that when the *Messiah* was first performed in London, King George II rose from his seat when he heard this imposing chorus, thus establishing a custom which has become traditional whenever it is sung.

It is interesting to note that while Bach and Handel were contemporaries, they represented two entirely different personalities. Both were considered among the greatest organists of their day; they both composed in the conventional style of their time, and they both produced lasting choral music. Bach admired Handel a great deal. He knew Handel's music and was anxious to know him personally. Handel, on the other hand, never had any desire to know Bach and probably knew very little of his music. The two men never met. Bach had no wish for fame and fortune. Handel wanted fame and luxury, and it was only after fate had made him poor that he found his true artistic expression.

Handel's music is always on a monumental scale. Having spent his apprenticeship in the school of Italian opera, he thought in elaborate and spectacular terms. His melodies are always broad, full of energy, and seldom obscured by technical devices. He often used the same melody many different times in different compositions, gaining variety and interest in the manner of treatment rather than in the originality of the material. He did not have the personal touch that marks the music of Bach. As a Baroque composer, Handel was indebted to the expressive content of music, but in a different way from Bach. Handel's expressiveness is in terms of broad, general emotions. Bach is more subtle, personal, and intensive. The appeal of Handel to the present listening generation is the appeal of realism, of a programmatic presentation. There are fewer demands on the intellect than in the music of Bach.

Both of these men represent the Baroque spirit in art. If they seem to contradict, such contradiction is a part of that spirit. The horizons of art were being widened, and both Bach, the idealist, and Handel, the realist, are universal in their appeal.

Summary

The Baroque was an age of systematic action in all areas of activity, intellectual, spiritual, technological, and artistic. It saw the beginning of the scientific method of inquiry that laid the foundations for our modern scientific age. All intellectual pursuits were concerned with the achievement of orderly systems, especially in mathematics, philosophy, and economics. There was also a wave of religious activity, and in both Catholicism and Protestantism sects arose that imposed strict rules of thought and conduct as an important part of the search for salvation.

The center of wealth had gradually shifted from southern Europe to northern Europe where foreign trade and shipping flourished. The extensive program of colonization, especially in the Americas and the East Indies, helped to build a middle class of wealthy capitalistic merchants who often became enthusiastic patrons of the arts. This rise of a wealthy middle class brought about a desire for magnificence, even to a point of vulgarity in ornamentation and decoration. This characteristic of overabundance of outward display of material wealth was partly responsible for the rejection of recognition of the true value of the Baroque until fairly recent times.

While the Church, especially Catholicism, still patronized the arts, it was more in the sense of a personalized religious experience than as an institution in the manner of the Gothic and Renaissance. The middle class became more and more of a patron, and everyday activities became suitable subjects with which the artist could appeal to the uncultivated emotions of the nonaristocrat and the common man as well. Music also reached out for a wider audience. Both sacred and secular music spoke with expressive singable melodies that could appeal to the average person.

Baroque painting can be characterized as full of vitality, movement, emotion, and often mysticism. Lines are usually made up of short curves with lost edges, showing vigor and merging of one figure with another. Colors are often monochromatic with varying hues, values, and intensities and the domination of one basic color. Space is expanding with unlimited recession and evidences of action extending beyond the visual limits of the canvas, vertically, horizontally, and in projection. Form is usually open without classic balance and symmetry. Moreover, expression and a show of emotion is achieved by the combination of color, diffused line, and space together with the emotional behavior of the figures. Baroque painters systematically explored the effect of light and shade on color, line, and space. The aim was to make the experience represent reality to the observer, to bring the observer into the canvas to partake of the action whether it be a religious scene, a landscape, or the everyday experience of ordinary people.

Baroque sculpture revealed the same action, expressiveness, and personalized feeling as painting. In comparison with the Renaissance, Baroque sculpture shows more strong emotion, more spatial quality, and more sense of movement in stone and metal. Deeply carved and flowing robes with elaborate decoration also enhanced the impression of movement. Sculptors did not hesitate to include sculptured backgrounds to make the illusion of space more real and to bring the observer into the scene.

It is in Baroque architecture that the desire for magnificence and dramatic spectacle shows itself in its most flamboyant form. While it remained classic in its basic forms, architects achieved vigor and motion by elaborate decoration of this basic design. Undulating facades, scrolls, twisting columns, and other ornamental decorations give a feeling of motion and light and shadow to an otherwise classic facade. Interiors are often complex variations on the curve of a round arch that leads the spectator from one point to another. They are also often filled with ornate ceiling paintings that give the illusion of being open to the very heavens.

Some of the more dramatic changes in Baroque art took place in music. While Baroque painting, sculpture, and architecture are in a sense dated in our time, Baroque music is almost timeless and even today remains as a foundation for much of our musical experiences. There were two main lines of development in Baroque music. One was the development of vocal dramatic music, both secular and sacred, that led to the cantata and the oratorio, as well as the opera. Opera, of course, has developed through the years into the musical theater of today. The other important development was that of pure instrumental music that was devoid of any verbal text. Emancipating instrumental from vocal music made it necessary to develop forms that were based solely on melodic and harmonic considerations. Composers systematically organized tonal material into such forms as the sonata, concerto, suite, fugue, and other polyphonic forms.

The Baroque also saw the technical development of most musical instruments. In fact the stringed instruments, violin, viola, and cello, reached such a high state of tonal perfection they still have not been surpassed. Keyboard instruments like the organ and harpsichord also reached a high state of excellence.

The homophonic texture in music became equal in importance to the polyphonic texture. In opera, oratorio, and cantata, the recitative and aria were homophonic, while choruses were more polyphonic in nature. In instrumental music, such forms as the fugue were totally polyphonic. Other instrumental forms like the sonata and concerto grosso often alternated homophonic and polyphonic textures. The development of tonal harmony was also a Baroque accomplishment. This gave rise to a number of new devices for handling tonal materials. The system of chordal relationships around a well-defined tonal center emphasized the importance of dissonant harmony that created tension and its release by consonant harmony. While Baroque music systematically developed the tonal resources of music, its expressive content was aimed at the emotional experience of the listener. Composers with their technical mastery of chromatic harmony and musically dramatic situations tried to lead the listener out and beyond the limits of ordinary existence and to open new aesthetic experiences through the emotions. An analogy can be drawn between the texture of tonal harmony and perspective in painting. The feeling of tension that comes from the dissonance and consonance of tonal harmony and the feeling of expanding space that comes from the effect of light and shade of Baroque painting can suggest such an analogy. The result of the many new musical developments during the Baroque brought an immense body of musical literature from such masters as Bach, Handel, Vivaldi, and Scarlatti, masters who became the inspiration for composers into our own time and even for the composers of twentieth-century popular music.

Musical examples

Monteverdi, *Orfeo*

Gabrieli, Giovanni, *Symphoniae sacrae*

Scarlatti, D., Sonata in c minor

Froberger, Suite in E Minor

Corelli, Concerto no. 7 *(Christmas Concerto)*

Vivaldi, *The Seasons*

Bach, *Fugue in d sharp minor, Passacaglia and Fugue in c minor, Christ Lay in the Bonds of Death, Sleepers Awake*

Handel, *Messiah*

Suggested readings

Bukofzer, Manfred F. *Music in the Baroque Era.* New York: W. W. Norton, 1947, pp. 1–18.

Grout, D. J. *A History of Western Music,* 3rd ed. New York: W. W. Norton, 1980, pp. 293–447.

Janson, H. W. *History of Art.* Englewood Cliffs, N.J.: Prentice-Hall, Inc., 1962, pp. 374–443.

Leichtentritt, Hugo. *Music, History and Ideas.* Cambridge, Mass.: Harvard University Press, 1940, pp. 113–33.

Upjohn, Wingert and Mahler. *History of World Art.* New York: Oxford University Press, 1949, pp. 241–78.

Wold and Cykler. *An Outline History of Music,* 5th ed. Dubuque, Ia.: Wm. C. Brown Company Publishers, 1982, pp. 99–150.

Suggested examples for further analysis

Painting: El Greco, *Descent from the Cross*; Hals, *The Drunkard*; Rubens, *Suzanne Fourmont*; Rembrandt, *Descent from the Cross* (etching)

Sculpture: Bernini, *Apollo and Daphne; Tomb of Alexander VII*

Architecture: San Carlo alle Quartro Fontane, Rome

Music: Bach, *Brandenburg Concerti*; Handel, Concerti Grossi; Corelli, Concerti Grossi; Scarlatti, Domenico, Sonatas for Harpsichord; Schütz, *Seven Last Words*

Film strips with sound

Baroque Music and Art. Educational Audio Visual Inc.

Additional sources for visual illustrations

Bronstein, Leo. *El Greco.* New York: Abrams, 1950.

Münz, Ludwig, and Hack, B. *Rembrandt.* New York: Abrams, 1966.

Sérullaz, Maurice. *Velazquez.* New York: Abrams, 1978.

9

Rococo and Classic
(1725-1800)

Chronology of the Rococo and Classic

1684	Antoine Watteau (1684–1721)	1748	Jacques Louis David (1748–1825)
1694	François Voltaire (1694–1778)	1749	Johann Wolfgang Goethe (1749–1832)
1696	Giovanni Tiepolo (1696–1770)	1751	Benjamin Franklin experiments with electricity
1703	François Boucher (1703–1770)		
1710	Louis XV (1710–1774)	1755	Marie Antoinette, Queen of France (1755–1793)
1712	Jean Jacques Rousseau (1712–1780)	1756	Wolfgang Amadeus Mozart (1756–1791)
1714	Willibald von Gluck (1714–1787)	1757	Antonio Canova (1757–1822)
1716	Etienne Maurice Falconet (1716–1791)	1760	George III of England reigned until 1820
1717	Maria Theresa Empress of Austria (1717–1780)	1769	Watt's steam engine patented
1723	Sir Joshua Reynolds (1723–1792)		Napoleon Bonaparte (1769–1821)
1724	Immanuel Kant (1724–1804)	1770	Ludwig van Beethoven (1770–1827)
1726	Charles Burney (1726–1814)		First New York performance of *Messiah*
1732	Jean Honore Fragonard (1732–1806)	1771	First Edition of the Encyclopedia Britannica
	Franz Josef Haydn (1732–1809)		

1774	Discovery of oxygen	1792	White House built
1776	American declaration of independence	1793	Louis XVI of France beheaded
	Burney's *History of Music* published	1794	Haydn's second trip to London
	Discovery of hydrogen	1795	Paris Conservatory founded
1788	Steamboat invented		
1789	Beginning of the French revolution	1799	Beethoven's First Symphony finished

Study Objectives

The objectives of this chapter are

1. To study the Rococo as an artistic style with delicate elegance, refinement, and sentiment, in contrast to the vigor of the Baroque.
2. To learn about the sonata as a classic form becoming the ideal abstract musical expression.

Pronunciation Guide

Amalienburg (Ah-mah′-lee-en-burg)
Antoinette (A-twoh-net)
Beaumarchais (Boh-mahr-shay)
Borghese (Bohr-gay′-ze)
Canova (Kah-noh′-vah)
Charpentier (Shahr-pen-tee-yay)
Cherubino (Kay-roo-bee′-noh)
Cosi Fan Tutte (Kos′-see Fan Too′-te)
Couperin, François (Koo-per-ă, Fran-swah)

Cythera (Si′-the-rah)
David, Jacques (Dah-veed, Zhahk)
Diderot (Dee-de-roh)
Falconet (Fall-koh-nay)
Fragonard (Frah-goh-nahr)
Mannheim (Mahn′-hihm)
Mezzetin (Me-za-tă)
Nymphenburg (Nim′-fen-burg)
Pompadour (Pohm-pah-door)
Val-d'Ogne (Vahl dohn-ye)
Versailles (Vayr-sih-ye)
Watteau (Wah-toh)

As the Baroque ran its course, there came a gradual revolution in all phases of life. The seventeenth-century urge for systematizing was carried to its ultimate. Reason was thought to be the key that would unlock the doors of utopias in every field, from politics to art. This philosophy was so commonly held that the eighteenth century has often been called the Age of Reason. Indeed, it was a century of order and symmetry. Everything was codified and formalized through the intellect; economics, science, religion, politics, art, even manners were affected. Diderot's *Encyclopedia* was a compendium of eighteenth-century logic that reduced all areas of human endeavor to mathematical exactness. It was a supreme symbol of the era.

Common people were also beginning to take their rightful place in society, and, by the latter decades of the century, freedom became the real object of reason. There was an urge for intellectual, political, economic, spiritual, and artistic freedom. This struggle for liberty reached its catastrophic climax in the French Revolution near the end of the century. The real artistic fruits of this struggle, however, are to be found in the Romantic movement, which will be studied in a later chapter.

Rococo

In the meantime, there was a style of painting, sculpture, and decoration called "Rococo" which flourished in the wealthy, despotic society whose greed and avarice was the object of the forthcoming revolution. The term *rococo* was probably derived from the delicate scroll of the seashell which was a conspicuous motif in ornamentation. It was especially the product of the courts of Louis XIV and Louis XV, but traces of it are also found in Italian and German aristocratic circles which imitated the French manner. The Rococo style dominated during the period from about 1725 to 1775. With emphasis on pleasantness and prettiness, it forms a marked contrast to the grandeur of the Baroque. It mirrored the beauty of life among the upper classes before the Revolution and the rise of democracy. Note that the Baroque and Rococo overlap in time. While the Baroque spirit was still strong in Germany until near the middle of the century, the Rococo had already come of age in France.

One of the dominant characteristics of the Baroque had been the intellectual activity, the demand for a systematizing of everything—economics, government, religion, art, and social intercourse. All this was most welcome and had a great many beneficial effects during the seventeenth and early eighteenth centuries. As you will remember, there was a tremendous vitality, a healthy activity, in almost every field of human endeavor. However, as is the case with almost any set of rules, in time they tend to become absolute, and instead of being a means to a better society and to progress for which they were first conceived, they often became millstones around the necks of more progressive thinkers.

It is easy to see how the seventeenth and eighteenth centuries flow into each other without any very definite line of demarcation, just as their two styles of art flow into each other without any great revolution in styles. The intellectual life of the eighteenth century produced a great many scholars, who as such were often more concerned with forms and niceties of expression than with the content of their works. The economic life had produced a very wealthy middle class which took on the attitudes of culture without ever discovering its real meaning. The absolutism of rulers was possible with the fruits of the mercantile system. Wealth was finally concentrated in a small group of people, with no provision or thought given to the welfare of the average person. The spiritual fires of both Protestantism and Catholicism had burned low by the middle of the century. The systematic advance in science, political absolutism, and economics had all but turned the hearts of the upper classes away from spiritual values. As can be readily seen, there was a marked change in emphasis between the healthy, vigorous seventeenth century and the decadent court society of the later eighteenth century.

This change in emphasis is nowhere so clearly evident as in the French court of Louis XV. At the royal residence in Versailles there were gathered the most elegant and, perhaps, the most mediocre people of France. Here the aristocracy lived in great leisure and in great luxury on wealth squeezed out of the common people by unscrupulous tax collectors. Rococo art was naturally colored by the patronage of this society, taking on the light and frivolous character of the court. Artists acceded to the amorous and playful whims of their clients. Painters, sculptors, and decorators created charming and sentimental works designed to flatter and please. The delicacy and fragility of their art was a mirror of the facade of aristocratic life, as artificial as its art.

Life itself came to be an art. Society and manners were reduced to a formula, with elegance, grace, refinement, and love as motivating forces. Here we have the Baroque carried to an extreme. The worship of wealth, pleasure, and power superseded the worship of God. The Baroque art of expression and spiritual values was cast out, for this society was interested in gossiping, conversing, dancing, and flirting. It preferred the tête-à-tête to large receptions; it preferred music for dancing to music for church; it preferred paintings of sentimental love to paintings depicting the reality of human experience. The secret of Rococo aristocratic culture lay in this mediocre manner of living that was open to everyone with wealth and was devoid of great passion and noble pleasures.

Painting

There were a few painters who were influenced by the spirit of their time whose works show more vitality and real expression than we would normally expect from such a decadent society. Watteau and Fragonard, both painters of the French Rococo, reveal a great debt to Rembrandt and Rubens in their styles. Boucher, who was a favorite at Versailles, painted in a delicately superficial manner that breathes the very air of aristocratic eroticism. The art of these painters was the feminine counterpart of the Baroque. Emotion gave way to sentimentalism and love to flirtation. Art had to meet the demands of a society that was articifial, with insistence upon luxurious display and elegance, no matter what the cost in money or morals. It is a wonder that a period of such mediocrity could produce art that had as much strength and vitality as it had.

Now that the functions of Rococo art have been suggested, what technique did the artists use to achieve those effects of grace and refinement? After the lessons of the Baroque in the use of light, shade, and expanding space, we would not expect any radical changes. The methods and organizations of the Rococo remain about the same but with less vigor and on a smaller scale. Spatial awareness is usually less strong. Lines are not quite so diffused, and there is a tendency to break the masses up into smaller fragments with shorter, more animated curves and more ornate detail. Formal organization is still multiple and color remains basically monochromatic, as it was in the seventeenth century. Formal organization is also less open than the Baroque, denoting less action as well as less space. As we examine the works of Rococo artists, we will find it more difficult to distinguish them from the Baroque on purely technical grounds. It is a matter of the degree of emphasis, coupled with subject matter and general attitude, that makes the style Rococo.

Watteau is perhaps the most important painter to mirror the fastidious life of the Rococo, for in his works the courtly customs and morals take on a grandeur of sentiment that transcends the actual conditions of the Rococo. Watteau lived from 1684 until 1721 and represented the period of change from the Baroque to the Rococo. He was still imbued with the vitality of the Baroque but, at the same time, he was meeting the artificial demands of the French court. His *Embarkation for Cythera* (fig. 9.1) is not only one of his best-known works but is highly representative of the era. The mythological subject tells the story of the successive courtly steps involved in convincing a lady to join the festivities and set sail for the mythical island of love. It was a kind of sentimental and amorous myth that court society loved to act out.

You will note that the basic concepts of the Baroque still hold in this work but differ in degree of emphasis. The lines are still diffused and edges are still lost in the mass of color, but there is a partial return of the clearly molded lines, as in the treatment of trees and the outlines of the figures. Formal organization is still multiple, though on a smaller scale. Mass melts into mass, but the fragments do not encompass as great an area as in the Baroque. This is due in part to the slight emphasis on clear-cut lines. The treatment of light and shade, so strong in the works of Rembrandt, has been thinned greatly. The light seems more evenly distributed, giving an almost pastel quality to the color. Tension of movement seems to be lost; open form is less direct and more static. Action is toned down; it is more delicate and restrained. There is little strong expressive appeal in this work. It speaks gently and softly, murmuring amorous sentiments in depicting the curious morals of the age.

Le Mezzetin (colorplate 24) is another of Watteau's delicate canvases that portrays the Rococo spirit. The subject is an actor singing a sentimental song of pathos, but one is more impressed by the effeminate costume than by the pathos. Here, also, the colors are a pastel quality of monochromaticism. Line

Colorplate 24 follows p. 210.

Figure 9.1 *Embarkation for Cythera* [1717]—Watteau. (Courtesy Editorial Photocolor Archives)

is broken up into fragments, and space seems carefully controlled. The gay costume belies the obvious heartbreak of the song in true Rococo style.

While Boucher (1703–1770) painted a great many miniature scenes of questionable taste for the King, his portrait *Madame de Pompadour* (fig. 9.2) is a happy combination of his consummate skill as a painter and the Rococo spirit of elegance. Boucher was the favorite artist of this woman of intrigue and power in French aristocratic circles. It is said that he was her constant advisor in matters of interior decoration, in selection of costumes, and in all matters pertaining to the purchase and commissioning of works of art. In this particular portrait of Madame de Pompadour—he painted many—he has captured the spirit of aristocracy in every detail. Her posture, her elegance of dress suggest her exalted position, even though she was not of noble birth. He has even given her an aura of intellectuality by including an open book in her hand. Through a skillful use of light and shade, he has painted the "feel" of the silken gown and has suggested a fragility to the lace and flowers that is very realistic. The Baroque technique is still present, as in Watteau, only on a miniature scale, without as much feeling or sentiment.

Sculpture

Rococo sculpture merits but a brief mention. The same general spirit prevails that is found in painting. Gardens were generously supplied with marble cupids coyly chaperoning amorous couples in their game of love. Even painters included such statues in their paintings, as in Watteau's *Embarkation for*

Figure 9.2 *Madame de Pompadour* [1758]—Boucher. (Courtesy Editorial Photocolor Archives)

Cythera. Falconet (1716–1791) was one of those artists who applied his whimsical and light touch to the Rococo scene. The *Punishment of Cupid* (fig. 9.3) shows the spirit of frivolity and superficiality that prevailed. There is no expression and no firm modeling of form. The statue served only as a reminder of a playful and insecure attitude toward love.

Architecture

The decorative aspect of the Rococo style is most obvious in interior decoration used in palaces and salons. The salon of Marie Antoinette (fig. 9.4) gives us a striking example of the use of delicately curved motifs in interior design. A floral wreath pattern is used on the carved wall paneling and on the ceiling. This same pattern is used again in the upholstery fabric of the chairs and divan. Another typical decorative item is the chandelier with its crystal prisms that sparkled like so many diamonds in the sunlight. Note also the huge mirror that, because of its height, could reflect the beauty and fashion of everyone in the room. This is a spacious and elegant setting for the charming conversation of a very elite segment of court society.

Rococo and Classic (1725–1800)   201

Figure 9.3 *Punishment of Cupid* [c. 1755]—Falconet. (Courtesy University Prints)

The salon of the Amalienburg Palace at Nymphenburg (fig. 9.5) is another example of the Rococo style that is lavish in the use of mirrors and delicate carvings that cover every bit of wall space and extend to the furnishings. This same filigreelike decoration can be found in almost every eighteenth-century palace, especially in France, Germany, and Austria.

Music

The musical counterpart of Watteau and Boucher is found in the delicately ornamented keyboard pieces of François Couperin (1668–1733). Here was a personal, intimate music in miniature. It avoided passion; it avoided the grand manner; it was fragile in texture and luminous in color, like the canvases of Watteau and Boucher. *La Galante*, with its exquisite style, its playful ornaments, and restrained manner, is a fine musical symbol of the Rococo. *The Bells of Cythera* is another fine example of the Rococo style.

Neoclassicism

There was another movement which, while it was a part of the Rococo, was also in opposition to it. This was Neoclassicism (new classicism)—a return to the Classic ideals of the ancients. The French Academy had been founded in the seventeenth century to serve as a guardian and purifier of French intellectual life. So far as the arts are concerned, the Academy controlled art,

Figure 9.4   Salon of Marie Antoinette [1762–1764]—Versailles.
(Courtesy Keystone View Company)

education, and exhibitions, and set the "official" standards of taste and style. In the latter part of the century, in protest against the superficial elegance of the Rococo, the Academy sponsored a return to Classic ideals. The movement gained real headway about the time of the Revolution when public opinion joined in the denunciation of almost anything that represented the court.

Neoclassicism sought to express Classic ideals by the use of models from Greece, Rome, and the Italian Renaissance. These models served a dual purpose. They reminded the observer of the need for patriotism and stiff morality in the struggle for liberty. They also served to make the modeling of forms more realistic and stripped art of its femininity. The calm, emotionless art of Greece and Rome became a symbol of a detachment from superficial feeling that was to be coveted during the deluge of blood that was to follow.

Figure 9.5   Interior Amalienburg Lodge [1734–1739]—Cuvillies-Nymphenburg-Munich. (Courtesy Marburg-Art Reference Bureau)

Painting

Jacques David (1748–1825) was the leader of this Neoclassic movement of the revolutionary period. After a visit to Greece and Rome, he returned full of enthusiasm for the glories of the ancient world. His first great success was the *Oath of the Horatii* (fig. 9.6), painted four years before the Revolution. Its subject is that of a Roman father pledging his three sons to fight against the enemies of Rome. Thus Roman virtue and readiness to die for liberty became the subject of Neoclassic French painting almost on the eve of the Revolution. Note the return to Renaissance classicism in the style and forms of the painting. The lines are shaply defined—severe and angular—denoting strength. Formal organization is not quite separate, but separate groups make up the whole—the three sons to the left, the father and the weeping women to the right. The focal point, the swords, is exactly in the center. Each group is framed against the background of a Roman arch set on Greek columns. For all its heroism, there is little expressive feeling in this canvas. Its subject is from a bygone age; its style is formal, intellectual, and unreal. Many of David's paintings emphasized the idea of dedication to freedom and the glory of the sacrifice necessary to attain it.

Figure 9.6 *Oath of the Horatii* [1785]—David. (Courtesy Editorial Photocolor Archives)

David occasionally produced a portrait such as *Mlle. Charlotte du Val d'Ognes* (fig. 9.7).[1] Compare this with Boucher's *Madame de Pompadour* (fig. 9.2) and the change from the Rococo will be obvious. This is realistic in its details, even to the broken pane in the window. The form is modeled firmly and clearly against the darkened background. The lines are sharply drawn to emphasize the severity of the figure, in contrast to the fragile quality of Boucher's portrait.

Sculpture

Neoclassic sculpture followed the lead of painting in its debt to the ancients. Canova (1757–1822) employed his technical facility in the task of making his patroness appear as the Greek goddess of love in *Pauline Borghese as Venus* (fig. 9.8). While the lines and plastic forms are classic in character, there is something missing. This is only the outward appearance of classic form for it does not portray the Greek ideal of beauty, but a woman of the world.

1. There is a question raised by recent scholarship whether this is by David or by Constance Marie Charpentier. In either case, it is still in the Neoclassic style.

Figure 9.7 *Mlle. Charlotte du Val d'Ognes* [1785]—Charpentier, formerly attributed to David. (Courtesy Metropolitan Museum of Art. The Mr. and Mrs. Isaac D. Fletcher Collection, Bequest of Isaac D. Fletcher, 1917)

Classicism in music

The art of music never succumbed so completely to the Rococo spirit that it could be thought of as a dominant influence. Rather, the Rococo ideal colored both the dying Baroque and the new Classicism in music in much the same way as the court practices of the Louises of France colored the social and artistic customs of every petty and great court in Europe during the eighteenth century. The great and lasting music of the classic period was a product of Germany, not France, and stresses perfection of form rather than the superficial lightness of the Rococo, though this was often present and recognizable. The French monarchy was an absolute one and extreme in its disregard for the average man. In Germany, we find an enlightened absolutism. This new absolutism was very active in all fields of cultural activity, and its patronage

Figure 9.8 *Pauline Borghese as Venus* [1808]—Canova. (Courtesy Editorial Photocolor Archives)

promoted artistic progress. Never was music more widely cultivated. This enlightened absolutism could boast as part of its enormous musical productivity the works of Mozart and Haydn. Both depended, either directly or indirectly, on the patronage of a court or aristocratic society which possessed a considerable degree of discriminating cultural, as well as musical, taste. In the works of these masters, one detects within the clarity and perfection of classic form the fantasy of the Rococo and the seriousness of the impending new Romanticism.

The Classic era, in its revolt against the multistylistic expression of the Baroque, depended on the wedding of lyricism and formal perfection to accomplish its success. The Baroque was the first period in western European music history which lacked a unity of style in all forms. In opera, the new music of the early Baroque had degenerated by the eighteenth century into an extravagant and shallow show for aristocratic society. Music in the Roman church was largely an imitation of Renaissance ideals.

In the seventeenth-century Lutheran church, music had become highly intellectualized through the use of a complex polyphonic style. Popular acceptance of this intellectualized Baroque style was not to be forthcoming for another one hundred years. Baroque instrumental music was still dependent to a major degree on vocal and dance models.

The lyric quality, whereby music reaches the understanding of the widest audience, was essentially lacking in the music of the Baroque. The folklike simplicity of the melodic invention of Haydn and Mozart supplied the lyricism which, when coupled with the formal perfection of their works, gave us a literature of the world's most beautiful music.

Composers after Bach found the complicated contrapuntal textures of music too involved to express the refinement of the social scene in which they moved and worked. As a result, they resorted to the use of clearly defined and expressive melodic material which could be readily grasped by the cultured aristocratic society which was their patron. This lyricism lent a new and fresh appeal to their art.

Composers of musical Classicism (eighteenth century) were more fortunate than the painters and decorators of the Neoclassic period in that they did not have models for the Classic ideal which they wanted to express. In music, Classicism was purely an ideal form, not a reworking of a Classic model as it so often was in the plastic arts. However, the operatic and instrumental forms of the Italian Baroque were influential in the development of classic forms. The Classicist used lyric and expressive melody, inventing a musical form predicated on the idea of one melody being contrasted with a second. The harmonic and rhythmic accompaniment was always in subordination to these melodic lines.

The most striking result was the instrumental form of music called the sonata. In this form, western European composers were able for the first time to embody their ideals of formal structure in an abstract instrumental form of large proportions. While the sonata is built upon ideas which come from music's long association with ritual, literature, and the dance, it is in the sonata form that music stands completely free from these associations. The sonata as a form of musical expression must stand or fall on the merits of the handling of abstract ideas in an abstract medium of instrumental music.

The sonata of the Classic period is an extended composition in three or four separate movements written for a single instrument, such as the piano, or for a combination of instruments. In some cases, the sonata has taken on the specific name of the group for which it has been written. For example, a sonata written for four stringed instruments (two violins, viola, and cello) is called a string quartet; a sonata written for an orchestra is called a symphony; a sonata written for a solo instrument and orchestra is called a concerto, etc. The composer of the sonata lends unity and variety to the several movements of the work by various means. Variety is achieved by contrasting tempos. The first movement is usually in a fast tempo; the second, slow; the third, stately to lively; the fourth, very fast. Harmonically, there is emphasis on unity, with the first, third, and fourth movements being in the same key and the second in a closely related key. Another means of achieving variety is in the selection of formal organization for each of the movements. With few exceptions, the first movement is in what is known as sonata-allegro form. The second movement is often in song or variation form. The third movement, the last to have been included in the sonata and the one often omitted, is a minuet. The fourth movement is most often a rondo or sonata-allegro form.

Of all these forms, the sonata-allegro is by far the most representative of the striving for the Classic ideal in music and represents most clearly the inventive genius of the Classic period. The fundamental structural idea of the sonata-allegro form is the presentation of two contrasting musical ideas, called the statement or exposition, their development, and the final reconciliation in a restatement, often called the recapitulation. The statement or A section is constructed of two contrasting key sections, each of which contains at least one melodic theme. In the classic sonata-allegro movements, these themes were generally contrasting in melodic outline and affective style, a more vigorous theme being presented first in the tonic key section and a more lyrical theme in the contrasting key section. The B section is called the development. Here, the themes are broken up into smaller bits and are subjected to various inventive musical techniques according to the ability of the composer. In the third section, A, the themes are repeated in the manner of the exposition, except that here the key difference is reconciled. This section, then, and with it the movement, is brought to a close in the original key.

The following is the plan of the Classic sonata-allegro form:

| Statement or Exposition | ‖:Th. I. (maj.) trans. Th. II. Dom. trans. Cl. Th.:‖ |
| | ‖:Th. I. (min.) trans. Th. II. Rel. trans. Cl. Th.:‖ |

| Development | Varied treatment of material of the exposition in distant keys followed by a cadence. |

Restatement or Recapitulation	Th. I. tonic maj. trans. Th. II. tonic trans. Cl. Th. tonic‖
	Th. II. tonic min. trans. Th. I. tonic maj. trans. Cl. ‖
	Th. tonic

(Th. I is first theme; trans. is transition; Th. II is second theme; Cl. Th. is closing theme. The outline below the line is the pattern when the movement is cast in a minor key.)

The sonata-allegro form gave composers the opportunity to present lyric melodies and tonal harmony so clearly that listeners could not fail to understand them. It also gave them opportunity to develop material so logically that the listeners could not easily forget it.

In much of the music of the Classic period, the Rococo spirit shows up in the manner in which the lyricism is treated. The music is often light, gay, full of rhythmic subtleties and bright melodies. The harmony is free-flowing, without the prolonged dissonant tension of the Baroque. In general, it is not "heavy" and does not pretend to delve into problems of philosophic expression. It is "occasional" music, moving freely, with grace and lightness to fit almost any cultural activity. It appeals to the concertgoer because of two primary attributes—the purity of melodic invention and the varied simplicity of form. This music reflects the well-regulated society of which it was a part. With the coming Romantic movement and its dramatic struggle for freedom, music became strong, violent, and full of personal passion. The Baroque had seen some of this in intense religious movements. The Classic period was a calm between the two great tides during which there was time for a brief bit of reflective thinking in the music of Haydn and Mozart.

While both vocal and instrumental music flourished in the Classic period, instrumental forms commanded the greater interest of important composers and represented the truly classic spirit in a more vivid way. Church music continued the tradition of the Baroque in the liturgical music of the Catholic church and virtually ceased to be of any importance in the service of the Protestant church. Even the secular choral works, such as Haydn's *Creation,* were in effect patterned after Handel but lacking in the virility of their Baroque models. The operas of Gluck and Mozart set a new ideal in this field. Even here, Mozart's consummate skill and inherent dramatic sense enabled him to write masterpieces in a form that differed little, if at all, from the Baroque models. In the Mozartian operas, it is the treatment of the form that sets these works apart from all their contemporaries and makes them the oldest and, perhaps, the most perfect in the repertory of the modern opera house. This treatment is that of classic balance and restraint.

Let us turn first, then, to some examples of the great literature of instrumental music. Because music is an art which moves in time, a great amount of time is needed for a listener to become thoroughly acquainted with a major work. Therefore the number of examples used must be held to a minimum in order to strike some reasonable balance with those of the other arts. Countless excellent examples must be omitted, and whole areas of compositions disregarded.

Haydn

Franz Joseph Haydn (1732–1809) is a fine example of the Classic composer who was in rapport with the social conditions of his time. Born in 1732 in a rural province village of the Austrian Empire, he early turned toward music. With the exception of a few months in which he was tutored by Nicolo

Colorplate 24 *Le Mezzetin* [1718]—Watteau. (Courtesy The Metropolitan Museum of Art, Munsey Fund)

Porpora, a very renowned Italian composer, he was chiefly self-taught, both in performance and in composition. His ability as a violinist and his early chamber music works caught the attention of an Austrian nobelman and, in 1761, he entered the service of Prince Esterhazy where he was to remain for the next twenty-eight years.

While this long period of employment in one household was perhaps not too typical of the fortunes of most performers and composers, Haydn's long life in the service of the aristocracy represents the normal career of the eighteenth-century musician. As one of the household servants, Haydn's work was the composition and direction of music for the court. In line with his duties, Haydn wrote a tremendous amount of music—solo works, chamber music, orchestral music, operas, church music of all sorts. Much of this great wealth of composition has been lost, but an enormous quantity has come down to us today. For example, there are over one hundred known symphonies of Haydn and some eighty-three quartets.

In 1790, Haydn, at the death of Prince Nicholas Esterhazy, was pensioned and relieved of the duties he had so long performed. A commission for the composition of a set of symphonies and their performance in London brought him to England for the first of two visits. While these last symphonies were more pretentious than most of the works written during his years with Esterhazy, they still serve as excellent examples of the mature Classic sonata as written for the orchestra. One of the best-known of the London symphonies is Symphony no. 101 in D Major, popularly known to concert audiences today as the *Clock Symphony*. It is scored for the mature Classic orchestra. Its instrumentation calls for the basic body of stringed instruments divided into four parts analagous to a mixed choir of sopranos, altos, tenors, and basses. The soprano and alto parts are played by the two groups of violins, the tenor part by the violas, and the bass part by the combined cellos and string basses. Depending on the wealth of the orchestral sponsor or patron and upon the physical conditions under which the orchestra was to perform, the strings were augmented so that there would be from four to eight performers in each of the four groups, making a total of approximately twenty-five string players. This group was established as the core of the symphony orchestra and has remained as such to the present time. To this string foundation the composer added wind and percussion instruments as he desired.

The *Clock Symphony* is scored for a full complement of woodwinds—two flutes, two oboes, two clarinets, and two bassoons. With the exception of the clarinets, these woodwinds were to be found regularly in various combinations in all the Classic symphonic works. The clarinets were the latest addition and were used only in a very few of the last Haydn and Mozart works for orchestra. The brass choir is made up of only two horns and two trumpets which are used principally for sustaining harmonies, reinforcing tonal volume, and marking rhythm. The percussion is represented by a pair of tympani which are used to stress rhythm and reinforce loud and full orchestral passages.

It will be noted that in general, even in such a late work as the *Clock Symphony*, Haydn does little in the way of exploiting the varied tonal qualities of the orchestral instruments. There is little dependence on instrumental color for affective expression. Passages where the particular qualities of an instrument or group of instruments are exploited stand out rather obviously, as in the trio of the minuet where flute and bassoon are used against a subdued string tone. All in all, it must be admitted that the Classic orchestra is essentially an organization in which the string section constitutes the aristocracy and the first violins are the ruling family.

The first movement of this symphony is an excellent example of the sonata-allegro form as described. At the beginning of the movement, however, Haydn has added a slow-moving introduction as a device to gain audience attention. This seems to act as a rather pompous foil to the sparkling and lively material out of which he fashions the actual first movement—something like the white wigs and liveried costumes he and all his musicians had to wear to dignify their artistic zest. Not only is this introduction put into a very slow tempo, but it is cast in a minor key, which tends to add to its solemnity or, at least, to add contrast to the first theme of the movement as it enters in the major tonality.

The first theme of the first movement proper (ex. 9.1), introduced by the first violins in very rapid tempo, is of a driving, dancelike character. Its main musical materials are to be found in the first few measures.

Example 9.1

This main theme is a completely lyrical idea which finds expression in the first violins accompanied by the other strings. Immediately, both melodic idea and accompaniment are enriched by the addition of the rest of the orchestra. Haydn then leads this first theme from its original key of D major to the key of A major in which he then exposes the second theme (ex. 9.2),

Example 9.2

which is very closely related, rhythmically as well as melodically, to the first. It also is introduced by the first violins, with only a string accompaniment.

The second theme is shorter and is rushed to a conclusion in the new key of A major by two descending figures in the strings. This comprises the A, or exposition, section of the first movement, which the composer, in the Classic tradition, asks to be repeated. In most modern performances, however, this is not done. Following the repetition, the B section, or development, is heard. If you are now familiar with some of the musical bricks and stones out of which the two principal themes are constructed, you will hear how Haydn treats these in the development section. At first, short motives from the second theme are traded back and forth between first and second violins. Eventually, violas and cellos are called into the action. Then a loud passage for full orchestra follows in which short bits of the musical materials of the first theme are subjected to musical exploitation. The development section ends with a very obvious full orchestral silence after a big climax. The first theme reappears as at the beginning of the A section, followed by the second theme. Both themes are now in their original melodic form, but Haydn avoids monotony by using different instruments and by the standard method of reconciliation of key difference, that is, by recalling the second theme in the same key as the first. A final farewell is sounded by a repetition of the first theme followed by a reiteration of the final chords so as to leave no doubt in establishing the key idea.

The second movement is the traditional slow movement based on a three-part song form with a simple device of statement, contrast, and restatement. Its key is that of G major, closely related to the main key of D. The second movement, with its insistent clocklike rhythm, suggests the name given to the symphony by Haydn's publisher. The lyrical songlike first part of the second movement is again carried by the first violins, aided at times by the oboe and flute. The middle section is marked by an abrupt change of key from G major to G minor and is characterized by less attention to lyrical quality and more to contrapuntal devices in handling short melodic fragments and rhythmic-melodic patterns from one part to another. A gradual transition back to the original key restates the melody of the first section in two repetitions. The first one is an example of the exploiting of tone color in that the first violins sing the theme against the accompaniment of flute, oboe, and bassoon. The second is a full orchestral repetition in which all the violins elaborately vary the opening theme with brilliant figuration in the manner of Rococo ornament.

The third movement, again in D major, is the traditional minuet, which serves as a good example of how a simple dance becomes a Classic form. Balance is neatly achieved by two independent three-part forms welded into a larger three-part form. The minuet and trio are essentially two independent minuets. Both are constructed on the same formal pattern as follows: (1) an A part repeated; (2) a contrasting B part plus the return of the A part, all of which is repeated. At the conclusion of the trio, or second minuet, the first minuet is repeated so that the following total scheme is realized:

A Minuet   (A repeated, B plus A repeated)
B Trio   (A repeated, B plus A repeated)
A Minuet   (A-B-A all without repetition)

The fourth movement, also in D major, is another basic dance form, the rondo. Essentially, the idea of the rondo is contrast and restatement. In this case, the thematic pattern is A-B-A-B-A. In contrast to the sonata-allegro form, the rondo lacks an actual development section, and, strictly speaking, the form is based on the dominance of the principal theme—in this case, A. In this movement, theme A is first presented by the first violins with only string accompaniment. A full orchestral transition follows this statement and leads to theme B in the key of A major. The opening measures of theme B are strikingly like A, but the syncopated form of the melody distinguishes it from A. It is introduced by the first violins and oboe. Another full orchestral transition leads back to A in the original key of D major. A digression to the minor key of D leads to the second appearance of theme B. The return to D major ushers in a return of theme A, this time treated in Baroque fugal fashion, showing that the Classic composer in no way had lost the skill of a past style. In fact, so skillful is Haydn in contrapuntal technique that this short section contains elements of both themes adroitly woven into the texture of the fugue. A full orchestral treatment of the fugal form of A, followed by a simple quiet statement of the original theme A, leads to a climax in the final cadence and brings the symphony to a close.

Here, then, is a musical work of rather large dimensions in which the composer depends entirely on the logic of formal treatment in abstract design for the communication of his aesthetic message. All the Classic ideals of restraint, balance, and formal design as expressed in the idealized art of Greek sculpture and architecture is now expressed in the purely abstract form of western European music. Unlike the architect, painter, and sculptor of the eighteenth century who turned not only to the spirit of the ancient Classic era, but to its subject matter as well, the composer had no models to follow. There were no examples of Classic Greek or Roman music. The composer had to invent the vehicle for the expression of the Classic ideals. The sonata and sonata-allegro form as developed in the symphony, concerto, and chamber music afforded the greatest opportunity for this expression. The abstract realization of Classicism in music became the ideal toward which all the other arts continued to strive during the next two centuries.

Mozart

Mozart (1756–1791) was perhaps the most nearly perfect musical creator in the history of Western music. His first cries of infancy must have had musical significance, for at four years of age he was already showing remarkable signs of musical precocity, and at ten he was composing works which ranked him with the masters of his time. Gifted as a performer both on the violin and the keyboard instruments of his day, he assayed every known field of composition with equal competency and genius. By the time of his death in 1791, at the early age of thirty-five, he had left behind a remarkable wealth of masterpieces. Their utter beauty and timelessness have kept them as alive and fresh during the two hundred years of their existence as they were at the time of their invention.

His works so faithfully embody the Classic ideal of objectivity and balance that it is difficult to realize the personal tragedy that haunted most of Mozart's short life. Here and there we sense a note of deep personal feeling in the works of this master, but the consummate artistry of the creative genius so beguiles us that somehow we are never conscious of the person Mozart, only of his musical spirit. His works make him the personification of immortal youthfulness. Perhaps the most outstanding characteristic of the incomparable genius is that of melodic inventiveness. Whatever musical material Mozart touches finds expression in lyric beauty. His magic makes everything sing, whether instruments or voices.

Mozart, unlike Haydn, was never successful in gaining the kind of a position that would have pleased him most—that of court composer. He had only one regular appointment during his lifetime, which was with the Archbishop of Salzburg, and he resigned that at an early age. This left him at the mercy of a society which was passing through a revolutionary period and had as yet made no provision for those artists who had no aristocratic attachments. Mozart was compelled, therefore, to spread his compositional activities in many directions—from the operatic stage to the chamber music salon, from the church to the ballroom. Perhaps we can be thankful that his great desire for an operatic post was never realized, for it forced him into many activities he might otherwise have passed by.

The Clarinet Quintet in A Major is a good representation of the personal detachment with which Mozart usually wrote. It was written within two years before his death and followed a bitterly disappointing tour of north Germany. He writes despairingly to a friend of the dismal outlook for himself and his family. Yet the work shows little but tranquil beauty in its musical expression. It is typical of the intimate mood of chamber music. The usual string quartet—two violins, viola, and cello—are joined by the clarinet, of which Mozart was especially fond.

The movements show the same general acceptance of the formal structure which marked the Classic style of Haydn. The key of the work is A major, and the first, third, and fourth movements are cast in this key, with the second in D major. The tempos follow the traditional pattern of fast, slow, moderate, and lively to fast.

The formal structure of the individual movements also shows little deviation from contemporary models. The first movement is a clearly defined sonata-allegro form. As an example of Mozart's great wealth of melodic invention, note how rarely he repeats a melodic idea, even a short one, without some very simple change sufficient to add a striking new beauty to the old idea. Listen carefully to the opening bars of the first movement (ex. 9.3), which present the first theme directly. Note the repetition of these same bars immediately after a very brief clarinet entrance. Only a single note of the melody (note marked with *) is changed in the repetition, and the harmonies are slightly altered, but what tremendous change in musical feeling is aroused by this inspiration.

Careful listening to Mozart will reward you with countless revelations in this master's work, and uncover the secret of his lasting quality.

The second movement is a simple song form in which the beauty of the clarinet tone is exhibited at length against a simple string accompaniment. The clarinet is used in the manner of a voice, and the whole reminds one of the lyric quality of an operatic aria.

The third movement is a minuet, but it foreshadows the romantic tendency to make this simple form into a much larger rondo form, since the use of two trios, alternating with the minuet, gives a scheme like this—A (minuet), B (first trio), A (minuet), C (second trio), A (minuet). The minuet and the first trio are quite characteristic of the stately aristocratic dance, but the second trio is certainly a typical Austrian country dance in every respect.

The fourth movement is a theme with variations. The theme is of folk song simplicity and charm. It is subjected to six variant treatments. The first one exploits the technical and idiomatic character of the clarinet. The second variation is almost entirely given to the string quartet. The third uses the minor key as a contrast. The fourth variation again exploits the clarinet in its agility to perform broken chord passages. The fifth variation sets a somber

Example 9.3 Clarinet Quintet in A Major

mood, which then gives way to a rollicking final variation which closes the work.

While there is no lack of expressive quality in this work its general impression is one of Classic restraint even in the sublime melodic line of the second movement. There are no abrupt clashes of melodic, dynamic, or harmonic contrasts. In general, notice that the transitions from phrase to phrase within the themes and the transitions from theme to theme are effected with the least possible disturbance to the musical continuity. The seams of composition, as it were, are carefully covered to avoid detection and to preserve the Classic restraint and balance.

The forty-one symphonies of Mozart represent a continuous concern with this form from early childhood to the last years of his life. The first thirty some symphonies, while typical of Mozart's individual style, follow the techniques of the Viennese and Mannheim schools and particularly that of Franz Josef Haydn. In these works orchestration, form, and harmonic design follow the early Classic models. Of the final ten symphonies, the last three stand out as landmarks in the history of this form. The Symphony in g minor, no. 40, is representative of Mozart, the mature orchestral composer. The Classic orchestra, though somewhat smaller than the full-blown orchestra of the nineteenth and twentieth centuries, has now been established. While Mozart does not use all the instruments in any one of his last works, the balance of woodwinds, brass, percussion, and strings is present in the orchestras of his symphonies, concertos, and operas. This instrumental force becomes the orchestra of the next 150 years. Expansion of the various instrumental choirs will occur in the Romantic and Modern eras, but the Classic balance will be maintained.

The Symphony in g minor is scored for the full complement of woodwinds, flutes, oboes, clarinets, and bassoons, but only two horns represent the brass choir, and percussion is entirely lacking. The strings are divided into four parts, first and second violins, violas, cellos, and string basses doubling the bass line. This symphony is one of the most compact of the last great works of Mozart. The entire work might be said to be based on the two-note figure which is heard at the very beginning, played by the violins. The first, second, and final movements are all in sonata-allegro. The third movement is the traditional minuet and trio. There are no slow introductory passages to any of the movements, for all of them begin straightaway with the thematic material upon which each is built. The development sections of the three sonata-allegro movements are concise and compact, based solely on the material of the main themes of each of the movements and employing contrapuntal treatment in bold fashion. There is extensive use of chromatic alterations, especially in the contrapuntal treatment of the development sections. The minuet, despite its general adherence to the traditional form and its overall feeling of symmetry, is rhythmically unusual in its juxtaposition of six- and four-measure phrases and in the overlapping of the end of one phrase with the beginning of another. Note, also, the bold harmonic dissonance that characterizes the second part of the minuet proper and the equally startling melodic dissonance in the opening of the development section of the last movement. Contained within the almost strict balance of Classic form, Mozart has achieved an expressive quality that foreshadows that of the Romantic composers of the nineteenth century in both quality of musical material and in the use of technical devices.

While the basic character of opera is essentially opposed to the Classic idea, even this form shows the strong influence of Classic restraint and formalism in the eighteenth century. The hybrid form known as opera was a child of the Baroque and assumed, during the seventeenth century, all the excesses of an era which was known for its emphasis on the highly emotional and spectacular. The late Baroque operatic composers found it difficult to achieve or maintain artistic value in the face of these excesses. As an example, Handel, after composing forty-three operas, abandoned the form in favor of oratorio. Gluck, in the last half of the eighteenth century, very determinedly set about to correct the abuses of opera. Mozart, on the other hand, had no preconceived ideas of reform, but his refined Classic taste, his innate feeling for, and love of, the theater led him to write what are perhaps the happiest solutions to the problem of combining pure music and extramusical ideas. These were his operatic works, among which *Don Giovanni, Cosí Fan Tutte, The Abduction from the Seraglio, The Magic Flute,* and *The Marriage of Figaro* are the finest examples. The genius of Mozart enabled him to keep his operatic works in the tradition of theatrical entertainment, while at the same time the music was cast in the finest Classical mold.

The overture and the first scene of *The Marriage of Figaro* will serve to illustrate the manner in which Mozart re-formed the decadent operatic form without in any way acting as a conscious reformer. The story of this opera is founded on a comedy by the French dramatist Beaumarchais. Figaro is about to marry Susanna, the Countess Almaviva's waiting maid. He realizes that Susanna is the object of the affection of the Count, his master (duets #1 and #2 of Figaro and Susanna). Figaro determines to effect a counterplot against his master, as well as Don Basilio, one of the Count's aides, in his designs on Susanna (cavatina of Figaro). A secondary plot is introduced in the persons of Marcellina and Dr. Bartolo, who desire revenge on Figaro and Susanna (aria of Bartolo and duet of Marcellina and Susanna). Cherubino, the Count's page, who has a secret passion for the Countess, becomes an apt assistant to Figaro. The page is in disfavor with the Count for flirting with Barbarina, a cousin of Susanna. He begs Susanna to intercede with the Countess (aria of Cherubino). During this scene, the Count arrives. Cherubino hides behind a large chair. The Count, not realizing that he is being overheard by Cherubino, tries to advance his designs on Susanna and, in turn, is interrupted by the arrival of Basilio. Not wanting to be found alone with Susanna, he hides behind the large chair, while Cherubino slips around and curls up in this same chair, where Susanna covers him with a dress of the Countess. Basilio enters and tries to advance the Count's cause with Susanna, mentioning also Cherubino's love for the Countess. The Count, unable to contain himself any longer, jumps from his hiding place and, in a rage against Cherubino, tells how he discovered the page concealed in Barbarina's room. He illustrates his action by snatching the dress off the chair, only to find Cherubino again (trio of Susanna, Basilio, and the Count). But Cherubino has heard too much, and the Count is forced to forgive them. However, the Count succeeds in ridding himself of the page by commissioning him as a captain in the army. Figaro bids Cherubino farewell (aria of Figaro). Thus the first act ends with the laying of a framework of intrigue which finally resolves itself in the happy marriage of Figaro and Susanna.

The music represented in the overture and vocal numbers is indicative of the same Classic design as is evidenced in the purely instrumental works of Mozart. The overture is a reduced sonata-allegro form lacking a development section. The vivacious spirit of the music makes a fitting prelude to the sparkling comedy which is to follow, though no attempt is made either through musical connection or extramusical device to connect the overture with the opera itself.

In speaking about the vocal numbers, no mention will be made of the recitatives which connect the various arias, duets, etc. The recitatives carry the narrative of the story in the traditional operatic manner and are of no significance as far as formal structure is concerned. Actually, Mozart employs the style of *secco*, or dry, recitative, which signifies the use of a keyboard instrument as an accompaniment to the sung declamation.

In the eight solo and ensemble numbers which occur in the first act, the importance of the vocal and instrumental ensemble, which is characteristic of all the operatic writing of Mozart, is noteworthy. Each of these numbers is a closed form quite complete in itself, even when removed from context. The same skill which Mozart evidenced in the handling of instruments in chamber music is characteristic of the handling of the voice and instruments in this work, for actually this opera, presented in the intimate surruoundings of the eighteenth-century court theater of Vienna, was also a sort of chamber music.

In addition to the formal beauty of each number, Mozart has voiced the musical counterpart of each theatrical situation so that we have a most happy wedding of extramusical idea (text) and pure musical utterance. Note how this is accomplished in the cavatina in which Figaro says, "If you want to dance, Sir Count, I'll play the tune." The first part is actually a minuet. This gives way to a contrasting middle section which voices the determination of Figaro to outwit his master, only to return again to the suave minuet form in which Figaro restates his confidence in being able to make the Count bend to his desires. The whole is formally a three-part song form with a striking contrasting middle section.

Cherubino's aria, in which he voices his disturbance over the fevers of love which beset him, is another example of Mozart's ability to frame the musical counterpart to the breathless utterances of the lovesick youth. The aria is a three-part song form with an extended coda[2] section. In the coda, the simple means of breaking the musical ideas into shorter and shorter repetitive patterns gives a feeling of musical frustration which reveals more of the tender self-pity and hopelessness of first love than the words of Cherubino themselves.

The trio which follows this aria is a masterful dramatic characterization of the three persons, within the formal musical structure of a free rondo form.

Figaro's final aria is another example of Mozart's use of a Classic form, in this case another rondo which serves to characterize the change that is to take place in the person of Cherubino. The first episode is in the rhythmic form of a march which serves to parade before Cherubino the soft and gay life of his past. This is done in the first section of the aria, A-B-A. A second episode, C, presents the more grim and bombastic military character of the life he is soon to lead in the army. The whole is rounded out formally with the repetition of the gay opening section.

Such is the skill of Mozart that perfection of musical form tends only to heighten the dramatic incident. Here we have a Classicist who by pure musical handling of his materials beguiles us into the dramatic situation so adroitly that we are willing, even eager, to accept the whole as an expression of a unified art form. Such has been the hope of every operatic composer, but few have been as successful as Mozart.

Summary

The Rococo style in the arts was a contrast to that of the Baroque. It was mainly the product of the French court, but because the court at Versailles became the model for aristocratic life and manners, the Rococo was imitated in other places, especially Germany and Italy. The Rococo was a natural development from the intense systematization of the Baroque. As a result of absolutism in government, wealth became concentrated in the hands of the nobility. Society and manners were reduced to a formula. There was an emphasis on elegance, refinement, amorous pursuits, and sentimental love. Gone were the great passsions and noble pleasures of the Baroque. Gone also were the intense spiritual values of the past. Life at the court was artificial and so was its art.

Amorous scenes, courtly life, and manners provided the most popular subjects for both painters and sculptors. The method and organization of the basic elements remained essentially as in the Baroque, however, there is less vigor and it is on a much smaller scale. Lines are not as diffused and are

---

2. Coda: A section added to a musical form as an ending.

broken up into smaller fragments. Spatial awareness is less, and color, while still monochromatic, is less intense and shows more of a pastel quality.

It is the decoration in architecture that reveals the Rococo style at its best where generous use is made of floral patterns with delicately carved motifs. This kind of decoration is also found in the design of furniture and in almost every kind of household furnishing, dishes, silverware, and other items found in the homes of the aristocracy.

The Neoclassic aspect of the Rococo-Classic was in direct opposition to the Rococo. In protest against the superficial elegance of the Rococo, the French Academy urged a return to the Classic ideals with models from the Greek, Roman, and Renaissance. This calm and emotionless art became a symbol of the revolt against the frivolity and elegance of the French court. In place of the amorous and artificial manners, the subjects of Neoclassic painters and sculptors were often patriotic, or at least revealed intellectual pursuits. Lines were clear with formal balance in keeping with the Classic ideals.

It is the music of the Rococo-Classic that has survived the test of time. Music never entirely succumbed to the Rococo, but it did respond to the ideals of Classic simplicity and clarity. In fact this music is referred to as the Classic style. The finest music of the period was mainly the product of Germany and stresses perfection of form, lyric melody, and the homophonic texture. While opera claimed the attention of the Classic composer, it is in instrumental music that the Classic style reached its culmination. The most important form was the sonata-allegro and the composite sonata. In it composers embodied their ideals of formal structure in an abstract instrumental form of large proportions. Repetition and contrast is the principle of design, that is, repetition of melodic material after contrasting melodies with varying tonal centers. Classic music is full of lyric melody and subtle rhythms, restrained emotional expression, and often light and gay. It is rarely profound or full of strong passion. It appeals to the concertgoer through its melodic invention and simplicity.

Musical examples

Haydn, Symphony no. 101 in D Major (*Clock*)

Mozart, Clarinet Quintet in A Major—*Marriage of Figaro* (Overture and Scene 1)

Mozart, Symphony in g minor, no. 40

Suggested readings

Grout, D. J. *A History of Western Music,* 3rd ed. New York: W. W. Norton, 1980, pp. 448–519.

Janson, H. W. *History of Art.* Englewood Cliffs, N.J.: Prentice-Hall, Inc., 1962, pp. 434–52.

Lang, Paul Henry. *Music in Western Civilization.* New York: W. W. Norton, 1941, chapter 12, pp. 530–52; chapter 13, pp. 618–74.

Leichtentritt, Hugo. *Music, History and Ideas.* Cambridge, Mass.: Harvard University Press, 1940, chapter 7, pp. 161–78.

Robb and Garrison. *Art in the Western World.* New York: Harper & Bros., 1942, chapter 29, pp. 752–66.

Sewall, John Ives. *A History of Western Art.* New York: Henry Holt & Co., 1953, chapter 18, pp. 844–52.

Wold and Cykler. *An Outline History of Music,* 5th ed. Dubuque, Ia.: Wm. C. Brown Company Publishers, 1982, pp. 153–178.

Suggested examples for further analysis

Painting: David, *Death of Socrates;* Fragonard, *The Lover Crowned, The Swing;* Gainsborough, *Mrs. Graham*

Sculpture: Canova, *Perseus;* Falconet, *The Bather;* Girardon, *Bathing Nymphs*

Music: Haydn, Symphony in G Major, no. 94 (*Surprise*) Quartet in C Major, op. 33, no. 3; Mozart, Symphony in C Major, no. 41, Quartet in d minor, K. 421, *Don Giovanni;* Gluck, *Alceste*

Film strips with sound

Eighteenth Century Music and Art. Educational Audio Visual Inc.

Additional sources for visual illustrations

Thuillier, J. *Fragonard, Biographical and Critical Study.* Geneva: Skira, 1966.

10
Romantic
(1800-1900)

Chronology of Romanticism (Including Realism, Nationalism in Music, and Impressionism)

1746 Franciso Jose de Goya (1746–1828)

1770 Ludwig van Beethoven (1770–1827)

1776 John Constable (1776–1837)

1782 Niccoló Paganini (1782–1840)

1786 Carl Maria von Weber (1786–1826)

1791 Theodore Gericault (1791–1824)

1792 Giacomo Rossini (1792–1868)

1796 Jean Baptiste Corot (1796–1875)

1797 Franz Schubert (1797–1828)

1798 Ferdinand Delacroix (1798–1863)

1803 Hector Berlioz (1803–1869)

1804 Napoleon becomes Emperor

1806 Lewis and Clark reach the Pacific

1808 Honore' Daumier (1808–1879)

1809 Felix Mendelssohn (1809–1849)

Abraham Lincoln (1809–1865)

Charles Darwin (1809–1882)

1810 Frederic Chopin (1810–1849)

Robert Schumann (1810–1856)

1811 Franz Liszt (1811–1886)

1812 Charles Dickens (1812–1870)

Fairy Tales by the Grimm Brothers

War of 1812 between England and the United States

1813	Giuseppe Verdi (1813–1901)	1840	Piotor Illyitch Tchaikovsky (1840–1893)
	Richard Wagner (1813–1883)		Auguste Rodin (1840–1917)
1815	Battle of Waterloo		Claude Monet (1840–1926)
1816	Froebel founds the first kindergarten.		First electric light
1818	Karl Marx (1818–1883)	1841	Pierre Auguste Renoir (1841–1919)
	First steamship, the Savannah, crosses the Atlantic		Saxophone invented by Adolphe Sax
1819	Gustav Courbet (1819–1877)	1844	Friederich Nietsche (1844–1900)
	Walt Whitman (1819–1892)		Nicolay Rimsky-Korsakow (1844–1909)
	Victoria, Queen of England (1819–1901)	1846	Ether used for the first time as an anesthetic.
1822	Louis Pasteur (1822–1895)	1848	Marx and Engels publish the *Communist Manifesto*
1823	Monroe Doctrine promulgated	1851	Georges Pierre Seurat (1851–1891)
1824	Bedřich Smetana (1824–1884)	1853	Japan opened to the West
1828	First performance of Goethe's *Faust*		First Chicago to New York rail connection
1831	Beginning of antislavery movement		Vincent van Gogh (1853–1890)
1832	Edouard Manet (1832–1883)	1854	Thoreau's *Walden* published
1833	Johannes Brahms (1833–1899)	1858	Giocomo Puccini (1858–1924)
1834	Edgar Degas (1834–1917)	1859	Darwin's *Origin of Species* published
	Mechanical reaper invented by McCormick	1860	Hugo Wolf (1860–1903)
1837	Morse invents the telegraph		Gustav Mahler (1860–1900)
1838	First photograph taken by Daguerre	1861	Russia emancipates the serfs
1839	Modest Moussorgsky (1839–1889)		American Civil War (1861–1865)
	Paul Cézanne (1839–1906)	1862	Claude Debussy (1862–1918)

1864	First Atlantic Cable Richard Strauss (1864–1949)	1877	Edison invents the phonograph
1865	Slavery outlawed in the United States by the Thirteenth Amendment Jean Sibelius (1865–1957)	1882	Koch discovers the tuberculosis germ
		1883	Automobile engine patented by Daimler
1867	Alaska purchased from Russia	1884	Universal adoption of solar day as unit of time
1869	First transcontinental railway in the United States	1886	American Federation of Labor organized
	Suez Canal opened	1895	Roentgen discovers the X ray
1870	Site of Troy excavated	1898	Spanish-American War starts
1876	Bell invents the telephone		

Study Objectives

The objectives of this chapter are

1. To study how the Revolution influenced the Romantic period.
2. To learn about the conflicts and contradictions as expressed by; the individualism and emotion of the Romantic artists.
3. To study the added tensions in harmony, melody, and rhythm as characteristic of most Romantic music.

Pronunciation Guide

Balzac (Bahl-zahk)
Baudelaire (Boh-de-layr)
Brahms (Brahms)
Chopin (Shoh-pa)
Corot, Camille (Koh-roh, Kahmeel)
Delacroix (Day-la-krwah)
Dvořák (Dvor'-zhahk)
Eroica (Ay-roh'-i-kah)
Gericault (Zhay-ree-koh)
Goethe (Goe'-te)
Goya (Goy'-ah)

Heine (Hih'-ne)
Hugo (U-goh)
Mendelssohn (Men'-del-zohn)
Paganini (pah-gah-nee'-nee)
Puccini (Poo-chee'-nee)
Rousseau, Jean Jacques (Roo-soh, Zhan Zhahk)
Sand (Săn)
Schubert (Shoo'-bert)
Schumann (Shoo'-mahn)
Verdi (Ver'-dee)

Romantic is the term used to designate the style of art and literature of a large part of the nineteenth century. The word itself has a rather vague and mysterious connotation of sentimentality. In fact, the first use of the term was to designate the chivalrous and sentimental writings of medieval Italy, France, and Spain. These "romances" had a marked predilection for moonlit forests, enchanted castles, dragons, and other devices to lend mythical atmosphere to the story.

By the turn of the nineteenth century, Romanticism had come to mean something very different. It was no longer seeking inspiration in the legends and myths of the Middle Ages, but rather it was seeking a new freedom in the expression of personalized feelings. Romanticism came to be a revolt against convention and authority, whether in personal, religious, civil, or artistic matters. The search for individual freedom in life and art was its motivating force, even when it was at the expense of formal perfection. This search distinguished the Romanticist from the Classicist, who sought perfection of form and design and who preferred intellectuality to personalized feelings. It must be clearly understood that Romantic artists did not completely ignore Classic design but used it only when it served their artistic purpose. Personal feeling came first and design came second in importance.

For a period of about one hundred years artists were concerned with the search for ways to express individualism and to intensify the emotional expressiveness of their art. One such trend was to impress the observer by being realistic, both visually and musically. This development became important enough to be called Realism. Another Romantic trend that became especially strong in music was Nationalism: the individuality of ethnic groups expressed in folk music, legend, and historical events of the past. It should be noted that the ingredients of the Romantic spirit will continue on through the following chapters of Realism and Nationalism in Music. Realism, especially in music, is only one facet of Romanticism. Nationalism in music is the application of the Romantic spirit to the sovereign state.

The eighteenth century had been an age of reason and all phases of intellectual activity were to a great extent dominated by the scientific attitude. The human element was almost eliminated from life. People believed they had worked out a perfect system and had extended this system to government, economics, art, society, and even religion. But they reckoned without human personality and emotions. The whole system exploded in the Revolution. Reason had not solved all of man's problems, nor had it been enough to satisfy his longing for spiritual consciousness. Man has both intellect and emotions. Had not reason been overcultivated at the expense of sentiment and liberty? This question was probably the one that directed the thinking which led to the Romantic attitude. The new way, called "Romanticism," produced new movements in religion, politics, art, and social life. The urge for freedom that had started in the eighteenth century was finally brought to a point where it had a real effect on human life. The realization that man was an individual, that he had feelings, that he had the right to agree or disagree is integral to the Romantic spirit.

Jean Jacques Rousseau is the figure that stands out as the popularizer of the Romantic movement. His *Social Contract*, written in 1762, sets forth his philosophy of individualism. Rousseau thus reflects one of the primary causes of the French Revolution, for his thesis is emotional individualism. He asserted that science and civilization had taken people away from nature and that natural instincts should be their guide. In order to "return to nature," the taboos and artificialities of civilization must be cast aside. Previous philosophies held that man is inherently evil and must be subordinated to the beneficial laws of society. Rousseau asserted that man is inherently good and is evil only to the extent that he is influenced by evil. To be one's natural self should be the guiding principle of life. The following lines from Rousseau's *Confessions* are representative of the whole Romantic spirit as it applies to individualism: "I am different from all men I have seen. If I am not better, at least I am different." Paganini, the great Romantic virtuoso of the violin, put it another way when he said, "Paganini avoids mediocrity in everything."

This emphasis upon individual feeling led to a feverish activity in all phases of life. European society was experiencing a demand for a fresh interpretation of man and nature. There was a revival of the "cult of feeling" which was to serve as a basis for much of the poetry, drama, art, and music of passion during the nineteenth century. To no creative activity could intense emotion mean so much as to music and the visual arts.

The philosophy of Romanticism gave men the freedom to give voice to their passion, fear, love, and longing. Artists could now celebrate natural man and break the bonds of formalism imposed by Classicism. This meant that new sources of subjects for art were now available. All kinds of subjects and experiences previously considered in bad taste now found artistic expression. There was a renewed interest in nature. Landscape again became a favorite theme, as it had been in the seventeenth century. Folklore and folk song found a place as expressions of the simple, unaffected peasantry. The mysteries of love and death brought passion and drama back into the arts. The new ideals of freedom were dramatized, both visually and tonally. The atypical experience fascinated the Romantic artist because of its mystery and supernaturalism. Violence and shocking events were often used because such subjects gave more opportunity for the projection of strong emotions. Romantic subjects were almost unlimited, for any subject seen through an individual temperament could be highly charged with passion and intense emotions.

There was a tendency to mix the arts. Painting and sculpture often depended upon literary and poetic ideas, even to the point of being illustrations of literary works, as was the case with Delacroix in his paintings of scenes from *Hamlet* and the *Divine Comedy*. Music entered into the realm of program music—music that recreated a story or scene in terms of melody, rhythm, and harmony. All Romanticists had emotional response as their immediate aim in revolt against the intellectual Classicism of the past. Whatever the subject or art, the listener or spectator was made to feel the whole scale of emotional sensations.

Because Romantic art expresses the individual temperament of its creators, the personal lives of artists take on a new importance. Biographical details can serve as keys to the motivating experiences that are intensified in their art. Their lives came to be as Romantic as their works. Freedom extended to personal behavior. Their love affairs, their relations with publishers and museum directors, their economic problems, and their eccentricities become an integral part of the record of their creative lives. Beethoven is such a case. Every scrap of information regarding his personal ideals, his love of nature, his illness, and his unfortunate love affairs colors our understanding of his music. Delacroix's literary associations with George Sand and Baudelaire, his friendship with Chopin, his travels, and his political friends reveal facts that influence our concepts of the Romantic qualities of his paintings. One must, however, be on guard against romanticizing the lives of artists at the expense of appreciating their message. After all, creative artists stand or fall on the quality of their works, not on the Romantic character of their personal affairs.

There was also a change in the patronage of Romantic art. No longer were artists attached to courts for the purpose of providing entertainment in keeping with courtly customs. Nor was the Church a particularly ambitious art patron. Romantic artists depended on their abilities to arouse the interest of a greater public—the common people. Composers and writers relied upon the sale of published works. Painters and sculptors depended upon the sale of their works to the public and upon fees for exhibitions. While composers, painters, and sculptors were not bound by the demands of the court or Church, they were influenced by public taste. Because there were very close economic ties with the general public, they were very sensitive to public reaction. Fortunately, the public generally accepted Romanticism as the artists had accepted it.

This new patronage also brought a change in the social status of creative artists. They were no longer servants but held a place in the social scene fairly commensurate with their artistic and economic success. Haydn was a servant at the court of Prince Esterhazy, but Beethoven, only a few decades later, was a free, independent, and financially successful composer. In general, successful artists came to be honored members of society and often gathered abundant funds for their efforts. Not all achieved financial success early enough to be of much satisfaction to them, however. This was the case with Schubert, who died at the age of thirty-one, apparently on the threshold of worldly success, though artistic success had come much earlier.

It is almost impossible to formulate a set of rules for evaluating Romantic art because it is a spirit of revolt, of individualism. There are many contrasts and paradoxes within the movement itself. If any guide can be suggested, it is contrast to the Classic. For example, the Classic tendency in music and visual arts is toward a centralization, toward closed form; in the Romantic, we find open form, the predilection for action and soaring emotions. The Classic is logical and intellectual, while the Romantic is irrational, untypical, and often experimental. The Classic deals in sharply defined lines and melodies; the Romantic in vague, shadowy, conjectural forms and suggestive harmonies. One can also contrast the strong positive objectivity of the Classic to the often loosely formed subjectivity of Romanticism.

As one returns to the art and music of previous epochs, it will be apparent that there were elements of Romanticism in all great art of the past. The Gothic cathedral, Leonardo da Vinci, Rembrandt, Bach, even Mozart show the tinge of the Romantic spirit. Perhaps this is what gave these works and artists expressive values that have made them almost timeless. It was not until the nineteenth century, however, that the Romantic spirit completely ruled and dominated the arts.

Painting

It has already been noted that the painters of Romanticism rejected the doctrine of Classicism and turned their attention to subject matters of a wide range, treating them with a greater individualism than the Rococo and Neoclassic. They also rejected the rigid system of Classical patronage. For the first time, on a large scale, artists were able to exist by selling their works after they were created. Art was finally free, unfettered by false standards of taste; it could express the personal feelings of the artist. The emotions of violence and excitement replaced the social niceties of the previous era. Painters turned to the Dutch art of Rembrandt and Rubens for inspiration in the use of color, light, and shade in depicting strong emotions.

Gericault

Theodore Gericault (1791–1824) was one of the first painters of the French Romantic movement with his *Raft of the Medusa* (fig. 10.1). The work was inspired by a newspaper account of the sinking of the ship *Medusa* off the coast of West Africa. After many days on a raft in the storm-tossed ocean, only a handful of survivors reached safety. Gericault, in an effort to recreate the emotions of the tragedy, revitalized in his imagination the scenes aboard the raft. It was reported that he even hired the survivors as models and made

Figure 10.1 *Raft of the Medusa*—Gericault. (Courtesy Editorial Photocolor Archives)

studies of corpses of the dead victims. He endeavored to express the despair, the hunger and thirst, the struggle for life aboard the raft. He tried to engulf the observer in the whole range of emotions of the disaster. Through color, twisting diagonal lines, and the emotional behavior of the participants, he made his painting a real experience in the minds of the spectators.

Delacroix

Eugene Delacroix (1798–1863) became the leader of the Romantic movement in painting. In his famous work *Liberty Leading the People* (colorplate 25),

Colorplate 25 follows p. 242.

Delacroix recaptures the spirit of the Romantic revolution. He has symbolized the struggle for freedom against the forces of tyranny in his portrayal of an allegorical figure of the goddess of liberty leading the people of France over the barricades. The event that suggested this work was the July Revolution of 1830 and not the Revolution of 1789, as is popularly supposed. Some of the Romantic aspects of the work are immediately apparent. This is more than a group of people engaged in a scene of violent action. The figure of the goddess, tall and placed in a central position, dominates the whole scene. She is not a static figure but is engaged in going forward, in raising the tricolor of France high above everything—in short, she is a symbol of the energy and action that are necessary not only to gain freedom but to retain it. The figures around her symbolize the various classes of people that make up a nation. They, too, under the leadership of the ideal, are forging ahead, trampling over the fallen bodies of their enemies and their own comrades.

The basic elements are arranged in much the same manner as in the Baroque style. While the goddess is the central figure, there is a generous amount of spatial awareness enhanced by the diffused lines and forms melting one into another in multiple organization. Color is still monochromatic in spite of the patches of color contrast. The use of the human form as a motive shows the theme and variation principle of design.

Delacroix himself was regarded as a flagrant revolutionary in his own day. As an artist, he was described as a barbarian and a savage with a paint-brush. He never thought of himself, however, as a leader of the new move-ment nor as a particularly savage Romanticist. He merely desired to express his unfettered feelings about subjects and scenes that attracted him. He came from a fine family background and was a well-read, sensitive, and intelligent person. He numbered among his friends such literary figures as Balzac, Victor Hugo, and George Sand. He was also a friend of the composer Chopin. Undoubtedly, these connections with fellow Romanticists served to fuse the elements of Romanticism more deeply into his personality. The hostility of the French Academy did not deter him; it served only to confirm his own ideals.

The Romantic tendency to mix the arts is shown in Delacroix's illustra-tions for Dante's *Divine Comedy. Dante and Virgil in Hell* (colorplate 26) depicts the two poets being ferried through a murky and bloody hell, with anguished and tortured souls clinging to the boat. He has shocked us with a painting of horror; even the two poets are appalled by the scene before them. Note some of the technical means by which Delacroix achieves his effects. The shadowy background with its faint spot of light gives a sense of the infinity of hell itself. There is action, both physical and emotional. The raised hand, the twisting torsos, the waves, and the flowing robes give a feeling of motion.

Colorplate 26 follows p. 242.

The agony of facial expressions provides a powerful emotional climax. He has used the mass of form without line drawing to mold his subject together. Color is basically monochromatic, with contrasts in shades to highlight the bodies clinging to the boat. It is the feeling which is most important; the forms are only a means to that end. The whole canvas has intensified the horror of a story which Dante already had painted verbally.

Goya

The Romantic movement was not confined to any particular country. Each brought forth its special brand of Romantic feeling and its own few artists who best portrayed that feeling. Francisco Goya (1746-1828) was one of the great Spanish individualist painters. He was an artist of tremendous imaginative and technical powers with the courage to paint whatever his feelings dictated. He used a wide range of subjects, from painstaking portraitures to scenes of violence and horror. As a Romanticist, Goya felt that art should do more than entertain or decorate. He was convinced that painting could, and must, focus attention on the moral issues. He made a set of prints called *Disasters of War* in which he suggests, with unbelievable literalness, the rape, mutilation, and desecration of men and women that took place during the French invasion of Spain in 1808. This series of prints is probably one of the greatest artistic comments on the tragedy of war. In each of his works, Goya appeals to the emotions through the power of suggestion. He is not a realist, but he expects the observer to supply the details out of his own imagination. Through this suggestive quality, Goya not only supplies the detail of action but intensifies the impact of the subject upon one's feelings.

May 3, 1808 (fig. 10.2) is a painting in which Goya displays his powers to suggest the drama, the terror, of blood and violence and to moralize upon the event at the same time. The subject is the execution of Spanish loyalists at the hands of the French. It is said that the artist, who witnessed the terrible event, went by night to sketch the pile of bloody corpses in preparation for his painting. Goya has used a great economy of line and color to suggest the impact of his message of horror. The monochromatic browns and greens give a feeling of terror and doom to the scene. The dim outline of the building and the sloping contour of the hill in the background impart a sense of spatial volume. There is little detailed line in either the soldiers or their victims. They are volumes of mass rather than realistic bodies. The upraised arms of one of the victims, highlighted in white, symbolize, in effect, the sacrifice of life for liberty. There is action in the line of soldiers with pointed rifles and the crowd which turns toward its executioners in resignation. Goya has used color and mass to intensify the drama of death for liberty.

Figure 10.2 *May 3, 1808* [1808]—Goya. (Courtesy Keystone View Company)

Corot

It has been suggested that one of the characteristics of Romantic painting was the return of the landscape as a favored theme. Camille Corot (1796–1875) was one of the prominent and prolific painters of Romantic pastoral scenes. There is a sentimental quality about his landscapes, for the mood is always gentle. His painted fields and trees seem to be immersed in mist and their forms seem to be dissolved in soft light, for color and lines are soft and pale. *A View Near Volterra* (colorplate 27) shows Corot's personal interpretation of nature. Here is a Romantic feeling for light, space, and color. A strong sense

Colorplate 27 follows p. 242.

of basic structure is shown in the solid mass of rocks and in the figure of horse and rider. Sentimentality, however, overtakes structure to create an escape from the stuffiness and turmoil of the city in favor of the quiet peace of a shepherd's world.

Romantic Architecture

As with the other arts during the Romantic period, there was no one architectural style to distinguish it as being Romantic. Most architecture consisted of revivals of past styles such as the Gothic, Renaissance, and Baroque. The Gothic revival is very apparent in the Neo-Gothic style of the Houses of Parliament in London (fig. 10.3), designed by Charles Barry and A. Welby Pugin and built during the period between 1840–1860. It has a symmetry about the main structure which encloses the governmental spaces. The Gothic influence is evident in the various towers which give it an irregular appearance.

Figure 10.3   Houses of Parliament, London. (1840–60) (Courtesy National Monuments Record, London—Art Reference Bureau)

Another example of revivalist architecture is the Paris Opera (fig. 10.4), built in 1861–74 and designed by Charles Garnier. It is often referred to as a Neo-Baroque structure, partly because of the multiplicity of its sculpture and ornaments, both outside and within. There is an opulence about the building which reflects the tastes of the newly rich and powerful captains of the Industrial Revolution.

There were a few structures that reflected the technological developments of the Industrial Revolution in their use of cast iron and glass. One of the most famous of these was the Crystal Palace in London, built for the Great Exhibition of the Works of Industry of all Nations, constructed in 1851. Unfortunately it was destroyed by fire in 1937. Another example is the famous Eiffel Tower in Paris, constructed in 1889.

Figure 10.4 *Paris Opera*, Paris. (1861–74) (Courtesy National Monuments Record, London—Art Reference Bureau)

Romantic music

In the Romantic period, music offers a far more effective medium for artistic expression than the visual arts. It is true that music deals only with abstract ideas and therefore lacks specific or concrete meanings. People have, however, in the past (they will probably continue this practice in the future) translated these purely musical ideas into specific personal feelings, if not specific ideas. Insofar as musical ideas are translated into personal feelings, music becomes a sort of universal language. In a period such as the nineteenth century, when emphasis was placed on the exercise of individual freedom, music, of all the arts, afforded the most liberal opportunity for the exercise of such freedom. The visual arts in their dependence upon subject matter either limited their appeal to a specific group or period of time, or, in their desire for wider expression, employed subjects of such trivial sentimental nature that the artistic value of their work suffered. It is difficult to find any great quantity of sculpture, painting, or architecture of the Romantic period that does not tend to become exaggerated, irrational, or sentimental in its desire to appeal to the individual's free exercise of emotional response. It is possible for music, however, to sustain a feeling of intensity which no visual art can do without becoming exaggerated or irrational. In fact, we often approve of things in music that would be intolerable in literature or the visual arts. Music is, then, the most Romantic of all the arts because it is the most abstract, and therefore less dependent upon objective facts that often are meaningful only to those who have experienced their history.

We have seen in earlier periods how the social and professional position of such men as Palestrina, Bach, and Haydn colored their creative efforts. With the Romantic struggle for freedom came the emancipation of the composer, as well as other artists, from the systems of Church or aristocratic patronage. From then on, the composer served either one or both of two patrons—himself and the general public. It is true that a great number of works in the nineteenth century were still written at the commission of a small, elite, and discriminating musical aristocracy. By and large, however, the great mass of works was written either for public performance or to satisfy the individual composer in his intense feeling for expression. Insofar as the Romantic composer wrote works that succeeded in appealing to the general musical public, he achieved a modicum of material success. Insofar as he wrote to satisfy his own personal desires, to express his own personal musical thoughts, he could experiment with new materials and forms, but should not have been surprised if such a path led to general disregard, if not to outright antagonism and obscurity, during his lifetime.

A more generally democratic society growing out of the revolutionary struggles of the late eighteenth century had replaced the cultured and discriminating aristocracy of the earlier periods. This democratic society now became the patron whose acceptance, or at least tolerance, the artist of the nineteenth century had to win. Failing this, the composer would have to write for a continually shrinking circle of admirers who were incapable of making it economically possible for him to continue as a creative artist. This is a condition which, we shall see, becomes more aggravated throughout the nineteenth and twentieth centuries.

In the nineteenth century we have, for the first time, a situation in which a composer's works fail to find performance before their intended audience. By whom were the last works of Beethoven heard during his lifetime? How many knew the great songs or instrumental works of Schubert until a generation after his death? With what personal sacrifice and expense of energy did Wagner succeed in gaining a hearing for his music drama? The Romantic composer either had to write potboilers or be a person of intense vigor and energy if he was to succeed in gaining public acceptance or even public performances.

As in the field of the visual arts, it is impossible to formulate a set of rules for Romantic music. However, all Romantic music is based on the premise that a feeling of musical tension is necessary to achieve a corresponding intensification of emotional response. Romantic music therefore concerns itself with the problem of achieving this tension. This means that the problem of sonority, dynamics, or the exploration of sheer masses of sound is one of deep concern to the composer. We shall see how true this was with all the Romanticists of the nineteenth century. It means also that the problem of tone quality (tone color)—the use of instruments in combination and the use of individual instrumental qualities heretofore untouched—also concerns the Romantic composer. It means that composers are interested in all the possibilities of setting up harmonic tension. The further exploitation of the duality of key, so neatly couched in the sonata-allegro form of the Classic period, now pushes on to plurality of key. This is reflected in the rich harmonic texture of Romantic music with its chromaticism or dissonance. Concomitant with this increased richness of harmony comes, of course, an increased richness of melodic line. Melodies are likewise intensified by choice of instrumental tone color and often seem inseparable from their initial association with a particular instrument or voice. Schubert's *Erlköniq* is unthinkable for a soprano voice, and anyone who has never heard the Largo movement of Dvořa'k's *New World Symphony* played on the English horn has not yet experienced the musical pathos of the original.

Finally, the composer seeks tension and, of course, its ultimate release in the problem of formal structure. The nineteenth century offers no essentially new formal plans, but the breaking-up of the thematic ideas into motives and the detailed development of both thematic and motival ideas is another indication of the concern with musical tension. Beethoven and Wagner, to mention only two, are particularly noteworthy in this respect.

Apart from these common concerns, it is difficult to stereotype musical Romanticism. There were Romantic idealists and Romantic realists. The idealists insisted that music could exist for its own sake; the realists insisted that music must tell a story that could be verbalized or possibly visualized. There were Romanticists who excelled in spectacular virtuosity, dazzling the listener by the brilliance of technique or by sheer number of participants. Then there were those who emphasized intimacy as the best approach to personalized feelings, writing chamber music and solo songs. Others combined literature and landscape with music in the invention of the symphonic poem.

There were three favorite media of expression for the Romantic composer—the orchestra, the piano, and the human voice. Most composers wrote in forms for all three. The orchestra grew into the favorite large instrument of the century. It had those qualities of bigness, colorfulness, and brilliance that went with Romantic expression. It could run the gamut of musical ideas from a whisper to an overpowering thunder, and therefore lent itself well to the descriptive desires of certain composers. The piano could do much the same in more confined quarters, and, what is more, it could be played by a single person. Consequently, the piano became almost a musical symbol of the Romantic spirit of freedom and individualism. The voice is also a personalized instrument, for it combines with the literary element of Romanticism to give an added intensity to the poetic text. Of course other instruments were also used during this period, particularly those which lent themselves to virtuoso exploitation, such as the violin.

Beethoven

While arguments can be justifiably made for placing Beethoven in the Classic period or between the Classic and the Romantic, it is clear from an analysis of his music that he is one whose compositions reveal those characteristics which are generally recognized as Romantic.

Beethoven (1770–1827), born in Bonn, Germany, exhibited strong musical gifts as a young boy. He suffered severely at the hands of his father, who, while he hoped to exploit his son's talents, was too incompetent a manager even to launch a career for his gifted son. Beethoven, despite his father's role of taskmaster, developed a deep love for music and acquired great skill as pianist, organist, and violinist. Because of his musical skill, he was employed as court musician in his early teens and was the sole family support until his final departure from Bonn in 1792. From then on, his residence in Vienna was interrupted only in the early years by concert tours of Germany and Austria. The last twenty years of his life were spent entirely within the city and suburbs of the Austrian capital.

While he began to devote himself to composition before his twentieth birthday, he was regarded in Vienna primarily as a magnificent concert pianist. Not until the overwhelming realization that his increasing deafness made such a career impossible did he forsake the concert stage and devote himself exclusively to composition. Beethoven's creative life falls conveniently into three periods. Roughly speaking, the first period ends about 1802.

This was the period of the pianist-composer, and while the works written during this time exhibit the seeds of the unfolding Romantic period, they still are of the Classic era of Mozart and Haydn. The composition of the Third Symphony in the years 1802–1804 ushers in the middle period, which was truly Romantic in character.

Classic restraint is now cast aside whenever intensity of expression demands. Because of his increasing deafness, Beethoven was forced to abandon his concert career and to accept his fate as a composer. What performance could have accomplished in personal expression must now find voice only through composition. Beethoven's works now became the vehicle for individualized personal expression.

Such a work is the Third Symphony in E flat Major, op. 55. Here we have a work which, in general, is based upon the Classic precepts of Haydn and Mozart but goes beyond the Classic style in its expressive quality. Countless pages have been written concerning the meaning of this work. Much has been made of the destruction by Beethoven of the dedication to Napoleon Bonaparte when he heard of the latter's assumption of the crown. All such attempts to bring understanding to the music of Beethoven are of little consequence. Nothing can take the place of a direct approach to the music itself with at least some elementary knowledge of what the composer was doing with his musical material. A thorough listening acquaintance with the Third Symphony and some appreciation of its musical composition will reveal the mind of Beethoven as that of one of the great revolutionary individuals of a great period of revolutionary thought. There is no need to assign political, theological, or economic ideas to such a work as the Third Symphony, or to resort to speculation of a literary nature as to the meaning of all, or any part, of this great masterwork. To one who has some appreciation of the temper of the last decade of the eighteenth century and the first of the nineteenth, this work will voice the spirit of Romanticism in its purely musical expression as surely as does *Liberty Leading the People* by Delacroix. Beethoven never felt the necessity of explaining his works by means of a descriptive narrative. The title *Eroica* given to this work was undoubtedly prompted by the desire to dedicate a work to Napoleon, whom he had admired purely as a liberator. Disgust with Napoleon's act of crowning himself Emperor prompted Beethoven to reword his dedication, but the title remained as a concession to the promise that remained unfulfilled. It is extremely doubtful if Beethoven ever had anything more in mind than this when he wrote the symphony.

The work itself is in the basic tradition of the Classic models. It has the traditional four movements, the first of which is in a very expanded sonata-allegro form. Particularly noteworthy is the fact that the musical materials of both the first and second themes are not melodies in the sense of the themes of the Haydn symphony or the Mozart quintet. These are themes made up of fragmentary ideas which lend themselves in a most spectacular way to development. The first theme group of Beethoven's Third Symphony is more a collection of melodic and rhythmic motives than a complete melody in itself. It first appears as a combination between cellos and violas (ex. 10.1). From these motives Beethoven typically constructs the first section of the exposition in the tonic key.

Example 10.1

There are not just two contrasting thematic melodies but two groups of themes, none of which can be lifted from context, as can a melody from Haydn or Mozart, and still remain a complete entity. Likewise, these are themes in a purely instrumental idiom. The second theme group is placed in the key of B flat, the dominant of E flat, in keeping with tradition. Beethoven feels no great need of harmonic deviation from tradition—as yet. He relies on striking dynamic contrasts and violent accentuations of regularly weak rhythmic beats to secure tension. This is particularly noticeable in the development section of this work, which is of extraordinary length. This section is no longer a place where the composer contrives a return to the tonic key for the purpose of restating the first theme in its original form. It is now the place where the composer's musical ingenuity and imagination can exploit every bit of musical value from the thematic material which he has previously stated. After this lengthy and violent development, Beethoven returns to the restatement of his thematic material but adds to it a very lengthy musical summary, which is termed in musical language a "coda." No longer content to close the restatement with a climactic cadence, he hammers home his ideas in ever new guises as if his inventive genius knew no limits.

The second movement, in the parallel key of c minor, is a funeral march with the distinctive rhythmic pattern always associated with this kind of music. It does not rely for its expressive character only on dynamic contrasts but exploits tone color in connection with melodic line, as in the opening melody which is first placed in the lowest register of the violins and then given to the oboe with its rather wailing quality. The form is loosely that of a march and trio. The trio in this instance is in the contrasting key of C major, which tends to accentuate the somberness of the C minor on its return. The conclusion of this movement is an excellent example of Beethoven's ability to accomplish a rather complete disintegration of the thematic material. Note how complete relaxation and repose are achieved by the gradual dissolution of the main theme.

The third movement is one of the most striking examples of Romantic transformation of what was originally a simple dance form into a vehicle for violent and intense action. Basically the form of the movement is that of the minuet, but its speed, length, and entire melodic character belie its origin. Beethoven employs the name "scherzo" (Italian for joke) to characterize the spirit of the movement. The trio, with its main theme given to three horns, shows Beethoven's interest in tone color as a means of Romantic expression.

The fourth movement is a brilliant set of variations freely contrived on a theme which he had used in three previous works. After an opening flourish of strings and full orchestra, the bass of the theme is given as a sort of skeleton over which the theme and its subsequent variations are stretched. The skill with which Beethoven adds contrasting material to this bass is remarkable. Again, dynamic contrasts, rhythmic complexities, and brilliance of thematic invention all unite in a blaze of spectacular musical expressiveness.

While Beethoven's expressiveness undoubtedly reveals itself most widely in his orchestral works, it is nonetheless equally present in other media of composition. This expressiveness can be readily observed in a piano sonata such as the Sonata no. 23, op. 57 or the String Quartet, op. 135.

The Sonata no. 23, also from the middle period of Beethoven's activity, is commonly known as the *Appassionata*. It exhibits certain compositional devices which Beethoven applied to the piano for the purpose of making this instrument an expressive vehicle for his music.

Various instruments have always differed from one another in technical and tonal characteristics. In the pre-Romantic periods, however, the composers gave greater consideration to the technical differences as far as the selection of one or another instrument was concerned. A keyboard instrument would do things with only one performer that no other single instrument could do. It could accompany a solo instrument or voice as effectively as a whole orchestra in every respect except that of tone color. For example, the recitative passages of most operas where instrumental tone color was of no concern were accompanied by the harpsichord. Beethoven, however, recognized the expressive potential of the piano, which had been in existence for over seventy-five years by the time he began composing for it. He made the piano an expressive medium such as it had never been before. Many other characteristics of Beethoven's romantic expressiveness are discernible in his piano Sonata no. 23. The terseness of the thematic material of the first movement and the driving motoric fashion in which the thematic material is used

Colorplate 25 *Liberty Leading the People* [1831]—Delacroix. (Courtesy Scala/Editorial Photocolor Archives)

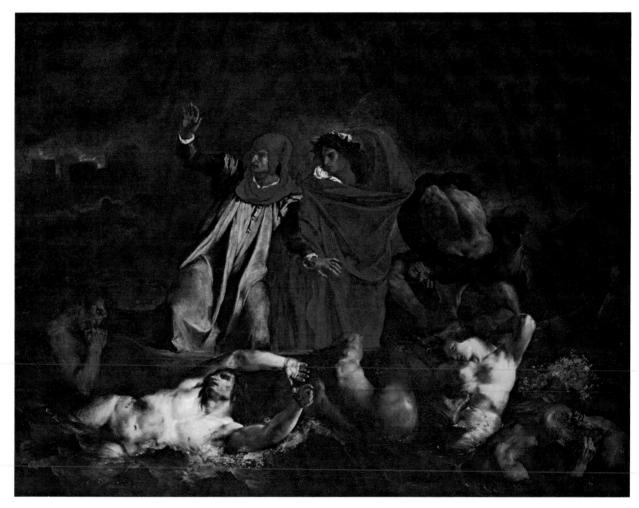

Colorplate 26 *Dante and Virgil in Hell* [1822]—Delacroix. (Courtesy Scala/Editorial Photocolor Archives)

Colorplate 27 *View Near Volterra* [1838]—Jean Baptiste Camille Corot. (Courtesy National Gallery of Art, Washington, D.C., Chester Dale Collection)

are as evident here as in the Third Symphony. In addition to this, however, Beethoven has written for the piano in a new way. Note the extended pitch range of the first twenty-five measures of the first movement, the great use made of the low register of the instrument, the heavy, thick chords placed low in the bass, the wide skips between consecutive motive groups, the abrupt dynamic changes, the sweeping chordal passages (ex. 10.2).

Example 10.2 Sonata No. 23, Op. 57

Example 10.2 (continued)

These are all pianistic devices which display Beethoven's command of the instrument as a means of expression and tend to set the stage for the Romantic exploitation of the piano, which made it second in importance only to the orchestra as a musical means of personal expression. By listening carefully to this sonata you will hear how Beethoven has, in a sort of musical ecstasy, molded his musical materials out of a very few short motives, two of which stand out as primary in importance. The first and second themes are actually very closely related, due to the use of these common motives. The sonata form of the first movement is quite obvious, though key relationships are somewhat different from the traditional sonata since the principal tonic key is in the minor mode. The long coda at the end of the movement is another example of Beethoven's expressive power in bringing this tumultuous movement to a climax—the second theme rising to the upper notes of the keyboard in a last vain effort, only to fall again to the very depths as the driving force appears to spend itself.

The second movement consists of a theme so simple as to be constructed almost entirely of two notes—the tonic and the dominant—and four subsequent variations. While there is an actual cadence at the end of the first movement, the appearance of the theme of the second movement low in the bass makes it seem to rise from the depths to which the first movement had sunk at its close. In this manner Beethoven links the first two movements together. He achieves an even closer linkage between the second and final movements in that there is no actual complete cadence at the end of the second movement.

The third movement grows out of a motive reminiscent of the second movement and finally presents its own thematic material in a rather irregular sonata-allegro form. This time, the motoric drive which characterizes the last movement is achieved by an almost uninterrupted pattern of sixteenth notes. Again the first theme illustrates Beethoven's expressive use of the low range of the piano. The coda is again a long one and uses not only an increased tempo but new thematic material. This, however, is soon discarded for the opening theme, which closes the work in another exhaustive presentation that exploits both the extreme upper and lower ranges of the keyboard.

The String Quartet no. 16, op. 135 is a work from the third period of Beethoven's life and was written only a year before his death. Shorter and, in some respects, less radical in deviation from Classical form than the other quartets of this period, it is nevertheless an example of the intensely personal style of late Beethoven. This is all the more striking when it is realized that here Beethoven packs into the rather limited medium of the string quartet a gamut of expressive qualities which runs from the wild incessant rhythm and leaping melody of the trio of the second movement to the tenderness of exquisite melodic line in the third movement. The continuous changes of rhythm and key which Beethoven employs in this work are typical of his late compositions. He seems to be searching for all means at his disposal in the desire to give full scope of expression to his inventive genius. No Romantic composer to follow Beethoven was able to handle the string quartet in such an expressive manner. All attempts on the part of the later Romanticists resulted either in weak imitations of Beethoven or in works which failed to realize the limitations of the medium.

Schubert

Another Romanticist, a contemporary of Beethoven, was Franz Schubert (1797–1828). He was the only great Viennese composer who could claim that city for his birthplace. Schubert's life was illustrative of a certain kind of bohemianism which is often associated with the age of Romanticism. He was never in the employ of any institution or aristocratic patron. Moreover, he did not even have the security of benevolent patronage that Beethoven enjoyed. He eked out a slim existence as a private teacher, sold a few compositions to publishers, and had a few commissions for works. His early death was unquestionably hastened by actual poverty. The greatest portion of his compositional output could be ascribed to art for art's sake. This is particularly true for his more than 600 art songs. These were not written on commission; few of them found publication during his life, and most of them were unknown and unsung until years after his death. While his chamber, piano, and orchestral works are significant contributions to Romantic music literature, it is the art songs of Schubert which illustrate another field of Romantic music expression.

Three short works from this great wealth of material will suffice to illustrate the manner in which Schubert treats this form. Individual solo songs were not the invention of the Romantic era, certainly not of Schubert. The great wealth of German lyric poetry, with its tendency toward the sentimental, however, stimulated the Romantic trend for combining music with extramusical ideas. This resulted in the great interest in art song settings from Schubert through the entire nineteenth, and even into the twentieth, century. Similarly, the Romantic love for the intimate and small form encouraged this medium of composition. Two distinct forms of the art song were used by Schubert. The first, known as the strophic song, is illustrated by the composition *Heidenröslein*. In this form, the several strophes or stanzas of the poem are set to the same melodic line. Actually, Schubert's song, though entirely original with him, is so much in the folk tradition that it is often thought to be a German folk song. The poem by Goethe is a simple one with its whimsical philosophizing. Schubert matches its simplicity with a charming straightforward melody and an accompaniment which, while written for the piano, might be realized on any chordal instrument such as the guitar or lute.

Another familiar song of Schubert, *The Trout*, is a slightly modified strophic song in which Schubert alters the strict repetition of melody where the words indicate the muddying of the waters. This bit of musical tone painting is typical of the Romantic tendency to fit music to the text. This charming song is used by Schubert a second time as the theme for a set of variations within the framework of a large sonata for five instruments; piano, violin, viola, cello, and bass viol. This famous *Trout Quintet* derives its name from the fourth movement, in which the simple song is set in a series of variations in which each of the instruments of the quintet exploits the theme according to its technical capabilities. This movement is, in fact, an interpolation between the normal third movement and the finale of the Classic sonata. This is an example of the liberal treatment with which the Romantic composer utilized the Classic form. The linking of song with the abstract instrumental form, and the richness of harmonic texture characterizes the Romantic treatment.

In contrast to *Heidenröslein* is the song the *Erlköniq.* This time, Schubert has chosen a dramatic ballad by Goethe. In this ballad, Goethe has related the story of an anxious father riding through the night with his sick son in his arms. As the father journeys through the dark forest, the erlking, the specter of death, entreats the child to come to him. Upon arrival at their destination, the father discovers the child is dead. This poem, Schubert felt, called for something more than a mere repetition of a suitable rhythmic melody for its eight stanzas. Here we have the second form of song writing, the "through-composed." Schubert is concerned, in this instance, with a musical characterization of the four persons involved in this story, and the repetition of a melody to each verse would have defeated such a treatment. There are repetitions of melodic idea, but they accompany the reappearance of the respective characters of this miniature drama. Underlying the entire vocal setting is the piano part, which in a true art song such as this is no longer a mere accompaniment but serves as a vital part of the musical expression of the total song. In the *Erlköniq* the piano part suggests, in both rhythm and melodic motive, a ceaseless and driving quality which sets up a musical tension that acts as the counterpart of the tenseness of the poetic idea. The four dramatic characters—the poet, the father, his son, and the erlking—are individually treated in appropriate melodic settings. The whole song, however, has a unity of melody which is remarkable. After a rather long piano introduction, the first stanza of the song is given by the narrator or poet. The second stanza is carried by the father and his young son. Schubert pitches their respective parts at levels appropriate to each one. With a specific indication of great softness and a change of melody and accompaniment, Schubert introduces the erlking in the third stanza as a wheedling enticer. With the further development of these characters, the song is rushed to its tragic end. This is a fine example of the combination of purely musical and extramusical idea in Romantic composition.

In addition to the wealth of song literature, Schubert was also very active as a composer of piano, chamber music, and orchestral works. His eighth and ninth symphonies give him a permanent place in the history of symphonic literature. The eighth symphony, known as the *Unfinished* is a work in only two movements which would normally be considered as the first and second movements of a typical symphony. Whether it was Schubert's intention to add two more movements or whether he considered the work complete remains forever a question. The continued inclusion of the *Unfinished* in the orchestral repertoire attests the satisfaction it gives as a complete work. Both movements are rich in lyrical melodic structure and representative of Schubert as a melodist. The C major Symphony, Schubert's last work in this form, is typically romantic in its great length, its contrapuntal treatment, and its deep expressive power, in which Schubert rivals Beethoven. The C major symphony is both a realization and a promise of Schubert's growing command of the symphonic form which his untimely death unfortunately left unfulfilled.

Schumann, Mendelssohn, Chopin

Schumann (1810–1856), Mendelssohn (1809–1847), and Chopin (1810–1849) are each representative in some individual way of the general Romantic trends of the nineteenth century. Like Beethoven and Schubert, they all represent a certain Classic restraint in an age of Romantic emphasis. Their respective lives are indicative of the new place that musicians were forced to find for themselves in the society of the nineteenth century. Schumann became a conservatory director and musical journalist. Both occupations became possible in the nineteenth century, which saw the founding of the first state music schools or conservatories in the face of the withdrawal of the Church and the aristocracy as musical patrons. Mendelssohn, privately wealthy, founded one of the first public orchestral societies and served as its director. Chopin made his living through widespread concertizing in which his own works were featured.

Schumann's most typical Romantic expression, perhaps, comes in his piano works. In these works, he employs the small forms, such as the three-part song form, as a vehicle for a poetic mood usually suggested in the title of the work. *Carnaval*, a series of such short works strung together by an extramusical idea, serves as a good example of Schumann's contribution to Romantic mood music. This work is a musical representation of a pre-Lenten carnival ball. As a consequence, most of the twenty-two short pieces are in dance rhythms, particularly that of the waltz. The individual names of the pieces are at least suggestive of Schumann's desire to give a musical characterization of certain individuals, both real and fictitious. Besides this descriptive quality, Schumann sets himself the task of using the notes A, E flat, C, and B, which in German represent the letters ASCH, the name of a town where an early sweetheart lived. They also represented the four letters of his own name which could be musically stated. Practically every one of these short pieces is based on the use of these four notes in one order or another. Each of the sections is simply constructed. Most of them are in some version of the three-part song form or simple rondo form. Harmonies are enriched with chromatically altered tones for the purpose of lending color through dissonance. There is no actual program to give specific meaning to the individual numbers other than the oftentimes ambiguous titles. The parts which are most stimulating to imaginative picturizations are those most dancelike in character, in which the listener probably projects the movement of appropriate dance figures into the musical work. *Pierrot et Arlequin* is an example of this. While in general this work is representative of nineteenth-century tonal painting at the piano, there is the obvious concession to formal considerations so characteristic of all of Schumann's compositions.

Though Schumann's piano works are usually considered his most Romantic medium of music expressiveness, he did make an impressive contribution to the literature of the German lied. One of the best known is the song cycle *Dichterliebe* (*Poet's Love*). In a series of sixteen songs, each on a text by the Romantic poet Heine, Schumann runs the gamut of the emotions of love from humor, intimacy, and irony to unrequited love and pathos. Each poem deals with one aspect of love and Schumann set most of them in a through-composed manner. A notable characteristic of these lieder is his use of the piano for more than mere accompaniment. In an expressive manner Schumann captures the mood of the text by purely musical means expressed in the piano part as well as in the vocal line.

Mendelssohn was almost more interested in conserving the Classical tradition than Schumann. The bulk of his great works—the symphonies, the piano and violin concertos, the oratorios—show a deep regard for Classic form. However, Romanticism is apparent particularly in one specific musical mood, the fanciful fairylike nature of his scherzo movements. In fact, this particular stylistic invention of Mendelssohn is often the distinguishing feature of many of his compositions, even where the term *scherzo* is not used.

The best example of this Romantic contribution is the scherzo from *A Midsummer Night's Dream*. Written to be used with the performance of the Shakespeare play, it has become one of the great orchestral virtuoso pieces of symphonic literature. The scherzo with Mendelssohn is no longer a piece of boisterous humor such as Beethoven wrote, but a dancelike bit of imagery in which the actual tones dance as if they were indeed the imaginative sprites of fairyland. To try actually to dance to this music would be like trying to clothe an abstract idea with some material form. The short movement is based on the alternation of two closely related themes, both of which are developed briefly and restated. This work represents another facet of nineteenth-century musical Romanticism, the invoking of literary fantasy through musical technique and invention.

Chopin is the poet of musical fantasy. With the exception of a few songs scarcely known today, Chopin composed exclusively for the piano. The fact that a composer of such enormous talent could find realization for it through a single instrument gives evidence of how greatly the piano had expanded its expressive qualities. This was not accomplished merely by mechanical perfection but by the newer concepts and exploitation of pianistic composition and performance. Composers for piano, who were almost always concert performers, exploited the new technical advances and had, by the middle of the nineteenth century, so thoroughly developed the varied possibilities of the instrument that a man like Chopin could find complete expression through its medium. For Chopin the piano became an instrument capable of expressing all varieties of musical moods and feelings. His more typical approach, however, tended to exploit the tender, singing quality of the instrument through compositions which shrouded the melodic line in patterns of harmonic fantasy. Most typical works were short, carried titles which suggested a mood, and were of rather intimate character meant for performance in the salons of the nineteenth-century aristocracy and literati rather than the large public concert hall. Such compositions were the nocturnes, scherzos, preludes, etudes, and many dance forms, such as the polonaise, mazurka, and waltz, which were elevated from their folk background to a level of sophistication. Besides Chopin's great importance in the development and exploitation of the piano, his command and use of harmony is noteworthy. In his small works, he affords good examples of the importance of harmony in achieving musical tension and release which is so readily translated into poetic feeling by the listener.

The Prelude no. 2 in a minor (ex. 10.3) is a rather extreme example of the dissonant harmonic idiom of Chopin's Romanticism. This is an exceedingly short work which employs no regularity of Classic construction melically, rhythmically, or harmonically. A short melodic idea repeated four times constitutes the entire thematic material, but is actually of little significance. The harmonic structure with its constant and complete indecision as to tonality is of central importance. Not until the next to the last measure does the composer actually establish a firm conviction of the ultimate tonality of this work. And yet, the final resolution coming so late is not unsatisfactory. Chopin has contrived so well harmonically that one has been led to expect this ending. Its long delay, however, has added tension to the work. This work is an excellent example of a technique of harmonic illusion and elusiveness which comes to be more and more employed by the Romantic composers for their expressive purposes. It depends particularly on the use of chromatic tones, actually dissonances, which heretofore required careful preparation and resolution. Chopin, however, in this short work, is content not only to introduce such dissonances without preparation but to follow one dissonance with another without resolution. Here is the use of notes quite outside the idiom of normal harmonic function. In this case, these dissonances are used without question to add confusion to the orderly traditional harmonic thinking, to heighten the tension created by the mere suggestion of a harmonic plan, and to make the eventual announcement of the key in the last two measures of tremendous emotional significance by its effect of musical release and repose. This device of harmonic suspense accentuated by rhythmic and dynamic effects is one of the principal methods employed by the Romantic realist and nationalists of the nineteenth century.

Another example of a musical device to create tension is the juxtaposition of two rhythmic patterns in the Valse in A flat, op. 42. The use of dance forms was common Romantic practice. It will be noted that, after a few introductory bars, while the triple meter of the waltz is maintained regularly in the left hand, the right hand is playing a melodic idea which divides the measure into an even two beats. At the same time, an inner part made up of a constant pattern of six notes to the measure is being maintained by the right hand. This ingenious rhythmic pattern results then in two strong patterns of three and two being opposed to one another, while a pattern of six (divisible by either the three or two) acts as a sort of mediator between the two basic

Example 10.3 Chopin, Prelude in a minor, no. 2.

Chopin

Example 10.3 (continued)

rhythms. This serves as a fine example of rhythmic tension such as was employed by many other Romanticists, particularly Brahms.

A final work, the Nocturne no. 17, op. 62, no. 1, illustrates still another device of musical expression employed by Chopin and destined to become almost commonplace with later Romanticists. This device made use of rapidly changing harmonies. Classical music was inclined to change its harmonies rather slowly. Illustrations of the rapidity of harmonic change are to be found in almost all of Chopin's works, but the opening of the coda of this nocturne illustrates harmonic change on every note of the measure. By this means, the Romantic composer secures additional driving power other than that of purely rhythmic devices. Moreover, the harmonies as used here are extremely chromatic, lending a very rich texture to the passage. Passages similar to this impart a feeling of lushness or even sweetness and sentimentality to the music of the Romantic composers. A singing melodic line is supported by an accompanying pattern of rich harmonic texture with the frequent rhapsodical figures so common to Chopin. The repetition of the opening section with the addition of trills and pedaling achieves an effect of rich sonority which was one of Chopin's distinctive contributions to the art of piano playing.

It should not be assumed that only the rather radical trends of Romanticism, i.e. Realism, Nationalism and Impressionism which are taken up in subsequent chapters, characterized the second half of the nineteenth century. A large number of composers continued the fusion of traditional forms and the romantic usages of the composers of the first half of the century. Such creative spirits as Brahms, Mahler, Verdi, and Puccini are still among the most widely performed in the concert halls and opera houses of the twentieth century.

They represent a large group of composers who neither broke with tradition nor repudiated the romantic practices of the nineteenth century. In general they expanded the traditional forms to greater length, called for added volume, especially in the enlarged orchestra; they adapted the harmonic and expressive traits of their own time, and made use of the romantic characteristics expressed in literature and art when employing texts for their works.

Brahms was perhaps the most given to employing the classic forms in his instrumental works. His four symphonies are among the greatest works in the orchestral repertoire, and follow the tradition of the classic form developed by Haydn and Mozart and expanded by Beethoven. The rich harmonic structure, the use of motival repetition throughout all the movements, as introduced by Beethoven in his Fifth Symphony, the introduction of folk-like melodic themes, and the frequent use of old forms and devices of composition such as the fugal passages and the passacaglia, are all to be found in his Fourth Symphony.

Mahler, known chiefly for his symphonies, takes his cue from Beethoven's Ninth Symphony, in his great love for combining choral and solo voices with the symphonic form. With Mahler the symphony often becomes a symphonic cantata. The selection of romantic literature and the frequent employment of folk tunes and poems are indicative of his devotion to romantic ideals. The formal structure of his symphonies reflect his respect for tradition, especially that of Beethoven. Mahler's Fourth Symphony uses a number of these characteristics, namely: (1) folk themes, (2) the solo voice, (3) the inclusion of romantic texts taken from the collection known as the *Knaben Wunderhorn* (*The Children's Horn of Wonder*), (4) the expansion of the individual movements of the symphony into enormous lengths, the obsession with death in the selection of literary as well as musical material. Note the funeral march in the second movement.

In opera Verdi shares the center of the stage with Wagner, whose works are dealt with in Chapter XII under Romantic Realism. Verdi remains faithful to the tradition of the Italian opera in which the solo voice is the dominating vehicle. However, Verdi, establishes a number of romantic trends within the tradition itself. His last operas, *Aida, Otello,* and *Falstaff* represent his ultimate achievement in the use of romantic trends within the Italian opera tradition. *Otello* and *Falstaff* are the epitome of tragedy and comedy on the opera stage; while both retain the vocal character of Italian opera, the orchestra has now become a vital part of the work. It is no longer a mere accompaniment. The individual characters of the opera still sing closed arias, but these are less differentiated from the continuous flow of melodic line, and the recitative passages as such has disappeared. There are fewer and fewer set arias which can be lifted from the work as independent songs. The libretti are chosen from dramas of great literary significance. While the Wagnerian device of leitmotif (see Chapter XIII) is not adopted by Verdi, he does make use of thematic material to relate certain dramatic events by means of music. Note the use of the same melodic theme in the love duet of act one of Otello, which is recalled in the death scene at the end of the opera, thereby providing both a psychological as well as musical formal link between the two scenes.

Puccini was the foremost Italian opera composer at the close of the nineteenth century; his style was labelled *verismo*. This referred to the choice of romantic realistic stories which were used by Puccini, and the melodramatic musical setting. Whether tragic or comic, they were not dramas about heroic figures of history, but rather about real persons, generally everyday character types. *La Bohème*, whose story is that of the life struggles of young artists in the Latin quarter of Paris, and the tragic love story of one of them, is representative of the verismo style in Puccini's works. Puccini retains the traditional predominant role of the singers with some set arias. The continuous musical line, however, does not differentiate recitative elements from aria; the very colorful orchestration and the use of chorus accentuates the role of these two facets of opera writing, which had been relegated to very minor roles in the classical Italian operas of the eighteenth century.

Still other nineteenth-century composers are to be treated in subsequent chapters under the special headings of Realism, Nationalism, and Impressionism. It must be remembered that these are special trends within the general course of Romanticism and serve as much for convenience in breaking this area into smaller parts as for distinguishing one kind of composition from another. It will be seen that music devices which are basic to Romanticism in general, along with some more particularized ones, are also characteristic of Realism and Nationalism.

Summary

The revolutions of the late eighteenth to the mid-nineteenth centuries caused a great upheaval in the political and economic systems of Europe. The urge for freedom of all kinds which had started in the eighteenth century finally had a profound effect on all activities of society. New movements in politics, religion, philosophy, social life, and the arts arose in a revolt against the past.

Romanticism in the arts was also a revolt against the past. It was anti-classic, repudiating symmetry, simplicity, and the restraint of emotional expression. Romantic artists strove for emotion rather than rationalism, for individualism rather than conformity. There was no typical Romantic style in any of the arts, for all creative artists had a personal way of expressing Romantic ideas and feelings.

The patronage of Romantic art had also changed. The courts of the nobility or even the wealthy merchant class were no longer the sole patrons. For the first time, the general public became the consumer of the arts. Creative artists sought to interest the common people in their works through literature, exhibitions and concerts.

The philosophy of Romanticism brought new sources of subjects for the arts. All kinds of subjects and experiences that were previously considered in bad taste were now acceptable. Violent and shocking scenes gave opportunity for strong emotions. There was a renewed interest in nature. The atypical experience fascinated the artists because of its mystery and supernaturalism. The arts were often mixed, with painting and sculptural illustrations of literary and poetic ideas. Even pure instrumental music attempted to recreate a story or a scene in terms of melody, rhythm, tone color, and harmony. Whatever the subject, the aim was to make the spectator, or listener, feel the whole range of emotional sensations, by whatever means the artist could muster.

Romantic painters often turned towards the Dutch and Flemish art of Rembrandt and Rubens respectively for their inspiration in the use of color, light, and shade in depicting emotion. Subjects often had a moral message or sometimes were propaganda for a political or social issue. Violent scenes of carnage captured the imagination of both artist and the public, especially if they were related to an actual event that had taken place during that time. Some artists turned their attention to scenes of nature in all its varied moods.

In any event, whatever the subject, there was usually asymmetrical balance, lost edges of line, and a variety of hues and intensities of one or two basic colors. Diagonal movement of line gave depth and recession which expanded space well beyond the center of the canvas.

Music is the most Romantic of all the arts because it is the most abstract and least dependent upon objective facts or scenes which often are meaningful only to those who have experienced their history. Like Romantic visual art, music was a revolt from Classic melody, harmony, formal balance, and restraint of expression. As in the visual arts the evocation of emotion was its principal aim. Romantic music is based on the premise that a feeling of musical tension is necessary to achieve an intensification of emotional response. As a consequence, Romantic music reveals a rich harmonic texture, with chromaticism and dissonance to suggest tension. Melody is not stylized, is sometimes fragmentary, is sometimes extremely long, and is intensified by a particular tone color that suggests its character and mood.

While formal organization of Romantic music is based on the Classic principle of the sonata-allegro form, the sections are often enlarged by detailed developments of motives and harmonic sequences.

The most popular media for Romantic music were the orchestra, the piano, and the human voice. Most composers wrote forms for all three, which suggests the wide variety of musical expression. The great bulk of music literature that is still viable and captures the imagination of present-day listeners comes to us from Romantic composers such as Beethoven, Schubert, Schumann, Mendelssohn, Chopin, Verdi, and Brahms.

Musical examples

Beethoven, Symphony no. 3 in E flat Major, op. 55 (*Eroica*); Piano Sonata no. 23, op. 57; String Quartet no. 16, op. 135; Chopin, Prelude no. 2 in a minor; Valse in A flat, op. 42; Nocturne no. 17, op. 62, no. 1; Mendelssohn, Scherzo from *A Midsummer Night's Dream*; Schubert, *Heidenröslein, Erlköniq, The Trout, The Trout Quintet*, Schumann, *Carnaval*, "Dichterliebe" song cycle.

Suggested readings

Einstein, Alfred. *Music in the Romantic Era.* New York: W. W. Norton, 1947, pp. 3–71.

Grout, D. J. *A History of Western Music*, 3rd ed. New York: W. W. Norton, 1980, pp. 520–681.

Hagen, Oscar. *Art Epochs and Their Leaders.* New York: Charles Scribner's Sons, 1927, chapter 5, pp. 231–71.

Janson, H. W. *History of Art.* Englewood Cliffs, N. J.: Prentice-Hall, 1962, pp. 453–88.

Lang, Paul Henry. *Music in Western Civilization.* New York: W. W. Norton, 1941, chapters 15 and 16, pp. 734–842.

Sewall, John Ives. *A History of Western Art.* New York: Henry Holt & Co., 1953, chapter 18, pp. 852–63.

Wold and Cykler. *An Outline History of Music,* 5th ed. Dubuque, Ia.: Wm. C. Brown Company Publishers, 1982, pp. 181–234.

Suggested examples for further analysis

Painting: Constable, *The Hay Wain;* Delacroix, *Massacre at Scio;* Millet, *The Man with a Hoe*

Music: Beethoven, Symphony no. 5 in c minor, Piano Sonatas, op. 109, 110; Brahms, Symphony no. 3 in F. Major; Schubert, Symphony in b minor (*Unfinished*); Schumann, Symphony no. 1 in B flat Major; Verdi, *Otello*

Film strips with sound

Romantic Art and Music. Educational Audio Visual Inc.

Romanticism: Its Age and its Art. Schloat

Pre-Modern Art: The Age and its Art. Schloat

Additional sources for visual illustrations

Corot, *Biographical and Critical Study.* Geneva: Skira, 1966.

Gudiol, Jose. *Goya.* New York: Abrams, 1965.

Serullaz, Maurice. *Delacroix.* New York: Abrams, 1971.

Walker, John. *Constable.* New York: Abrams, n. d.

11
Realism
(1800-1900)

Chronology of Realism (including Romantism, Nationalism in Music, and Impressionism)

1746	Franciso Jose de Goya (1746–1828)	1808	Honoré Daumier (1808–1879)
1770	Ludwig van Beethoven (1770–1827)	1809	Felix Mendelssohn (1809–1849)
1776	John Constable (1776–1837)		Abraham Lincoln (1809–1865)
1782	Niccolo Paganinni (1782–1840)		Charles Darwin (1809–1882)
1786	Carl Maria von Weber (1786–1826)	1810	Frederic Chopin (1810–1849)
1791	Theodore Gericault (1791–1824)		Robert Schumann (1810–1856)
1792	Giacomo Rossini (1792–1868)	1811	Franz Liszt (1811–1886)
1796	Jean Baptiste Corot (1796–1875)	1812	Charles Dickens (1812–1870)
1797	Franz Schubert (1797–1828)		Fairy Tales by the Grimm Brothers
1798	Ferdinand Delacroix (1798–1863)		War of 1812 between England and the United States
1803	Hector Berlioz (1803–1869)	1813	Giuseppe Verdi (1813–1901)
1804	Napoleon becomes Emperor		Richard Wagner (1813–1883)
1806	Lewis and Clark reach the Pacific	1815	Battle of Waterloo

1816	Froebel founds the first kindergarten.	1841	Pierre Auguste Renoir (1841–1919)
1818	Karl Marx (1818–1883)		Saxophone invented by Adolphe Sax
	First steamship, the Savannah, crosses the Atlantic	1844	Friederich Nietsche (1844–1900)
1819	Gustav Courbet (1819–1877)		Nicolay Rimsky-Korsakow (1844–1909)
	Walt Whitman (1819–1892)	1848	Ether used for the first time as an anesthetic.
	Victoria, Queen of England (1819–1901)	1848	Marx and Engels publish the Communist Manifesto
1822	Louis Pasteur (1822–1895)	1851	Georges Pierre Seurat (1851–1891)
1823	Monroe Doctrine promulgated	1853	Japan opened to the West
1824	Bedřich Smetana (1824–1884)		First Chicago to New York rail connection
1828	First performance of Goethe's Faust		Vincent van Gogh (1853–1890)
	Suez Canal opened	1854	Thoreau's Walden published
1831	Beginning of antislavery movement	1858	Giocomo Puccini (1858–1924)
1832	Edouard Manet (1832–1883)	1859	Darwin's Origin of Species published
1833	Johannes Brahms (1833–1899)	1860	Hugo Wolf (1860–1903)
1834	Edgar Degas (1834–1917)		Gustav Mahler (1860–1911)
	Mechanical reaper invented by McCormick	1861	Russia emancipates the serfs
1837	Morse invents the telegraph		American Civil War (1861–1865)
1838	First photograph taken by Daguerre	1862	Claude Debussy (1862–1918)
1839	Modest Moussorgsky (1839–1889)	1864	First Atlantic Cable
	Paul Cezanne (1839–1906)		Richard Strauss (1864–1949)
1840	Piotor Illyitch Tchaikovsky (1840–1893)	1865	Slavery outlawed in the United States by the Thirteenth Amendment
	Auguste Rodin (1840–1917)		Jean Sibelius (1865–1957)
	Claude Monet (1840–1926)	1867	Alaska purchased from Russia
	First electric light		

1869	First transcontinental railway in the United States	1884	Universal adoption of solar day as unit of time
1870	Site of Troy excavated	1886	American Federation of Labor organized
1876	Bell invents the telephone		
1877	Edison invents the phonograph	1895	Roentgen discovers the X ray
1882	Roch discovers the tuberculosis germ	1898	Spanish-American War starts
1883	Automobile engine patented by Daimler		

Study Objectives

The objectives of this chapter are

1. To study program music as a means of suggesting Realism.
2. To learn how the photographic image influenced the visual arts as a means of portraying social Realism and natural scenes.

Pronunciation Guide

Berlioz (Bayr-lee-ohz)
Courbet, Gustave (Koor-bay, Gus-tahv)
Daumier, Honoré (Dohm-yay, Hoh-nor-ay)
Dies Irae (Dee'-ays Ee'-rih)
Eulenspiegel (Oy-len-spee'-gel)
Idée fixé (I-day feex)

Lamartine (Lah-mahr-teen)
Liszt (List)
Preludes, Les (Pray-lüd, Lay)
Strauss (Shtrows)
Wagner (Vahg'-ner)

Romanticism had focused attention on feeling and sentimentality in the arts. Artists, both visual and musical, had been viewing the world through a misty atmosphere of sentiment and fantasy. As the century progressed, there emerged those who, while still Romantic, were beginning to be concerned with actualities. There was a growing consciousness of the facts and problems of a world of reality, not fantasy. Why not express their feelings about the real world in art?

The Industrial Revolution had brought a great many social and economic problems, and its impacts upon society was both good and bad. The poverty of industrial workers gave increased point to social theory and made people more conscious of social problems. The concentration of population in urban centers also had a tendency to draw further attention to problems of human relationships. The problems of the mid-nineteenth century were the problems of the masses and all society, and the artists of Realism made them their problems.

Realism was not anti-Romantic. On the contrary, it was an integral part of the Romantic ideal, but applied to more objective subjects. Artists sought to be more "photographic," to view things with a closeness denied them by Classicism. Feeling was still a primary consideration, but it was feeling about a specific problem or event that touched the lives of people. Because of sentiment, form was still of secondary importance and the feeling about the subject was the motivating force of art.

Visual Realism is perhaps the easiest to grasp because it could deal with the burning issues of social injustice, poverty, labor, and morals. In laying bare the facts of these issues in simple realistic forms, it could intensify public sentiment regarding them. Visual art also could deal in a realistic manner with other subjects, such as simple acts of everyday living, portraits, or scenes from nature. Music, being an abstract art, found it more difficult to tell a story in tone or at least to suggest a story or a poetic idea. Various realistic devices were used: the most common was to identify a melody or harmonic sequence with an idea or object. The composer could then tell or suggest a story realistically by the use of these symbols and could reach the sensibilities of the audience through both the music and the literary suggestion.

In a sense, Realism is not an epoch of art in the manner of the Gothic or the Baroque. It was a style within a style, for it continued the basic tenets of Romanticism. Its aim was the same, and its patronage was essentially the same. One might say that because of its realistic devices art was a little less vague and sentimental. Music was more firmly knit together by means of extramusical connotations. Visual arts were more prone to straightforward lines and more visual objectivity.

Gustave Courbet (1819–1877) was one of the first painters actually to use the term "Realism" in connection with his art. He chose subjects from nature and from simple acts of ordinary people. As a Romanticist, he was a supreme egoist, taking great care that he, personally, as well as his works, should have the greatest possible publicity. He was well aware of his own talent and did not hesitate to proclaim his Realism. He is said to have told a friend, "Show me an angel, and I'll paint one." One of his famous pieces of Realism is the *Burial at Ornans* (fig. 11.1). There is nothing literary or spectacular about this work. It is a simple, straightforward account of a natural act of life, the burial of the dead, and its function is to portray this act. Its message is one of nobility and unashamed humility. The lines of the faces, however, are more clearly drawn to emphasize the sentiment of the moment. Formal organization is

Figure 11.1 *Burial at Ornans* [1849]—Courbet. (Courtesy Editorial Photocolor Archives)

multiple, but again the faces are quite separate. The blue sky and the gray and violet coloring of the figures give a monochromatic effect, broken by the patches of red. Space is controlled by the vertical arrangement of the mourners around the grave. There is, however, a realistic sense of spatial volume in the forms themselves. The painting is a realistic portrait of those who mourn a departed member of their group. Its sentiment is Romantic, but the feeling is aroused through Realism.

Honoré Daumier (1818–1879) was one of those Realists who emphasized the social and economic inequality which came as a result of the Industrial Revolution. *The Third Class Carriage* (colorplate 28) is not a pretty picture. It depicts the weariness, the poverty, and the futility of the working class. Crowded into the dark carriage are people with tired, bitter, and insolent faces. They are poor, but with their tall hats as symbols of respectability they are imitators of the elite. The woman in the front contemplates a life of toil and hardship, and the youth at her side seems destined to live out the same kind of existence. The lines denoting form are vague, but short curved lines are used to emphasize the facial and physical features of weariness. Monochromatic browns fill the atmosphere with a drabness not unlike that of its occupants. Most of Daumier's works show this class, the hardworking and miserable. They go through their weary days, a protest against the social and economic conditions of their time.

Colorplate 28 follows p. 274.

Realism in music

It has been pointed out earlier in this chapter that Realism in music lay in the rise of program music, music with a specific extramusical idea which was generally literary in nature but could be represented by plastic form as well. A number of factors tended to make realistic, or program, music the criterion by which all music of the Romantic nineteenth century was judged. The most suitable medium for program music was the orchestra with its very colorful tonal palette. The rise of the orchestra as a concert organization was an important phenomenon of the nineteenth century, as important as the opera. Listeners were impressed by the seeming ability of composers to portray specific ideas by means of the orchestra. Since the harmonic, melodic, and rhythmic devices used by the Realists to effect their aims were essentially those of the Romantic period in general, the listener was led to believe that all nineteenth-century music had a specific meaning. He even read into the works of Beethoven and Brahms the same kind of programs that Berlioz and Wagner consciously tried to express in their compositions. The works did not have to be in the orchestral field. Simple nocturnes and preludes of Chopin were given realistic subjects by the listener.

Berlioz

How did the Realists achieve, or at least attempt to achieve, the idea of program music? Examples from three of the most significant composers of this era will serve to illustrate the technique employed. First, let us turn to the *Fantastic Symphony* by Hector Berlioz (1803–1869). It is noteworthy that both Berlioz and his great contemporary, Wagner (1813–1883), were men of distinct literary abilities. As a music critic Berlioz wrote a great deal for the Parisian newspapers. His *Evenings in the Orchestra* is a collection of important essays expressing his philosophy of music as well as the current musical ideas of the nineteenth century.

The *Fantastic Symphony* was avowedly written to give a musical representation of a literary idea. The following is the translation of Berlioz's statement published with the musical score of the work:

Program of the symphony

A young musician of unhealthy sensitive nature endowed with vivid imagination has poisoned himself with opium in a paroxysm of lovesick despair. The narcotic dose he had taken was too weak to cause death, but it has thrown him into a long sleep accompanied by the most extraordinary visions. In this condition his sensations, his feelings, and his memories find utterance in his sick brain in the form of musical imagery. Even the Beloved One takes the form of a melody in his mind, like a fixed idea which is ever returning and which he hears everywhere.

First movement—[Dreams, Passions]

At first he thinks of the uneasy and nervous condition of his mind, of somber longings, of depression and joyous elation without any recognizable cause, which he experienced before the Beloved One had appeared to him. Then he remembers the ardent love with which she suddenly inspired him; he thinks of his almost insane anxiety of mind, of his raging jealousy, of his reawakening love, of his religious consolation.

Second movement—[A Ball]

In a ballroom, amidst the confusion of a brilliant festival, he finds the Beloved One again.

Third movement—[Scene in the Meadows]

It is a summer evening. He is in the country musing when he hears two shepherd lads who play, in alternation, the *ranz des vaches* (the tune used by Swiss shepherds to call their flocks). This pastoral duet, the quiet scene, the soft whisperings of the trees stirred by the zephyr wind, some prospects of hope recently made known to him—all these sensations unite to impart a long unknown repose to his heart and to lend a smiling color to his imagination. And then She appears once more. His heart stops beating; painful forebodings fill his soul. "Should she prove false to him!" One of the shepherds resumes the melody, but the other answers him no more . . . sunset . . . distant rolling of thunder . . . loneliness . . . silence.

Fourth movement—[March to the Scaffold]

He dreams that he murdered his Beloved, that he has been condemned to death and is being led to execution. A march that is alternately somber and wild, brilliant and solemn, accompanied without modulation by measured steps. At last the fixed idea returns—for a moment a last thought of love is revived, which is cut short by the death blow of the axe.

Fifth movement—[Dream of a Witches' Sabbath]

He dreams that he is present at a witches' revel, surrounded by horrible spirits, amidst sorcerers and monsters in many fearful forms who have come together for his funeral. Strange sounds, groans, shrill laughter, distant yells, which other cries seem to answer. The Beloved melody is here again, but it has lost its shy and noble character; it has become vulgar, trivial, a grotesque dance tune. It is she who comes to attend the witches' meeting. Riotous howls and shouts greet her arrival . . . she joins the infernal orgy . . . bells toll for the dead . . . a burlesque parody of the *Dies Irae* . . . the witches' round dance . . . the dance and the *Dies Irae* are heard together.

It is not necessary to go beyond this detailed program of Berlioz except to point out some of the means whereby these details find their musical counterpart. The opening of the first movement, which is entitled *Dreams, Passions*, obviously tries to portray the ephemeral quality of dreaminess through the vague manner in which the thematic material is presented. Actually, the principal theme, Berlioz's *idée fixe*, is not presented in its complete form until about four minutes of the first movement have passed. He keeps hinting at it in the use of fragmentary motives derived from the theme itself.

The opening two measures constitute a cadence in the key of C minor such as one would expect at the close of a composition. Berlioz apparently hopes to evoke the vague feelings one has in remembering a dream—something has gone before, but the ending is all that can be recalled. So it is here—a cadence implies something preceding it, but here we have only the cadence, and it opens a work rather than closes it. There is no question but that the musical mind interprets this as a peculiarly vague musical reference to something nonexistent. When this musical vagueness is coupled to an explicit literary program, or even to the title *Dreams*, we are easily persuaded that the music has realistically portrayed an actual event. Strictly speaking, the composer has merely made use of a simple and usual cadential device in a very unusual place. Besides using the device in an unusual place, he has scored it for instruments which give the passage a certain hollow tone quality, particularly when he demands that they play with extreme softness. All of this heightens the connection between musical effect and literary allusion, and we can say that Berlioz has in a measure succeeded in persuading us of the realism of his work.

This first section in the minor key acts as an introduction and leads to the major key of C which presents the main theme, not only of this movement, but of the entire symphony. Again Berlioz attaches a definite extramusical meaning to this theme by means of his program. While the first movement itself has the general outlines of the sonata-allegro form, traditional with symphonic first movements, Berlioz feels no compulsion to restrict himself to formal devices. The principal theme, the *idée fixe* (ex. 11.1), serves as the source of musical material for the whole movement.

Example 11.1®

Allegro agitato e appassionato assai

Its presentation in various episodic passages is the musical counterpart of the literary program Berlioz has used to justify his treatment of it. There is no difficulty in following Berlioz's program as applied to the music. It must be realized, however, that the success of this application rests upon a purely musical treatment of thematic material. Berlioz's success is not only achieved by the mere realistic combination of musical and extramusical ideas. His success is achieved by the masterly use of techniques of harmony, rhythm, dynamics, and instrumentation as applied to the compositional device of thematic and motival development.

Listen to the music carefully, quite apart from its program, and the unity achieved through the use of a central theme will be recognized. Likewise, one will be struck with the inventive genius of Berlioz in the way he exploits this single theme by various musical devices. Form is not discarded; it is, however, made subservient to the expressive desires. Whether these desires are dictated by purely musical or extramusical ideas is difficult, if not impossible, to say. It was probably difficult for the composer to determine also. Perhaps it would be safest to say that the broad general concept of the program acted as a point of departure for the composer. The realization of this concept through music was possible only if the composer first acceded to musical principles of composition. The details of the program had to be fitted to the musical result. The reverse procedure could only give us a sound track that had little or no artistic value as a work of art. A good example of the latter kind of procedure is the writing of music for motion pictures. After more than fifty years of such endeavor by some of our best composers, we have yet to hear an artistic piece of music that has come from the association with motion pictures.

In the second movement of Berlioz's work, the fixed idea (ex. 11.2) is but a rather slight reminder of the connection, both musical and programmatic, of the several movements.

Example 11.2

The choice of a waltz rhythm is an obvious one, as can be realized from Berlioz's program notes as quoted. The opening makes use of vague harmonic progressions of a chromatic character which are finally resolved to the key of A major in which the waltz proper is cast. The first part of the dance has its own theme closely allied to the fixed idea. The fixed idea itself is soon introduced to form a contrasting middle section. The first part returns, this time almost in a frenzied manner. A coda, in which the fixed idea is once more recalled in dramatic fashion, brings the movement to a fiery and impetuous close.

In the third movement, Berlioz is concerned almost exclusively with instrumental tone color. Thematic idea is of secondary importance. Particularly indicative of this treatment are such sections as the pastoral duet displayed by the English horn and the oboe at the opening of the movement, the thunderstorm played by the tympani, and the lonely utterance of the oboe at the very close of the movement when this instrument plays only its portion of the opening duet. All of these sections provide more sound effect than thematic construction. Even the fixed idea is used only as a faint reminiscence of the "Beloved One" in the tonal atmosphere of a pastoral scene (ex. 11.3).

Example 11.3

Through the use of woodwind instruments, traditionally associated with the outdoors, and with the use of high strings, Berlioz paints a touching musical scene of nature.

The fourth movement is a grotesque and a noisy march. Its grotesque quality is achieved mainly by the use of unusual instrumental combinations and even more unusual demands upon these instruments. Note the opening measure in which two sets of tympani, employing two performers, together with cellos and string basses, set the march rhythm. The basses are called upon to fix the tonality by having to play the tonic chord of G minor in a closed chord form at the extreme depth of their range. The first theme of the march grows out of this ominous-sounding background. By the use of certain extreme ranges of the bassoon and string basses, Berlioz effects weird tonal colors that lend credence to his program. The second theme of the march is a noisy, blatant one employing the brasses and woodwinds as if they were an actual wind band. These two themes alternate in brilliant treatment, which is made particularly significant to the program by the use of contrasting instrumental groups in cleverly contrived distribution of rhythmic patterns. The fixed idea comes into this movement only as a pure piece of Realism explained completely by Berlioz's program (ex. 11.4).

Example 11.4

In the final movement, Berlioz stakes everything on the virtuosity of his orchestration. This is particularly true in the opening measures where the entire intent is to set a mood through sound effect achieved by fantastic demands upon the orchestral instruments. Not only are the demands made upon the individual performer, but the orchestra is now made into a huge palette with enormous resources. The opening measures, for example, divide the string section into ten separate parts; and the full score calls for such unusual instruments as the E flat clarinet, valve cornets, tuba, four tympani, bells, bass drum, etc. What a change from the Classical orchestra of the eighteenth century! Berlioz calls for other new effects also, such as muted horns, the strings to be played with the wood of the bow instead of the hair, tympani to be played with sponge mallets, etc. The grotesque is heightened in this movement by parodying and burlesquing two thematic ideas: one, the fixed idea (ex. 11.5) which he uses to portray the "Beloved One," and the other, the solemn chant of the *Dies Irae* from the *Mass for the Dead* (ex. 11.6), and its parody (ex. 11.7).

Example 11.5

Example 11.6

Example 11.7

This parody is attained by rhythmic and melodic distortion of these two themes. The last movement is climaxed by a witches' dance which, strangely enough, Berlioz commences in fugal fashion, a formalism which one suspects is used for emphasizing the parody, for Berlioz is known to have disliked the fugue as a musical form. This vigorous fugue subject is finally joined by the *Dies Irae* and the symphony ends in a wild setting of musical frenzy.

Such is the Realism of one of the most revolutionary composers of the nineteenth century. By the deliberate association of a nonmusical idea with a specific musical theme, and the subsequent musical treatment of this theme in accordance with the development of this associative nonmusical idea, Berlioz achieved a convincing Realism as well as a musical work of art which could justify its existence independently of all extramusical ideas.

Wagner

Richard Wagner's Realism is achieved in much the same manner as that of Berlioz. Wagner, even more than Berlioz, sacrifices formal musical considerations to the end that all the arts, including music, should be synthesized into a new and compelling medium of artistic expression. His last great music dramas (he disliked the term "opera") are examples of his realization of such an "artwork of the future."

One of these later music dramas, *The Mastersingers of Nuremberg,* illustrates Wagner's theories concerning the "artwork of the future." The technique employed by Wagner in gaining a Realistic expression is well illustrated in this music drama. In this work, as in his later works, he employed the device of the leitmotif both as a means of musical organization and construction and as a means of making the music realistically express the literary-dramatic implications of the work. These leitmotifs are short melodic and harmonic ideas to which a certain literary or dramatic idea is attached. This association is achieved by means of the libretto, dramatic action, or even manipulation of stage properties or lighting. Each leitmotif gains in this way a definite extramusical meaning. In *The Mastersingers,* there are such motifs as the one which opens the prelude and represents the mastersingers themselves or the one immediately following this which is associated with the lovemaking of Walter. The overture itself contains many more, such as the motifs of David, of the apprentices, of the call of spring—all of which become extramusically significant in the course of the drama.

Musically, these motifs are used in the course of the music drama just as themes are used in any piece of absolute music. They are subjected to repetition, development, variation, and similar musical treatments, as are the themes of a symphony or sonata. In this respect, they are used by Wagner in much the same way as Berlioz used his *idée fixe.* However, Wagner has need for many more motifs because they have very specific dramatic significance and their use is dictated by the necessities of the dramatic action. Their musical treatment, however, calls for more than mere vocal use. In fact the music as a single part of this "new complete art" is to express the inner meaning, while the literature, drama, and even architecture and painting are to express the outward meaning. Wagner uses the orchestra rather than the voice as the vehicle for musical expression. As a consequence, the motifs are rarely sung in their pure simplicity but are treated symphonically by the orchestra.

The voice parts are conceived as a continuous decorative melody which assists in expressing the outward meaning of the drama by means of a text. Generally there are no complete forms within the course of the work. The vocal part is neither aria nor recitative, as in the traditional operas, but a sort of spoken melody.

Wagner's Realism is convincing to the degree that we are persuaded that the leitmotifs are, or are not, satisfactory musical expressions of the literary and dramatic ideas to which they are attached. If the musically strong rhythmic and harmonic quality of the leitmotif representing the mastersingers can be persuasively linked to the actual mastersingers as they are dramatically presented and developed, then we are likely to be willing to accept Wagner's Realism. If the musical device of long-delayed resolutions, achieved by the use of continuously altered and dissonant harmonies, can be represented as Realistic expression of longing, renunciation, and other psychological states, then again Wagner's Realism is successful. It would seem that, despite great opposition to his works in the latter half of the nineteenth century, Wagner not only persuaded the listening public as to the validity of his aesthetic principles but, generally speaking, he persuaded most of the composers of his own time and those immediately following him, particularly those who wrote music dramas.

The Mastersingers of Nuremberg is the only work of Wagner which is a comedy. His intuitive feeling for the stage led him to write this work in a less labored style than is felt in works such as *Tristan and Isolde* or *Parsifal*. Wagner comes close to the closed form of the aria in such a passage as the "Prize Song" of Walter. This, however, does not contradict his idea of continuous melody and motif development when one considers that the dramatic story calls for the creation and singing of an actual closed song.

Wagner not only creates a Realistic work by the deliberate association of musical idea with extramusical meaning, but he makes this association most convincing in several ways. First, he invents motifs which in their melodic outline seem to have a real relationship to the idea with which they are associated. He then strengthens these melodic ideas with rhythmic, harmonic, and tonal qualities—all of which seem eminently suitable in enhancing the illusion of Realism. For, in the last analysis, we must admit that we have allowed ourselves to become the victims of a fascinating and delightful illusion. The tones making up the opening theme of the prelude to the *Mastersingers* do not actually depict the mastersingers, but we are willing to let this musical conjurer, this tremendous creative spirit, convince us that they do. Not only are we convinced, but we even go so far as to delight in this illusion.

No other nineteenth-century Romanticist ever achieved such convincing Realism and, at the same time, such well-knit musical expression. The fact that Wagner's works are heard in large part on the concert stage, apart from all dramatic action, settings, even voice, indicates the musical solidity with which he constructed them. On the other hand, this very fact also indicates that despite Wagner's contention that the "art of the future" was to be a synthesis of all the arts and that his own works were of this nature, he actually failed to achieve this goal. The music still is the main medium in the total drama.

Two other Realists of the nineteenth century should be mentioned: Franz Liszt (1811–1886) and Richard Strauss (1864–1949). Liszt combined virtuosity with Realism, both in his composition and in his performance as a pianist. He was recognized as the greatest technical artist of his age, and his piano compositions, whether in a purely Realistic vein as *La Campanella* or in a more Classical form such as the Piano Concerto in E flat, exploit the virtuosity of the pianist. In the field of symphonic composition his thirteen tone poems are virtuoso pieces for the orchestra which were deliberately Realistic in their intent. In these works, he uses the leitmotif to effect his Realistic purpose, the motifs being related to the poem or other program which he attaches to the work. *Les Préludes* is such a composition in which Liszt contrives to express, through the musical idiom of nineteenth-century Romanticism, the poetic ideas of the French poet Lamartine in his poem *Les Préludes,* the text of which Liszt attaches to the published score of the work. By use of leitmotifs, which correspond to the ideas of the poem, and by use of technically elaborate and spectacular orchestration of these motifs, Liszt weaves a musical counterpart of the poetic idea.

Richard Strauss, a follower of the Wagner and Liszt tradition, uses the same devices of musical construction and the same principles of Realistic expression as Wagner and Liszt, both in his operas and in his symphonic tone poems. Harmonies become richer and more dissonant; the orchestra becomes a still more expanded medium. The tone poem *Till Eulenspiegel* is a remarkable example of wit and humor in music, quite apart from any program that has been attached to it. Actually, Strauss never wrote an explicit program, but he implied one through the complete title, *The Merry Pranks of Till Eulenspiegel,* and never denied the association of extramusical idea with the work. Till was a sort of half-real character of the German low countries, and every one knew his more famous pranks. It was easy to associate them with their obvious musical counterparts.

Without driving the analogies too far, the traditional pranks ascribed to Till such as the upsetting of the market ladies baskets, the parading as a priest, his love affair, and finally his trial, judgment, and execution at the close of the work, these and many others can be supplied by the listener who is familiar with the prankster and his many escapades. Strauss refused to write an explicit program for the work but gave a title which when translated reads: *Till Eulenspiegel's Merry Pranks, in an Old Roguish Manner—in Rondo Form.* Furthermore when he was pressed for an explanation of the work, he merely said that he would leave it to the listeners to crack the nuts that the rogue gives them. He indicated that the two motives (ex. 11.8 and 11.9) were representative of Till in his many disguises, moods, and situations, and that the whole ends up in a catastrophe when he is condemned and strung up on the gibbet. In Strauss's time, one must remember, the immediate audience for this work actually knew the stories of Till. He was a folk figure as well known to all Germanic peoples as is Robin Hood to those of English tradition.

Example 11.8 Richard Strauss, Themes from *Till Eulenspiegel*®

Example 11.9

Musically the work is a free rondo form in which the two motives constantly recur in various guises, changed in their melodic and harmonic forms, put into new tempos, rhythmically and tonally altered, always in a gay or wistful manner. This is a rondo unlike the Classical rondo where the themes maintain their forms quite consistently, for the motives of Till undergo many transformations.

Till Eulenspiegel illustrates the fact that no piece of music, no matter how detailed its Realistic expression or how successful its relation to extramusical ideas, can base its success as a work of art solely on its Realism. It must first be a piece of music. In the case of every successful Realist in music, success rests primarily upon his artistic skill as a creative musician and only secondarily on his ability as a storyteller or painter in tones.

Summary

As was pointed out in the preceding chapter on Romanticism, Realism is only a facet of the Romantic spirit. Realism is an integral part of the Romantic ideal, but applied to more objective subjects. Emotion was still a primary consideration, but it was to arouse feelings over a specific problem, or a specific event, often mundane, that touched the lives of ordinary people. Visual realism often dealt with the issues of poverty, social injustice, labor, or morality. Most Realistic painters tried to present their subjects in an almost photographic manner, and there was little mysticism or imagination, only the objectivity of the scene as they saw and experienced it.

Music, being an abstract art, found it more difficult to be objective, to tell a story or convince the listener of a particular scene. Program music was the result of the composer's attempt to be realistic. Various realistic devices were used to try to convince the listener of objectivity. The orchestra, with its vast resources of tone color and harmonic possibilities was the most popular media for program music. By suggesting that certain melodic configurations, certain harmonic progressions, certain tonal colorings, or rhythmic patterns were identifiable with poetic ideas, physical movement, or specific personalities, composers could in fact tell a story or paint a picture in tone. However, their music had to be based on a firm foundation of formal structure in order to survive. In most of the more successful program music, the music was probably conceived before the program it was to illustrate was completed.

Musical examples

Berlioz, *Fantastic Symphony*

Liszt, *Les Préludes*

Strauss, Richard, *Till Eulenspiegel*

Wagner, *The Mastersingers of Nuremberg* (overture and selections)

Suggested readings

Grout, D. J. *A History of Western Music*, 3rd. ed. New York: W. W. Norton, 1980, pp. 549–680.

Lang, Paul Henry. *Music in Western Civilization*. New York: W. W. Norton, 1941, chapter 17, pp. 843–94.

Robb and Garrison. *Art in the Western World*. New York: Harper and Bros., 1942, chapter 30, pp. 788–93.

Wold and Cykler. *An Outline History of Music*, 5th ed. Dubuque, Ia: Wm. C. Brown Company Publishers, 1982, pp. 184–233

Suggested examples for further analysis

Painting: Courbet, *The Wave*; Daumier, *The Washerwoman*

Music: Berlioz, *Romeo and Juliet*; Liszt, *Faust Symphony*; Strauss, Richard, *Death and Transfiguration*; Wagner, *Rhinegold, Tristan and Isolde*; Moussorgsky, *Night on a Bald Mountain*; Dukas, *Sorcerer's Apprentice*.

Film strips with sound

Romantic Art and Music, Educational Audio Visual Inc.
Romanticism: Its Age and its Art, Schloat
Pre-Modern Art: The Age and its Art, Schloat

Additional sources for visual illustrations

Rey, Robert. *Daumier.* New York: Abrams, 1966.

Colorplate 28   *Third Class Carriage* [c. 1862]—·Daumier. (The Metropolitan Museum of Art. Bequest of Mrs. H.O. Havemeyer [1929]. The H.O. Havemeyer Collection)

12

Nationalism in Music
(1800-1900)

Chronology of Nationalism in Music (Including Romantism, Realism, and Impressionism)

1746	Franciso Jose de Goya (1746–1828)	1804	Napoleon becomes Emperor
1770	Ludwig van Beethoven (1770–1827)	1806	Lewis and Clark reach the Pacific
1776	John Constable (1776–1837)	1808	Honoré Daumier (1808–1879)
1782	Niccoló Paganini (1782–1840)	1809	Felix Mendelssohn (1809–1849)
1786	Carl Maria von Weber (1786–1826)		Abraham Lincoln (1809–1865)
1791	Theodore Gericault (1791–1824		Charles Darwin (1809–1882)
1792	Giacomo Rossini (1792–1868)	1810	Frederic Chopin (1810–1849)
1796	Jean Baptiste Corot (1796–1875)		Robert Schumann (1810–1856)
1797	Franz Schubert (1797–1828)	1811	Franz Liszt (1811–1886)
1798	Ferdinand Delacroix (1798–1863)	1812	Charles Dickens (1812–1870)
1803	Hector Berlioz (1803–1869)		*Fairy Tales* by the Grimm Brothers
			War of 1812 between England and the United States

1813	Giuseppe Verdi (1813–1901)	1840	Piotor Illyitch Tchaikovsky (1840–1893)
	Richard Wagner (1813–1883)		Auguste Rodin (1840–1917)
1815	Battle of Waterloo		Claude Monet (1840–1926)
1816	Froebel founds the first kindergarten.		First electric light
1818	Karl Marx (1818–1883)	1841	Pierre Auguste Renoir (1841–1919)
	First steamship, the Savannah, crosses the Atlantic		Saxophone invented by Adolphe Sax
1819	Gustav Courbet (1819–1877)	1844	Friederich Nietsche (1844–1900)
	Walt Whitman (1819–1892)		Nicolay Rimsky-Korsakow (1844–1909)
	Victoria, Queen of England (1819–1901)	1846	Ether used for the first time as an anesthetic.
1822	Louis Pasteur (1822–1895)	1848	Marx and Engels pronounce the *Communist Manifesto*
1823	Monroe Doctrine promulgated		
1824	Bedřich Smetana (1824–1884)	1851	Georges Pierre Seurat (1851–1891)
1828	First performance of Goethe's *Faust*	1853	Japan opened to the West
1831	Beginning of antislavery movement		First Chicago to New York rail connection
1832	Edouard Manet (1832–1883)		Vincent van Gogh (1853–1890)
1833	Johannes Brahms (1833–1899)	1854	Thoreau's *Walden* published
1834	Edgar Degas (1834–1917)	1858	Giocomo Puccini (1858–1924)
	Mechanical reaper invented by McCormick	1859	Darwin's *Origin of Species* published
1837	Morse invents the telegraph	1860	Hugo Wolf (1860–1903)
1838	First photograph taken by Daguerre		Gustav Mahler (1860–1911)
1839	Modest Moussorgsky (1839–1889)	1861	Russia emancipates the serfs
	Paul Cézanne (1839–1906)		American Civil War (1861–1865)
		1862	Claude Debussy (1862–1918)

1864	First Atlantic Cable Richard Strauss (1864–1949)	1877	Edison invents the phonograph
1865	Slavery outlawed in the United States by the Thirteenth Amendment Jean Sibelius (1865–1957)	1882	Koch discovers the tuberculosis germ
		1883	Automobile engine patented by Daimler
1867	Alaska purchased from Russia	1884	Universal adoption of solar day as unit of time
1869	First Transcontinental railway in the United States Suez Canal opened	1886	American Federation of Labor organized
		1895	Roentgen discovers the X ray
1870	Site of Troy excavated	1898	Spanish-American War starts
1876	Bell invents the telephone		

Study Objectives

The objectives of this chapter are

1. To study Nationalism as a type of Romantic program music applied to ethnic groups.
2. To learn about the conscious effort to incorporate folk melody and folklore into musical composition.

Pronunciation Guide

Glinka (Gleen'-kah)
Grieg (Greeg)
Godounov, Boris (Goh'-doo-nuf, Boh'-ris)
Moussorgsky (Moo-sohrg'-skee)
Pater (Pay'-ter)

Pushkin (Poosh'-keen)
Smetana, Bedřich (Sme'-tah-nah, Bedr'-zheekh)
Tchaikovsky (Chai-kof'-skee)
Vltava (Vul'-tah-vah);
Moldau (Mohl'-dow)

We have seen Romantic and Realistic art as the expression of individualism, as an expression of the struggle for freedom and liberation from all kinds of tyranny. So far those struggles have been on a personal basis, but when the collective efforts of a people are directed toward freedom and liberty from oppression, we have Nationalism. Nationalism is the application of the Romantic spirit to the sovereign state. It is the natural development of individualism on a national scale.

After the defeat of Napoleon, it had been necessary to completely redo the map of Europe. His conquests had so changed the political map that in order that each country could gain back some of its territories, innumerable treaties had to be made. In the ensuing process, there was a tendency to draw lines according to nationalities. One after another of those smaller groups of European states and districts began the slow process of national unification. Germany, the last of the major national groups to achieve unity, finally became united in 1871 under Bismark. The smaller states like Poland, Bohemia, Norway, and Finland did not realize this aim immediately, but a growing patriotism kept the problem alive.

How did this Nationalism influence the arts? This is our immediate problem. All that was true of Romanticism and Realism is still true of the new movement. The difference is in emphasis and subject matter. Anything that could inspire the person in the street with pride and patriotism was a legitimate subject. Folklore made its debut in serious music. For centuries it had been ignored because of its association with the common people; hence it had not been a fit subject for the courtly life. It was both natural and romantic that the rise of the common person should also bring folklore and folk music into the realm of creative art.

Nationalist art had a propaganda value for the sovereign state in that it glorified the traditions of the state. Jealousy of national power and culture has been both a blessing and a curse to society as a whole. The German Nationalism which was born with Bismark has been one of the major causes of two world conflicts. Nationalism is not a period of time, but an attitude that will remain as long as there are strongly nationalistic feelings among nations. Most often, the smaller the state, the stronger the Nationalist movement in art. Small nations cannot boast of military, political, or economic power, but art is something which is not dependent upon large armies.

It is in music that we find the most powerful and lasting romantic Nationalism. Patriotism is a feeling and can best be expressed by music, the art which best lends itself to intensified emotions.

The student must remember that the artists were individuals and also Romanticists. There were no marked changes in techniques or organizations of the basic elements of the arts. Nationalism appears only in the function and in the use of materials that were indigenous to a particular country. For example, we identify Spanish music by a particular rhythmic pattern, Russian music by a certain oriental quality of melodic intervals, and Polish music by the use of folk dances, such as the polonaise and mazurka.

As is the case in Romanticism, the visual arts of Nationalism have a lesser appeal to the world today than its music. The use of contemporary events limits the appeal to those who are familiar with their history. But beyond the borders of the specific country and beyond the span of memory, these events often lose their power and significance. However, the musical means whereby Nationalism was expressed in the compositions of nineteenth-century Romanticism were already familiar to all peoples of the western European tradition, since they were much the same as those used by the Realists. In addition, while the Nationalistic extramusical ideas would never impress the nonnational public, the purely musical values remained the same for all groups. Where music of artistic worth was combined with Nationalistic Realism, it therefore found wide audiences: one within the confines of its own immediate national group because it spoke to a people sympathetic with its musical and extramusical subjects, and one outside its own national confines because it used both an artistic medium and a certain strange and unusual idiom which appealed to the romantic sense of all people. Walter Pater defined "romanticism" as "the combination of the beautiful and the unusual." This is perhaps the key to the widespread acceptance of the works of Nationalistic composers, even where people are entirely unsympathetic, or even opposed, to the patriotic ideas the composer tries to express.

Nationalism in music was not only an attempt to express the political independence of national groups, but it was also a conscious revolt for musical independence. German music has grown in its domination over European music, particularly that of central and eastern Europe, since the beginning of the eighteenth century. By the beginning of the nineteenth century, Germany provided practically all the performing musicians and teachers, as well as the music itself for the numerous smaller national groups. These groups now felt a need to parallel their hopes of independence with musical independence.

The same basic elements that were responsible for Wagner's use of old epics and legends brought about this new trend of Nationalism. Composers began to identify themselves with their own environment. Music had always contained the elements of Nationalism. There were always traces of Italian, German, and Spanish influence, but never before had there been such a conscious effort to exploit the national traits of their immediate society as there was during the last half of the nineteenth century.

Nationalism, as would be expected, was strongest among those who were politically and culturally dominated by foreign forces. The largest national groups to feel such domination were the Slavic peoples. As a consequence, we have a very conscious Nationalism in the music of the Russians, the Poles, and the Czechs.

The latter group was the smallest numerically and represented the most complete domination by a foreign people. Since the first part of the seventeenth century, Germanic culture and political organization had been imposed upon the Czechs. The liberating tendencies of the Romantic nineteenth century, however, gave hope to an unquenchable desire for freedom which could find expression only in art, and particularly in music, until the twentieth century. As a result, Czech music in the middle of the nineteenth century was intensely Nationalistic.

Bedřich Smetana (1824–1884) was a strong fighter for Czech independence, particularly in artistic and musical matters. He was, in many respects, a disciple of the musical aesthetics of Wagner and Liszt. He hoped to use their techniques, coupled with the idiom of the Czech national folk song and dance, to express the extramusical ideas of Czech nationalism through the folktales and acts of patriotism cherished by the Czech peoples. His great cycle of tone poems under the title *Ma Vlast* (*My Fatherland*) represents the adaptation of Romantic musical procedures to this purpose. This work consists of six individual symphonic poems, each dealing with a certain aspect of Czech countryside, life, mythology, and history.

Vltava (*The Moldau*), the second poem of the cycle, is a fine example of Nationalistic expression which has won itself wide acceptance in concert halls everywhere. Fundamentally this work is a typical symphonic poem in the Lisztian tradition with several leitmotifs, the most important of which is the first main theme depicting the river Vltava itself. This theme is closely allied to Czech folk song. In the course of the work, and in keeping with a detailed descriptive analysis published in the score, Smetana describes the course of this beautiful river by appropriate musical episodes through which the principal theme continues to flow. A reading of Smetana's own program will reveal as detailed Realism as is found in Berlioz's *Fantastic Symphony*. This time, however, the composer is playing upon the patriotic sentiment of his compatriots. The Vltava, which flows through the length of Bohemia, stood as a symbol of Czech strength and patriotism long before this work was written. The castles on its banks, the countryside along its broad valley, the rapids which interrupt its swift course—all these are very close to the hearts of a people who, for three centuries, symbolized their unity and strength in this river. Smetana, by his association of these "real" objects of patriotic feeling with music which was often closely related to the rich folk music tradition of his homeland, appeals to the deepest sympathies of his compatriots. This is the extramusical idea which can never, in Nationalistic music, find much more than mild understanding by one who is not "of the nation." For those who are outside this intimate relationship, the work must hold its own almost solely by virtue of its musical artistry. Its program is understood, but only as a passive observer from a distant city might view a baseball game between the Dodgers and the Yankees. If you were from Los Angeles, a Dodger victory would be all that mattered. To the visitor, a skillfully played game would be of prime importance. To the Czech who listens to *Vltava*, whatever clichés of Romanticism Smetana may have fallen into are irrelevant. The story and its musical counterpart, the beauty of the melodies and their likeness to folk song—the whole sentiment is of prime importance. The skill of workmanship is secondary in consideration.

In this respect, no one can ever have a deep attachment to, and understanding sympathy for, the National music of any others than those people with whom he or she is intimately related. As a result, much Nationalistic music is never heard outside the confines of the country in which it was composed. That which is successfully performed abroad is valued because, in addition to its peculiar Nationalistic idiom, it has intrinsic musical worth.

Russia, while it was not under the political domination of a foreign power, felt a complete and utter dependence on western Europe in the realm of art music until the advent of Glinka's opera *A Life for the Czar* in 1836. After this first essay into the field of musical Nationalism, Russia soon produced a number of composers who were determined to free Russian music from the bondage of German Romanticism.

Actually, their efforts resulted in adaptations of the techniques of this same Romanticism, flavored with the melodic, harmonic, and rhythmic idiom of Russian folk music, for the purpose of expressing some nationalistic program. Two groups of composers arose, rather strongly antagonistic to one another. The one group, the Russian Five, felt themselves to be the true representatives of Russian Nationalism, as opposed to Tchaikovsky who, in their minds, represented an alliance with German Romanticism.

A work of Tchaikovsky and one of Moussorgsky, the most original genius of the Russian Five, will reveal the difference between these two groups. The Fourth Symphony by Tchaikovsky (1840–1893) is a good example of the continued use of the Classic forms by the Romantic composer with whom the traditional forms give way to his personal expressive desires. In this work, there is evidenced the close relationship of Tchaikovsky with the German symphonic tradition of Haydn, Beethoven, and Brahms. However, his Nationalism is also very evident in the use of melodies idiomatic of Russian folk songs. This is especially apparent in the second theme group of the first movement and in the trio of the scherzo. In the finale he actually uses a popular Russian tune (ex. 12.1). While there is no program given for this symphony, nor is one intended, Tchaikovsky in his letters written at the time of its composition acknowledges its Russian Nationalism.

Example 12.1 *In the Field there Stood a Birch Tree*, Russian folk song

Such Nationalism as Tchaikovsky reveals in the Fourth Symphony was not acceptable, however, to the Russian Five, who felt that Russian composers must not only employ the idioms of Russian folk music but must link the musical idea to Russian subject matter and, above all, must create a musical tradition of their own. Perhaps the most original example of such purpose is the opera *Boris Godunov* by Moussorgsky (1835–1881). The first two scenes from this work reveal the connection of extramusical idea, as represented by the dramatic situation, with musical expression in the magnificent orchestral and choral writing—all based upon an idiom that reveals Moussorgsky's intimate knowledge of Russian folk and liturgical music. In this opera, Moussorgsky portrays the Russian people as the central heroic character. It is truly a work of Nationalistic significance. While the musical language is that of the Romantic nineteenth century, Moussorgsky does not pay tribute to Wagner by employing his aesthetic principles of music drama, nor does he follow the Italian tradition. He sets out on a rather narrow Nationalistic path and, despite the dangers of such a restrictive procedure, succeeds in writing a work of musical artistry and magnificence. Its Nationalistic ideas, musical and extramusical, are evident throughout. It is in essence a set of choral-symphonic scenes, of which the first two scenes serve as the Prologue to Act 1. Scene 1 takes place in the courtyard of a monastery near Moscow, and through its folklike melodic and harmonic idiom gives a setting of true Nationalistic meaning. Interesting to note, also, is the irregularity of meter which is so characteristic of the eastern European and Slavic folk music. The song of the pilgrims which ends the first scene brings in the liturgical music of the Russian church, which had a long history prior to the nineteenth century and was a close part of the life of every Russian person. The second scene, commonly called the "Coronation Scene," is made realistically National by the skill with which Moussorgsky simulated the sounds of the great bells of Moscow, not only through the employment of orchestral bells, but by careful orchestration and harmonic understanding. The use of folk and folklike melody likewise strikes a Nationalistic note. Beyond these musical means, he had based his libretto on a drama by Pushkin which, in turn, was based on an actual period in Russian history, so that the whole dramatic side of the opera was of intense National character.

Countless Nationalistic works ranging from short piano pieces in the folk dance idiom of various peoples to such large forms as those described above engaged many composers in the nineteenth century and continue to do so in the twentieth century. Sometimes, as with Smetana, Moussorgsky, Grieg, and others, the traits of Nationalism never seem absent from the composer's music. Others, such as Chopin and Liszt, pay some respect to this phase of Romanticism but are not entirely given over to it. All in all, it represents another facet of Romantic Realism, the importance of which can only be appreciated by realizing that here is an enormous mass of musical works only a fraction of which ever find performance outside their very restricted national areas. Only occasionally do any of these works overcome the restrictive confines of their National messages. However, their purpose was never felt to be for any others than their own people. For those groups who were struggling for cultural independence, this great musical literature was, and still is, of tremendous significance in its expression of Nationalism.

Summary

As was stated in the chapter on Romanticism, Nationalism is merely a phase of the Romantic spirit. The basic ingredients of nationalistic music are the folk songs and dances of a particular country, or ethnic group. If true folk material is not always used, composers created their own melodies in the spirit and style of folk music. In addition, legends or stories of historical events were often used as programs in the same manner as the musical Realists tried to tell stories or suggest scenes in terms of music. In any case, it is the extramusical ideas of Nationalistic interests, added to the music itself, that makes such music dear to those who are of that particular nationalistic origin. The acceptance of such music by those who are outside a specific national culture is due mainly to its musical worth in its own right and to the Romantic and exotic interest of all people.

Musical examples

Smetana, *Vltava*

Tchaikovsky, Symphony no. 4

Moussorgsky, *Boris Godunov* (scenes 1 and 2)

Suggested readings

Einstein, Alfred. *Music in the Romantic Era.* New York: W. W. Norton, 1947, chapter 17, pp. 293–336.

Grout, D. J. *A History of Western Music,* 3rd. ed. New York: W. W. Norton, 1980, pp. 549–681.

Lang, Paul Henry. *Music in Western Civilization.* New York: W. W. Norton, 1941, chapter 19, pp. 938–60.

Salazar, Adolfo. *Music in Our Time* (translated from the Spanish by Isabel Pope). New York: W. W. Norton, 1946, chapter 1, pp. 22–26, 60–70.

Wold and Cykler. *An Outline History of Music,* 5th ed. Dubuque, Ia.: Wm. C. Brown Company Publishers, 1982, pp. 184–233.

Suggested examples for further analysis

Music: Grieg, *Norwegian Dances;* Dvořák, *Slavonic Dances;* Sibelius, *Finlandia;* Glinka, *A Life for the Czar*

13
Impressionism
(1860-1900)

Chronology of Impressionism (including Romanticism, Realism, and Nationalism in Music)

1746   Franciso Jose de Goya
  (1746-1828)

1770   Ludwig van Beethoven
  (1770-1827)

1776   John Constable
  (1776-1837)

1782   Niccoló Paganini
  (1782-1840)

1786   Carl Maria von Weber
  (1786-1826)

1791   Theodore Gericault
  (1791-1824)

1792   Giacomo Rossini
  (1792-1868)

1796   Jean Baptiste Corot
  (1796-1875)

1797   Franz Schubert
  (1797-1828)

1798   Ferdinand Delacroix
  (1798-1863)

1803   Hector Berlioz
  (1803-1869)

1804   Napoleon becomes
  Emperor

1806   Lewis and Clark reach the
  Pacific

1808   Honoré Daumier
  (1808-1879)

1809   Felix Mendelssohn
  (1809-1849)
  Abraham Lincoln
  (1809-1865)
  Charles Darwin
  (1809-1882)

1810   Frederic Chopin
  (1810-1849)
  Robert Schumann
  (1810-1856)

1811   Franz Liszt (1811-1886)

1812   Charles Dickens
  (1812-1870)
  Fairy Tales by the Grimm
  Brothers
  War of 1812 between
  England and the
  United States

1813	Giuseppe Verdi (1813–1901)	1840	Piotor Illyitch Tchaikovsky (1840–1893)
	Richard Wagner (1813–1883)		Auguste Rodin (1840–1917)
1815	Battle of Waterloo		Claude Monet (1840–1926)
1816	Froebel founds the first kindergarten.		First electric light
1818	Karl Marx (1818–1883)	1841	Pierre Auguste Renoir (1841–1919)
	First steamship, the Savannah, crosses the Atlantic		Saxophone invented by Adolphe Sax
1819	Gustav Courbet (1819–1877)	1844	Friederich Nietsche (1844–1900)
	Walt Whitman (1819–1892)		Nicolay Rimsky-Korsakow (1844–1909)
	Victoria, Queen of England (1819–1901)	1846	Ether used for the first time as an anesthetic.
1822	Louis Pasteur (1822–1895)	1848	Marx and Engels pronounce the *Communist Manifesto*
1823	Monroe Doctrine promulgated		Paul Gauguin (1848–1903)
1824	Bedřich Smetana (1824–1884)	1851	Georges Pierre Seurat (1851–1891)
1828	First performance of Goethe's *Faust*	1853	Japan opened to the West
1831	Beginning of antislavery movement		First Chicago to New York rail connection
1832	Edouard Manet (1832–1883)		Vincent van Gogh (1853–1890)
1833	Johannes Brahms (1833–1899)	1854	Thoreau's *Walden* published
1834	Edgar Degas (1834–1917)	1858	Giocomo Puccini (1858–1924)
	Mechanical reaper invented by McCormick	1859	Darwin's *Origin of Species* published
1837	Morse invents the telegraph	1860	Hugo Wolf (1860–1903)
1838	First photograph taken by Daguerre		Gustav Mahler (1860–1911)
1839	Modest Moussorgsky (1839–1889)	1861	Russia emancipates the serfs
	Paul Cézanne (1839–1906)		American Civil War (1861–1865)

1862	Claude Debussy (1862–1918)	1876	Bell invents the telephone
1864	First Atlantic Cable	1877	Edison invents the phonograph
	Richard Strauss (1864–1949)	1882	Koch discovers the tuberculosis germ
1865	Slavery outlawed in the United States by the Thirteenth Amendment	1883	Automobile engine patented by Daimler
	Jean Sibelius (1865–1957)	1884	Universal adoption of solar day as unit of time
1867	Alaska purchased from Russia	1886	American Federation of Labor organized
1869	First transcontinental railway in the United States	1895	Roentgen discovers the X ray
	Suez Canal opened	1898	Spanish-American War starts
1870	Site of Troy excavated		

Study Objectives

The objectives of this chapter are

1. To study Impressionism as both the final stage of and a revolt against Romanticism.
2. To learn about the use of tone color in music and color in the visual arts as the primary vehicles of artistic expression.

Pronunciation Guide

Debussy (De-boo-see)
Grande Jatte (Grahnd Zhaht)
Mallarmé (Mahl-lahr-may)
Monet, Claude (Moh-nay, Klohd)
Moulin de la Galette (Moo-lan du lah Gah-let)
Nuages (Noo-ahzh)
Ravel (Rah-vel)

Renoir, Auguste (Ren-wahr, Ow-goost)
Rodin (Roh-da)
Scriabin (Skree-yah'-been)
Seurat (Soe-rah)
Verlaine (Ver-layn)
Vétheuil (Vu-too-ee)
Webern (Vay'-bern)

As the Romantic spirit ran its course, there was an increasing effort of all artists toward "feeling." "Art is an expression of the soul, a communication of emotional states from one soul to another"—this was the creed of the later Romanticists, an attitude that sensitized the whole field of art to the Impressionist movement. The passionate, violent outpourings of the Romanticists slackened off; in their place there arose the vague suggestions of mood and atmosphere.

Even before the turn of the twentieth century it became evident that there was little left in the Romantic conventions of art. One writer calls it a period of culture-weary art because there had been such a concentration of emotional forces that people's feelings were almost immune to further effort. The first half of the nineteenth century, however, found emotional release and spiritual values in the Romantic offerings of its artists. As the century advanced, there was an intensification of materialism that brought forth Realism and Nationalism. Finally, the shift is complete. From its subjective point of view, art goes to a completely objective point of view by the beginning of the twentieth century.

Impressionism is the connecting link between these two extremes. It is a protest against the exuberance and the excess of Romanticism, and yet it is still Romantic in that it is based on feeling. It is Realistic and objective in that it attempts to portray the subject as seen through the eyes of the artist at a particular moment and under the particular conditions of that moment. Its final aim is to evoke an image, to suggest an emotion. There is no passion, no deep feeling; it is a cult of suggestive colors, lines, and sounds, a fleeting glance, an incomplete melody; the viewer and the listener must supply the details and complete the picture. Impressionism is a sensuous art without a moral quality.

Literature provided both the painter and the composer with suggestive poetry with which to fuse their arts. Just as the painters and composers had rebelled against the structural patterns of Classic and Romantic art, the Impressionistic poets rebelled against the restrictions of poetic forms. Words were used for their musical qualities rather than for their intellectual meanings; they were used as visual symbols rather than for thought content; they were more than just words—they became a means of suggesting musical sounds and visual colors. Both painters and composers were strongly influenced by the symbolic imagery of Verlaine and Mallarmé, who headed a group of "symbolist" poets. Theirs was a fragile, erotic poetry that stimulated the imagination of their fellow artists.

The relationship between the artists and the public was also a factor in the rise of Impressionism. Artists had been gradually drifting away from the public. Some of the functions of artwork were no longer valid. Photography, for example, was taking away the job of portraiture from the painter. Courtly life was on the decline, and composers could no longer look forward to the kind of patronage enjoyed by Haydn. Official Academy painting and sculpture was stilted and stagnant, but it had public approval. The musical public, likewise, was still tied to Romantic sentiment. In an effort to entice the public from its normal path of artistic taste, artists were experimenting with new theories and new methods. One of these experiments resulted in the Impressionistic style. New vistas of art were the theoretical goal of its innovators, but public attention was also a strong motive.

Painting

The initial innovations which led to Impressionism in art were made by a group of painters in France. In their protest against the traditional methods and the exuberance of Romanticism, they concerned themselves with the objectivity of the eye. They painted only what their eyes really saw under specific conditions of light and shade. At first glance, Impressionism seems very unreal, but when one observes nature closely, it is evident that this can be a very realistic art. Color changes according to the atmospheric conditions which control the intensity and amount of light. Notice the difference in the color of grass in sunlight and in shade. The grass itself does not change, but the atmosphere causes it to take on different hues of green. Distance not only has the effect of making objects appear smaller, but it also cuts out details which we may know to be present but cannot actually see with our eyes. The Impressionists explored almost every possibility of the effect of light on color and on volume of mass.

By calling attention to the delight of instantaneous vision, the Impressionistic painters opened a new area of human experience for the artist to explore. This was to play an important part in the development of the various "-isms" of twentieth-century painting.

Landscapes, houses, people—anything that could be observed was a legitimate subject for Impressionistic painting. The only stipulation was that it must be presented as it appeared at the moment of artistic creation. This made artists change their techniques. Design was no longer of major concern. Even line, space, and formal organization were subordinated to color. Artists no longer confined painting to the studio; now they brought their work out into nature, and they had to devise a method of working that was quick and sure. They used only a few basic colors and brushed them on quickly with bold strokes, for they realized that blending of color hues could take place in the eye of the spectator. A canvas must be finished at once before the light effects changed. At times it was necessary for the artists to wait days, even weeks, for the same conditions of light and atmosphere to return. Landscapes with water were particularly popular with painters because of the fact that water responds to the slightest change of light and wind.

Claude Monet (1840–1926) was one of the successful painters using the Impressionistic technique. In fact, it was his painting *Impression: Sunrise,* which he exhibited in 1874, that gave the movement its name. The *Banks of the Seine, Vêtheuil* (colorplate 29) is a coloristic study of the effect of light and atmosphere on water, trees, and foliage. There are no people, and there is no emotion, no action, no social problems—only the quiet beauty of the shimmering reflections on the water. Note how Monet has applied the color in bold patches, with no effort to integrate them on the canvas. Details of the trees and foreground foliage are vague and obscure. Space is made apparent in various ways. One is by bringing the horizon high in the painting and by having a large area of foreground foliage. Another technique is the use of

Colorplate 29 follows p. 290.

clearer brush marks on the foreground, but each is only a bit of color, not the linear outline of leaves or flowers. There is little sense of formal organization, for the painting is an impression of a segment of real life and not a carefully arranged pattern.

In *Rouen Cathedral* (colorplate 30), Monet has caught the full force of bright sunlight on the facade of the cathedral. This is one of many canvases painted of the same subject, each under a different light condition. The intense light has a tendency to break down the massiveness of the building. Lines are shadowy. There is no idea of ordered structure or calculated design except that determined by the architectural subject itself. Color is in patches of grays and tans that mean nothing when viewed closely but integrate into a whole when viewed from a distance. Monet only suggests to the spectator the idea of the cathedral in the brilliance of a noonday sun.

Auguste Renoir (1841–1919) is another French painter who was sympathetic to the Impressionistic school. Renoir was not wholly concerned with color, however, for he carried on the tradition of structural form from the Romanticists. Consequently, we have more emphasis on the plastic quality of figures, but he painted them with the realistic technique of Impressionism. *By the Seashore* (colorplate 31) is such a canvas. Renoir places his subject against the background of sky and water. There is a fragile and scintillating quality about the landscape. Pastel colors scarcely define anything except the rocky cliff. The lady, however, is boldly modeled in a most traditional fashion, but the effect of light and color is apparent in the soft tones of flesh and in the reflecting folds of her dress.

Le Moulin de la Galette (fig. 13.1) shows Renoir's treatment of a group of figures. There is an intentional blurring of outlines, for here he has paid little attention to the details of form. The effect of light on color and form is again the most important impression one receives. Note how the patches of light fall on the dark shadows. The stripes of the dress of the figure at the table are bleached by light. The background figures become merely brushstrokes of pastel color. There is no feeling of formal balance or organization. Renoir has painted only the gaiety of color with a realistic impression of a whirling throng in the sunlight. If it has any sense of motion, it is that of including the observer in the creative process. Unlike the Baroque, in which the spectator is sometimes drawn into the picture, Impressionism forces the viewer to synthesize and complete the picture.

Paul Gauguin (1848–1903) can be called a Post-Impressionist. After being disenchanted with the industrial civilization of his time he escaped to Tahiti in search of the simple primitivism of the South Seas. Here he began to use color as flat surfaces without three dimensional modeling, with the aim of decorative organization. Unity came as the result of the juxtaposition of patterns of color that were symbolic of primitive forms. His *Mahana No Atua* (*Day of the Gods*) (colorplate 32) gives us a vicarious experience of a simple life style in an exotic setting. It is a quiet two dimensional decorative design devoid of action or sensuousness.

Colorplates 30, 31, 32 follows p. 290.

Figure 13.1 *Le Moulin de la Galette* [1876]—Renoir. (Courtesy Editorial Photocolor Archives)

George Seurat (1859–1891) is sometimes called a post-Impressionist. He seemed to exploit the impressionistic theories to their logical end as a bridge to the twentieth century. He was still mainly concerned with color and light, but in a more disciplined manner. He reduced brushstrokes to thousands of small dots of color of uniform size that were designed to merge into shapes in the eye of the beholder much like the bold patches of color used by Monet. Seurat's style is often called "pointillism" and is sometimes compared to the fragmentary musical fabric of Anton Webern. *Sunday Afternoon on the Island of La Grande Jatte* (colorplate 33) is one of his best-known paintings. The forms become almost geometrically stylized through the integration of dots of color in varying hues and values. A strong sense of spatial recession is achieved by the progressively smaller size of background figures. There is no sense of movement, merely a static family portrait of people in a park.

Colorplate 33
follows p. 290.

Colorplate 29 *Banks of the Seine, Vétheuil* [1880]—Monet. (Courtesy National
Gallery of Art, Washington, D.C., Chester Dale Collection)

Colorplate 30   *Rouen Cathedral, West Façade, Sunlight* [1894]—Monet. (Courtesy
National Gallery of Art, Washington, D.C., Chester Dale Collection)

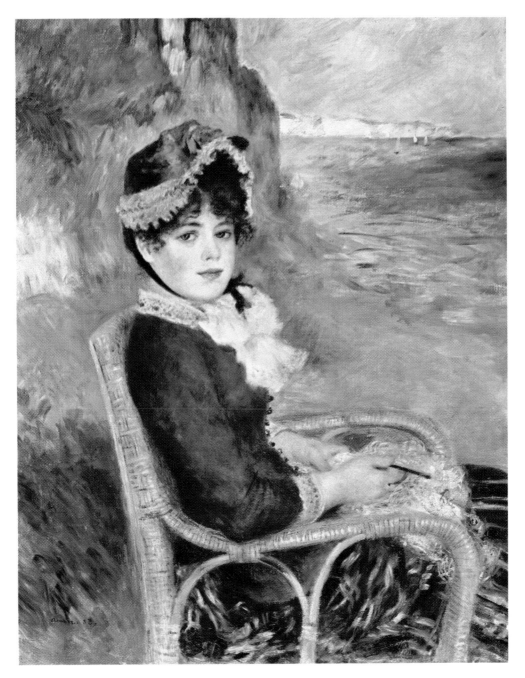

Colorplate 31 *By the Seashore* [1883]—Renoir. (Courtesy The Metropolitan Museum of Art, bequest of Mrs. H. O. Havemeyer, 1929. The H. O. Havemeyer Collection)

Colorplate 32 *Mahana No Atua (Day of the Gods)* [1894]—Gauguin. (Collection of
the Art Institute of Chicago)

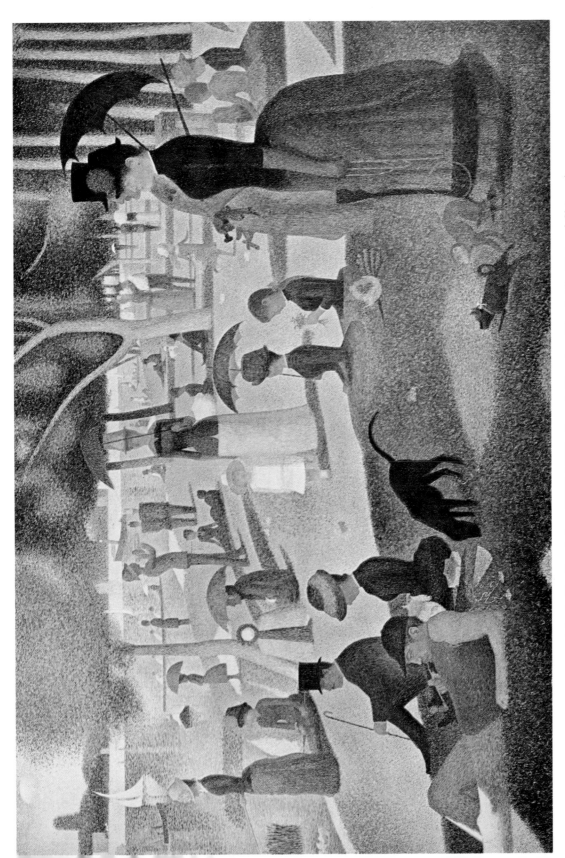

Colorplate 33 *Sunday Afternoon on the Island of La Grande Jatte* [1884–1886]—Seurat. (Courtesy The Art Institute of Chicago)

It is impossible to discuss all the Impressionistic painters. There have been thousands of paintings in this style, all following the same formula of visual reality. Only a few artists, however, have achieved success in this stylistic medium. It is too restricting, too specialized, and too lacking in spiritual and moral values. There seems to be little except a fleeting pleasure to be gained. The history of art has shown us repeatedly that to be alive, art must present values which are more important and more universal in their appeal.

Sculpture

The feeling for luminous color and fragmentary form was primarily a technique of painting, but sculpture was also touched by the spirit of Impressionism. Auguste Rodin (1840–1917) was, without a doubt, one of the greatest sculptors of the nineteenth century. While he cannot be truthfully called an Impressionist, his later works show this influence. He began to "suggest" in stone and bronze. He liked to leave something to the imagination of the spectator—something that could be completed only in the visual experience of the beholder. To achieve this effect, Rodin sometimes left the plastic modeling of form incomplete and let his figures emerge out of the material. He also tended to dematerialize form by using light and shade in the modeling of surfaces into hollows and projections which caught light and thus produced shadows.

The Kiss (fig. 13.2) is a fine example of this influence of Impressionism on sculpture. The play of lights and shadows over the surfaces of the entwined figures gives a feeling of the warm flesh tones. The same effect of light seems to lessen the sense of weight and hardness of the marble, and it also breaks up the volume into suggested fragments. Rodin has made his figures almost abstract by the lack of classic-type detail, by veiling the heads by the woman's arm, and by the use of shadow. While the subject is sensual, the passion of the scene is only suggested to the spectator.

Music

Impressionism was also carried over into the realm of music. Composers experimented with new ways and means of achieving coloristic effects in response to the luminosity of the painters. Many of these experiments seem fantastic to us today. Cyril Scott, the English composer, went so far as to work out a scientific analogy between the color spectrum and vibrations of sound. He then proceeded to compose according to this analogy. Scriabin, the late nineteenth- and early twentieth-century Russian composer, decided to include the sense of smell in his onslaught against sense perceptions. The performance of his last work, *Mysterium*, which he never completed, was to include a screen with changing colors and the release of certain perfumes as

Figure 13.2 The Kiss [1886]—Rodin. (Courtesy Editorial Photocolor Archives)

an accompaniment to the music. Needless to say, these experiments were generally failures. However, Impressionism did find its successful counterpart in the music of Claude Debussy (1862–1918).

Like French painters, Debussy raised his voice in protest against the exuberance of Romanticism. In this case, music was directly influenced by painting and literature, for Debussy was greatly stimulated by the paintings of Monet and also by the literary Impressionists. Debussy was also influenced by the music of the Orient, especially from Bali and Indonesia which was performed at the Paris Exposition of 1889. Naturally, the materials and techniques of music differ greatly from those of the visual arts, and Debussy did not attempt to imitate the effects of coloristic scenes. He did, however, try to suggest the same kind of feelings in his music as his colleagues did in painting and poetry. He sought to express the shimmering effects of light and shades in painting by means of tone color and chordal structure in music.

Debussy sacrificed lyric melody, traditional form, and polyphonic complexities for suggestive harmonic progressions. In order to achieve a more luminous tonal coloring, he destroyed the traditional relationships of the successive scale steps and, in the whole-tone scale, he endowed each note with a subtle persuasion all its own. He weakened his musical cadences by parallel chord progressions which helped to dissolve harmonic tensions. Debussy's music is almost formless in its vague meandering of melody and harmony.

His *Prelude to The Afternoon of a Faun,* written in 1894, was the first of a series of Impressionistic compositions and, perhaps, the most successful of all. It is a brief symphonic poem based on Mallarme's poem of the same title dealing with a mythical creature, a faun, half man and half beast. It describes the awakening of a faun in the forest and his recollection of the previous day, in which he wonders whether his experiences were dreams or whether the visit of the nymphs was real. Debussy has captured the fanciful spirit of the poem with a tonal fabric that suggests the feeling of the poetic idea.

There is no obvious formal organization in this music, but Debussy implies the use of the repetition-after-contrast device by using three quite contrasting melodic ideas and repeating the first more than once. This main melody (ex. 13.1), played by the flute, rises and falls gently and chromatically, at first alone, then weaving in and out of subtle harmonic progressions that seldom seem to reach a complete cadence.

Example 13.1

Climaxes are only anticipated, for they never reach the full force of tonal power that is promised. Rhythm is exceedingly complex, moving in and out of measures of nine, six, twelve, and four beats without establishing an easily recognizable pattern for any one of them. The fragile and lazy melodic line of the flute, the soft sweep of slightly dissonant chords on the harp, the restrained climaxes of the full orchestra—all of these serve to suggest to the listener just such a feeling of blissful drowsiness as the poet implies.

An analysis has already been made in chapter 2 of another of Debussy's works, *Nuages.* Refer to it again, and listen to the music in light of what we have said about Impressionism. Note that Debussy uses the same techniques in both *The Afternoon of a Faun* and *Nuages,* and he achieves much the same degree of coloring and subjective feeling in both. Like Monet's paintings, *Rouen Cathedral* and the *Banks of the Seine,* Debussy's music is evasive. It suggests a "feeling," thereby forcing us into the creative process. The music is cradled in the soft glow of pastel harmonies, outlined by delicately shaded melodic lines which fade into the shadow of musical imagery.

Debussy reflects the oversensitive, restless mind of the late nineteenth century. He avoids the passion and sentiment of earlier composers and, at the same time, there is little hint of the harsh, brittle materialism which was to come. He is the very quintessence of musical Impressionism; in fact, he was the whole movement. No other composer, with the possible exception of Ravel, so consistently created works in this style. Suite I and II from Ravel's ballet, *Daphnis and Chloe,* are excellent examples of his impressionistic style and skill in orchestration. Because it was oversensitive and lacking in vitality and spiritual ideals, Impressionism in music, as well as in painting, was destined to be short-lived. All the arts were to enter a period of radical revolt against the nineteenth-century traditions of music and art, including Impressionism.

Summary

Impressionism can be thought of as a bridge between Romanticism and the twentieth-century abstract art. On one hand, it is a revolt against the emotional exuberance of the Romantic and, on the other hand, is an art of color and the technique of achieving coloristic objectivity, both visually and in terms of tone color in music. Impressionistic painters were interested in the phenomena of instantaneous vision; that is, the integration of color and line in the eye of the spectator. Artists painted what they actually saw at a particular moment, under the immediate conditions of atmosphere, light, and shade, and from a specific angle or perspective of vision. Impressionists usually went out of doors for their subjects. Landscapes, especially water where the play of light and wind could change color and forms, were the favorite subjects. There is little movement, for the subject remains static. There is no passion or deep feeling evoked by emotional behavior. Line, spatial concepts, and formal organization were subordinated to the technique of juxtaposing bold strokes of color that would blend in the eye of the beholder.

Music came under the influence of Impressionistic painters and poets. In fact, some composers consciously tried to suggest the same kinds of feeling in music as in painting and poetry. Tone color and harmonic progressions took precedence over formal organizations, polyphonic complexities, and even over lyric melody in many instances. Composers weakened the strong tonal center of earlier music and thereby lessened the sense of tension and release that is associated with the emotion and passion of the Romantic. Impressionistic music suggests "feeling" with its vague melodic lines, static harmonies, and rhythmic complexities that invite listeners into the creative process in music in the same manner as color and line in painting invite the beholder to complete the scene.

Musical examples

Debussy, *Prelude to The Afternoon of a Faun, Nuages*

Suggested readings

Austin, William W. *Music in the 20th Century.* New York: W. W. Norton, 1966, pp. 1–53.

Grout, D. J. *A History of Western Music*, 3rd. ed. New York: W. W. Norton, 1980, pp. 636–681.

Janson, H. W. *History of Art.* Englewood Cliffs, N. J.: Prentice-Hall, 1962, pp. 489–511.

Lang, Paul Henry. *Music in Western Civilization.* New York: W. W. Norton, 1941, chapter 20, pp. 1014–23.

Robb and Garrison. *Art in the Western World.* New York: Harper & Bros., 1942, chapter 30, pp. 793–802.

Sewall, John Ives. *A History of Western Art.* New York: Henry Holt & Co., 1953, chapter 18, pp. 863–74.

Wold and Cykler. *An Outline History of Music*, 5th ed. Dubuque, Ia.: Wm. C. Brown Company Publishers, 1982, pp. 184–233.

Suggested examples for further analysis

Painting: Degas, *Ballet Dancer;* Manet, *Picnic on the Grass;* Renoir, *Three Bathers*

Music: Debussy, *La Mer;* de Falla, *Nights in the Gardens of Spain;* Griffes, *The White Peacock;* Respighi, *Fountains of Rome*

Film strips with sound

Impressionism in Art and Music, Educational Audio Visual Inc.
Pre-Modern Art: The Age and its Art, Schloat

Additional sources for visual illustrations

Courthion, Pierre. *Manet.* New York: Abrams, 1963.

———. *Seurat.* New York: Abrams, 1968.

Jacobus, John. *Matisse.* New York: Abrams, 1973.

Peck, Walter. *Renoir.* New York: Abrams, 1950.

Rich, Daniel Cattan. *Degas.* New York: Abrams, 1951.

Seitz, William C. *Monet.* New York: Abrams, 1960.

14
Modern to 1945

Chronology of the Twentieth Century

1839	Paul Cézanne (1839–1906)	1879	Raoul Dufy (1879–1953)
1853	Vincent Van Gogh (1853–1890)		Paul Klee (1879–1940)
			Josef Stalin (1879–1953)
1856	Sigmund Freud (1856–1939)		Albert Einstein (1879–1955)
1864	Leoš Janáček (1864–1928)	1881	Pablo Picasso (1881–1973)
1866	Vasily Kandinsky (1866–1944)		Wilhelm Lehmbruck (1881–1919)
1868	Scott Joplin (1868–1917)		Béla Bartók (1881–1945)
	Henri Matisse (1869–1954)	1882	Igor Stravinsky (1882–1971)
1869	Frank Lloyd Wright (1869–1959)		James Joyce (1882–1941)
1871	Georges Rouault (1871–1958)	1883	Walter Gropius (1883–1969)
1873	W. C. Handy (1873–1958)		Anton Webern (1883–1945)
1874	Winston Churchill (1874–1965)	1884	Franklin D. Roosevelt (1884–1945)
	Arnold Schoenberg (1874–1950)	1885	Alban Berg (1885–1935)
	Charles Ives (1874–1954)		Edgar Varese (1885–1965)
1875	Maurice Ravel (1875–1937)	1887	Charles Eduard Jeaneret (Corbusier) (1887–1965)
1876	Constantin Brancusi (1876–1957)		Marc Chagall (1887–)
1877	Piet Mondrian (1877–1944)	1888	Jean Arp (1888–1966)
			T. S. Eliot (1888–1965)

1890	Naum Gabo (1890–1977)	1914	First World War starts
1893	Joan Miró (1893–)	1915	Panama Canal opened
1895	Paul Hindemith (1895–1963)	1917	First printed use of the term "Jazz"
1897	Ragtime from c.1897 to 1915	1918	First World War ends
1898	Alexander Calder (1898–1976)		Leonard Bernstein (1918–)
	Henry Moore (1898–)	1923	Gyorgi Ligeti (1923–)
	Bertold Brecht (1898–1956)	1925	Gunther Schuller (1925–)
	Ernest Hemingway (1898–1961)	1928	Karlheinz Stockhausen (1928–)
	George Gershwin (1898–1938)	1933	Krzysztof Penderecki (1933–)
1899	"Duke" Ellington (1898–1974)	1934	Peter Maxwell Davies (1934–)
1900	Aaron Copland (1900–)	1938	Nuclear fission discovered
1901	Alberto Giacometti (1901–)	1945	Atomic bomb destroys Hiroshima and Nagasaki
1904	Salvador Dali (1904–)	1946	First assembly of the United Nations
	Willem de Kooning (1904–)	1950	Pop and Op art (c. 1950)
	Luigi Dallapicolla (1904–1975)	1957	First satellite (sputnik) launched by Russia
1906	Peter Blume (1906–)	1960	Rock and roll (c. 1960)
1908	Elliott Carter (1908–)	1969	First man landed on the moon
	Olivier Messaien (1908–)		
1912	Jackson Pollock (1912–1956)		
	John Cage (1912–)		

Study Objectives

The objectives of this chapter are

1. To learn about the influence that mass media has on all the arts.
2. To study the technical development of new materials and new sounds.
3. To learn about the revolt against the excesses of Romanticism.
4. To learn about the rise of jazz as a phenomenon of the early twentieth century.

Pronunciation Guide

Arp, Jean (Ahrp, Zhahn)
Bartók (Bahr'-tok)
Bauhaus (Bow'-hows)
Berg (Bayrg)
Bloch (Blokh)
Brancusi (Bran-koo'-zee)
Cézanne (Say-zan)
Chargall (Shah-gahl)
Corbusier (Kohr-boo-see-ay)
Dali (Dah-lee)
Freud (Froyd)
Gabo (Gah'-boh)
Giacometti (Jah-koh-met'-tee)
Gropius (Groh'-pee-oos)
Guernica (Gwer'-nee-kah)
Haba (Hah'-bah)
Jas de Bouffan (Zha de Boo-fà)
Kandinsky, Wassily (Kahn-din'-skee, Vah-see-lee)

Klee (Klay)
Koussevitsky (Koo-se-vit'-skee)
Lehmbruck (Laym'-brook)
Mahler (Mah'-ler)
Matisse (Mah-tees)
Miro (Mee'-roh)
Mondrian (Mon'-dree-ahn)
Petrouchka (Pe-troo'-shka)
Picasso (Pee-kah'-soh)
Pogany (Poh-gah'-nee)
Rimsky-Korsakov (Rim'-skee Kor'-sah-koff)
Rouault (Roo-ahlt)
Schoenberg (Shoen'-berg)
Stravinsky (Strah-vin'-skee)
Van Gogh (Van Gokh)
Webern (Vay'-bern)

We have been following a thesis based on art as a reflection of the cultural forces of the age. What, then, are some of these forces in the twentieth century, and how have they placed their imprint upon the art of our day?

The first fifty years of the twentieth century saw the most drastic changes in our way of life. Almost all of these changes can be laid directly at the door of technological and scientific advances. We are conscious that we do live in an age almost entirely given over to technical experiments and developments that have resulted in a scientific concept of life. It has also led us to the threshold of a chaos of overorganization and to an almost brutal indifference to the individual as a human personality. Our last two world conflicts have shown that we also live in an age of doubt and distrust, in an age of uncertainty, dissatisfaction, and disillusionment. We live in an atomic age, and we are deathly afraid of the consequences. In spite of more scientific research and more mechanical devices to make life easier and give us more leisure, the world is suffering more pain and hunger than we have ever known before.

We are all somewhat aware of the changes which are, and have been, taking place in the economic, social, and moral spheres of our life; there have been so many it is hardly possible to even note them here. These changes represent signs of a new era with which we are not yet familiar, but an era which we have the power to mold. Future historians will determine whether we reached a higher artistic level than those before us. It will depend on our own faith and moral fiber, on our efforts and sacrifices for a better world.

In spite of our recognition of the technical nature of our civilization and in spite of our distrust and disillusionment, somehow we have expected our artists to continue, as they did in previous times, producing a romantic art of feeling and sentiment. While we live in a mechanical world, we often condemn modern artists when they are only trying to embody in their art the intellectual, spiritual, social, scientific, and economic trends of our time. If we are to grow and avoid cultural death through stagnation, we must seek to learn what they are trying to express. Artists have always been prophets of the future and reliable indexes of the present, for they have the intuitive power to sense relationships and trends which we often miss. If we continue to close our eyes and ears to this, we are guilty of ignorance, of denying our own culture, and thereby giving strength to an already noticeable tendency toward decay.

Artistic growth, like physical growth, is essential to life. Any standstill or stagnation will result in a devitalization and eventual decadence of art. Thus we see that the modern trends in music and art are nothing more than an attempt to stimulate growth and avoid sterility through stagnation. This growth, or change, is usually made by breaking down old boundaries and widening the horizons of artistic expression. We have already seen that the Renaissance was a revolt against the Medieval, the Romantic a revolt against the Classic, and the Impressionistic a revolt against the Romantic. Modern art is also a revolt. It is a revolt against the sentimentality of Romanticism and, at the same time, an affirmation of the scientific attitude.

After the turn of the century, we began to question the wallowing in emotionalism and sentimentalism of the Romantics. We also began to question the realistic and materialistic world which had seemed so real and permanent to our predecessors. There rose a demand for some sort of artistic explanation of the scientific phenomena which were being explored and their integration into the entire society. The results of research with X rays and the microscope, the splitting of the atom, the new concepts of time and space, the psychological research of people such as Freud—all of these phenomena challenged the artists. Artists were looking for some expression that would mirror these results in a new conception of the world based on inward, not outward, appearances. The result was a rejection of the Renaissance theory that art must be based on natural representation. In an attempt to understand and express what lay behind natural appearances, the essence of things came to be of greater importance than their outward forms to the modern artist as well as the scientist. Creative minds tried to follow science. They tried to make of art some sort of universal vision, freed from physical appearances and, at the same time, a truthful mirror of their age.

How can we tell whether contemporary artists are really incorporating truthful remembrances of our time into art? This is a difficult question, for only the slow and cumbersome, though infallible, processes of time can state with finality: "Here is a rich consummation of the spiritual influences and tendencies of a hectic age." We who live in that hectic age do not want to wait; we desire a final statement immediately. If we cannot have it, we are likely to retreat to the work of those artists on whom time has already placed its stamp of approval. We must have the tolerance and the courage to face our artistic future. We must endeavor to understand what modern artists are trying to do, and we must set values on their work.

While we cannot state with finality that this or that artist is "great," there are certain trends which we can observe and evaluate. As in other periods, moderns artists, whether painters, sculptors, architects, or composers, can be grouped into three types, all based on the premise that art must continue to grow in order to stay alive. Since we are so close to our artists and cannot always separate the great from the less than great (a process that has already been completed for the older periods), it will be advantageous to know at least what these three types are like.

One type of artist can be called "sensationalist." Sensationalists break down convention and throw overboard the ballast of accepted methods and values. They are often brilliant, but, because their art is most often aimed at gaining attention through shocking subjects and techniques, their works frequently lack expressive qualities and sometimes even sincerity.

The second type can be called the "experimentalist." As is the case with most innovators, they are seeking new methods and combinations of materials to express themselves. They are treading on new ground and are basing their art on untried theories. They are sincere, but their art often lacks unity and coherence. Experimentalists pay the price of most innovators, for they seldom perfect what they invent.

The third type is artists who are great enough to combine that which is good from the first two types and what is valid from the past into personalized expressions. Their art is usually less brilliant but it shines with a more steady light than that of the sensationalist or experimentalist. It may be a more accurate reflection of our age. Unfortunately we cannot always segregate our artists into these types. This can come only through a faith in, and an understanding of, our art and the assurance that the greatest creators will integrate truthful remembrances of today with their creations.

Like the Romantic, twentieth-century art is difficult to reduce to a set of rules. There have been a great many experimental styles that have left their mark. Furthermore, because of the rapid tempo of our life, there has been a speedy change of these "-isms" in modern art. There has been such a general overlapping of styles that one can hardly separate them chronologically. There are, however, a few basic principles that seem to be common to most twentieth-century artists. These principles can be stated as a sort of creed that serves as a general guide for almost all artists in their effort to grow and avoid stagnation. Naturally, this creed is not subscribed to by all our artists, nor are all portions of it necessarily applicable to those who do accept it. It is merely a generalization of what most of them believe.

The first principle holds that artists must break with the past, especially with nineteenth-century Romanticism. The modern movement is a revolt against all that the Romantics stood for—their techniques, their subjects, and their expressions. If contemporary artists have any real attachment to the past, it is to the Classic ideal, for they are more concerned with method than with subject.

Second, modern artists reject subjective emotion as a basis for art. They reject the idea that personal feeling, or emotion, has a place in artistic expression. In the case of Stravinsky and Picasso, we have a flat denial of emotion of any kind. This attitude is perhaps born of our own scientific age, for we are dominated by the machine, which is made of steel and has no feelings. Even men in business and politics have a tendency to deny feelings in their impersonal organizations.

The third item in the creed of contemporary artists is the rejection of the concept that art must be realistic or literal. They insist that art is a matter of representing abstract patterns—something that can exist as an absolute thing in itself rather than as a means for suggesting ideas, experiences, or definite objects. This seems also to be a demonstration of the scientific attitude of understanding the world in terms of mathematical formulas.

The last principle that seems to be a part of the creed is the rejection of unnecessary ornaments and of attempts to "dress up" art. "Form follows function" is a motto for modern artists. As a result, there is a demand for simplicity, terseness, and often brutality of expression. There is little attempt to please or to entertain, only a desire to present our age simply and unashamedly.

From the above creed, it would appear that most twentieth-century art would be cold, intellectual, and perhaps a bit cynical. This was generally true during the early decades, but the last few years have seen a softening, a realization that feelings do have a place in art. It is fair to say that from about 1930, art has had a tendency to swing back toward the Romantic ideal, not to a point of sentimentality, but to the recognition that man has a soul and even the machine must be guided by human hands. The tendency is increasing.

Another factor that should be taken into consideration in our study of contemporary art is the relation of artists to their public. Creative artists of today are even further alienated from their public than Romantic artists. This is due to a number of factors. First, the public cannot keep pace with the speed with which art styles change. It takes time to become acclimated to an art style and, today, the public barely comes to a point of acceptance of a particular style when that style is no longer valid. Consequently, the gulf between patron and artist is widened and the patron seeks aesthetic pleasure in something more firmly established in the past.

The second reason for the alienation of creative artists from their public is closely related to the first. Because of the technical advance in mass production of copies and because of the availability of recordings, the public no longer has to depend upon the gallery or concert hall for artistic experience. There is less urge to explore the new and the untried. Mass education and mass communication have tended to place a premium on conservatism. Trade publishing, recordings, radio, television, and motion pictures—all business enterprises—give the public "artists" and old masters whose reputation has been established and is unquestioned.

Because contemporary art is often an unknown quantity, it is by-passed, leaving artists to retreat into teaching or some other means of making a living, for they seldom can live by their own creative efforts.

The Architects are the only contemporary artists whose works have received broad recognition and who have generally reaped reasonable rewards from society. This has been due in part to the functionalism of architecture, which has evoked an enthusiastic response from a society that worships efficiency and usefulness. In just what way architects do this, we shall find out later.

Painting

It is impossible to say there is an exclusive modern style in painting. Because life is so complex, there are bound to be those artists who are endeavoring to reflect this or that aspect of contemporary life. Furthermore, because we are so close to these artists, it is impossible to pick out for study only those who will stand the test of time. We therefore will confine our study to what seem to be the most important movements, and to the analysis of the works of a few artists who seem to have had great influence on their contemporaries and who seem, from this vantage point, to have endowed their art with something of the spirit of the modern age.

Expressionism

The desire of contemporary artists to get behind natural appearances and to present the inner meaning of natural phenomena has already been mentioned. One aspect of this influence can be called "Expressionism." These artists were seeking to express the elemental feelings inherent in a real world. They were not sentimental Romanticists, nor were they stark realists. They were often dissatisfied with the world as they saw it and were aware of the conflicts inherent in it—conflicts in both nature and human nature. In a real sense, they were the prophets of the world conflagrations which we have since experienced.

The forerunner of this "ism" lived out his short life before the turn of the twentieth century. Vincent van Gogh (1853–1890) was a deeply religious man—a man aware of the cosmic, or divine, forces of the universe. He attempted to paint his feelings about the natural world—not only what he could see of it, but what he knew of it. Van Gogh thought of himself as a missionary of kindness. He lived a simple, humble life with miners, giving away his meager funds to the needy. He even shared his rooms with a prostitute and her child because he could not bear to let their suffering go unheeded. He was tormented by the suffering and agony of the human race and finally, to escape the reality of life, ended his own life in suicide. Like Beethoven, van Gogh had a profound conviction of his destiny in bringing the brotherhood of man closer to reality.

Starry Night (colorplate 34) shows van Gogh's feelings about nature. The twisting cypress, the stark simplicity of the horizon and houses, and the swirling forces of the atmosphere of night combine to make this canvas an expression of the rhythm of the universe. Indeed, one can almost experience the movement of the earth against the stars. The realism, however, is not photographic, it is the realism of his feelings about the scene. Van Gogh sought to reveal the mysteries and the moving forces of nature. He used heavy oil paint in pure colors, which he applied in bold strokes. He did not bother with detailed drawings but preferred to portray the elemental character of nature with strong contrasting curves of color. Note the inconsistency of the direction of the curves, which give the canvas a swirling rather than a directional motion. He has even painted the motion of atmosphere, which we know exists but cannot actually be seen. His coloring is very polychromatic, with brilliant blues, yellows, and oranges. In fact, the most obvious elements of this work are color and line. All other elements seem quite unimportant, for van Gogh could, and did, express his feelings about the internal forces of the universe through color and line.

An example of late Expressionism is found in the works of Georges Rouault (1871–1958). His *Christ Mocked by Soldiers* (colorplate 35) is not only in the Expressionistic style but is one of a small number of religious paintings in the modern idiom. The artist has used broad heavy lines of black to give a forceful linear quality to his figure. He has expressed the pathos of Christ and the brutality of the soldiers by deep red and cobalt blue, colors characteristic of stained glass windows. In fact, Rouault worked at the trade of stained glass for a time and carried this technique over into his paintings. Somewhat like van Gogh, the "feeling" for his subject is conveyed by heavy colors and forceful line. Organization and spatial depth seem secondary. The realism of the incident was of no concern, for Rouault saw in the mocking of Christ a symbol of the mocking and brutality of our own ideological conflicts.

Cubism

Another result of the urge to get behind natural appearances and to present the inner meaning of natural phenomena is called "contructionism," or, as it is better known, "Cubism." Cubism is the style of contemporary art that reduces nature to its basic geometric patterns, such as circles, squares, and rectangles, and to volumes of mass, such as the cone, sphere, and cube. Like scientists, artists saw the mechanical side of nature in recurring geometric

Colorplates 34, 35
follows p. 306.

forms, and they eliminated all superficial detail in order to reveal these forms. Again we have artists painting what they knew, not what they saw. In pursuing this style, they became more closely associated with the Classic idea, for they began to be concerned again with how they painted and less with what they painted.

Like Expressionism, Cubism goes back to the last decades of the nineteenth century for its beginning. Paul Cézanne (1839–1906) was the first to explore the possibilities of the constructional idea. For Cézanne, nature was not what she seemed when photographed but was something that could be reduced to simple and monumental forms. He tried to reveal the character of objects, people, and landscapes through cylinders, cubes, cones, and spheres. While landscapes were his favorite subjects, Cézanne also painted still lifes and group pictures. In the *Card Players* (fig. 14.1), he has achieved a sense of the monumental by his arrangement of figures and has emphasized an architectural quality. The figures at the table form an arch as they lean over their cards. This arch is imitated in each figure by a hat. Contrast comes through the angular plane of the table and through the standing figure at the rear, who reiterates the same geometric pattern by his shoulders and hat. Cézanne has brought the two figures at either side closer, both by size and by use of dark colors. The artist is not interested in the act of card playing but strives only to make an interesting pattern by volumes. He does not distort nature but simplifies it by bringing out its natural forms.

Chestnut Trees at the Jas de Bouffan in Winter (colorplate 36) is an example of constructive technique in landscape painting. Compare the photograph of the same scene (fig. 14.2) with the painting, and notice the amount of detail Cézanne has eliminated in order to bring out the natural forms of the trees and background. Many limbs have been left out to emphasize the cylindrical shapes of the trees. Buildings have been used sparingly, and then only as volumes of mass. The mountain, Ste. Victoire, shows clearly through the trees as a block of earth in nature. Cézanne's painting differs from the photograph in that it has become a pattern of angular lines that define volume and mass of structural form.

The best-known name in contemporary painting is Pablo Picasso (1881–1973). He has not limited himself to any one aspect of the modern idiom but has experimented and changed his style many times. He was one of the first artists to be influenced by the sculpture of primitive Africa and also by artifacts from other non-Western cultures. Taking up where Cézanne left off, Picasso made notable advances in the technique of Cubism. In addition to breaking natural forms into geometric design, he expressed a new kind of space relationship by creating instead of imitating. He rejected all rules of perspective and showed several points of view at the same time. *Girl Before a Mirror* (colorplate 37) is one of Picasso's best-known paintings in the Cubist tradition. He has not only dissected the female figure into its elemental forms, but he has presented it from different points of view simultaneously. He has

Colorplates 36, 37
follows p. 306.

Figure 14.1 *Card Players* [1891]—Cézanne. (Courtesy Keystone View Company)

reflected the recent scientific discoveries in the field of time-space relations by destroying the traditional sense of time and space in this painting. Note how he has superimposed a profile view on a frontal view of the face and then reflected the image in the mirror. In reducing the figure to geometrical form, Picasso has greatly enlarged those portions which are symbolic of womanhood. His lines are sharply delineated with brilliant colors of black, red, yellow, green, and purple, suggesting the technique of stained glass, like Rouault. Picasso has given us a nonrealistic painting in which he presents the idea of woman in its basic geometric forms.

Colorplate 38 follows p. 306. An example of Cubism carried to the point of abstraction is *Composition in White, Black, and Red* (colorplate 38) by Piet Mondrian (1872–1944). Mon-

Colorplate 34 *Starry Night* [1889]—Van Gogh. (Courtesy The Museum of Modern Art, New York, Lillie P. Bliss Bequest)

Colorplate 35   *Christ Mocked by Soldiers* [1932]—Rouault. (Courtesy The Museum of Modern Art, New York)

Colorplate 36   *Chestnut Trees at Jas de Bouffan in Winter* [1886]—Cézanne. (Courtesy The Minneapolis Society of Fine Arts)

Colorplate 37 *Girl Before a Mirror* [1932]—Picasso. (Courtesy The Museum of Modern Art, New York, Mrs. Simon Guggenheim Fund)

Colorplate 38   *Composition in White, Black, and Red* [1936]—Mondrian. (Courtesy The Museum of Modern Art, New York, Gift of the Advisory Committee)

Colorplate 39 *Panel Number Three* [1914]—Kandinsky. (Courtesy The Museum of Modern Art, New York, Mrs. Simon Guggenheim Fund)

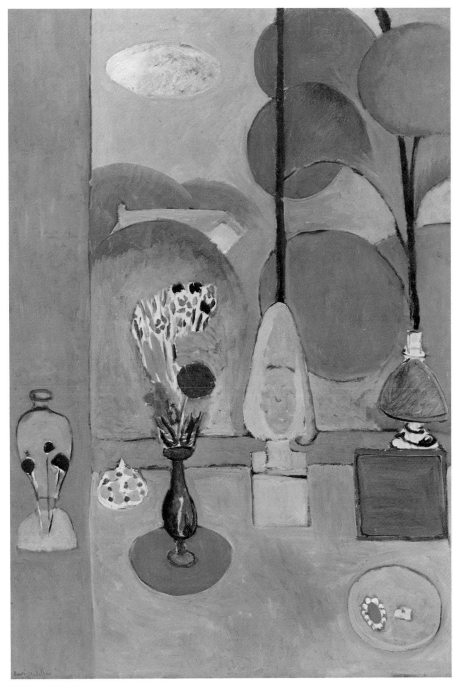

Colorplate 40 *Blue Window* [1911]—Matisse. (Courtesy The Museum of Modern Art, Abby Aldrich Rockefeller Fund)

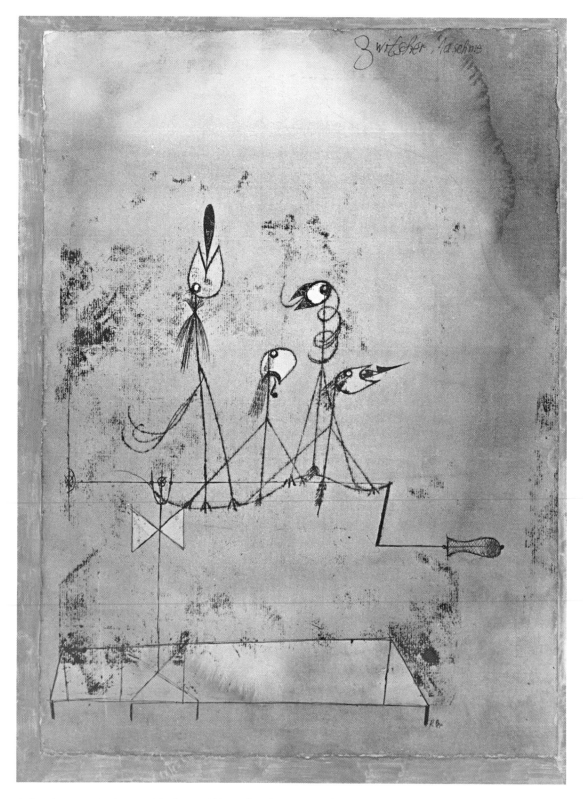

Colorplate 41   *Twittering Machine* [1922]—Klee. (Courtesy The Museum of Modern Art, New York)

Colorplate 42 *Persistence of Memory* [1931]—Dali. (Courtesy The Museum of Modern Art, New York)

Colorplate 43   *Eternal City* [1934–37]—Blume. (Courtesy Collection The Museum of
Modern Art, New York)

Colorplate 44 *I and the Village* [1945]—Chagall. (Courtesy The Museum of Modern Art, Mrs. Simon Guggenheim Fund)

Colorplate 45 *Person Throwing a Stone at a Bird* [1926]—Miró. (Courtesy The Museum of Modern Art, New York)

Figure 14.2 Photograph of scene of Avenue of Chestnuts—Cézanne. (Courtesy Keystone View Company)

drian dispensed with all suggestion of real objects and even eliminated an objective title. This is purely abstract painting. After all, music is abstract, so why not painting? If music can appeal through its melody, harmony, and rhythm, why can't painting appeal to one's aesthetic sense through pure line, color, and organization? While this painting looks simple, it is really very complex, for every line is of a different thickness and each area of white is of a different size. The whole is organized and balanced with mathematical exactness.

Wassily Kandinsky (1866–1944) was an important figure in the artistic politics of the 1917 Russian revolution. He was forced to leave Russia when the Soviets decided that nonrepresentational art did not fit their plan of Marxist propaganda. He went to Germany, where he taught at the Bauhaus School until the Nazi regime closed it down. He eventually went to Paris, where he worked until his death.

Kandinsky's abstractions are unlike those of Mondrian in that he used color as the basis of his artistic expression. In fact he wrote extensive essays on the psychological and expressive meaning of color. His *Panel Number Three* (colorplate 39) is one of a series of nonobjective paintings in which he used a complex rhythmic flow of line and color that seems to move from the bottom to the top with energized movement and dramatically contrasting colors. The viewer's eye constantly moves along the line from color to color in much the same manner as the ear absorbs the line and tonal coloring of much of twentieth-century music by composers such as Schoenberg and Webern.

Henri Matisse (1869–1954) was a contemporary of the Impressionist painters, of Cezanne and Van Gogh, but he seemed hardly aware of their styles. His simple, but strong forms, together with an innovative use of color was startling to his contemporaries. He used color without reference to three dimensional forms or to the reality of forms. His *Blue Window* (colorplate 40) demonstrates his concern with strong color harmonies and decorative motifs. It is an abstract still-life study that blends into a kind of stylized landscape. A sense of recession is suggested by a lessening of the intensities of color in the background. The colors do not fuse into a scheme of color harmony, but seem to retain their own intense identities.

An important painter whose works seem to be on the verge of Surrealism, but are based on Cubism, is Paul Klee (1879–1940). His art is one of delicate but nonrepresentative line, used with subtle pastel coloring. His *Twittering Machine* (colorplate 41) is almost a comic-strip drawing. By linear means he amuses us with the subject of symbolic birds operated by a mechanical device as a satire on the mechanistic world. By the same devices he even suggests the experience of sounds, such as loudness by the exclamation point coming from the beak of one of the birds. The sensation of piercing shrillness is suggested by one of the twitterers with an arrow through its beak.

Surrealism

Perhaps the most spectacular of all the "-isms" of the twentieth century is "Surrealism," a style of art which aims to portray the reality of the subconscious mind. This movement in art is also inspired by modern scientific research, for it is linked closely with post-World War I developments in Freudian psychology and the interpretation of dreams. Surrealism frees those drives that are usually suppressed in normal life and lays bare the motivating forces behind our thoughts, actions, and desires. It utilizes the stream-of-consciousness technique to record feelings or thoughts that we normally consider outside the realm of expression, using symbols to convey the meanings of visual dreams. As a result, all sorts of fantastic and unreal forms appear in its art.

Colorplates 39, 40, 41 follows p. 306.

Salvador Dali (1904–   ) is the best-known and most sensational of the Surrealists. His *Persistence of Memory* (colorplate 42), with its fantastically limp watches, is an unforgettable painting. Dali paints everything with the greatest detail; even the rocks in the distance are almost photographic in their realism. His sense of space becomes limitless by the elimination of atmosphere and by making the distant objects as detailed as the closer ones. The most unnatural parts of this painting are the limp watches hanging over a barren tree limb and over the edge of a table. The humanoid figure and the crawling ants are symbolic of the infinity of time itself. The observer may not immediately understand all that Dali symbolizes, but he will never forget the painting. Perhaps this is what Dali had in mind when he gave it the title *Persistence of Memory.*

Contemporary events have provided many subjects for modern artists of all "-isms." This is especially true of the rise of Fascism, Nazism, and Communism. Modern wars have also been subjects of Expressionism and Surrealism for our artists. In the early thirties, a young American artist, Peter Blume (1906–   ), spent some time observing the rise of Fascism in Italy, and came home to put on canvas what he had seen and felt. *Eternal City* (colorplate 43), an allegorical picture of modern Rome, complete with the Church, Mussolini, and the crushing weight of Fascism, was the result. Blume gathered together a great variety of symbols which were to remind the spectator of the lost beauty and tradition, the decadence, and the violence of Mussolini's Rome. The picture is allegorical in that it represents more than the gruesome scene: it represents the forces that were to lead eventually to carnage and war. Every symbol is painted in minute detail, and every color is sharply contrasted. The bright-green head of Mussolini contrasts with the blinding white of broken marble. Christ, dressed with the symbols and medals of war, overlooks the great chasm into which humanity has been plunged and from which the monster jack-in-the-box originates. Blume has used the technique of realistic detail to achieve his effects. His message is transmitted by the impact of incompatible forms which symbolize the various forces of Fascism. This is an ugly picture, but that is just what the artist wanted, for he wanted to make clear his prophecy of the end of Mussolini and Fascism years before it happened.

Another shocking picture which came out of the war came from the studio of Picasso. We have already mentioned that Picasso did not subscribe to any one style; he changed as the times changed and grew as his insight into life grew. It is still too early to tell but, of all the painters of our day, Picasso seems most likely to be remembered the longest. *Guernica* (fig. 14.3) is a huge mural depicting the horrors of an air raid. In 1937, the German air force, flying for Franco in the Spanish civil war, bombed the Spanish village of Guernica as an experiment in modern warfare. Judging from the number of people killed and the destruction, the experiment was a success, and the technique was to be used again. Picasso, a Spaniard, was shocked by this brutality and set about to create a great canvas in protest against all war.

Colorplates 42, 43
follows p. 306.

Figure 14.3 *Guernica* [1937]—Picasso. (Copyright © SPADEM, Paris/VAGA, New York, 1982)

He used linear drawings of fragments to symbolize the manifold horrors of destruction. There is no spatial depth, for these are patterns on a plane. The colors are gray, black, and white—colors which are symbolic of death and mourning. Some of the allegorical forms seem quite obvious; others, again, are clothed in the mystery of a dream world. A woman with her dead child, a broken sword, a dying horse—all these, and many more, make up Picasso's artistic protest against twentieth-century brutality. Despite his strong feelings about his subject, Picasso retains the abstract quality of contemporary painting. Every symbol does more than suggest a scene of terror—it also fits into the organization of abstract patterns of pure design.

Marc Chagall (1887–) is a Russian artist who never abandoned his affinity for Russian life and its folk-lore. While he was influenced in his early works by cubism and its geometric forms, he revolted against its rationalism. His preference for irrational arrangements of natural objects led to a dream imagery in his paintings. Perhaps he can be associated with cubism and surrealism in his creative works. *I and the Village* (plate 44) grew out of memories of his youth. Here he transports the viewer magically into the world of childhood dreams associated with Russian folklore. The composition consists of simple peasant figures, roosters and floating cows with a rich colorized and irrational organization of figures that seem to float in space. Chagall has also been responsible for numerous theatrical sets, including decorations for the opera house at Lincoln Center in New York, as well as the Paris Opera.

An artist who demonstrates both Surrealism and Abstractionism is Joan Miró (1893–). He suggests surrealistic symbols by forms that appear as if they had developed as living organisms. These forms are often called bio-morphic in modern art. In Miró's *Person Throwing a Stone at a Bird* (colorplate

Colorplate 44
follows p. 306.

45), the title stimulates the viewer by whimsical fantasy created by color and almost childlike biomorphic forms. Its most striking aspects of formal organization are its sharply defined curvilinear lines and the brightly contrasting colors.

Early twentieth-century artists were combining truthful remembrances of their time. If we try to understand their messages and prophecies, we may be moved to exert our influence in molding a better world. If we do not like the *Eternal City* or *Guernica*, we should see to it that conditions which brought forth this art do not repeat themselves.

Sculpture

Sculptors have reacted to the contemporary scene in much the same manner as painters. Cut loose from the patronage of the Church and the aristocracy, they also have been led to seek new functions and new markets for their works. They too have been alienated from their public because of the non-objectivity of art and public conservatism. Consequently, sculptors, like painters, have been experimenting with new techniques and new materials in seeking new expressiveness and a sensitive patronage.

There appears to have been at least one important trend in the function and patronage of sculpture. Artists are now creating works in scale and design that fit into the modern home. In the past, they conceived monumental pieces for the Church, for palaces and gardens of nobility, or for public buildings and memorials. With the decrease in this type of market, they turned to the home as a gallery. As a result, sculptors are creating works especially designed as decorative pieces for modern living. New timesaving tools with which to work and new processes of reproduction have also helped to bring the pleasure of sculpture within the economic possibilities of those with modest incomes, whereas in the past, it was only the more wealthy who could afford this pleasure.

There is another factor that has influenced the techniques and expressions of comtemporary sculptors. Unlike painters, who have in general used the same materials as in the past, sculptors have a variety of new materials and new processes at their disposal. Aluminum, chrome, and plastic are but a few that have been successfully used in recent years. The physical character of these new materials has provided artists with many new possibilities of form and surface finishes with which to express modern life.

In general, contemporary sculptors have followed the lead of the painters in their attempts to get behind natural appearances and to express the inner meanings of our world. They also subscribe to the same artistic creed—the revolt against Romanticism, the rejection of emotion, the rejection of objectivity, and the rejection of ornamentation. Expressionism, Cubism, and Surrealism in painting have their counterpart in contemporary sculpture, for sculptors are trying to express their feelings about our times in the same

Colorplate 45
follows p. 306.

manner as their colleagues of the canvas and brush, except that they use different techniques and a different medium.

The Expressionistic movement in sculpture is well represented by Wilhelm Lehmbruck (1881–1919). He distorted and elongated forms in order to realize the expressive feeling which he was seeking. In the *Kneeling Woman* (fig. 14.4) of cast stone, Lehmbruck endowed his figure with a feeling of simplicity and naturalness without being literal or objective. He has distorted the neck, torso, arms, thighs, and legs to give an almost medieval feeling of asceticism. The open spaces only add to the linear quality and to the feeling of elongation. Like van Gogh, Lehmbruck was not realistic about anything except the expression of the humanity, the pathos, and serenity of his subject.

Many sculptors employed the style of Cubism in their works. Some broke up the forms into cubes and spheres retaining the recognizable features of the subject. Others reduced their forms to almost complete abstractions. Henry Moore's (1898–   ) *Family Group* (fig. 14.5) typifies a style of organic free forms, but with enough objectivity to be representational. Moore was strongly influenced by primitivism, and this work shows a predilection for smooth,

Figure 14.4 *Kneeling Woman* [1911]—Lehmbruck. (Courtesy Collection, The Museum of Modern Art, New York)

Figure 14.5 *Family Group* [1945–49]—Moore. (Courtesy Collection, The Museum of Modern Art, New York. A. Conger Goodyear Fund)

rounded forms that symbolize the basic shapes that are synonymous with the human figure without going into detail. Moreover there is multiple unity of the figures that gives strength to the expressive idea of the family unit.

Constantin Brancusi (1876–1957) used polished surfaces of silver and bronze to show the play of light and dark in bringing out the natural shapes of his geometric forms. *Mlle. Pogany* (fig. 14.6) is one of his best pieces in the Cubist tradition that still retains identifiable features. The young lady's head is a prolate spheroid, and the eyes become two great curves which meet at the nose. The neck is envisioned as two entwined cylinders. Here is simple Cubism using curved forms. There is no decoration, no emotion, and no realism; but there is a play of light and shadow over the surface of the metal

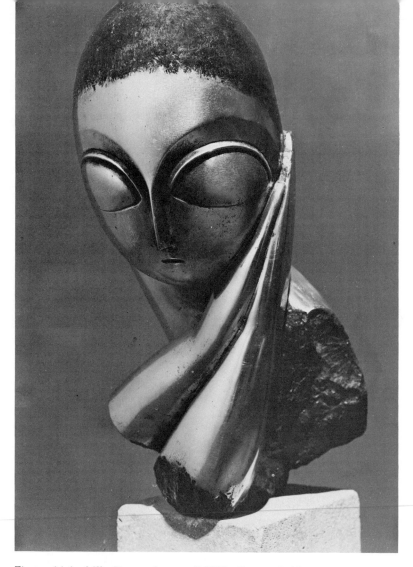

Figure 14.6 *Mlle. Pogany*, bronze [1920]—Brancusi. (Courtesy Collection, The Museum of Modern Art, New York)

which gives rhythmic movement to the volumes of mass. There is also a formal organization of the sculptural masses that clearly suggests the visual idea of a human head.

An even more abstract piece of Cubism in sculpture is *Spiral Theme* (fig. 14.7) by Naum Gabo (1890–1977). Using only plastic, he has experimented with both time and space in the manner of Picasso's *Girl Before a Mirror*. The translucent quality of the material makes it possible to impose one plane upon another simultaneously. This quality gives a sense of rhythm and motion in both time and space.

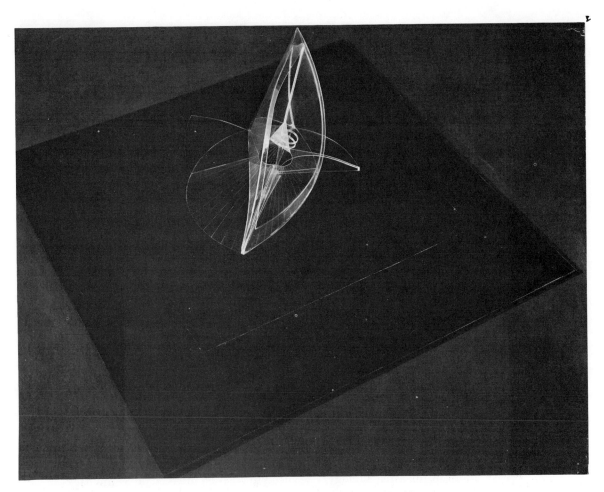

Figure 14.7 *Spiral Theme*, construction in plastic [1941]—Gabo. (Courtesy Collection, The Museum of Modern Art, New York)

Human Concretion (fig. 14.8) by Jean (Hans) Arp (1888–1966) is related to the Surrealistic technique of symbolic imagery. The softly molded forms are abstract and are rhythmically balanced by the repetition of similar shapes of different sizes. These would be purely abstract but for the title, *Human Concretion*, meaning the concreteness of something that is human. Thus we relate the forms to some organic or protoplasmic matter. Arp has brought Surrealism into his work by his title, perhaps creating both interest and confusion, but nevertheless introducing an element of the subconscious.

Albert Giacometti (1901–) is one of the important sculptors who has joined the Surrealistic movement. His *Palace at 4 A.M.* (fig. 14.9) is a fantasy in constructivism that gives a Surrealistic expression to a variety of subconscious memories. The artist says its details were suggested by a variety of

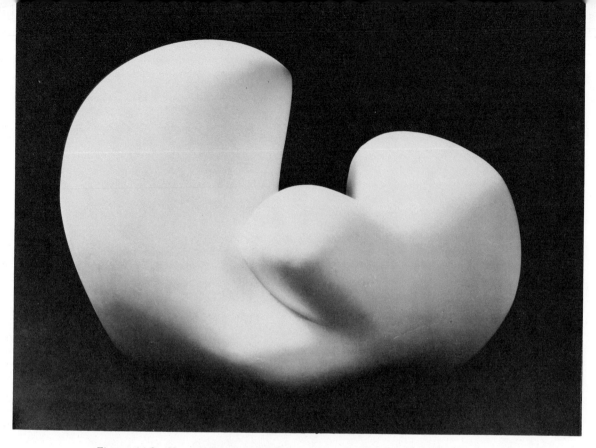

Figure 14.8 *Human Concretion* [1935]—Arp. (Courtesy Collection, The Museum of Modern Art, New York)

incidents ranging over a long period of time. Each detail of the construction is symbolic of the artist's imagery reduced to abstract ideas, such as the backbone hanging from the scaffold of a tower and the abstract figure representing womanhood. It all seems to be within a spatial area enclosed by symbolic walls.

Architecture

It is on architecture that the scientific and mechanical influences of the twentieth century have had their most obvious and most practical effects. Changes in industrial life, in transportation, in communications, as well as in our economic and social life, have had a great influence on the function of contemporary architecture. Builders have tried to adapt the planning, style, and construction of their architecture to meet the demands of a mechanistic and complex society. The new standards of living that make it possible for the average family to own its own home have challenged architects to build

Figure 14.9 *Palace at 4* A.M. [1932–33]—Giacometti. (Courtesy Collection, The Museum of Modern Art, New York)

efficient, comfortable, and low-cost dwellings. In urban society, the large apartment house has been developed into an economic and efficient machine for modern living. Mass education has brought the problem of building a suitable plant in keeping with our philosophy of an education. The supermarket and large department store have been created to assist in the distribution of the enormous production of our farms and factories. The factories themselves have become magnificent architectural achievements, providing open space for the machines of production and safe, pleasant surroundings for the workers. In the cities, the skyscraper has become the symbol of the scientifically organized business life of our age.

In solving these manifold problems, architects have subscribed to the motto "Form follows function." For example, architects have viewed the home from a sociological point of view. They have sought to make their plans according to the personality of the owners, taking into consideration their profession, hobbies, social and cultural life. Consequently, the home is functionally designed to fit the needs of its occupants. This is also true for other kinds of structures. Architects have let the efficient *function* of their buildings—whether home, apartment house, supermarket, factory, or skyscraper—determine their outward *form*. They have eliminated sentimental decoration; they have rejected traditional or derivative styles; they have dared to let the inside speak for the outside. In general, the appearance of our new buildings is a straightforward and simple expression of their functions. For their efforts the contemporary architects have received more recognition and more patronage than any other contemporary artists. True, conservatism was their great barrier for a time, but the efficient practicability of their design soon won the approval of the doubtful.

These innovations have been possible only because of the materials and processes that have been developed in recent years. Steel, aluminum, reinforced concrete, glass, plywood, and plastics are but a few of these new materials that are used today. In addition, the perfection of central heating, the elevator, and electrical appliances have helped to make new designs more practical. The influence of the automobile on modern building is so great that it is almost immeasurable.

New materials bought new methods of construction, notably the cantilever method and the steel-cage construction (fig. 14.10). The cantilever is the projection of a slab, or beam, anchored at only one end. This is done by the use of steel and reinforced concrete material that has great tensile strength. The steel cage is just what the name implies—a cagelike skeleton with steel beams. Both of these new methods make it possible to use glass for outside wall surfaces, for the weight is not borne by the walls but by the steel cage or the cantilevered projection and its anchor.

Another great influence, especially in domestic housing, is the trend toward the outdoors in building. Nature is no longer shut out of the house but is brought inside with large windows of glass. Nature also becomes a part of the living space, with enclosed patios for outdoor living. The public is becoming more conscious of "view" also, and there is a tendency to integrate their homes with the natural surroundings and to use materials indigenous to their locale. One of the finest examples of this is the famous "Falling Water" House (figs. 14.11 and 14.12) in Bear Run, Pennsylvania, built by Frank Lloyd Wright (1869–1959) for Edgar Kaufmann. Wright made the most of a stream and a waterfall that were on the site. He used cantilevers for overhanging balconies and brought nature into the house with large expanses

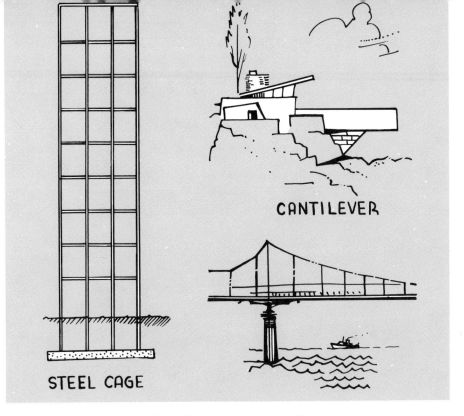

CANTILEVER

STEEL CAGE

Figure 14.10 Steel cage and cantilever construction—Sandgren

of glass. Note that the outside appearance is Cubistic. Wright has used elemental forms without decoration to express the function and simple beauty of the house in its natural surroundings.

Another striking example of integration with natural surroundings is the Watzek House (fig. 14.13) in Portland, Oregon, designed by the firm of Yeon and Doyle. The house is built on a hill overlooking the city and majestic Mount Hood. The lines of mass imitate the contours of the distant mountain, making the building a form in a well-organized visual design. An exterior finish of natural wood helps to blend the building into its setting among the shrubs and towering fir trees.

The Bauhaus (fig. 14.14) at Dessau, Germany, is not only important from an architectural point of view, but also because of its function. It was designed by Walter Gropius (1883–1969) as a technical school for the specific purpose of creating designs and techniques for the twentieth century. Each workshop was a separate unit and, as such, had its own design commensurate with its activities, but all the units were connected with covered passageways. Gropius used the cantilever method of basic construction with glass for the outer walls. The exterior gives the appearance of a curtain of glass hung over a masonry frame. Note the lack of ornament and the simple, angular pattern of the bands of glass and masonry. This is also an architectural realization of the motto "Form follows function."

Figure 14.11 Kaufmann House [1936]—Wright. (Courtesy Keystone View Company)

Frank Lloyd Wright utilized glass and concrete in solving the problems of an industrial office building in the Johnson Wax Building (figs. 14.15 and 14.16) in Racine, Wisconsin. To support the great weight of the ceiling, he used hollow concrete piers that taper at the bottom and mushroom at the top. Indirect lighting through a diffused glass ceiling gives equal illumination without glare. The tapered piers provide a maximum of space for the desks, which were also designed by Wright for their specific function in the office.

Figure 14.12   Kaufmann House [1936]—Wright. (Courtesy Keystone View Company)

Music

At the opening of the twentieth century, music like the plastic arts was influenced by a number of forces, all of which tended to be used to affect the desire to break with the nineteenth century and its Nationalistic, Realistic, and Impressionistic tendencies. This revolt was evidenced not only in the area of concert and serious music but also in the production of popular music, the music of the concert hall and theater.

The musical techniques employed to achieve such ends as represented in the output of the nineteenth century had been pushed as far as possible by the opening of the twentieth century. If composers were to be creative

Figure 14.13   Watzek House [1938]—Yeon and Doyle. (Courtesy Boychuk Studio)

artists they must find new ways to say new things. Musically this meant that melody, harmony, rhythm, and tone quality must be reassessed and studied if composers were to keep pace with their artistic colleagues in other media of expression.

Melodically and harmonically, there were two ways out: divide the twelve tones of the scale into smaller intervals and thereby create new material out of which to build or find new principles of construction so that the old materials would create new ideas. While the former was attempted by such men as Hába and Barth and used to a slight degree by others such as Bloch and Bartók, so far it has not succeeded in winning any significant place as a solution of modern melodic or harmonic problems. The other solution, to find new principles of construction, has been applied in various

Figure 14.14   Bauhaus at Dessau [1925–26]—Gropius. (Courtesy Keystone View Company)

Figure 14.15   Johnson Wax Building [1937]—Wright. (Courtesy Johnson Wax Company)

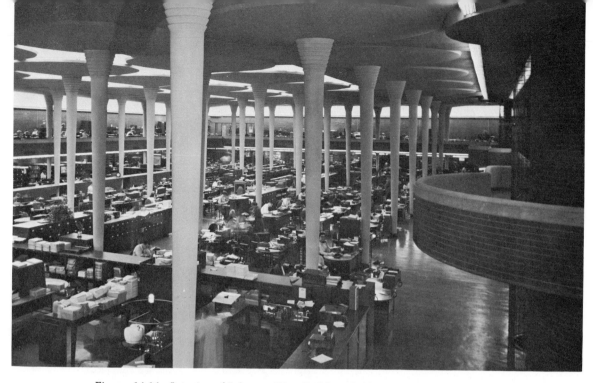

Figure 14.16   Interior of Johnson Wax Building [1937]—Wright. (Courtesy Johnson Wax Company)

ways. In a sense, all these grow out of the practices of the nineteenth century. Harmonically as well as melodically, the Romantic composer piled dissonance upon dissonance to the end that musical tension or expressive quality might be heightened. Yet these dissonances were all a part of a scheme of harmony which functioned within the feeling of a central tonality. No matter how reluctant Chopin might have been to reveal the tonality in a short prelude, or how interminable might be the delayed resolutions and ultimate establishment of key in a Wagnerian opera, the fact remained that these works, whether long or short, were governed by tonal considerations, and dissonances were used only to intensify them. However, twentieth-century composers came to appreciate the musical value of such dissonant treatment for the mere sake of the dissonance itself. They found a certain expressive beauty in dissonance that was compatible with twentieth-century ideas and justified its use by various principles of construction. Among these were polytonality (the use of two or more keys simultaneously); the use of free dissonant tones, whereby the traditional harmonic principles were adhered to but the use of dissonance was greatly expanded; the principle of the twelve-tone row, or "composition with twelve tones," as Schoenberg called it; or the deliberate denial of tonality as a principle, without any formalized system.

The total result of these practices is the evident dissonance which characterizes all twentieth-century music to a greater or lesser degree—usually greater. Perhaps the most ready answer that would be given by a group of persons asked to listen to, and describe, three or four typical twentieth-century works would be "extreme dissonance." The inability to reconcile the harmonies of twentieth-century compositions with the harmonic practices that everyone accepts as socially correct by virtue of growing up exclusively with eighteenth- and nineteenth-century music, leads to the general regard for contemporary music as dissonantly ugly.

In the realm of rhythm, composers revolted not only against the regularity and symmetry of phrase, but against the regularity of meter. Some indications of this are already apparent in some late nineteenth-century composers. As usual, the seeds of destruction are to be found within the thing destroyed. Nationalism particularly exploited the unusual rhythmic and metric patterns of folk music, especially of the eastern Europeans, who were less affected by the regularity of centuries of art music. Odd rhythms of 5/4 were commonly found in the music of numbers of the Slavic composers, notably Tchaikovsky and Moussorgsky. Twentieth-century composers have expanded these rhythmic irregularities to an enormous degree. In the works of some composers, there is scarcely a set meter, and some have written without metric signature. Such patterns as 5/4, 7/16, and 11/8 are commonly used, not always consistently, but rather liberally interspersed with the other conventional patterns so that the total effect is one of great irregularity. Moreover, many works achieve rhythmic complexity by the juxtaposition of one or more independent rhythms. While such rhythmic complexities make great difficulties for the performer, average listeners are not so disturbed by them as they are by dissonances. Difficulties of performance, however, militate against widespread acceptance of contemporary music by many musicians and result in poor performance by others.

Exploitation of tone quality is a province in which even the most traditional twentieth-century composers dare to indulge themselves. In fact, this is the cloak for much pseudomodernism in twentieth-century composition. Witness the extreme distortion to which such instruments as the trumpet, the trombone, the saxophone, and the clarinet have been subjected by the popular dance musician. The modern audience does not seem to resent cacophony if it is only cacophony of tone quality. Some more serious composers have added immeasurably to the orchestral tonal palette by making new demands on old instruments or calling for new sound devices such as wind machines, electronic instruments, sirens, and noisemakers of all sorts—even to the dropping of glass in a bucket and shaking it!

In addition to these developments concerned with traditional materials of music, several others have arisen in the twentieth century. One of these was the new popular style known as jazz. Its characteristics will be discussed later in this chapter, but suffice to say, it played a distinct part in influencing a number of twentieth-century composers.

Another influence was that of a revived interest in the music and instruments of the medieval and Renaissance eras. This interest in tonal color was also reflected in the use of instruments of non-European origin, such as the African drums of all types, the sitar from India, and the Balinese instruments from the gamelan orchestras. These interests were taken up by both the serious and the popular composers and purveyors of music.

The beginnings of the use of electronic media in recordings and amplification began in the first half of the twentieth century, though its main influence was not felt until the post-World War II era.

In each of these ways, and by the combination of two or more, twentieth-century music has challenged the intellect of the twentieth-century listener. Until the emergence of an accepted style on the part of composers, there will be no general acceptance on the part of the listener. As yet, such a unity of style as made possible the designations Classic, Baroque, or Romantic has not emerged, or at least not clearly enough. This is readily understandable. We have come scarcely seventy-five years since Romanticism, with its phases of Realism, Nationalism, and Impressionism, was the accepted style. Most early twentieth-century composers were more actively interested in doing away with Romanticism than they were in creating expressive artworks. Hundreds of works were written by countless composers. Most of them were already forgotten by the middle of the century. But out of these rise a number of works which are landmarks, if not for posterity at least for three-quarters of the twentieth century. A style is in the making and we as listeners, as well as creators, must interest ourselves in the works of our own times if we are to have a continuing cultural growth. Composers do not set styles by themselves. Society as a whole sets styles, and when there is no longer any participation by the whole society, then the art form will die, just as any other social phenomenon must.

Let us look briefly at a few representative examples of twentieth-century music. In each case, the composer mentioned has wielded great influence not only on the musical audience, but also on the composers of the third quarter of the twentieth century. Omission of significant composers or works is only an admission of the impossibility to deal with anything more than an example here and there of some few particular and obvious stylistic traits.

Schoenberg

Arnold Schoenberg (1874–1951) is probably one of the most controversial composers of the twentieth century. At first a vigorous follower of the Wagnerian tradition, he soon felt the necessity for a new system of composition. As a result he constructed a new technique of musical composition based on the independence of each of the twelve tones of the chromatic scale, often referred to as dodecaphonic. In it, harmonic and melodic relationships were not governed by procedures of traditional and functional harmony, but by the arbitrary pattern of the twelve tones. This "tone row" was the unifying element of the composition. It served as a sort of theme for countless variations; it made tonality unnecessary in that it was the nucleus out of which all musical material grew and, hence, the germ of the form itself. Its constant reappearance served as the basis of unity, its constant variation as the basis of variety. The result was a composition in which the listener must not seek to relate sounds in the harmonic style of the eighteenth and nineteenth centuries, but one in which the harmony was the result of a closely knit formal organization based primarily on contrapuntal practices. One must remember that tonal harmony can be dissonant as well as consonant, even in the traditional sense. The harmony of Schoenberg's work purposely avoids any implications of tonality, and consequently sounds consistently dissonant if one uses the traditional harmonic idea as a frame of reference. For this reason it is often referred to as "atonal" music.

One of the early works of Schoenberg from the period 1921 to 1923 is the *Serenade*, op. 24. In this Expressionistic work, Schoenberg has gained full mastery over his new technique. Each of the seven movements is based on a different arrangement of the twelve tones of the octave. It will be noted that the formal organization of each movement is traditional—in fact, in most instances, somewhat archaic. March, variation, minuet, song, dance—these are forms long employed by composers. But the treatment of harmonic material is in no way traditional. Melody, even when given to the voice as in the fourth movement, is no longer subservient to vocal considerations. Melody and harmony must move in deference to the principles established by the composer, and whatever difficulties this raises for instrument or voice must be mastered. Rhythm is one of the principal means of varying the tone row and is therefore very free and irregular. The unusual combination of instruments for which the *Serenade* is scored is an indication of the interest the composer had in tonal color. Moreover, each of the instruments used is exploited tonally in most extraordinary ways.

Movements one, two, four, five, and seven are all based on strict application of the principle of composing with twelve tones, as Schoenberg called his system. Movement three uses only eleven tones, and movement six employs a theme of eighteen tones in which six of the twelve are repeated. Movement four, which is a setting for voice and instruments of a sonnet by Petrarch, is written so that the voice consistently repeats the twelve-tone row throughout the movement while the instruments accompany it. In this instance, the tone row consists of the notes E, D, E flat, B, C, D flat, A flat, G flat, A, F, G, B flat (ex. 14.1).

Example 14.1®

One syllable is set to each note and, since the sonnet has eleven syllables to each line of verse, each line begins with a different note of the repeated row. For example: the first line starts on the first note of the row, E; the second line on note twelve, B flat; the third on note eleven, G; the fourth on note ten, F, etc. This gives great variety to the verse settings, which is heightened by the fact that the notes can be in any octave within the possibilities of the vocal range and can be treated in various rhythmic fashion—all within the rigid repetition of the basic row. The total effect of the whole work is one of intense expressive power through dissonance, rhythmic strength, and unique tonal colors. Like all new ideas in music, this work must be heard many times until its first impression of unusualness no longer is a disturbing element in our appreciation of it.

Unfortunately a great number of factors join together in keeping modern music of this kind from frequent performance. Among these are difficulty of actual execution, lack of sympathetic and willing performers among those technically capable, and reluctance of those who control music commercially to essay new ideas. An analogy can be drawn in the failure of the first stream-lined automobile, put out by the Chrysler corporation in the 1930s, to capture the public's acceptance. When a number of companies in the post–World War II period turned to streamlining, however, the uniqueness wore off in the first year, and all cars competed with each other in achieving new extremes in this style. Acceptance of new art styles moves more slowly, and music meets, perhaps, the greatest opposition to a wide understanding of new stylistic trends.

One composer, however, has been able in a large degree to break through the public opposition to contemporary idioms. Analogous to the increasing decorative design in architecture of the mid-twentieth century, following a period of decidedly stripped and functional form, is the Violin Concerto of Alban Berg (1885–1935), one of the most successful of Schoenberg's pupils. Berg was an exponent of the twelve-tone system of composition and used it in the varied areas of his work: opera, chamber music, orchestral and vocal compositions. In all of these he succeeded in tempering the strict dissonance of the twelve-tone system with a freedom that has made his works widely accepted in the opera houses and concert halls of the world. The Violin Concerto, written in 1935, was his last completed composition. It was a commission by the American violinist, Louis Krasner, and was dedicated to the memory of Manon Gropius, the eighteen-year-old daughter of Alma Mahler, the widow of Gustav Mahler, and Walter Gropius, the architect. The young girl had died after a year of painful infantile paralysis, and the concerto's form and expression was in a great part determined by the affection and admiration Berg held for this lovely girl.

The work is based on a most extraordinary tone row (ex. 14.2) which enabled the composer at the same time to incorporate the modern dissonance of twelve-tone music with traditional harmony. It will be noted that if certain successive notes of the tone row are played together or successively they constitute traditionally sounding harmonies: 1,2,3; 5,6,7; 2,3,4; 7,8,9; and 3,4,5,6. Also the alternating notes 1,3,5,7 constitutes the tuning of the strings of the violin, and the last four notes of the tone row are each one whole step apart from one another forming a segment of the whole-tone scale. Berg makes use of all these potentialities of the tone row. In addition to the tone row he employs a Bach chorale.

Example 14.2   Tone Row; Alban Berg: Violin Concerto®

Example 14.3   Tone Row as it appears in the Solo Violin passage of the First Movement, Berg: Violin Concerto.®

The concerto falls into two large parts or movements. Each of the movements is divided into the further sections joined together without pause. The first movement is an attempt to describe the beauty of the young Manon, and the second movement her suffering and death. In the first movement the opening introduction is a sort of dialogue between the violin and the orchestra exposing the tone row in various forms. The first section then presents a development of the tone row in a slow andante tempo. Particular note should be made of the four note whole-tone figure for it becomes a most important part of the second movement. The second section of the first movement depicts the youthful character of the young girl with its ready reference to Viennese waltz rhythms and the eventual inclusion of an actaul Austrian folk dance toward the end of the movement.

The second movement is a presentation of the tragic death and the ultimate deliverance of the "Angel." The four note whole-tone scale which was already heard in the first movement now assumes more and more importance, and finally leads to a full presentation of the choral tune, *O Ewigkeit, du Donnerwort* (*Oh Eternity, Thou Thunderous Word*) in the original Bach harmonization. The four last notes of the tone row in the whole-tone scale are the opening four notes of the chorale tune. Their importance is now revealed. The superb dramatist, Berg, has made full use of the modern idiom in tying the present with the past and at the same time has not hesitated to draw upon the romantic emotional power of music and its tradition to realize his purpose as stated in the dedication of the concerto.

While Schoenberg will probably always mark a period and a school of musical thought, one of his pupils, Anton Webern (1883–1945), if often looked upon as one of the most gifted and influential composers of the twentieth century. Webern is recognized as a composer who not only adopted the twelve-tone technique of his teacher but extended its implications to what could be called completely organized serialism. That is to say, not only is each of the twelve tones used before any one is repeated, but the tonal qualities were organized so that no instrument plays two successive tones of a theme. Dynamics are similarly treated. The thematic material is extremely epigrammatic and terse so that the compositions seem to be a counterpart of the paintings of such an artist as Klee.

The *Five Orchestral Pieces*, op. 10 were written in 1913 before Webern had adopted the twelve-tone system of composition. They are most suitable as illustrative of the succinct manner of Webern's writing which he never abandoned, and which in turn was extremely influential on other composers of the twentieth century. This was particularly true of Stravinsky in the 1950s as well as the whole school of electronic composers.

Some facts concerning the fourth piece (ex. 14.4) of the set will give an idea of the terseness and economy of means which Webern used. The work is only six measures long with a metronomic marking of sixty beats to the minute. Allowing for the two ritardandos (slowing-down) passages, the total playing time would not exceed twenty-four seconds. Only solo instruments are used making a total of nine performers. There are fifty-seven printed notes in the score, many of these are sustained or repeated. The mandolin has the greatest number of different pitches to play, a total of seven. Two instruments play only one pitch, three play two pitches, and of the remaining three instruments two have four and one has five different pitches. If one is to analyze the work technically it will be discovered that two intervals which have been traditionally treated as dissonances constitute the basic motives of the work; the major second (two half steps) and the long feared tritone (six half steps). The latter had been known for centuries as the diabolical interval. Based on such economic structural and formal means, Webern has fashioned as extremely concise expression of fleeting kaleidoscopic tonal changes. Only an art form whose presentation takes place in time could become truly analogous to Webern's work. Subliminal vision in motion pictures and television perhaps offer the best analogy.

Music and painting have also been analogous in many ways in the twentieth century. In fact a number of composers have been quite successful painters and a number of painters have shown intense interest in musical symbols and ideas. Schoenberg, for example, was a close friend of Kandinsky and was a talented painter with a number of public showings of his works. Moreover, the close friendship between Picasso and Stravinsky is well known.

Example 14.4　Webern: *Five Orchestral Pieces,* op. 10, no. 4

Example 14.4   (Continued)

Stravinsky

Igor Stravinsky (1882–1971) has unquestionably been the most successful twentieth-century composer in winning acceptance from the general public. This was not accomplished easily, however, and many of his finest early works are, after forty years, still rarely heard. Stravinsky stems from quite a different tradition than that of Schoenberg. His musical education was in the school of the realistic Nationalism of the Russian Five, of whom Rimsky-Korsakov was his teacher. This is particularly evident in the works of the first twenty-five years of the century, of which all the important ones were ballets or at least stage works, many with Russain themes—*Firebird, Petrouchka, The Rite of Spring, Les Noces,* and *Mavra,* among others.

Stravinsky neither followed nor formulated any set theory of composition. His music is characterized by a free use of dissonance which reached the extreme of atonality in only a few rare instances. Rhythmic drive often resulting in brutal reiteration within very complex and irregular patterns characterizes his works. Tonal qualities of great effectiveness, running the gamut from those of great beauty to those of cruel ugliness, are found.

The ballet music to *The Rite of Spring* is one which established the young Stravinsky as the *enfant terrible* of the twentieth century. The first performance in Paris created a scandal. The same kind of reception was accorded it in other capitals of Europe. Despite these early difficulties, the work has lasted and become accepted; in fact, it was looked upon as somewhat mild by the middle of the century. Harmonically, its dissonant effects are chiefly the result of a basic bitonality, a superimposition of two chords with their fundamental tones a half step apart. This gives rise to a very biting dissonance. Formally, the work relies on a kind of restricted thematic development which avoids to the utmost any literal repetition, so that the old principle of statement, digression, and restatement is substantially nonexistent. The result is a type of thematic variation which is very limited as well as monotonously insistent. In securing effective expression, the rhythmic freedom within a strict metronomic beat is all-important. All of these purely musical techniques are woven into a musical design which, however, never loses sight of the theatrical use for which the whole work is written—music for the ballet. The idea is the portrayal of primitive rites, following the long winter season, by means of which the people beseech the gods for a bountiful and kindly year.

Bartók

Béla Bartók (1881–1945) is another twentieth-century composer who set up no theory or formula but arrived at results quite as opposed to nineteenth-century Romanticism as either Schoenberg or Stravinsky. His background is the folk idiom, not only of his native Hungary, but of all the Balkan peoples. So great was his interest in folk music that he even studied in very serious fashion the folk music of North Africa. The harmonies and rhythms of the untutored folk musicians of the Balkan states, untouched by the tradition of western Europe, intrigued Bartók. Great quantities of his piano pieces are very original settings of simple folk songs and dances. However, his large works in the more traditional forms are likewise influenced by the long and serious study of folk music which led him to collect over 10,000 of these works.

The Sonata for Two Pianos and Percussion dates from 1937. Not only is it indicative in melody, harmony, and rhythm of Bartók's deep knowledge and love of the folk idiom, but its very use of the piano is illustrative of his close affinity with the music of the people. The Hungarian cimbalom, a folk form of the psaltry, of which the piano is a highly mechanized type, is an instrument struck with hammers. Bartók frequently, if not always, feels the piano to be a descendent of this percussive instrument and treats it in this fashion. It is not unusual, then, that he should combine it here with other percussive instruments.

In this work, percussion and piano blend into a tonal texture in which they are remarkably complementary. Dissonant quality, the earmark of twentieth-century music, is the result of various techniques. Sometimes it is bitonality, as in the opening of the first movement where the pianos enter, each in a different key. Sometimes it is the result of free dissonances used to heighten the harmonic tension. Sometimes it is the result of very free contrapuntal treatment, as in the final movement. Basically, it is the result of the folk background in which Bartók discovered unusual scale patterns which produce dissonances when used harmonically.

The Concerto for Orchestra is one of the last great works of Bartók composed during those terrible final years of illness in New York. It was written for the Boston Symphony on commission by its conductor, Serge Koussevitzky. Bartók explained the use of the term *concerto* as a title in that he wished "to treat the single instruments in a concertante or soloistic style." This was a reversion to the Baroque concerto style of the early eighteenth century.

The Concerto consists of five movements. The first contains a slow introduction in the grand manner of the eighteenth-century symphonic introduction, which is then followed by an allegro vivace section. The introduction is based on the intervallic motive of a fourth. Bartók was particularly fond of using this rather dissonant interval in many of his compositions since it frequently occurred in the folk song tradition with which he was familiar. The first movement proper is built on the traditional sonata-allegro form and the use of the interval of the fourth is prominent in the thematic material. The second movement is given the title *Game of Pairs*, since he presented five pairs of wind instruments in a series of short sections. Each pair is combined at a specific and individual interval; bassoons at the sixth, oboes at the third, clarinets at the sevenths, flutes at the fifth, and trumpets at the second. During the restatement of the five sections, Bartók uses an elaborate instrumentation. The third movement is called *Elegia* and is a song of death. The fourth movement is called *Interrupted Intermezzo*. A folksong-like tune followed by a lyric melody is interrupted in mood and melodic idiom by a more popular style tune after which the first part returns. Characteristic of the rhythm of the entire movement is its alternation of 2/4, 3/4, 5/8, 6/8, and 7/8, making an obvious asymmetrical scheme. The *Finale* marked *pesante* (heavy), which brings the work to a close, is filled with primitive folk tune material. The interval of fourth is again prominent and the movement employs a fugue, making use of all the devices of counterpoint.

Bartók's complicated rhythmic patterns are the result of deep interest in the fine subtleties of rhythmic feelings as expressed in folk song and dance. All of these—dissonances, rhythmic complexities, clang of tonal quality—contrive to give this music a freshness and spontaneity which marks it as typical of the twentieth century.

Ives

In much the same way that Hungarian folk music served Bartók as a point of departure in his compositions, so did the folk songs and gospel hymns of his native New England serve Charles Ives (1874–1954). Ives is one of those creative spirits who arose out of a very traditional background and foreshadowed musical events that only became widely used and accepted years after he had used them. Almost his entire compositional output predates World War I, yet most of it was never heard until after World War II. *Central Park in the Dark Some Forty Years Ago* is representative of Ives's predilection for quoting folk tunes and popular songs in his compositional structure. These tunes are used contrapuntally against one another, usually in different simultaneous tonalities and polyrhythms. Written early in the twentieth century (the composing of the work lasted from 1898 to 1907), this is, in the words of Ives, "a picture in sounds of the sounds of nature and of happenings that men would hear when sitting on a bench in Central Park on a hot summer night."

Gershwin

The person of George Gershwin (1898–1937) poses something of a problem in the attempt to place him in this chapter. While his style is distinctly related to the popular jazz idiom, he has achieved the definite stature of a serious composer through both his concert works and his theatrical compositions. *Rhapsody in Blue, An American in Paris,* and his Piano Concerto in F have taken the jazz idiom of his time and successfully incorporated it into the more or less traditional forms of concert music. His musicals, such as *Of Thee I Sing* and *Girl Crazy,* supplied a number of the hit tunes that were popularized throughout the world by jazz bands, but they also instilled a new life into the fading romantic operetta form that resulted in a whole new era of so-called Broadway musicals. His opera *Porgy and Bess* is a successful amalgam of jazz, blues, spiritual, and folk song idiom with a highly dramatic quality that makes this work a true folk opera whose musical achievement places it in favorable comparison with any of the traditional operatic masterworks.

Jazz

Since jazz is a musical practice, not a form of composition, it tends to be ever-changing in character and style. In its earliest appearance it was known as ragtime, a name which was generally used for the first two decades of the century. The work of Scott Joplin, which has been rediscovered and revived in the post–World War II period, is a good example of this early ragtime. The period after World War I began to designate this popular style of dance music as jazz, and this term has been generally used to denote all the various phases of popular music down to the present time.

Two of the most important elements of jazz, blues, and ragtime were derived from the *spirituals* and *hollers* of the black religious communities and the black field-workers. Blues were typically twelve measure songs with instrumental accompaniment in which a good deal of improvisatory option was left to the instrumentalists. Certain alterations in the major scale, namely the lowering of the third and seventh degrees, gave rise to the term *blue notes*, which in turn led to the term blues as a name for this type of song. *Memphis Blues* and *St. Louis Blues* by W. C. Handy are examples of this style which have become "classics" in the repertoire of popular music.

Ragtime was largely a style of piano playing in which syncopation and improvisation was applied to the marchlike rhythm of dance music. The work of Scott Joplin, such as *The Maple Leaf Rag* and *Pineapple Rag,* are typical of this style.

The term jazz came to be applied to the popular eight- and sixteen-measure phrased tunes into which ragtime and blues were incorporated. These were regularly performed by small groups of instrumentalists consisting of cornet, clarinet, trombone, drums, and piano. Some of the performances of such groups was known as Dixieland style in which there was emphasis on the polyphonic improvisation of the performers. In the 1920s jazz came to be the accepted name for all types of popular music and remained so until challenged by the *rock and roll* style of the post World War II era.

The movement of blacks to northern urban centers after the First World War moved the centers of jazz from New Orleans to such cities as St. Louis, Chicago, and Kansas City, each of which developed a style of its own. The saxophone was added to the instrumental combination and some of the earlier instruments were superseded; for example, the banjo which had been occasionally used was replaced by the guitar, the cornet by the trumpet, and the tuba by the string bass. The band was divided between a melody and harmony section. The clarinet, trumpet, and saxophone were essentially parts of the melody section, and the piano, string bass, and percussion parts of the harmonic section.

The form of the jazz tune was that of the traditional three-part song which was to be found in the music of western Europe since the sixteenth century. This was the so-called chorus or refrain of the popular song. The verse was rarely used as a part of the instrumental rendition. Four eight-measure phrases (A-A-B-A) made up the dance tune and these were repeated a number of times allowing for improvisatory solos based on the tune by various members of the ensemble. Two styles of jazz were the generally accepted modes of performance in the 1920s: hot jazz and sweet jazz. Personal appearances as well as recordings made such performers as Louis Armstrong, "Duke" Ellington, and Bix Biederbecke, among many others, known to a worldwide audience. Paul Whiteman directed a jazz orchestra which had the distinction of premiering Gershwin's *Rhapsody in Blue* and thereby established itself as one of the leading groups in the 1920s.

Jazz in the period preceeding World War II ended in the era of the big bands and swing. Improvisation gave way to some extent to arrangements, and the big bands of Guy Lombardo, Benny Goodman, "Duke" Ellington, Tommy Dorsey, Harry James, and Glenn Miller, to name but a few, ruled the world of jazz before the onset of bop, funky jazz, and the small combo, all of which led into the rock and roll era of post–World War II.

Summary

The problem of a summary of twentieth-century art and music is made exceedingly complicated by the tremendous speed of change that has come about in every area of twentieth-century life. This change has included the massive technological and scientific developments, as well as the dramatic economic, political, intellectual, and social changes that have come about since the turn of the century. The arts responded to and are affected by all of these developments. The technological innovations have had an especially important impact on the arts, both in terms of patronage and in terms of communication of the artist's message to the public. The advances made in transportation, in the media of communication, including radio, television, and reproductions through recordings and color photography have made it possible for great masses of the public to experience artworks that in the past were in effect available only to a few people.

Unfortunately the mass media has led to an abundance of "kitsch" or popular art that appeals to the aesthetically uneducated public, created by sensationalists and those who try to give the public what they think it wants and will buy. In spite of this, however, there have been a number of "isms," especially in visual art, that have indeed captured the spirit of the twentieth century in one way or another. Expressionism, Cubism, Abstractionism, and Surrealism have in their own way focused attention on some of the important facets of twentieth-century culture. While music cannot be defined in terms of the same "isms" as visual arts, there are certain analogous relationships that can be discerned. For example, some music by Webern can be said to be analogous to the art of the Cubists and Abstractionists. Schoenberg was not only a composer, but a painter as well, and was closely associated with the ideas of Kandinsky and the members of the Bauhaus School of Design. Moreover Picasso and Stravinsky were good friends and were aesthetically very compatible.

The rise of jazz with its varied styles of blues, ragtime, and Dixieland is also a facet of the spirit of the early twentieth century. Its improvisational style in which the music was composed during the performance was reminiscent of the Gothic and Renaissance periods.

There are a few abiding principles that seem to prevail in almost all of twentieth-century art. One is the denial of the emotional excess of Romanticism. Instead there seems to be an emphasis on the technical development of handling the basic elements, both visual and musical, according to new principles of construction. Another is the functionalism of most twentieth-century art. "Form follows function" is a creed that can be observed in architecture, painting, sculpture, and even in music. Decoration and ornamentation seem to be discarded in favor of the aesthetic beauty of basic materials of stone, metal, plastic, color, simple lines, and even individual sounds in music. New concepts of time and space are suggested by various means in all the arts including music.

The arts of the first half of the twentieth century were a revolt against the Romanticism and Impressionism of the nineteenth century and revealed the spirit of changes that were taking place in the technological and sociocultural climate. World War II and its dramatic aftermath was to precipitate art and music into a series of more accelerated "isms," fads, and avant-garde artists and composers.

Musical examples

Bartók, Sonata for Two Pianos and Percussion, Concerto for Orchestra

Berg, Violin Concerto

Gershwin, *Porgy and Bess*

Ives, *Central Park in the Dark Some Forty Years Ago*

Schoenberg, *Serenade*, op. 24

Stravinsky, *The Rite of Spring*

Webern, *Five Orchestral Pieces*, op. 10

Suggested readings

Austin, William W. *Music in the 20th Century.* New York: W. W. Norton, 1966, pp. 178–370, 523–38.

Barr, Alfred Jr. *What is Modern Painting?* New York: Museum of Modern Art, 1952.

———. *What is Modern Architecture?* New York: Museum of Modern Art, 1946.

Grout, D. J. *A History of Western Music,* 3rd ed. New York: W. W. Norton, 1980, pp. 662–714.

Janson, H. W. *History of Art.* Englewood Cliffs, N.J.: Prentice-Hall, Inc., 1962, pp. 512–45.

Lang, Paul Henry. *Music in Western Civilization.* New York: W. W. Norton, 1941, chapter 20, pp. 1023–30.

Machlis, Joseph. *Introduction to Contemporary Music.* New York: W. W. Norton, 1961.

Saltzman, Eric. *Twentieth-Century Music: An Introduction,* 2d ed. Englewood Cliffs, N.J.: Prentice-Hall, 1974.

Sewall, John Ives. *A History of Western Art.* New York: Henry Holt & Co., 1953, chapter 19, pp. 893–942.

Wold and Cykler. *An Outline History of Music,* 5th ed. Dubuque, Ia.: Wm. C. Brown Company Publishers, 1982, pp. 221–80.

Suggested examples for further analysis

Painting: Burchfield, *The Night Wind;* Cézanne, *Bathers;* Picasso, *Les Demoiselles d' Avignon*

Sculpture: Archipenko, *Medrano;* Brancusi, *Bird in Space;* Zorach, *Mother and Child*

Architecture: Wright, Frank Lloyd, Goetsch-Winkler House, Okemos, Michigan; RCA Building, Rockefeller Center, New York City

Music: Berg, *Wozzeck;* Copland, *Rodeo;* Schoenberg, Third String Quartet

Film strips with sound

Twentieth Century Artistic Revolution, Educational Audio Visual Inc.

Twentieth Century: The Age and its Art, Schloat

Surrealism in Art and Music, Educational Audio Visual Inc.

Additional sources for visual illustrations

Courthion, Pierre. *Rouault*. New York: Abrams, 1977.

Deschanes, Robert. *Dali*. New York: Abrams, 1976.

Finn, David. *Henry Moore*. New York: Abrams, 1977.

Graohman, Will. *Klee*. New York: Abrams, 1967.

Haftmann, Werner. *Chagall*. New York: Abrams, 1974.

Jaffe, Hans L. C. *Mondrian*. New York: Abrams, 1970.

———. *Picasso*. New York: Abrams, 1964.

Penrose, Roland. *Mirô*. New York, Abrams, 1978.

Popper, Frank. *Agam*. New York: Abrams, 1976.

Schapiro, Meyer. *Cézanne*. New York: Abrams, 1952.

Schwarz, Arturo. *Duchamp*. New York: Abrams, 1978.

15
The Arts Today

Chronology of the Twentieth Century

1839	Paul Cézanne (1839–1906)
1853	Vincent Van Gogh (1853–1890)
1856	Sigmund Freud (1856–1939)
1864	Leoš Janáček (1864–1928)
1866	Vasily Kandinsky (1866–1944)
1868	Scott Joplin (1868–1917)
1869	Frank Lloyd Wright (1869–1959)
	Henri Matisse (1869–1954)
1871	Georges Rouault (1871–1958)
1873	W. C. Handy (1873–1958)
1874	Winston Churchill (1874–1965)
	Arnold Schoenberg (1874–1950)
	Charles Ives (1874–1954)
1875	Maurice Ravel (1875–1937)
1876	Constantin Brancusi (1876–1957)
1877	Piet Mondrian (1877–1944)

1879	Raoul Dufy (1879–1953)
	Paul Klee (1879–1940)
	Josef Stalin (1879–1953)
	Albert Einstein (1879–1955)
1881	Pablo Picasso (1881–1973)
	Wilhelm Lehmbruck (1881–1919)
	Béla Bartók (1881–1945)
1882	Igor Stravinsky (1882–1971)
	James Joyce (1882–1941)
1883	Walter Gropius (1883–1969)
	Anton Webern (1883–1945)
1884	Franklin D. Roosevelt (1884–1945)
1885	Alban Berg (1885–1935)
	Edgar Varese (1885–1965)
1887	Charles Eduard Jeaneret (Corbusier) (1887–1965)
	Marc Chagall (1887–)
1888	Jean Arp (1888–1966)
	T. S. Eliot (1888–1965)

1890	Naum Gabo (1890–1977)	1915	Panama Canal opened
1893	Joan Miró (1893–)	1917	First printed use of the
1895	Paul Hindemith		term "Jazz"
	(1895–1963)	1918	First World War ends
1897	Ragtime from c.1897 to		Leonard Bernstein
	1915		(1918–)
1898	Alexander Calder	1923	Gyorgi Ligeti (1923–)
	(1898–1976)	1925	Gunther Schuller
	Henry Moore (1898–)		(1925–)
	Bertold Brecht	1928	Karlheinz Stockhausen
	(1898–1956)		(1928–)
	Ernest Hemingway	1933	Krzysztof Penderecki
	(1898–1961)		(1933–)
	George Gershwin	1934	Peter Maxwell Davies
	(1898–1938)		(1934–)
1899	"Duke" Ellington	1938	Nuclear fission discovered
	(1899–1974)	1945	Atomic bomb destroys
1900	Aaron Copland (1900–)		Hiroshima and
1901	Alberto Giacometti		Nagasaki
	(1901–)	1946	First assembly of the
1904	Salvador Dali (1904–)		United Nations
	Willem de Kooning	1950	Pop and Op art (c. 1950)
	(1904–)	1957	First satellite (sputnik)
	Luigi Dallapicolla		launched by Russia
	(1904–1975)	1960	Rock and roll (c. 1960)
1906	Peter Blume (1906–)	1969	First man landed on the
1908	Elliott Carter (1908–)		moon
	Olivier Messaien	1977	Yale University Center
	(1908–)		for British Art opens
1912	Jackson Pollock	1981	"Guernica" by Pablo
	(1912–1956)		Picasso is returned to
	John Cage (1912–)		Spain
1914	First World War starts		

Study Objectives

The objectives of this chapter are

1. To learn about the influence of pop culture on both the visual and musical arts.
2. To study about the disintegration of traditional principles of design and composition.
3. To understand the problem of immediate evaluation in a wide diversity of styles.
4. To study the spirit of post-World War II culture as revealed in rock music.

Pronunciation Guide

Agam (Ah'-gahm)
Berio, Luciano (Bay'-ree-oh, Loo-
    chee-ah'-noh)
Bernstein (Bern'-stihn)
Boulez (Boo-lez)
Dallapiccola (Dahl-lah-peek'-koh-
    lah)
Henze (Hen'-tse)
Krenek (Kre'-nek)
Lichtenstein (Likh'-ten-stihn)
Ligeti (Li-get'-ee)
Messaien (Mes-ah-ee-yǎ)

Milhaud (Mee-loh)
Nono (Noh'-noh)
Pei (Pay'-ee)
Penderecki (Pen-der-et'-skee)
Rauschenberg (Row'-shen-berg)
Rochberg (Rokh'-berg)
Rothko (Roth'-koh)
Schuller (Shool'-ler)
Stockhausen (Shtock'-how-zen)
Tinquely (Tin'-ke-lee)

The end of World War II in 1945 marks a genuine crisis in the development of artistic expression. It was about this time that the arts embarked on new courses which may have been difficult to foresee in 1939. With the world greatly altered politically, economically, socially, and technologically, the arts could hardly expect to continue untouched by the events of the war. It would be an error, however, to suggest that postwar art and music represented something entirely new and unprecedented. As has been suggested in earlier chapters, all artistic development has its roots in the past and in the case of postwar art, its roots lay deep in the soil of the modernism which got its start in the late nineteenth and early twentieth centuries.

A survey of some of the more important nonartistic developments that have affected the lives of everyone since the war will suggest a number of ideas that have captured the imagination of our recent creative artists.

A veritable explosion of postwar technology has drastically changed the life-style of people the world over. While the mass media had been a powerful factor before 1939, it has become even more efficient as the result of television and world communication via satellite. Data processing and the computer have made possible instant information on almost everything that touches our lives. The refinement of the techniques and the psychology of advertising and packaging have made household words of a vast variety of products and processes over the entire world. The mobility of people has increased dramatically since the war. Not only the automobile, but jet air transportation has made every nook and cranny within easy access of almost everyone. As a result there has been a cross-fertilization of cultures taking place that threatens to destroy the integrity of races and their indigenous cultural heritage. Terms such as Coca-Cola, jazz, and countless others which in the first half of the twentieth century had been symbols of an American culture have now become symbols of a worldwide cultural leveling. What was formerly peculiar and exclusive to the people of a certain nation or race has been torn from its native soil and spread worldwide.

Not only have the techniques of civilization been altered but also the moral and ethical values by which people understand themselves and relate to each other. The revolt of youth has always been present in the relationships of older and younger generations, but its extreme evidence in the post–World War II period is represented by such violent outbursts as the worldwide opposition to the Vietnam War, which was more apparent in the United States since it was engaged directly in the conflict. Further evidences of the revolt of youth have been the use of hallucinogenic drugs as a protest and escape, the breakdown of expressive language to the point of pornography, and the social concern with civil and human rights that are expressed in some countries by racial enmities and in others by the denial of individual freedom. All these conflicts are represented in the painting, sculpture, and musical expression of the postwar period. Such an event as the Kent State killings was the direct result of these events in the United States. The Bader-Meinhof gang and its kidnappings and murders was a similar experience in Europe.

Another important development of post–World War II is the emphasis on environmental issues—issues that have focused on clean air, land use, preservation of wilderness areas and endangered species, and, of prime importance, the arguments over the effects of nuclear power. In addition there has been a concentration on consumer protection, an issue which has had an important influence on the health and economic welfare of people over a wide area of the world. All of the above have had a significant impact on the sociocultural climate of the world since 1945.

What then are some of the connections between the results of technological developments and the social and economic concerns that have affected the life-styles of postwar people and the creative activities of music and art? It would be unwise to try to relate specific works of art and music to specific ideas and events. It can, however, be shown that creative artists have been, and still are, influenced by such events, but they interpret and relate to them in their own individual ways and within the confines of their elected medium. Certainly Penderecki's *Threnody for the Victims of Hiroshima* was the result of the atomic bomb, and Benjamin Britten's *War Requiem* was a musical comment on war itself with its tragedies and victories. The marvels of the computer and electronic synthesizer have been the catalysts for a variety of electronic music such as that of Otto Luening and Stockhausen.

The protest movements of the fifties and sixties that were part of the civil and human rights movements, and opposition to the Vietnam war with all its ramifications, spawned a wave of protest songs in popular music. Pop culture, which earlier saw the popularity of jazz, ragtime, Dixieland, comic books, and so forth, has been even more exploited by the mass media which has championed the rise of rock, rock and roll, as well as hard and acid rock with all their fads and styles. In the visual arts, the mass media and mass production caught the attention of the pop artist who turned to banal, everyday subjects such as are portrayed in Warhol's *Green Coca-Cola Bottles* and *Brillo Boxes*. Pop culture, both musical and visual, has consumed ideas at a tremendous rate; the speed of change seems to require that no idea be fully developed. It is easier to drop a fad and replace it with another.

What can be seen as a plus for the cultural activity in the arts has been the federal, state, and foundation support for the arts of all kinds. Laws that require a certain percentage of monies for public buildings to be given over to the visual arts have provided opportunity and support for many artists. Foundations and business corporations have become aware of the public relations impact in supporting the arts. This has resulted in the purchase of the individual artist's works and cultural activities such as symphony concerts in bank buildings. The cultural exchange programs with all parts of the world have dramatically widened the horizon for artistic creativity. Serious art and music as well as the popular arts have been benefited by these programs with such diverse events as the New York Philharmonic concertizing in Russia and Louis Armstrong on worldwide tours.

Dealing with this post–World War II period, however, poses a problem which did not arise in the earlier chapters of this book. For the first time we are not only faced with the artistic paintings, sculpture, architecture, and musical works, but we are living within the social, economic, and cultural conditions out of which they grow. This fact, combined with the technological media of communications, presents us with a situation that we have not experienced before.

The examples of art and music which have been considered as representative of past eras have been influenced, obviously, by the selectivity of past generations. The works of only a few of the most highly regarded artists and composers have been used as examples. The art and music patrons of past centuries have done much of the selection, as has always been the case. It should be pointed out that those artists and composers whose works are used were not necessarily always the most celebrated or even most widely known in their own day. This was especially true in the case of music and musicians. Countless musical works and composers were popular only in their own day and quickly disappeared from the scene when their works had to stand the test of time and history. According to Arnold Schoenberg, one of the great composers of the early twentieth century, "Contemporaries are not final judges, but are generally overruled by history."[1]

Rapid communication, which has been so highly developed in the twentieth century, has tended to encourage the ever widening dissemination of the popular art and music to the exclusion of the more aesthetically demanding. Again music is the most directly influenced of the arts in this respect.

1. Arnold Schoenberg, "Composition with Twelve Tones" in *Style and Idea* (1941) p. 103.

On the other hand, it is unjust to say that popular art and music did not exist in earlier times. In fact, there is no question but that popular art and music have always been present in people's lives. The innate desire on the part of all people, of all economic and intellectual levels, from prehistoric times to the present, to participate in, and enjoy these cultural aspects of life has undoubtedly always been present and likely will always continue to be present. We are at a loss, however, to reconstruct or reproduce much of the popular art and music of the past since those media which we possess today, the printing press, the phonograph, the tape recorder, and television, did not exist in any extensive form until after 1950. The means of reproduction which did exist in earlier times were either largely unavailable or so slow in function that popular art and music, because it always had a short life span, was rarely recorded in any way. We know very little about folk songs, for example, until the first collections were begun in the middle of the nineteenth century.

Moreover, we have no information about the composers of folk music of earlier times though it is obvious that someone had to compose it. We know almost as little about the popular songs and dances except as they were occasionally used by composers as the basis for some of their compositions (see Isaac, *Innsbruck, I Must Leave Thee*). We do know that these two kinds of popular music existed because the words were frequently recorded. The tunes of the minstrel singers of the eleventh and twelfth centuries were rarely written down, whereas there are hundreds of song lyrics recorded in elaborate manuscript books. The generations of fifteen or more centuries have winnowed out the lasting gems from among this great wealth of folk and popular music and art and we are indebted to them for that which remains.

In contrast, we are now in the midst of an overwhelming abundance of all art forms, popular and serious. It pours out on us at every moment of the day and night through radio, television, phonograph, tape recorder, color printing press, etc. We must make our own selection from this super abundance.

As an example, folk songs composed by such composers as Pete Seeger, John Jacob Niles, and Woody Guthrie are not only widely known, but are copyrighted and protected. They are heard and learned by millions of avid folk singers since they are available in printed form as well as heard on all types of audio media. Some of these songs will live for a few months or years, some will probably live for many generations, and some will die aborning. The life span of the works of serious composers will also vary, just as it did in the past.

In this chapter we have decided to present briefly the artistic and musical situation as we find it today. No attempt has been made to evaluate individual works or present one style of production as more important than another. A few works and a few creative artists seem to stand out as representative. We have briefly mentioned persons and some works which seem to have this distinction. Others might have served as well, perhaps better. Only the wear and tear of time will tell.

Visual art

As has been mentioned earlier, it would be too much to claim that post-1945 art represented something new. The series of "isms" and fads of the earlier twentieth century were still viable, but those which have become a series of even more narrow "isms" have succeeded each other in more rapid tempo. Expressionism became Abstract Expressionism to be succeeded by Pop art, Op art, Kinetic art, Minimal art, Superrealism, and even Nonart. However, it must be noted that all these latest "isms" are rooted in the modernism of the early twentieth century. Abstract Expressionism came out of Expressionism and Surrealism. Pop art developed out of Surrealism, Op and Kinetic art are related to the works that were derived from the Bauhaus School of Design in the 1920s and 1930s.

There has been an emphasis on the artist's own uniqueness, on originality at any cost, in what appears to be an effort toward sensationalism. Artists often try to be far-out, socially shocking, erotic, and antiestablishment, as is often found in the performance of rock musicians. Art happenings (almost like aleatoric music), assemblages, minimal art, even nonart, caught the attention of the public. In an industrial technological age, the distinction between art and nonart, between manual craftsmanship and mechanical technology, is no longer an absolute one. Neither painting nor photography, light shows nor motion pictures, sculpture nor industrial design can be any longer jealously separated from each other. The arts began to overlap. Pictures became three-dimensional and may even produce sounds. Sculpture moves and sometimes makes sounds and projects images. Even architecture extends to regional planning. All of these "isms" and fads vie with each other for attention and acceptance. Because of the proliferation of styles and "isms" only the most prominent will be treated here.

Abstract expressionism

Abstract Expressionism, sometimes called action painting, is related to earlier Surrealism, to the Expressionism of the early twentieth century, and to the Abstractionism of Mondrian, Kandinsky, and others. It is a free and spontaneous kind of abstraction which emphasizes color, energetic and emotionally suggestive line, together with dynamic spatial qualities which led to the creation of very large canvases. Even the method of line and color application is a part of the expressive character of this work. Jackson Pollock (1912–1956), Willem de Kooning (1904–   ), and Mark Rothko (1903–1970) became the principal protagonists of this new style.

Pollock, with his technique of drip painting, placed his canvases on the floor and brought his whole body into action while he splashed and dripped colors in swirling configurations according to his own feelings at the moment, without any set pattern or classic design. In his *Number I* (colorplate 46), his splashed and spilled lines appear to have been created in an intense and unrehearsed fury of action. However, the structure seems to be carefully organized. Color combinations are emotionally charged and the design is developed through the rhythm of his own bodily movements. Pollock's lines of color take our eyes into the painting and encourages the viewer to explore the swirling paths of line and color that are woven into the surface. Nothing is static, there is movement physically and emotionally.

De Kooning also uses violent strokes of color which seem to have been angrily splashed on the canvas. His *Woman I* (colorplate 47) is probably more closely connected to the Expressionism of van Gogh and Rouault. Through the use of slashing line and heavy coloring he has expressed the vulgarity of his subject in an almost completely abstract manner. De Kooning seems to have captured both the inner feeling about the woman as well as the outer condition. He has, in effect, gone beyond the realistic appearance and visual meaning of his subject.

Rothko was moving out of Abstract Expressionism when he painted *Number 19* (colorplate 48) in 1958. In his search for expression, he abandoned all reference to objectivity, and color became both content and form. The work is completely lacking in objectivity of real forms. Patches of color are superimposed one upon another with a lack of hard edges. Color spreads from one form to another because the hues and values are closely related to each other. There is little spatial consciousness, but the colors do set up a gentle rhythmic movement of abstract forms and gradations of hues that evoke a mystic kind of expressionism.

Pop art

The sources of Pop art lay in our so-called pop culture. But just what is pop culture? It is the result of bringing together the effects of mass production, the leveling of social strata, and fashion. In earlier times high fashion was for the wealthy and elite. However, with more money, more leisure, and mechanization, fashion is available to a worldwide market for all people. Democracy has led to the idea that everyone has the right to be fashionable if they wish. Fashion uses visual ideas at a ravenous rate and there is a constant search for novelties and gimmicks to further intrigue the public and make what they now have obsolete. Almost all the objects we use or wear are mass produced by the millions. Pop artists have seized on this phenomenon as a source for their artistic activities.

Pop art emphasizes man-made objects and symbols of the mass media. It can be said that Pop art is opposed to the so-called fine arts. It is almost the opposite of Abstract or Expressionist art in presenting the commonplace, mass-produced visual experiences of our society in a blatantly realistic manner. Posters, soup cans, comic strips, and banal objects of everyday existence

Colorplates 46, 47, 48
follows p. 354.

become subject matter for the artist's efforts. These items are usually depicted with photographic realism, often in exaggerated sizes. It is an art that seems to parallel the subliminal images of television commercials. Because of size, or repetitive images, there is an intensity so that we, as spectators, often for the first time, become conscious of what we see around us in our everyday existence.

Robert Rauschenberg (1925–   ) was one of the artists whose works precipitated the Pop art movement and is a kind of link between Abstract Expressionism and Pop art. He attached real objects, or groups of objects to his canvases in a kind of collage technique. Sometimes the objects were covered with paints and sometimes not. In one of his early works, he exhibited a real bed that was all made up and covered with paint. In *Quote* (fig. 15.1), painted in 1964, he portrayed a review of passing events and symbols of momentary happenings, the varied ideas and events that affected our lives at a particular moment in time. Using a silk-screen technique he juxtaposed the images of a series of events and common experiences, such as the well-known photo

Figure 15.1 *Quote* [1964]— Rauschenberg. (Courtesy Leo Castelli Gallery, New York)

of President Kennedy, parachute jumping, and other common visual experiences. He also used color to intensify the expressive quality. The association of dissimilar images, the unusual placement of the images, and the irrational spatial character suggest a connection with both Surrealism and Abstract Expressionism.

Andy Warhol (1930–), also one of the pioneers of Pop art, uses multiple images of symbols of mass-produced items that characterize our culture. His *Green Coca-Cola Bottles* (colorplate 49) proclaims the skills of the world of advertising that has more respect for the container than the material contained. His subjects in other works range from multiple images of Marilyn Monroe to Brillo boxes and Campbell soup cans—all symbols of American pop culture.

Another Pop artist is Robert Indiana (1928–) who uses word images and symbols of commercialism. His *American Dream* (colorplate 50) shows a painting of stenciled signs with such words as "tilt" and "take all" to suggest the pinball machine syndrome and a comment on the American dream of getting rich quick. Like Warhol, there is nothing personalized about the work, only a bland statement about the commercialism of today.

Roy Lichtenstein (1923–) startled and shocked the public with his giant comic book illustrations. In an era when the comics are an integral part of our culture for people of all ages, he has exalted such heroes as Steve Canyon and others. His technique even includes the dots which are a part of the cheap color-printing process. In his *Drowning Girl* (fig. 15.2) the exaggerated teardrops and the verbal message suggest the melodrama of the scene.

One can hardly discuss Pop art without reference to Claes Oldenburg (1929–) who was more a maker of objects than a painter. Influenced by Warhol, he created giant hamburgers and fur-lined cups. He distorted the reality of almost every object he portrayed. He took them out of context, changed their forms from hard to soft, and usually exaggerated their size. His *Giant Soft Fan* (fig. 15.3) is constructed from metal, wood, foam rubber, vinyl, and plastic tubing. The work comes through as a satire on the efficient machine culture of today.

Op art

Optical art, or Op art as it is generally called, is a term usually applied to those two- and three-dimensional works which explore the optical illusion generated by color and line. It is abstract, without representationalism and yet essentially formal and exact. It is a trend that grew out of the ideas developed in the Bauhaus School of Design in the 1930s. Nonobjective patterns of line, shape, and color act as stimuli to the eye and mind of the viewer. Whatever the expressive result, it is a new kind of subjective experience in which illusion, afterimages, and visual movement are real in the mind of the observer, but do not exist objectively in the artwork. Op art does not lend

Colorplates 49, 50 follows p. 354.

Figure 15.2 *Drowning Girl* [1963]—Roy Lichtenstein. (Courtesy, The Museum of Modern Art, New York. Philip Johnson Fund and gift of Mr. and Mrs. Bagley Wright)

itself to intellectual exploration or explanation. Its impact is usually only that of a unique experience.

Double Metamorphosis II (colorplate 51) by Agam (Yaacov Gipstein) (1928–) shows various nonrepresentational patches of color that seem to undulate three-dimensionally behind a screen of closely textured vertical lines. The whole visual pattern changes as the viewer moves from one point of view in the room to another.

Colorplate 51 follows p. 354.

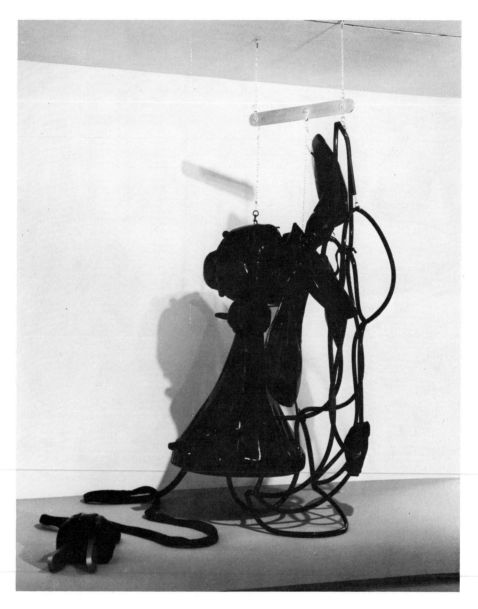

Figure 15.3 *Giant Soft Fan* [1966–67]—Claes Oldenburg. (Courtesy, The Museum of Modern Art, New York. The Sidney and Harriet Janis Collection, gift to The Museum of Modern Art)

Figure 15.4 *Current* [1964]—Bridget Riley. (Courtesy, The Museum of Modern Art, New York. Philip Johnson Fund)

A further example of Op art is that of Bridget Riley (1931–   ). Her *Current* (fig. 15.4) is black-and-white undulating stripes and a formal progression of line. The work depends on the phenomenon of optical illusion to suggest movement.

More recently, psychedelic light shows are an obvious attempt to intensify this kind of visual experience by adding both movement and artificial lighting in the same manner as rock music intensifies the experience of sound by electronic amplification and the movement of the performers themselves.

Kinetic art

Kinetic art, art that employs movement, has opened new avenues of creativity for the artist, especially the sculptor. Some kinetic art moves by means of motorized units and others by depending on the movement of air against delicately balanced forms. Alexander Calder (1898–1976) was a pioneer in kinetic art and is the best-known artist to use this media. Using the movement of air currents for the motive power in his mobiles, which he introduced in the 1930s, he created what amounted to a new art form. He suspended metal plates, painted with primary colors and black and white, from metal rods in such a way that they could move in any direction. When set in motion by currents of air they revolve, exhibiting a varied pattern of forms and colors in their motion. His *Lobster Trap and Fish Tails* (fig. 15.5) is one of his earlier works of kinetic sculpture. His last monumental mobile was created for the new East Wing of the National Gallery of Art and is shown in colorplate 42 of the Central Courtyard of the National Gallery. The idea of Calder's mobiles became very popular and are widely imitated as home decorative items. While Calder's mobiles get their energy from natural sources, there are some sculptors who resort to artificial means of providing motion, using such devices as electric motors and clock springs. In an attempt to reflect our mechanized society some have even created machines that add noise to the artistic experience. As was noted earlier, this idea was suggested by the painter Paul Klee in his *Twittering Machine* (colorplate 41).

Len Lye (1901–   ) in his *Fountain* (fig. 15.6) uses a mechanized motor to make the vertical metal rods sway gently to suggest the flow of water affected by currents of air.

There are others who have created machines that move, rattle, and groan that have no relationships to anything except our mechanized culture. One of the more sensational of these was called *Homage to New York* by Jean Tinguely. Its many parts clanged, rattled, and screeched. It was even programmed to self-destruct, which it did, in a cloud of smoke, according to reports, supervised by the New York Fire Department and witnessed by a large audience.

Minimal art

Minimal art, or primary structures as it is often called, grew out of the work of the constructivist sculptors. In some ways it is related to cubism. Minimal art is three-dimensional and consists of either a single unit or a series of identically shaped primary forms, not necessarily of the same size. It is a reduction to basic shapes without ornament or an attempt to improve the geometry or volume of the basic form. Most often this kind of sculpture seems to penetrate the space we occupy. The work can intrigue the spectator by evoking responses to spatial openings, to volumes and enclosures. David Smith's (1906–1965) *Cubi X* (fig. 15.7) is over ten feet in height and, because

Colorplate 46 *Number I* [1948]—Jackson Pollock. (Courtesy, The Museum of
Modern Art, New York, Purchase)

Colorplate 47   *Woman, I* [1950–52]—Willem de Kooning. (Collection, The Museum of Modern Art, New York, Purchase)

Colorplate 48   *Number 19* [1958]—Rothko. (Courtesy, The Museum of Modern Art, New York, Given anonymously)

Colorplate 49 *Green Coca-Cola Bottles* [1962]—Warhol. (Courtesy the Whitney Museum of American Art, New York)

Colorplate 50   *The American Dream, I* [1961]—Indiana. (Courtesy The Museum of Modern Art, New York. Larry Aldrich Foundation Fund)

Colorplate 51 *Double Metamorphosis II* [1964]—Agam (Yaacov Gipstein). (Courtesy, The Museum of Modern Art, New York, Gift of Mr. and Mrs. George Jaffin)

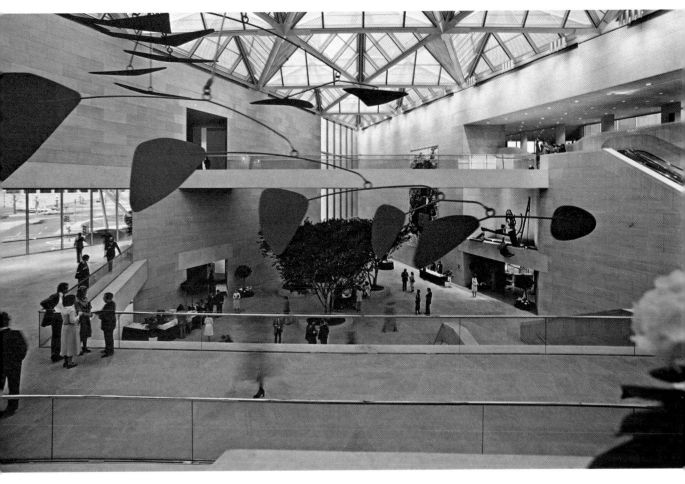

olorplate 52   Central Courtyard of National Gallery of Art in Washington, D.C.,
st Building [1978]—I. M. Pei. (Courtesy Robert Lautman)

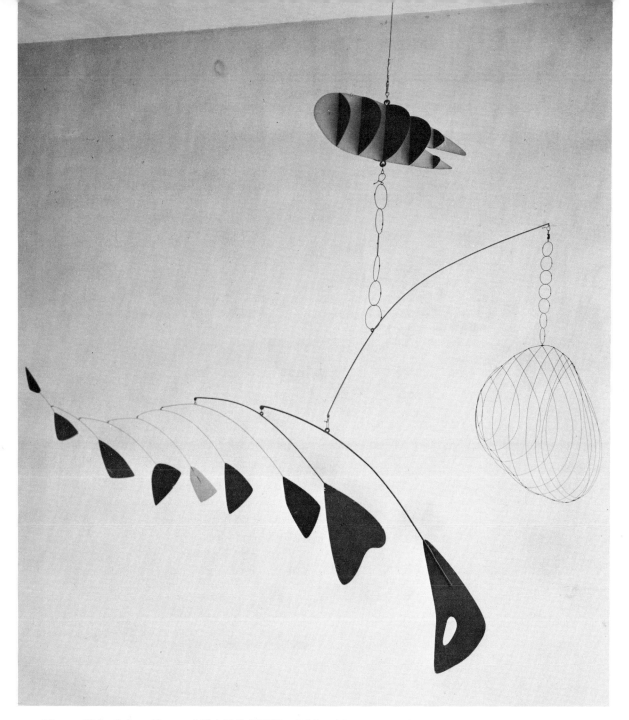

Figure 15.5 *Lobster Trap and Fish Tails* [1939]—Calder. (Courtesy Collection, The Museum of Modern Art, New York)

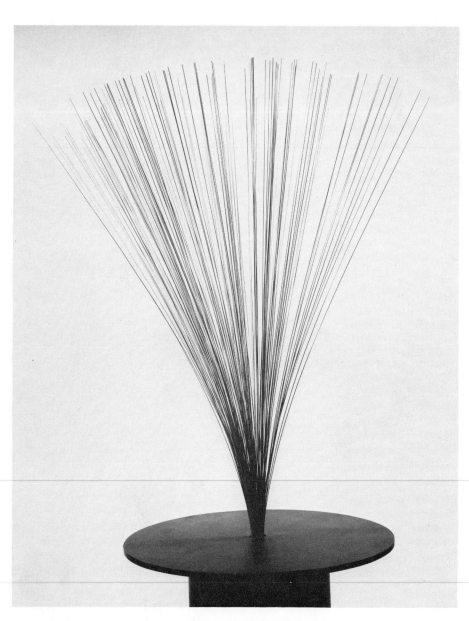

Figure 15.6   *Fountain* [1959]—Len Lye. (Courtesy of Whitney Museum of American Art, New York. Ford Foundation Purchase Program)

Figure 15.7 *Cubi X* [1963]—David Smith. (Courtesy, The Museum of Modern Art, New York. Robert O. Lord Fund)

of its narrow base, gives a sense of balance and counterbalance of one primary form against another.

Untitled Cube (6) (fig. 15.8) by Sol Lewitt is a steel cage construction with painted metal rods. It makes no statement beyond cubical shapes and the volume encompassed within these cubes. It expresses nothing more than itself, a series of cubes connected together. The artist probably intends that the spectator will have the idea of cubes—hence, the idea of cubes becomes, not only the subject matter, but the artwork itself.

Architecture

Post–World War II architecture continued on the course of functionalism that marked the best and most exciting prewar architecture. With emphasis on technology, architects have searched for the practical solution for a given function or set of needs. In recent years this has taken into consideration environmental compatibility and land use, as well as the aesthetic quality. Efficiency of operation has emphasized such things as climate control, solar energy, and ease of ingress and egress. In spite of the idea that a building must be an efficient, functioning machine, architects have managed to find a basis for unique individual expression. Moreover, in recent years architects have utilized the talents of sculptors and painters to enhance and symbolize the function of the building and relate it to the human activities by their creative efforts.

One of the most exciting and artistic solutions to the problem of function and aesthetics is the East Building of the National Gallery of Art in Washington, D.C., designed by I. M. Pei and completed in 1978. It was designed to achieve harmony with the other buildings along Pennsylvania Avenue. Moreover, Pei was able to orient the structure in such a manner that the dome of the Capitol is visible from almost any window or corner. The Central Courtyard (colorplate 52) gives an idea of what the visitor can experience. Geometric forms of triangles and cubes confront one everywhere, the stairwell, exhibit space, the ceiling, walls, and floor. Suspended from the eighty-foot-high ceiling is Calder's last monumental kinetic sculpture with a huge Miró tapestry hanging in the background.

The skyscraper has continued to be the symbol of twentieth-century economic life and a unique American contribution to architecture. The congestion in the city of New York made it necessary to build vertically in order to house more operations on a small piece of ground. The Headquarters of the United Nations Building (fig. 15.9) shows the use of steel cage construction in a skyscraper. Note the horizontal bands of windows that run completely across the face of the building, one band for each of the thirty-nine stories. The arrangement of the well-lighted airy offices and suites makes this a functional building for the transaction of business and government in the important branches of the United Nations. From the exterior it appears

Colorplate 52
follows p. 354.

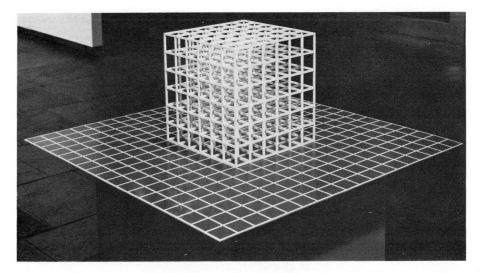

Figure 15.8 *Untitled Cube* (6) [1968]—Sol Lewitt. (Collection of Whitney Museum of American Art, New York. Gift of Howard and Jean Lipman Foundation, Inc.)

almost abstract in design, like Mondrian's *Composition in White, Black and Red*. The General Assembly Building of the United Nations is shown in the background (fig. 15.9). The main lobby of the General Assembly Building (fig. 15.10) shows the use of cantilevered balconies in free organic forms, a sharp contrast to the geometric design of the exterior of the Headquarters Building. The figure of Zeus in the foreground is a gift of the Greek government.

These examples by no means exhaust the innovations in post–World War II architecture. They do, however, demonstrate that architects have responded to their time. They have kept their art alive and vital by incorporating new materials and new techniques, in order to meet today's functional demands and at the same time be expressive of our contemporary culture.

Another architectural structure which emphasizes the very recent tendency to do more than merely enclose a space with a steel and glass cage, is the *Crystal Cathedral* in Garden Grove, California. This edifice grew out of the desire of the pastor of a large congregation to embody not only the "drive-in" portion of his flock to which he had been preaching for a number of years, but also to house another large portion of his people in an enclosed space, but an enclosed space that must retain the "openness" of the drive-in theater where the congregation first met. What resulted was a spectacular building that retained the open air character of the minister's desire and at the same time captured the religious character of a Gothic cathedral, not by imitation of style, but rather by skillful employment of engineering structure to achieve a spiritual serenity on an enormous scale.

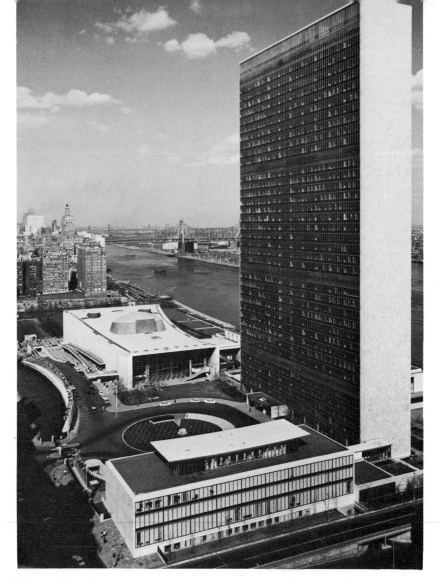

Figure 15.9   Headquarters of the United Nations New York [1950]—
Wallace K. Harrison, Architect in Charge. (Courtesy United Nations)

The structure (Figs. 15.11 and 15.12) is essentially a steel frame covered with more than ten thousand specially fabricated glass panes which give a feeling of light and "out-of-doorness" to both the interior and exterior views. The *Crystal Cathedral* is one solution to the combination of religious purpose to twentieth century uses and techniques: the out door "drive-in" element induced by the automobile, the beauty of interior setting as a consideration of T.V. broadcasting, the use of structural steel frame and glass, the solving

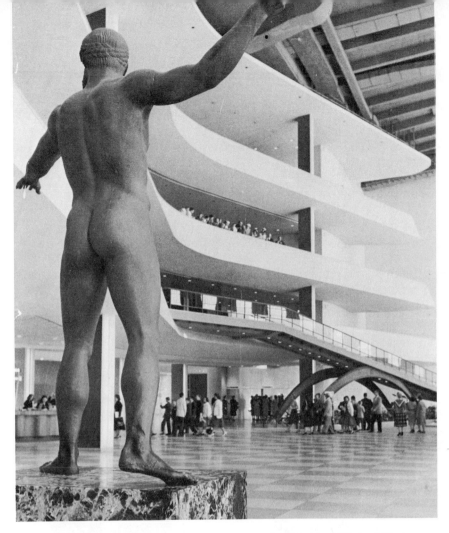

Figure 15.10   Main lobby of the General Assembly Building United Nations, New York [1950]—Wallace K. Harrison, Architect in Charge. (Courtesy United Nations)

of acoustical problems both within and without the building by the most recent electronic systems rather than by any restrictions placed on the structural elements. All in all this fantastic building is "in truth—extraordinary architecture: with its magic of light and structure, it is a building that reaches out to people and that people reach out to—a fair litmus test for any serious piece of architecture."[2]

2. Robert E. Fishcher, *Architectural Record*, November 1980.

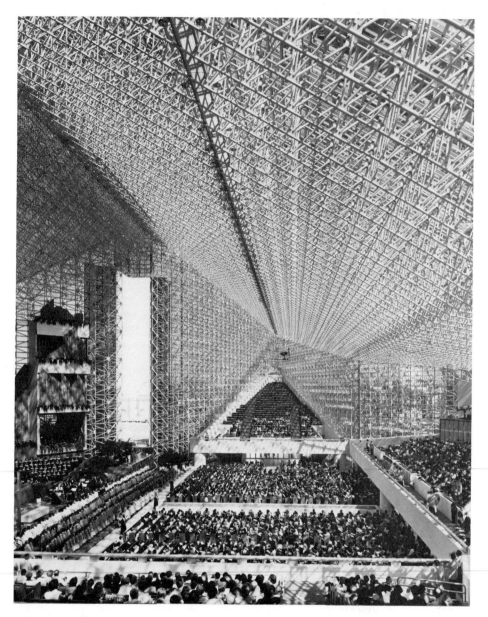

Figure 15.11 "Interior of *Crystal Cathedral*," Johnson/Burgee, Architects. (Courtesy Gordon H. Schenck, Jr.)

Figure 15.12 "Exterior of *Crystal Cathedral*," Johnson/Burgee, Architects. (Courtesy Gordon H. Schenck, Jr.)

General considerations concerning music

While the technical media of communications have tremendously influenced the dissemination of musical performance of all kinds, no aspect of musical creativity has been so proliferated as popular music—jazz, rock, country, bluegrass, and so forth. Phonograph reproduction and radio broadcasting were already widespread before World War II, but the addition of tape recording made both phonograph recording and radio broadcasting more efficient and productive, not to mention the sudden appearance of television after the War.

The universal availability of technical media that receives or reproduces music has made the dissemination of music one of the biggest industries in the world, particularly in the United States. The desire and intent of the producers of both technical media and the communications which they are made to receive is to sell as great an amount of their products as possible. The greater the number of machines—tape recorders, phonographs, radios, and television sets—the greater the demand for communication production— tapes, recordings, and radio and television programs.

Like folk music, popular music, in order to be of universal appeal, must be readily recognized and understood. In many cases, music is not an independent medium; it is rather a vehicle for a verbal message, the text. In some cases, the words maintain their predominant importance over the music as in protest songs and country-western music; while in others, the words may be soon relegated to a secondary position if not forgotten entirely in improvisatory performances, particularly evident in most jazz works of the post–World War II period. Progressive, west coast, and third-stream jazz, in which the main interest centers on the free improvisatory instrumental variations, are created on tunes derived from a variety of sources—original, gospel, folk, and so forth. The technical skill of some popular music performers has achieved a level of sophistication in creativity that has given their productions the stature of works of art. The high level of artistic performance, however, is not an exclusive mark of distinction for the popular music performer. Technical media has made an extremely high level of technical skill and interpretive artistry a condition for success in the performance of concert and theater music, recordings, and broadcasting, just as worldwide personal appearances, made possible through rapid transportation, have made a small group of performing artists the standards of the industry.

In the field of concert and theatrical music, recordings have given a vast audience standards against which they are inclined to judge all interpretation and performance skill. In the field of popular music, the situation is peculiar in that a recorded performance is unique in much the same way as a painting is unique. Unlike the painting, the original performance cannot be distinguished from the reproductions since all recordings are identical and can be reproduced indefinitely. Every original performance of popular music is unique by virtue of the fact that spontaneous improvisation is the sine qua non of the popular idiom in jazz, in its many forms, as well as in rock and roll. In contrast to the traditional art forms which exist in notated scores, the works of jazz and rock artists find a lasting existence only in recorded performances.

A number of significant sociocultural, as well as artistic effects and expressions, are reflected by the whole field of popular music. Perhaps the greatest one is the emphasis upon the performer as creator. One must not forget that such a creative element existed in the music of previous eras, particularly in the music of the Baroque period when the performer not only took liberties with the music of the composer, but was expected to do so. Perhaps this is one of the reasons for the current popularity of Baroque music since the 1950s. Its improvisatory possibilities and expectations are in direct keeping with twentieth-century performance. The liberties taken by the modern jazz artist are a direct reflection of the revolt of youth against the traditions of the older generation. The nineteenth-century musical works dictated in great detail every pitch, rhythm, tone color, and dynamic for the obedient performer to follow, and, to top all this, tradition put a director over the orchestral performance to see that directions were faithfully followed.

Twentieth-century jazz in all its forms succeeds in making the performer-musician the composer. The performer is once again a whole musician, much as he was in the Baroque and pre-Baroque eras. Musically this characteristic of popular jazz is present in the art music of the post–World War II period as well. Many modern composers have provided the opportunity in one or more works for purely improvisatory performance. Aleatory or indeterminate music is also a kind of improvisation. These are attempts to satisfy the compositional urge to which the performing musician feels he should be entitled. The modern composer of serious works has used a number of new devices of notation which are, in effect, indications for directed or even free improvisation.

Another sociocultural factor in the performance of both popular and art music is the mass audience. Music is no longer to be regarded as the property of a few highly selected persons as it was traditionally. The mass media of broadcasting via radio and television, the proliferation of recordings, and the electronic amplification of instruments and voices to reach the mass audience of tens of thousands are all indications of the desire of the performer and the masses to come together. Obviously the audiences for popular music performance are by far the larger—Newport Jazz Festival and Woodstock—but the number of outdoor music festivals in which concert music and opera are performed for mass audiences is also enormous—Hollywood Bowl, Wolf Trap Farm, and Tanglewood.

One of the essential features of popular music is, of course, the rhythmic emphasis. The regularity of rhythmic beat is countered by a certain freedom resulting from the improvisatory character of the performance. This accent upon the rhythmic element stems naturally from the dance with which jazz was first exclusively associated. The rhythm of jazz has intrigued composers since the beginning of the century and continues to do so even in the post–World War II period. Emphasis upon percussion ensembles derived in some degree from the rhythmic emphasis of the jazz band and the highly developed technique of the jazz band drummers.

Tone colors achieved upon such traditional instruments as the trumpet, trombone, saxophone, and others have been exploited by the serious composers as well as the performers of popular music. The interest in non-European cultures as a phenomenon of the late twentieth century has its counterpart in the inclusion of the musical instruments of non-European societies in the performance of both popular and serious music. A great variety of drums and percussion instruments from the South Pacific and African areas, as well as instruments from East Asian countries, have made their appearance in some popular bands and have had an effect on the art music of today.

The whole socio-political movement of protest against the abrogation of civil and human rights has given rise to an enormous wave of protest songs that rightfully belong in the area of popular music. The musical vehicles are regularly very simple and traditional for the most part so that the message conveyed by the words might be easily grasped and the whole widely performed, not only by musicians but, even more importantly, by many people. In some cases, the tunes have in themselves become the message as in the civil right's song *We Shall Overcome*. Large numbers of concert and theatrical compositions have also carried the message of protest—Schoënberg's *Ode to Napoleon* and Penderecki's *Threnody for the Victims of Hiroshima*.

Two other areas of traditional music have been highly influenced by popular music, the musical stage and the church. The influence of rock and roll is exemplified in the stage works *Hair* and *Jesus Christ Superstar*, while Bernstein's *Mass* for the opening of the Kennedy Center in Washington, D.C., contains a great quantity of popular idioms.

Popular music — The people's music

The post–World War II era has seen two predominant styles of pop music, at first antagonistic and divergent and finally combining in their efforts.

Jazz of the 1940s continued to flourish, even though it was overshadowed for the most part by rock and roll. This decade saw the height of the big bands and "swing" which gave way to the smaller combos with their jam sessions and bebop style. In the 1950s jazz cultivated the styles of funky jazz, soul music, and cool jazz. The latter was already an approach to the sophistication of free-form jazz and third-stream jazz. In free-form jazz the dependence on the harmony or melody of an already popular tune was abandoned and the performance was that of a highly skilled multiple improvisation. Even the consistent pattern of rhythm, so characteristic of previous jazz, was rarely present in this style. Third-stream jazz was an attempt to bring together the traditional "classical" forms and styles with the freedom and rhythmic characteristics of jazz. A number of composers, such as Gunther Schuller and Rolf Liebermann, wrote works which spanned the gamut from highly chromatic, harmonically and rhythmically complex sounds to actual combinations of the elements of jazz with traditionally serious forms of composition.

Performers and composers associated with the above styles of the 1940s are "Duke" Ellington and Benny Goodman (big bands); Charlie Parker and "Dizzy" Gillespie (funky jazz and bebop); John Lewis, Dave Brubeck, and Miles Davis (cool jazz); and Gunther Schuller (third-stream jazz). Examples of the various jazz idioms of the post–World War II era can be found in the countless recordings made at the time by these and other performers. The very nature of the jazz improvisatory idiom makes it impossible to separate the composer from the performer. In almost all instances they are one and the same.

"Rock and roll took the tension of a fast, up-tempo rhythm and its hard-driving beat from rhythm and blues. This was mixed with a vocal style of country and western, which was superimposed on the rhythm. The lyrics were adaptations of the blues and popular music. The only other need was a new source of sound to make it distinct form the tradition of popular music. This was supplied by the electrified and electronic innovations in the instruments."[3]

The forms of earlier blues, mainly the twelve-bar measure, was characteristic of rock and roll, but a repeated bass figure often destroyed any semblance of formal balance of phrases. Essentially rock and roll was an expression of adolescence in defiance of the traditional mores in dress, vocabulary, and music. The earliest of the rock and roll stars, Elvis Presley, personified this revolt for millions of youth not only in America but all over the world. Among the factors which stimulated the rapid spread of this style in the 1950s and 1960s were the disc jockeys of the radio stations, most of whom had close connections with publishing houses and recording companies controlling the reproduction of rock and roll combos and bands. This control of popular music by "big business" often led to illegal practices. Another factor was the spread of the use of drugs which went hand in hand with the type of presentation and costuming—both of which were important, integral parts of rock and roll performance. A third factor was the dominating volume of sound that was only possible through the use of electronic amplification that added immeasurably to the hallucinatory character of rock and roll. Unlike jazz, this was not dance music. Rock and roll was almost exclusively a music for performance to large admiring audiences of youths whose activity consisted of a kind of hypnotic, nervous, gut response to the amplified sounds and glaring lights. Such a performance had all the aspects of a "happening" in which light, sound, movement, and words were combined into a single emotional impression.

3. Andrew J. Broekema, *The Music Listener* (Dubuque, Ia.: Wm. C. Brown Company Publishers, 1978), p. 238.

In the 1960s the Beatles represented a phase of rock and roll that was marked by its interest in philosophical and social aspects, particularly those of Eastern religions. Another English group, the Rolling Stones, represented a more violent emotional phase of rock and roll which eventually led to a style known as acid rock in which the drug culture was emphasized as well as the social revolt of youth. Groups such as the Grateful Dead and Jefferson Airplane represent such a style also.

The 1970s have seen something of retrenchment of the excesses of rock and roll. There have been attempts at various degrees of eclecticism. Jazz, East Indian music, electronic music, and blues have all been combined in one way or another in many of the rock and roll performances. Even modal harmonies and scales outside the major-minor area have been used by the more enterprising bands. In general, the trends, while yet indistinguishable, seem to be toward a more mild form of presentation as well as musical effect. The apparent turn to nostalgia of the early 1970s has affected all aspects of rock and roll.

Music in the concert hall, theater, and ballet

The general trends of the first half of the twentieth century continue and are further developed and exploited in the post–World War II period. The twelve-tone construction of Arnold Schoenberg became a tool of almost every composer, some of whom used it occasionally, often in a rather free manner. The complete serialism of Anton Webern was seized upon by a number of the avant-garde composers, and Webern's pointilistic style was a kind of forerunner of composing with electronic sounds of the newly invented synthesizer. The development of the synthesizer and computer as tools for achieving new tonal colors and rhythmic complexities that were unobtainable through any other media is one of the most novel and influential trends of this period. The improvisatory techniques of the jazz performers and the rhythmic freedom of popular music was reflected in serious music as well. A further expansion of new and free techniques is that type of music known as aleatoric, chance, or indeterminate. The terms refer to musical composition which is only partially dictated by the notation of the composer. In fact, the composer merely suggests certain patterns of sound, if any, in a notation which varies from that of the traditional kind to that completely lacking in definite rhythm or pitch. The performer, following very broad and general instructions, uses these suggestions as a basis for a controlled type of improvisation. In some instances, only the duration of the improvisatory section is indicated.

As in any age, the list of composers active in the latter part of the twentieth century is one of enormous length. It is impossible to select any one or more as being the most representative. In this period of rapid change and great diversity, each composer reflects his or her own personal idiom along with one or more of the common, and almost universal, characteristics of musical composition. A few composers have already had rather widespread recognition. Whether they or other comtemporaries will be most representative of the last half of this century remains to be seen.

In the following pages, certain obvious trends of the post–World War II era have been indicated and representative examples have been listed. In some instances, composers may be found under one or more categories, since they have participated in several of the trends.

A development which has taken place mainly in the post–World War II era is that of electronic music. Most electronic music is in the nature of experimental exercises, with tonal materials gathered from various sources. Electronic composers first recorded and manipulated all manner of sounds and noises and composed these by means of tape recording into theoretically organized forms. In some instances, the sounds are those of musical instruments distorted through the manipulation of the tape recorder. The development of the synthesizer, however, gave composers the opportunity to use sounds generated directly by means of electrical equipment. Experiments in combining such manipulated sounds with traditional instruments are also a part of the electronic composer's expression. Many composers have used electronic devices of one kind or another. Karlheinz Stockhausen (1928–   ), a German musician, is one of the leading composers in this field. A pupil of Messaien, his work has centered around the electronic studio of the Cologne radio and the Darmstadt Center for Contemporary Music. In his *Gesang der Jünglinge* and *KONTAKTE*, Stockhausen has combined both natural sounds with electronically generated ones. Edgard Varése (1883–1965), who was one of the earlier exploiters of tonal color, also used the synthesizer in his works *Deserts* and *Poeme Electronique.*

Composers using electronic music were often closely allied to the principles of twelve-tone construction; albeit, they extended these principles beyond the practice of Schoenberg and Webern. Twelve-tone composition was serialism confined to the element of musical pitch. Most of post–World War II composers were content to keep within the restriction of this concept though they often treated the technique with considerable freedom. A notable example of such twelve-tone composition was the work of the Italian Luigi Dallapiccola (1904–1975). Among his many works the opera *Il Prigioneri (The Prisoners)* manages to combine the twelve-tone technique with the lyrical tradition of the Italian operas. Dallapiccola never abandoned his close relation with traditional Italian lyricism throughout all his loyalty to the principles of Schoenberg and twelve-tone composition.

A number of composers, however, contrived to extend the idea of pitch serialism to the other elements of music, such as duration, intensity, timbre, texture, and even silence. A series of pitches might be combined with a series of another element or even all other elements to a state of "total serialism." Such music lacks the traditional aspect of thematic basis and development, and the result is one of great complexity of sounds. The unifying element of serialism will be recognizable only to someone who has devoted much study to such works and who has had the opportunity to hear them repeatedly. Stockhausen has used such total serialism in his work *Zeitmass* in which all the elements of music are controlled by detailed markings of every note for the five woodwind instruments employed in the work. Milton Babbitt (1916–) is an American composer who has worked with electronic composition and in total serialism. His *Ensembles for Synthesizer* is a representative work in this style.

Closely allied to these techniques are those of aleatoric (random or indeterminacy technique) composers. Stockhausen is also a prime example of this trend. His work, *Klavierstück XI* (*Piano Piece XI*) written in 1956, is an example of aleatoric or chance composition. The work consists of nineteen fragments of notation which are printed on a large cardboard placed on the piano music rack. The performer plays any one of these nineteen patterns that he or she happens to see, and may play this pattern and any succeeding ones that his or her eye catches, treating each and any one of them in accordance with certain suggested directions. Any segment may be repeated and all need not be played. The piece ends when the performer finds that he or she has repeated any segment three times.

Another composer whose musical aesthetics has been so revolutionary that, driven to its ultimate, it becomes nonmusic is the American John Cage (1912–). He has "composed" a work entitled *Imaginary Landscape*, which calls for twelve radio receivers tuned by chance to different radio frequencies. The resulting sounds become the musical composition. In a sense, this performance becomes an aural "happening" paralleling the visual happenings of the avant-garde.

These developments all suggest a parallel with the arts of painting and sculpture in which new materials, improvisation, and chance play a controlling part. Cage has gone so far as to compose nonmusic, works in which neither the composer or the performer contributes a sound, but endeavors to get the audience to "compose" those natural sounds and noises which they might hear into a piece of "music." In his *Four Minutes and Thirty-three Seconds* Cage asks the "performer" only to sit before an open piano with a stopwatch and allow the natural sounds of life to be "composed" into a musical expression by the participating audience.

Multimedia expression consists of the combination of various art media such as music, dance, dramatic movement, light, painting, and sculpture into a synthesis. Generally, such attempts have ended in the predominance of the musical element, though the other media have added to the expressive quality of the whole composition. This is, of course, the old desire of the operatic thesis of Monteverdi, Gluck, and Wagner, which was also never completely realized. The late twentieth century saw many such attempts in both the serious and popular fields of musical production. Rock and roll depends in great part on movement (the gyrations of the performer), light, and costuming, which are essential parts of the performance. Serious composers have used some of these elements, mainly in the area of choral compositions. An example of multimedia expression in which physical movement and music are combined is the composition *Circles* (ex. 15.1) by Luciano Berio (1925–) in a setting of poems by E. E. Cummings for voice and percussionists, in which the performers' physical movements are calculated to give shape to the composition.

Gunther Schuller (1925–) has also composed a kind of multimedia work in *The Seven Studies on Themes of Paul Klee,* composed in 1959. This is a musical translation of the "musical" elements in some of Klee's paintings. Klee was an amateur musician and frequently used musical terms and forms in his paintings. Among the paintings that Schuller chose was *The Twittering Machine* (colorplate 33). He made the music "twitter" by use of mechanical application of the twelve-tone technique in a manner analagous to the pointillism of Webern. Schuller seems to realize the aural experience of the sounds of the symbolic mechanical birds that Klee expressed visually.

Popular music, particularly jazz, has influenced a number of composers of the twentieth century. Even in the first half of the century several composers wrote works which showed a rather naive attempt to incorporate ragtime and jazz into their works, notably Debussy in *Golliwog's Cake Walk;* Krenek in his opera, *Johnny Strikes up the Band;* and Milhaud in his ballet, *The Creation of the World,* among many others. Continued efforts of this kind can be found in the work of Gunther Schuller who is not only known for his expressionism in which serial technique, highly imaginative tonal coloring, and chromatic atonality are employed, but also for his interest in jazz. Schuller was deeply engaged in the setting up of the *third-stream* jazz movement with John Lewis. He founded the Third Stream Performance Ensembles at the New England Conservatory where he taught. The results were a cross-fertilization of classic forms with all the modern techniques including jazz and its improvisatory elements.

The theater has provided the opportunity for two types of performance employing music to flower in the period since the Second World War, namely the musical theater and the ballet. The ballet has achieved a spectacular popularity in the second half of this century in America. A great part of the music used, however, has been works which were not immediately written for ballet performance, such as instrumental works extending from Bach to Schoenberg. A few contemporary composers such as Copland and Sessions have written specifically for ballet. A number of popular musicians have written short works using modern popular dance styles.

The musical theater, a descendent of the Viennese operetta has provided a large number of composers of popular style music an opportunity to write for dramatic entertainment. Such works vary from the more traditional musical comedy type such as *My Fair Lady* and *Fiddler on the Roof* to outright rock musicals such as *Hair* and *Jesus Christ, Superstar.* These works often contain considerable amount of ballet music, some of which has become the basis for independent ballet performance.

Example 15.1 *Circles*, page 21 of score from the setting of E. E. Cummings's poems [1923–1945]—Luciano Berio. (Courtesy of Universal Editions, London, England, copyright owners.)

Leonard Bernstein (1918–   ), an internationally known American conductor and composer, is equally at home in the serious as well as in the popular idioms of composition. The former is represented in such works as his *Jeremiah Symphony* and the latter in several stage works among which are *Wonderful Time* and *West Side Story*. His *Mass*, written for the opening of the John F. Kennedy Center in Washington, D.C., represents an acknowledgment of the incorporation of jazz and popular idiom into one of the oldest forms of church music, the mass.

There have been a number of composers who have experimented in many of the techniques of the post–World War II era but who have not adopted any one of them exclusively, and thereby have avoided becoming advocates of any one school of thought. Most of them have exploited one or another or even several of the modern idioms, such as electronic music, serialism, multimedia, jazz, and so forth, or at least have been influenced by these trends. They do not necessarily represent the only successful composers of the second half of the twentieth century, but they appear to be representative of a kind of composer for whom the maintenance of personal identity and individuality supercedes the necessity of alliance with a particular trend or school. The composers who represent this individuality have been selected since their works have attracted international attention.

Olivier Messaien (1908–   ) is a French composer of unique abilities and techniques whose works date from the 1920s, but whose greatest compositions and influence as a teacher came after the middle of the century. His interest in tonal color and rhythmic complexities combined with a deeply religious sense and highly developed literary capabilities give his music a very personal flavor. An example of his religious intensity is reflected in the numerous works for organ and church performance. His interest in rhythmic problems is characteristic of such works as *Chronochromie* and *Mode de Valeurs et d'Intensité*. Among those works which display his preoccupation with tonal colors is the long list of piano pieces under the title *Catalog of the Birds*, in which Messaien's lifelong interest in nature and particularly in the songs and calls of birds is exploited to the utmost. This work is based on actual bird songs and calls notated by Messaien in countless field observations of birds in their natural habitats. His influence as a teacher is indicated by the fact that among his students at the Paris Conservatory were such important young composers as Stockhausen, Boulez, Nono, and many others.

Elliott Carter (1908–   ) is an American composer whose modern use of highly contrapuntal style gave way in the 1950s to a serialism of intervals and rhythms which characterize his later works. Among his large number of compositions his string quartets have probably achieved a wider audience that any of his other works.

Gyorgi Ligeti (1923–   ), a Hungarian who lives in Germany, has worked closely with the electronic studio in Cologne and with the International Courses in New Music in Darmstadt. His works cover the whole gamut of compositional genres, both vocal and instrumental. He has employed electronic devices, serialism, chance, and experiments in tonal color, but has managed in all his works to maintain a personal idiom. His *Wind Quintet* and the vocal work for sixteen solo voices, *Lux Aeterna,* are both indicative of his mastery of tonal coloring whether for instruments or voices.

Peter Maxwell Davies (1934–   ) is an English composer whose compositional techniques reflect an interest in styles that range from pre-Bach polyphony to serial and improvisatory styles. A number of his works deal with sacred themes, among these a cycle of carols and instrumentals sonatas based on the plainsong version and text of *O Magnum Mysterium.*

Krzysztof Penderecki (1933–   ) is a Polish composer who has been probably the most widely heard of the post–World War II period. He is one of a rather large number of young Polish composers who have adventured in the most advanced styles and idioms of the time. His works embrace all genres, and his orchestral and choral compositions have won international attention and acclaim. He has chosen both old texts, as in the *St. Luke Passion,* and modern subject matter, as in *A Threnody for the Victims of Hiroshima.* This latter work, while scored for traditional instruments—fifty-two string instruments—is representative of Penderecki's concern with sound groups and instrumental coloration. Much of the score (ex. 15.2) does not even indicate definite pitch, and there is actually no traditional indication of rhythmic pulse or meter. These are indicated rather by blocks of time. The figures 15″, 11″, 4″, 6″, and so forth in example 15.2 are the number of seconds that the notation is to be played. The symbols are explained in a preface to the score. The figure ▲ indicates the highest pitch possible on the respective instrument (indefinite pitch), and the only traditional indications are those of dynamic change. The work is obviously not built on melodic or harmonic patterns, motifs, or themes but rather in blocks of tone colors achieved by all sorts of manipulations by the performers—striking on the wood of the instruments, playing behind the bridge, and slow vibrato with wide pitch differences, playing on the tailpiece of the instrument. The overall effect is one of striking tonal combinations through which Penderecki tries to transmit his deeply felt reaction to the Hiroshima holocaust. Tone color, improvisation, and absence of thematic statement in the traditional sense are all characteristics of this new music of the second half of the twentieth century and are to be found in the works of countless composers of this time.

In the works of these composers we can see several aspects of twentieth-century music. Yet all of these composers have certain common traits. There are many other composers equally characteristic of this period. While time and space do not allow for the mention of all of them or their works, it is important that the person interested in music become acquainted with as many works of as many contemporary composers as possible. Among other important creators who have made, and are making, valuable contributions to the present-day scene are Boulez, Henze, Britten, and Krenek, among the Europeans, and Piston, Sessions, Rochberg, and Copland among the Americans.

Example 15.2 *Threnody for the Victims of Hiroshima*, Penderecki

Summary

The rapidity of change in all aspects of life-styles since the end of World War II has been even greater than in the first half of the twentieth century. The impact of this accelerated change on the creativity of art and music has led to a proliferation of "isms" and fads that preclude the establishment of consistent stylistic characteristics in any of the arts.

The sophistication of technology has led to tremendous advances in the area of communication and in the psychology and techniques of the mass media. Technology has also led to the development of new synthetic materials for visual art and new resources of sound and sound amplification.

The sociocultural forces that have affected the arts have not only been numerous, but have come within a short time span. The Vietnam war with its widespread protest movements; the anti-nuclear movement; the environmental issues; the civil and human rights movement; the general revolt of youth against the status quo—all of these developments have had a powerful impact on the artistic creativity with a variety of new and sometimes exotic subject matters for the artist to deal with. Another important factor is the fact that the economic conditions place a tremendous buying power, not in the hands of the elite as in previous times, but in the hands of the mass society, especially the youth. The mass of society is an indifferent and passive population whose interest is to consume. Many artists and composers, especially composers of popular music, have focused their efforts on supplying the consumer with what the artist wants to sell. The effect of this relation between the consumer and creative artists is seen most clearly in the area of popular music. Rock, rock and roll, hard and acid rock music have become big business with literally billions of the consumer's dollars being gathered in.

There has been a tendency toward the improvisatory character of all the arts since World War II. While the visual arts have been influenced by the element of chance in the arrangements of the basic materials to some degree, it is music that has been affected more directly. Post–World War II composers have experimented extensively with aleatory, or chance music, in which all elements of music were to be determined by the uncontrollable chance happenings of sounds.

Another important development has been the use of new materials from which to construct works of art. These have ranged from the synthetic materials of plastic, stainless steel, reinforced concrete to new developments in paints and the means of putting them onto a variety of surfaces. In music new sounds, some produced by electronic means, such as sound generators and computers, as well as the new sounds directly from the world of industry, have given composers a whole range of tonal possibilities with which to work.

There seem to be many paradoxes in twentieth-century art. One paradox proclaims a strict and systematic discipline of materials and technique on one hand and an aleatory or haphazard combination of materials and elements on the other hand. Another paradox is the apparent denial of emotion in art, especially in the early part of the century, and a move towards an almost hysteria of emotion in the post–World War II period. This is most apparent in recent popular music where a complete freedom of emotional expression is the popular mode. These paradoxes are partly the reasons why it is impossible to place all post–World War II art into a strict stylistic framework.

There are indications, some of them rather distinct as in the case of architecture, others more covert as in painting and music, that the desire for some element of emotional interest and expressive quality is softening the earlier tendencies of the twentieth century to make technique and structure the dominating elements of works of art. The music of the electronic synthesizer, for example, has already lost its novelty and is becoming a means to an end rather than an end in itself. The same can be said of compositional devices such as serial construction. Even in the area of popular entertainment music there are indications of less emphasis on the frenetic and psychedelic elements of hard rock, disco, etc., and a return in many instances to the sweeter combinations such as the big bands of the first half of the century. Painting, too, has its representational advocates, although not in the strict traditional techniques.

Artists of every media have tried, or are trying, to be compatible with and reflect the dramatic changes that have taken place in our understanding of ourselves and the universe in which we live. Nothing is so permanent as change. This, in effect, can be the key to the understanding of the art of our century. Only time will sift the worthy from the unworthy, the good from the "kitsch." Only time will put its stamp of approval on the few great creative artists of our time who have, or will create, truthful remembrances of the important exigencies of our time. If our cultural heritage is to be maintained and furthered, it is incumbent upon a society that gives its creative artists a fair reception and a fair criticism, whether they be painters, sculptors, architects, or composers. Only in this manner can the arts be kept alive and flourishing.

Musical examples

Babbitt, *Ensembles for Synthesizers*

Berio, *Circles*

Bernstein, *West Side Story*

Dallapiccola, *The Prisoners*

Davies, *O Magnum Mysterium*

Ligeti, *Lux Aeterna*

Messaien, *Catalog of the Birds*

Penderecki, *A Threnody for the Victims of Hiroshima*

Schuller, *Seven Studies on Themes of Paul Klee*

Stockhausen, *Gesang der Juenglinge, Piano Piece XI*

Varése, *Poême Electronique*

Suggested readings

Austin, William W. *Music in the 20th Century.* New York: W. W. Norton, 1966.

Broekema, Andrew J. *The Music Listener.* Dubuque, Ia: Wm. C. Brown Company Publishers, 1978, pp. 223–45, 439–83.

Grout, D. J. *A History of Western Music*, 3rd ed. New York: W. W. Norton, 1980, pp. 682–752.

Lippard, Lucy R. *Pop Art.* New York: Praeger, 1966.

Lucie-Smith, Edward. *Late Modern*, 2d ed. New York: Praeger, 1976.

Machlis, Joseph. *Introduction to Contemporary Music.* New York: W. W. Norton, 1961.

Pellegrini, Aldo. *New Tendencies in Art.* New York: Crown, 1966.

Richardson, Tony, and Nikos, Stangos. *Concepts of Modern Art.* New York: Harper and Row, 1974.

Saltzman, Eric. *Twentieth-Century Music: An Introduction,* 2d ed. Englewood Cliffs, N.J.: Prentice-Hall, 1974.

Wold and Cykler. *An Outline History of Music,* 5th ed. Dubuque, Ia.: Wm. C. Brown Company Publishers, 1982, pp. 238–304.

Suggested examples for further analysis

Painting: De Kooning, *Woman and Bicycle;* Jasper Johns, *Numbers in Colour;* Jackson Pollock, *Ocean Greyness*

Sculpture: Robert Mooris, *Untitled;* Robert Indiana, *Love*

Architecture: Lincoln Center, New York; J. F. Kennedy Center, Washington, D.C.

Music: Boulez, *Les Marteau sans Maitre;* Carter, 2nd String Quartet; Messaien, *Chronochromie;* Bernstein, *Mass;* Sessions, 8th Symphony.

Film strips with sound

Twentieth Century Artistic Revolution, Educational Audio Visual Inc.

Twentieth Century: The Age and its Art, Schloat

Surrealism in Art and Music, Educational Audio Visual Inc.

Additional sources for visual illustrations

O'Connor, Francis V. *Jackson Pollock*. New York: Museum of Modern Art, 1967.

Rosenberg, Harold. *De Kooning*. New York: Abrams, 1978.

Waldman, Diane. *Rothko*. New York: Abrams, 1978.

Appendix

Instruments

There are three general groups of instruments used in a modern orchestra—
(1) string, (2) wind, and (3) percussion. These are subdivided as follows:

Stringed instruments

Instruments played with a bow:
Violin
Viola
Violoncello ('cello)   String Choir
Double bass

Instrument played by plucking the strings: Harp

Wind instruments

Woodwinds
Flute   Sounded by blowing across
Piccolo   a hole near the end of tube.

Oboe   Wood-
English Horn   wind
Bassoon   Double-reed instruments   Choir
Contrabassoon

Clarinet
Alto clarinet
Bass clarinet   Single-reed instruments
Saxophone

Brass winds (instruments with cupped or conical mouthpieces):
Trumpet
Cornet
French horn   Brass Choir
Trombone
Tuba

Percussion instruments played by striking

Kettledrums (tympani)   Triangle
Side drum (snare drum)   Castanets
Bass drum   Gong
Tambourine   Glockenspiel (bells)
Cymbals   Piano

In a large symphony orchestra (ninety to one hundred players), the approximate proportion of instruments will be about as follows:

16 or 18 1st violins   1 contrabassoon
14 or 16 2nd violins   3 clarinets
12 or 14 violas   1 bass clarinet
10 or 12 'cellos   4 French horns
8 or 10 string basses   3 or 4 trumpets
1 harp   3 trombones
3 flutes   1 tuba
1 piccolo   3 or 4 kettledrums
3 oboes   1 snare drum
1 English horn   bells, cymbals, and other
3 bassoons   percussion instruments

String Choir

Violin

The violin is the soprano member of the string choir and queen of the orchestra. It is the smallest of the stringed instruments, and its tone is very brilliant and penetrating.

The first violins are required to play the greater part of the leading themes of a piece, although they often play minor parts.

The second violins usually play a part that corresponds to the second soprano part in choral music. They also reinforce the first violins in many passages.

Viola

The viola has the same general appearance as the violin, but upon close inspection it will be found to be a little larger. Its tone is not so brilliant, but is deep and resonant. The viola plays a part that corresponds to the alto in choral music.

Violoncello ('cello)

The violoncello is a tenor member of the string choir. It has a greater variety of tone color than the viola and is used more often as a solo instrument. It is the most flexible of the tenor instruments.

Double bass

The double bass, often called the bass viol, is the lowest pitched member of the string choir. The chief function of the double bass is to furnish a bass foundation for the orchestra.

Harp

The harp consists of a large, triangular frame of wood and metal, within which are stretched forty-six strings. The wide, hollow side of the instrument that rests against the player is a wooden soundboard; the purpose of which is to increase the tone by its resonance. The tone of the harp is rather weak, and it is used in the orchestra to accompany solo passages. In some cases, it is used as a solo instrument.

Woodwind choir

Flute and piccolo

The flute is a slender tube with a system of keys for the fingers, by which the player can open and close holes in the instrument to produce different pitches.

All wind instruments are sounded by setting in vibration columns of air. A flute player causes the column of air within the flute to vibrate by directing a flow of air across a hole near the end of the tube. Its tone is very clear and pleasing in sound, and its variety of tone makes it a fine instrument for solo passages.

The piccolo is nothing more than a small flute and its tone is very high and shrill. This instrument is rarely used in soft passages, but it is used when the full orchestra is playing loudly to add tone color.

Oboe

The oboe is a double-reed instrument. These instruments produce tones by means of a double reed, which consists of two thin strips of cane placed together with a small passage between them for air. The oboe, soprano member of the double-reed family, is a slender wooden instrument with finger holes and keys. It has a penetrating nasal quality of tone suggesting oriental, melancholy, and pastoral scenes.

English horn

The English horn is really an alto oboe. Its tone quality is dark and melancholy, and it is often used in solo passages to express sadness or mystery.

Bassoon

The bassoon, also a double-reed instrument, is considerably larger than the English horn, its wooden tubing being so long that it must be doubled upon itself for convenience in holding and playing. Its tone is very low and it is often used in solo passages to express grotesqueness or humor.

Contrabassoon

The contrabassoon is the bass member of the double-reed family of instruments. It plays sustained tones in the bass and is rarely heard as a solo instrument.

Clarinet

The clarinet, alto clarinet, bass clarinet, and saxophone have single reeds made from strips of cane. The reed is placed over an oblong-shaped opening in the mouthpiece and rests against the player's lower lip.

The clarinet has somewhat the same appearance as the oboe at a distance, but it is larger than the oboe and has a different system of fingering. The tone quality of the clarinet is exceptionally clear and beautiful, and it is therefore often used for solo passages. Frequently it takes alto parts when the flute plays the melody, since the tones of the two blend well. The alto clarinet and bass clarinet serve to fill out the lower register of the clarinet section. While they are used in orchestras, they are more common in bands.

Saxophone

The saxophone is not regularly a member of the orchestra, but it is used in modern music frequently and effectively. Like the clarinet, it is played with a single reed in a chisel-shaped mouthpiece. Unlike the clarinet, it has a conical bore, a relatively large and up-turned bell, and is made of brass.

Brass choir

The player of a brass-wind instrument not only blows air into the horn but causes his lips to vibrate in a certain manner upon the cupped or conical mouthpiece; by this means, the column of air within the instrument is set in vibration. A considerable amount of practice and training is necessary to develop the muscles of the mouth properly and to attain skill in breathing.

Trumpet

The trumpet is composed of about eight feet of tubing coiled so that the length of the instrument is about eighteen inches. The tone of the trumpet is very brilliant and has a wide range. It is valuable for reinforcing the other instruments in loud passages and also for expressing military triumph or jubilant, festive moods. It adds sonority and brilliance to the playing of the orchestra that is very effective.

Cornet

The cornet has the same range as the trumpet, but has a slightly different tonal color, due to the difference in the bore of tubing. The tone of the cornet is coarser and lacks the brilliance of the trumpet. However, there are many passages in orchestral literature for both of these instruments.

French horn

The French horn has sixteen feet of brass tubing curled in a circular form. Its tone, pitch, and various effects are more dependent upon the skill of the performer than upon the mechanism of the instrument. It is, perhaps, the most beautiful voice of the brass choir.

Four horns are regularly employed in a symphony orchestra, although some compositions call for more or less than that number. The horn sounds to best advantage when used for sustained tones, but it is useful in many other ways.

Trombone

The slide trombone is an important member of the brass-wind family. It is not only capable of extreme power of tone, but has a rich, resonant quality which is very effective.

The trombone is a tube about nine feet long that is doubled on itself to about half that length by means of a sliding U-shaped tube so that the length, and therefore the pitch, of the instrument can be altered.

Tuba

The tuba or bass horn is the largest of the brass-wind family and capable of the deepest tone. Its tone blends very well with that of the trombone and it is often used with three trombones to form a brass quartet. It is a flaring tube of brass about eighteen feet long, expanding to a large bell at its final opening, and is equipped with valves like the trumpet for varying pitches.

Percussion

The kettledrums or tympani are the most important of the percussion section. They resemble large copper bowls and across the tops are stretched membranes called "heads." Kettledrums, unlike other drums, can be tuned so that varied pitches can be played upon them. They play a dramatic role in the orchestra. In loud passages they intensify the excitement or accent the rhythm; in soft parts they can be used to produce an effect of mystery.

The side drum (snare drum) is a small drum upon which can be played a variety of rhythmic patterns by means of two drumsticks.

The bass drum is used to accent the rhythm of loud passages.

The piano is a stringed instrument whose strings are struck by hammers through a series of levers attached to keys, hence the classification as a percussion instrument. The piano is one of the most versatile of all instruments. It has a wide range of pitch and is capable of many degrees of loudness. Furthermore, it can produce a great many tones at one time and has great agility of action. This versatility, coupled with the fact that one performer can achieve these varied musical effects, has made it the most popular of all instruments. When the piano is used as a part of the orchestral fabric it is usually employed as a percussion instrument to enhance the element of rhythm. When it is used as a solo instrument, either with or without orchestra, its capacity for melody is usually exploited.

Other percussion instruments include the tambourine, a small drum played by striking with the hand; the cymbals, large discs of brass played by striking together; the triangle, a small steel bar bent in the shape of a triangle and played by striking with a short steel rod; castanets, small pairs of clappers held in the hands and clicked together; the gong, a suspended metal plate sounded by striking with a bass drumstick; and the glockenspiel (bells), a set of metal bars played by striking with small metal hammers.

Notation

Note values

Note name   *Relative value*

Staff notation

Time Chart

		VISUAL ARTS	MUSIC	HISTORICAL FIGURES & EVENTS
500 B.C. ↕ 100 B.C.	GREEK	Phydias Praxiteles	Pythagorus Greek Modal Scales	Aeschylus Pericles Plato Aristotle
↕ 500 A.D.	ROMAN AND EARLY CHRISTIAN	Colosseum Pantheon		Julius Caesar Virgil Hadrian Constantine
↕ 1100 A.D.	ROMANESQUE	St. Vitale Ravenna Notre Dame Le Grande Poitier Pisa Cathedral	Liturgical Gregorian Chants	Pope Gregory 2nd Council of Nicaea
↕ 1400 A.D.	GOTHIC	Gothic Cathedral Amiens Chartres Salisbury Etc. Stained Glass Windows	Troubadors Trouveres Minnesingers Organum Perotin Machaut	Crusades St. Francis St. Thomas Aquinas Dante Petrarch Chaucer
↕ 1600 A.D.	RENAISSANCE	N. Pisano El Greco Martini Giotto Verrochio Donatello Botticelli Bramante da Vinci Grünewald Dürer Michaelangelo Giorgione Raphael Paladio Tintoretto	Dufay Des Prés J. Walter A. Gabrielli Palestrina Lassus Marenzio Gesualdo	Columbus Da Gama Lorenzo de Medici Machiavelli Savanarola Copernicus Luther Pope Julius II Council of Trent Shakespeare
↕ 1725 A.D.	BAROQUE	Rubens Bernini Boromini Velasquez Rembrandt	G. Gabrielli Monteverdi Schütz Corelli Vivaldi J. S. Bach Handel D. Scarlatti Couperin	Lord Bacon Kepler Harvey Descartes Milton 30 Yrs. War Moliere Spinoza Louis XIV Newton

		VISUAL ARTS	MUSIC	HISTORICAL FIGURES & EVENTS
1800 A.D.	ROCOCO CLASSIC	Tiepolo Watteau Boucher Falconet Gainsborough Fragonard David Canova	Gluck Haydn Mozart	Voltaire Louis XV Frederick the Great Rousseau Maria Theresa Goethe Marie Antoinette American Revolution French Revolution
1900 A.D.	ROMANTIC	Goya Constable Corot Delacroix Daumier Courbet Manet Degas Rodin Monet Renoir Seurat	Beethoven Schubert Berlioz Mendelssohn Schumann Chopin Liszt Verdi Wagner Smetana Brahms Moussorgsky Tchaikovsky Debussy Richard Strauss	Byron Schopenhauer Longfellow Tennyson Darwin Lincoln Dickens Waterloo Whitman Queen Victoria Pasteur Nietzsche Communist Manifesto
	20th CENTURY	Cezanne Van Gogh Kandinsky F. L. Wright Roualt **B. Fuller** Brancusi Mondrian Picasso Klee Corbusier Gropius Gabo App. Moore Miro Dali Giacometti Pollock Blume Op Art Pop Art	Schoenberg Ives Bartok Stravinsky Webern Hindemith Copland Carter Jazz Cage Stockhausen Penderecki Electronic Music Berg Dallapiccola Messiaen Rochberg Ligeti	S. Freud W. Churchill F. D. Roosevelt Stalin James Joyce B. Brecht T. S. Eliot Hemingway Motion Pictures 1st World War Radio Television 2nd World War United Nations Atomic Fission Hiroshima Sputnik 1st Moon Landing Space Shuttle launched

Glossary of Art Terms

Abstract art	Art that is not concerned with realistic representation of nature.
Abstract Expressionism	A style of painting that combines personal expression with abstract representation.
Acropolis	A hill town or fortified hill, usually applied to a Greek city that contained Greek temples.
Action painter	A painter who uses his whole body to achieve rhythm and line, usually on a large canvas.
Aesthetic	Any work of art, music, or literature that emphasizes beauty rather than usefulness.
Analogous colors	Color hues that are close to each other on the color wheel.
Apse	A semicircular part of a plan terminating at the main axis of a church.
Arcade	A row of arches supported by piers or columns.
Atrium	An enclosed but unroofed courtyard.
Baptistry	A building used for baptism, usually circular in shape.
Barrel vault	A semicylindrical vault.
Basilica	A rectangular hall flanked by aisles.
Beam	A horizontal member to support a weight over an opening.
Buttress	A masonry support built against a wall to support the outward thrust of a wall and roof.

Cantilever	A method of construction in which beams project beyond their support and are anchored by weight on the attached end.
Capital	The top part of a column wider than the upright section and usually decorated.
Casting	The process of pouring a liquid material into a mold where it hardens to take the shape of the mold.
Catacombs	Subterranean tunnels used for burial places.
Chancel	The area of a Christian church around the high altar, usually reserved for the clergy.
Choir	The portion of a church between the altar and the nave and reserved for the lower clergy and singers.
Cloister	A rectangular courtyard along the side of a medieval church to provide a sheltered walkway.
Collage	Compositions created by glueing bits of paper and/or other material on a flat surface.
Colonnade	A row of columns supporting beams or lintels.
Column	An upright support, usually cylindrical, for a roof or upper part of a building.
Complementary colors	The hues that are opposite of each other on a color wheel, such as green and red, or blue and orange.
Contour	The shaping edge of a form in sculpture or painting.
Design	The structure or organization of the various components of a work of art.
Dome	A hemispherical vault supported on columns or walls.
Entablature	The portion above the columns and below the roof in Greek architecture.
Expressionism	A style of art in which the artist's expression of emotions is the principal concern.
Facade	The front or main entrance of a building.
Flying buttress	A half arch used to counteract the outward thrust of the nave vault and transfer the thrust to the piers outside the walls.
Fresco	A technique of painting on wet plaster.
Frieze	The decorated horizontal band of the entablature in architecture.

Groined vault	A type of vault created by the intersection of two barrel vaults.
Hue	A particular gradation of color, tint, or shade.
Impressionism	A style of painting that tries to capture the effects of the quality of light on objects.
Intensity	The degree or strength of a color hue.
Keystone	The central stone in a round arch that forces the stones of the arch together.
Kinetic art	Art that depends on the movement of its various parts for its artistic message.
Linear perspective	A method representing the size of objects as they recede into space by the use of parallel lines.
Lintel	A beam over the rectangular opening between two posts or columns.
Medium	The techniques or material used by an artist to create a work of art.
Minimal art	A style of art that uses a very limited range of colors and shapes.
Mobile	A kind of sculpture that utilizes movement to achieve relationships between its various components.
Monochromatic	A color arrangement that uses only one hue with varying degrees of intensity.
Mosaic	A design composed of small units of stone, glass, or porcelain set in mortar.
Mural	A painting on a wall that may use any kind of paint or technique and is usually very large.
Nave	The central aisle of a church.
Op art	A style of painting that uses lines of contrasting colors in such a way as to evoke vibrations in the eye.
Pier	An architectural support, usually masonry.
Pop art	A style of art that uses commercial and popular images as subject matter.
Portico	A porch whose roof is supported by columns or piers.

Post and lintel	A system of construction in which vertical supports carry horizontal beams.
Primary colors	The hues that can be mixed to produce all other hues. The primary colors are red, yellow, and blue.
Relief sculpture	Sculpture in which three-dimensional forms are achieved from a flat background.
Rib	An arch used to support a vault.
Steel cage	A construction method in which steel supports in a post and lintel system are made as a self-supporting framework.
Texture	The surface character of an object or its representation by paint or other material.
Thrust	The lateral pressure of an arch or vault.
Tympanum	The surface above the door and below an arch, usually filled with sculptural figures, especially in medieval architecture.
Value	The measure of darkness or lightness of a color.
Vault	A method of roofing an area based on the principle of the arch.

Glossary of Music Terms

A cappella	Unaccompanied choral singing. Music written for voices alone.
Absolute music	Music that has no extramusical implications. The opposite of program music.
Accidental	A symbol used to raise or lower a pitch by one semitone (sharp ♯ , flat ♭ , natural ♮).
Aleatory	A type of composition in which the performer has been given more or less liberty in choosing pitches, rhythms, durations, and so forth. Chance improvisation.
Antiphonal	Music in which alternating choirs are used.
Aria	An extended solo song usually with orchestral accompaniment as in opera, oratorio, and cantatas.
Atonality	Denial of fixed tonality.
Bar	The vertical line separating the measures in written notation. The term is often used as a synonym for measure.
Cadence	The point of rest in a melody or harmonic progression that marks the end of a phrase or section.
Cadenza	Most generally, a highly ornamental cadence played by the soloist at the end of a movement of a concerto.
Canon	A contrapuntal device in which the melody of one voice is imitated exactly by one or more other voices. The term also refers to an entire composition using this device. (*See* round.)

Cantus firmus	A basic melody either composed or taken from another source upon which certain polyphonic works are constructed.
Chamber music	Music written for small ensembles, such as duos, trios, and quartets. Usually refers to instrumental music but may employ vocal forces as well.
Chorale	Traditionally, the hymns of the German Protestant churches. Lutheran chorales.
Chord	A pitch complex of two or more simultaneously sounded tones. The study of harmony deals with chordal functions.
Chromaticism	The melodic or harmonic use of tones not in the seven-tone diatonic scale of a composition.
Clavier	A term loosely used to designate a keyboard instrument usually of the clavichord or harpsichord variety.
Clef	The sign used at the beginning of the staff to designate the pitch of one note; hence, the terms c clef, g clef, f clef.
Cluster	An effect in modern music achieved by striking a number of adjacent keys of the piano or organ, or by having several instruments play tones within a close proximity of one another.
Coda	A section of a composition that brings it to a conclusion. Codas are considerably long in the movements of a symphony and some sonatas.
Color	Tonal quality as represented by each individual instrument or voice or a combination of instruments or voices. (*See* timbre.)
Consonance	Traditionally, a combination of tones that are pleasing or restful in distinction to dissonance.
Contrary motion	In contrapuntal compositions the movement of two voices in opposite directions, one ascending and one descending.
Counterpoint	A texture achieved by the simultaneous setting of one melodic line against one or more other lines.
Development	The section of a sonata-form in which the thematic material is exploited rhythmically, melodically, harmonically, dynamically, and color-wise.
Diatonic	The eight tones of the octave forming a major, minor, or modal scale.
Dissonance	A harsh combination of tones that, because of its tension, requires resolution to a restful consonance.

Dodecaphonic	The method of composing in which the twelve tones of the chromatic scale are used in some prearranged form throughout the composition.
Dominant	The fifth degree of the diatonic scale or key.
Drone	A consistently sustained tone or tones in the bass used throughout a section or even a whole composition.
Dynamics	The gradations of tonal power indicated in a composition.
Enharmonic	Tones in equal-tempered scales that are identical in sound but are notated differently, i.e., f♯ and g♭.
Ensemble	A term applied to any group of performers and to the performance itself.
Equal temperament	The tuning of the octave in twelve equal parts.
Exposition	The first section of sonata-allegro form in which the thematic material is exposed or stated. (*See* statement.)
Fugue	A style of contrapuntal composition in which the entire work is generally based on a single short theme called the subject.
Half tone	The smallest interval used the division of the octave in equal temperament.
Harmony	The simultaneous combination of sounds. The use of chords.
Heterophony	The simultaneous singing of a melody in both a simple and ornamented form by 2 or more performers.
Homophony	Music in which a dominant melodic line is supported by chordal accompaniment. The music is vertical in structure as opposed to polyphony, which is horizontal.
Imitation	A device of polyphonic texture in which one voice restates the melody of another voice. The imitation can be strict (exact) or free (similar).
Interval	The melodic or harmonic distance between two tones.
Intonation	The accuracy of playing or singing on pitch.

Inversion	Melodic inversion requires that every ascending interval be replaced by an equal descending one, and every descending interval by an equal ascending one. Chordal inversion implies that some tone other than the root of the chord is in the bass.
Key	The tonal center of a composition. The key note is the first note of the scale upon which the composition is based. The term "key" is also used for the levers or elements that are manipulated by the fingers of an instrumentalist, such as the keys of the flute or the black-and-white keys of the piano.
Libretto	The text of an opera, oratorio, or cantata.
Lied	The German word for song. Generally used to refer to the German song literature of the late eighteenth, nineteenth, and twentieth centuries accompanied by piano.
Major	A pattern of steps and half steps within the octave in the following order—two whole steps, a half step, three whole steps, and a half step. Defined another way, a scale of eight tones in which the third and fourth tones and the seventh and eighth ones are separated by half steps while all the others are separated by whole steps.
Measure	The smallest rhythmic unit in a composition that is divided into a number of beats as indicated in the meter signature.
Meter	The organization of rhythmic accented and unaccented pulses within the measure.
Minor	A second scalar pattern that has three forms—harmonic, melodic, and natural. The distinguishing feature of all minor scales is the half step between the second and third notes of the scale.
Modality	The use of the system of medieval modes rather than the use of major or minor scales.
Modulation	Changing from one key to another in the course of a composition. For example, the change from the tonic key to the dominant in the statement section of a sonata-allegro form movement.
Monophony	Musical texture consisting of a single unaccompanied line of melody.
Motive	The smallest unit of musical form.

Note	The symbol of musical writing that directs the performer to produce a tone of specific pitch and duration.
Opus	A numbering scheme introduced in the early nineteenth century that indicates the order of publication and the general order of composition of a composer's works.
Ornament	Notes added to a melodic line either by the composer specifically through proper symbols or by the performer improvisatorily.
Ostinate	A melodic or rhythmic figure repeated consistently throughout a complete work or section of a composition.
Parallel motion	Two melodic lines moving at the same interval.
Pentatonic	A division of the octave into five intervals. Normally the pattern consists of whole step, step and a half, whole step, whole step, step and a half. Note there are no intervals smaller than a whole step.
Phrase	A musical melodic idea corresponding to a sentence in prose. A phrase consists of one or more motives, and ends in a cadence.
Polyphony	A texture in which two or more melodic lines are interwoven, as in a canon or fugue.
Polytonality	The use of two or more keys simultaneously in a composition.
Program music	Music that attempts to convey an extramusical idea, such as a story, landscape, painting, etc.
Recapitulation	A synonymous term for restatement. The third section of sonata-allegro form in which the themes of the statement or exposition are repeated.
Recitative	A type of vocal performance in which the words are tonally declaimed with a bare minimum of melodic interest.
Resolution	The harmonic progress from a dissonance to a consonance; i.e., movement from tension to release.
Round	A canon for voices that is repeated ad libitum.
Rubato	A slight variation of the rhythmic beat made by the performer for expressive purposes.
Scale	The arrangement of the tones of the octave as used in a composition; i.e., major and minor scales.

Score	The notation of the complete parts of an instrumental or vocal ensemble composition in a composite form from which the entire work can be conducted or studied.
Serialism	The method of composition by which the composer extends the technique of twelve tone composition to other areas, such as rhythm, dynamics, timbre, duration, etc.
Sequence	A compositional technique in which a melodic figure is repeated a number of times at different pitch levels.
Signature	The symbols set on the staff at the beginning of a piece of music to designate the tonality or key and the metric organization.
Statement	Synonym for exposition. (*See* exposition.)
Stretto	A section in a fugal composition in which the subject and its answer overlap each other.
Subject	A theme, particularly that of the fugue.
Syncopation	The displacement of the accent from a strong beat to a weak beat or weak part of a beat.
Tempo	The speed of performance of a piece of music suggested either by a metronomic rate (i.e., the number of beats per minute) or by a more general term, such as adagio, andante, presto, etc.
Texture	The density of a composition dependent upon the use of one or the other techniques of monophony, homophony, or polyphony.
Theme	Generally used to describe the tune or melodic subject of a work. Could be used, however, to describe a rhythmic or harmonic pattern out of which the composition is built.
Timbre	*See* color.
Time signature	The symbol written on the staff at the beginning of a composition indicating the number of beats per measure and the note value receiving a beat. For example, 3/4 time or meter signifies that there are three beats per measure and that each quarter note receives one beat.
Tonality	The central tonal organization of a part or the whole of a composition.

Tone	The sound received by the ear due to the vibrations set up by a resonating body. Musically, tones have the properties of pitch, intensity, duration, and timbre.
Tonic	The first or key note of a scale; i.e., "c" in the c major scale.
Triad	The simplest harmonic chord consisting of three tones sounded simultaneously; i.e., c-e-g; f-a-c, etc.
Trio	A composition for three performers. Also the second part of a minuet or scherzo in the classic sonata.
Tritone	The interval of a fourth containing three whole tones (known as an augmented fourth). An interval forbidden in strict counterpoint.
Twelve tone music	Music consistently constructed on a pattern of the twelve chromatic tones selected prior to composition.
Tutti	A term applied to passages in which all performers play in contrast to solo passages.
Vibrato	A device of performance used by singers and instrumentalists, especially string players, to achieve expressive quality by alternately deviating from the prescribed pitch and returning to it.
Voice	The human sound production. Also applied to the vocal as well as instrumental lines in polyphonic music.
Well-tempered	A system of tuning in which all tones of the octave are separated by equal half steps. This tuning makes it possible to play in all keys on a single keyboard instrument.
Whole tone scale	A scale dividing the octave into six equal whole tone intervals.

Index